# THE STORY OF TEXAS


**Series Authors**

Dr. Richard G. Boehm

Claudia Hoone

Dr. Thomas M. McGowan

Dr. Mabel C. McKinney-Browning

Dr. Ofelia B. Miramontes

**Consultant for Texas History**

Dr. David C. DeBoe

Texas State Historical Association

**Series Consultants**

Dr. Alma Flor Ada

Dr. Phillip Bacon

Dr. W. Dorsey Hammond

Dr. Asa Grant Hilliard, III



HARCOURT BRACE & COMPANY

Orlando Atlanta Austin Boston San Francisco Chicago Dallas

New York Toronto London

## SERIES AUTHORS

**Dr. Richard G. Boehm**
Professor
Department of Geography and Planning
Southwest Texas State University
San Marcos, Texas

**Claudia Hoone**
Teacher
Ralph Waldo Emerson School #58
Indianapolis, Indiana

**Dr. Thomas M. McGowan**
Associate Professor
Division of Curriculum and Instruction
Arizona State University
Tempe, Arizona

**Dr. Mabel C. McKinney-Browning**
Director
Division for Public Education
American Bar Association
Chicago, Illinois

**Dr. Ofelia B. Miramontes**
Associate Professor
School of Education
University of Colorado
Boulder, Colorado

## SERIES CONSULTANTS

**Dr. Alma Flor Ada**
Professor
School of Education
University of San Francisco
San Francisco, California

**Dr. Phillip Bacon**
Professor Emeritus of Geography and Anthropology
University of Houston
Houston, Texas

**Dr. W. Dorsey Hammond**
Professor of Education
Oakland University
Rochester, Michigan

**Dr. Asa Grant Hilliard, III**
Fuller E. Callaway Professor of Urban Education
Georgia State University
Atlanta, Georgia

## CONSULTANT FOR TEXAS HISTORY

**Dr. David C. DeBoe**
Texas State Historical Association
The University of Texas
Austin, Texas

## MEDIA AND LITERATURE SPECIALISTS

**Dr. Joseph A. Braun, Jr.**
Professor of Elementary Social Studies
Department of Curriculum and Instruction
Illinois State University
Normal, Illinois

**Meredith McGowan**
Youth Librarian
Tempe Public Library
Tempe, Arizona

## GRADE-LEVEL CONSULTANTS AND REVIEWERS

**Joyce Billings**
Teacher
R. L. Thornton Elementary School
Dallas, Texas

**Theresa H. Escobedo**
Associate Professor
Department of Curriculum and Instruction
The University of Texas
Austin, Texas

**Gary J. Gabehart**
Director
Inter-Tribal Council of American Indians
San Antonio, Texas

**Dr. Sara R. Massey**
Educational Specialist
Institute of Texan Cultures
The University of Texas at San Antonio
San Antonio, Texas

**James Olson**
Chair
Department of History
Sam Houston State University
College of Education and Applied Science
Huntsville, Texas

**Dr. Linda Kerrigan Salvucci**
Associate Professor
Department of History
Trinity University
San Antonio, Texas

**Ronald W. Shafer**
Teacher
Frazier Elementary School
Houston, Texas

**Willie Earl Tindall**
Teacher
San Augustine Independent School District
San Augustine, Texas

**Dr. Cary Wintz**
Professor
Department of History
Texas Southern University
Houston, Texas





Acknowledgments and other credits appear in the back of this book.

Printed in the United States of America

ISBN: 0-15-302041-5

3 4 5 6 7 8 9 10 032 99 98 97

# CONTENTS

Lady Bird Johnson

Young Pueblo girl

Hernando Cortés

Stephen F. Austin

Lorenzo de Zavala

Sam Houston



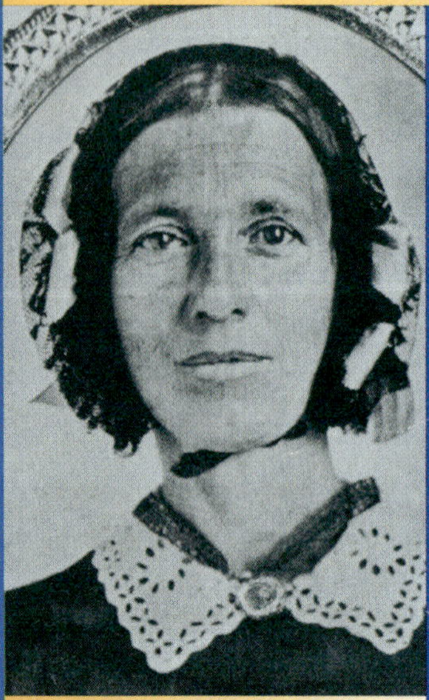

Elise Waerenskjold

Satanta, Kiowa chief

CHAPTER 8

## The Years After the Civil War



UNIT 5

Jovita Idár

CHAPTER 9

Barbara Jordan

Rose Chin Wong

George W. Bush

# F.Y.I.

## Literature, Primary Sources, and Documents



## Learning from Visuals

### Geography Skills



### Chart and Graph Skills



## Building Citizenship

### Reading and Writing Skills

## Thinking Skills



## Citizenship Skills



# Features

## Counterpoints



## Making Social Studies Relevant



# Maps

## Charts, Graphs, Diagrams, Tables, and Time Lines

# ATLAS

## CONTENTS

# ATLAS

## THE WORLD: POLITICAL

### CENTRAL AMERICA AND THE CARIBBEAN

National border

**Abbreviations**

| | |
|---|---|
| **EQU. GUINEA** | EQUATORIAL GUINEA |
| **NETH.** | NETHERLANDS |
| **N.Z.** | NEW ZEALAND |
| **U.A.E.** | UNITED ARAB EMIRATES |
| **U.K.** | UNITED KINGDOM |
| **U.S.** | UNITED STATES |

# ATLAS

## THE WORLD: PHYSICAL

### NORTHERN POLAR REGION

ARCTIC OCEAN
Severnaya Zemlya
New Siberian Islands
Svalbard
Barents Sea
Novaya Zemlya
Arctic Circle
Iceland
URAL MTS.
Ob River
Yenisey River
Lena River
SIBERIA
Volga R.
British Isles
North Sea
Baltic Sea
North European Plain
EUROPE
Mt. Elbrus 18,510 ft. (5,642 m)
Aral Sea
Irtysh River
Lake Baikal
Amur R.
Sea of Okhotsk
Kamchatka Peninsula
Kuril Is.
Mont Blanc 15,771 ft. (4,807 m)
ALPS
Danube R.
Pyrenees
Iberian Peninsula
Balkan Peninsula
Black Sea
Caucasus Mts.
Caspian Sea
Asia Minor
ASIA
TIAN SHAN
GOBI (DESERT)
Hokkaido
Sea of Japan
Honshu
Mediterranean Sea
HINDU KUSH
K2 28,250 ft. (8,611 m)
Huang He
Shikoku
Kyushu
Madeira Islands
Atlas Mts.
Tigris R.
Euphrates R.
Plateau of Tibet
HIMALAYAS
Indus R.
Chang Jiang
East China Sea
PACIFIC OCEAN
Canary Islands
SAHARA
Nile R.
Persian Gulf
Mt. Everest 29,028 ft. (8,848 m)
Ganges R.
Thar Desert
Taiwan
Red Sea
Arabian Peninsula
SAHEL
Lake Chad
Arabian Sea
Deccan Plateau
Bay of Bengal
Hainan
South China Sea
Philippine Islands
Micronesia
Niger River
AFRICA
Ethiopian Highlands
Sri Lanka
Malay Peninsula
Zaire River
Mt. Kenya 17,058 ft. (5,199 m)
CONGO BASIN
Lake Victoria
Maldives
Seychelles
Sumatra
Borneo
Celebes
New Guinea
ATLANTIC OCEAN
Lake Tanganyika
Mt. Kilimanjaro 19,340 ft. (5,895 m)
Java
Melanesia
INDIAN OCEAN
Lake Nyasa
Madagascar
Fiji
Kalahari Desert
AUSTRALIA
GREAT VICTORIA DESERT
GREAT DIVIDING RANGE
Darling R.
Murray R.
Mt. Kosciusko 7,316 ft. (2,230 m)
Tasmania
Cape of Good Hope
Cape Agulhas
N
S
E
W
0 1,000 2,000 Miles
0 1,000 2,000 Kilometers
Robinson Projection
Scale accurate at equator
ANTARCTICA
Ross Sea
20° W
0°
20° E
40° E
60° E
80° E
100° E
120° E
140° E
160° E
180°
80° N
60° N
40° N
20° N
0°
20° S
40° S
60° S
80° S

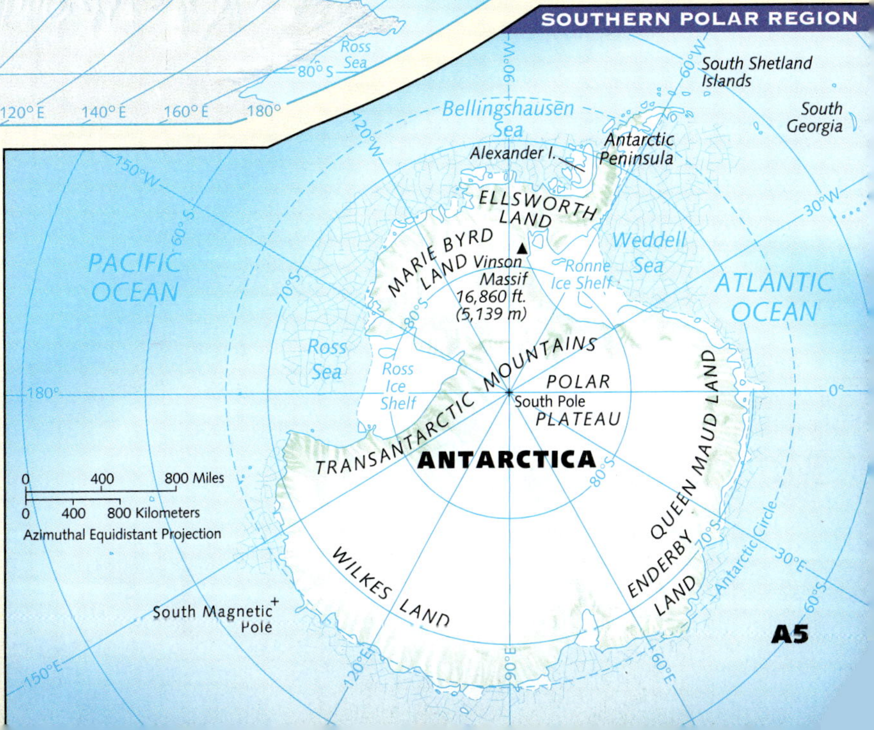
SOUTHERN POLAR REGION
South Shetland Islands
South Georgia
Bellingshausen Sea
Antarctic Peninsula
Alexander I.
ELLSWORTH LAND
PACIFIC OCEAN
MARIE BYRD LAND
Vinson Massif 16,860 ft. (5,139 m)
Weddell Sea
Ronne Ice Shelf
ATLANTIC OCEAN
Ross Sea
Ross Ice Shelf
TRANSANTARCTIC MOUNTAINS
POLAR PLATEAU
South Pole
QUEEN MAUD LAND
ANTARCTICA
0 400 800 Miles
0 400 800 Kilometers
Azimuthal Equidistant Projection
WILKES LAND
ENDERBY LAND
Antarctic Circle
South Magnetic Pole
180°
150° W
120° W
90° W
60° W
30° W
0°
30° E
60° E
90° E
120° E
150° E
60° S
70° S
80° S

# ATLAS

## WESTERN HEMISPHERE: POLITICAL

# ATLAS

## WESTERN HEMISPHERE: PHYSICAL

# ATLAS

## UNITED STATES: OVERVIEW

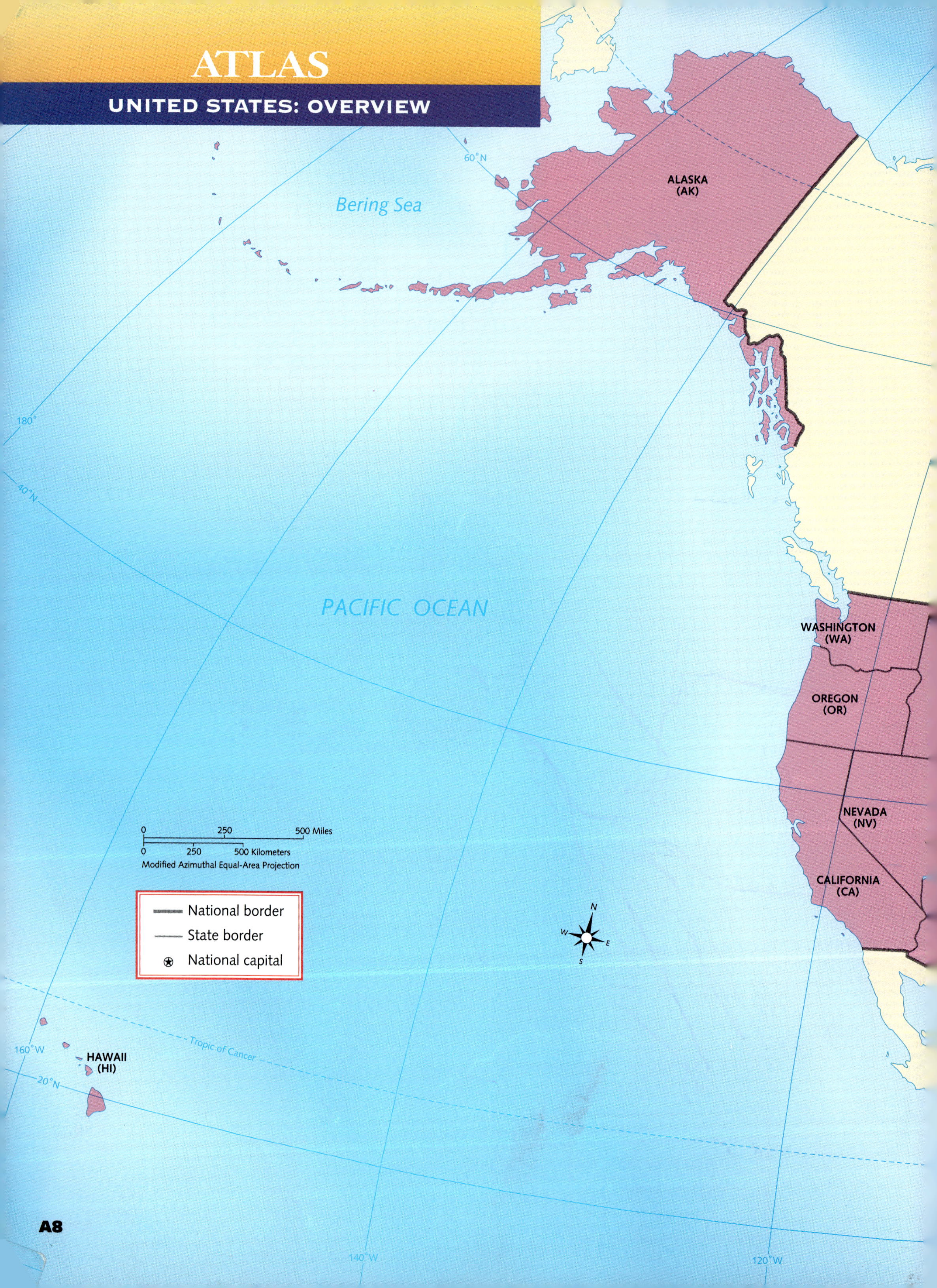

ICELAND
Arctic Circle
Greenland
60° N
40° W
Hudson Bay
CANADA
MONTANA (MT)
NORTH DAKOTA (ND)
MINNESOTA (MN)
Lake Superior
MICHIGAN
Lake Huron
VERMONT (VT)
MAINE (ME)
NEW HAMPSHIRE (NH)
60° W
IDAHO (ID)
WYOMING (WY)
SOUTH DAKOTA (SD)
WISCONSIN (WI)
Lake Michigan
(MI)
Lake Ontario
NEW YORK (NY)
MASSACHUSETTS (MA)
RHODE ISLAND (RI)
40° N
NEBRASKA (NE)
IOWA (IA)
Lake Erie
PENNSYLVANIA (PA)
CONNECTICUT (CT)
NEW JERSEY (NJ)
ILLINOIS (IL)
INDIANA (IN)
OHIO (OH)
Washington, D.C.
DELAWARE (DE)
UTAH (UT)
COLORADO (CO)
KANSAS (KS)
MISSOURI (MO)
WEST VIRGINIA (WV)
VIRGINIA (VA)
MARYLAND (MD)
KENTUCKY (KY)
NORTH CAROLINA (NC)
TENNESSEE (TN)
ARIZONA (AZ)
NEW MEXICO (NM)
OKLAHOMA (OK)
ARKANSAS (AR)
SOUTH CAROLINA (SC)
MISSISSIPPI (MS)
ALABAMA (AL)
GEORGIA (GA)
ATLANTIC OCEAN
TEXAS (TX)
LOUISIANA (LA)
FLORIDA (FL)
Gulf of Mexico
MEXICO
CUBA
DOMINICAN REPUBLIC
20° N
PUERTO RICO
HAITI
100° W
80° W

# ATLAS

## UNITED STATES: POLITICAL

100°W
90°W
80°W
70°W
50°N
40°N
30°N
70°W
80°W
90°W
100°W
CANADA
ATLANTIC OCEAN
Gulf of Mexico
BAHAMAS
CUBA
Lake Superior
Lake Michigan
Lake Huron
Lake Erie
Lake Ontario
St. Lawrence River
Mississippi River
Missouri River
Platte River
Arkansas River
Red River
Ohio River
Tennessee River
Lake Okeechobee
NORTH DAKOTA
Grand Forks
Fargo
Bismarck
SOUTH DAKOTA
Pierre
Rapid City
Sioux Falls
NEBRASKA
Lincoln
Omaha
KANSAS
Topeka
Wichita
MINNESOTA
Duluth
St. Paul
Minneapolis
IOWA
Sioux City
Cedar Rapids
Davenport
Des Moines
MISSOURI
Kansas City
Jefferson City
St. Louis
Springfield
WISCONSIN
Green Bay
Madison
Milwaukee
ILLINOIS
Rockford
Chicago
Peoria
Decatur
Springfield
MICHIGAN
Sault Sainte Marie
Grand Rapids
Lansing
Flint
Detroit
INDIANA
Gary
South Bend
Indianapolis
Evansville
OHIO
Toledo
Cleveland
Akron
Columbus
Dayton
Cincinnati
Wheeling
KENTUCKY
Louisville
Frankfort
Lexington
TENNESSEE
Knoxville
Nashville
Chattanooga
Memphis
ARKANSAS
Fort Smith
Little Rock
LOUISIANA
Shreveport
Baton Rouge
New Orleans
MISSISSIPPI
Meridian
Jackson
Biloxi
ALABAMA
Huntsville
Birmingham
Montgomery
Mobile
GEORGIA
Atlanta
Macon
Columbus
Savannah
FLORIDA
Tallahassee
Jacksonville
Orlando
Tampa
St. Petersburg
West Palm Beach
Miami
SOUTH CAROLINA
Columbia
Charleston
NORTH CAROLINA
Winston-Salem
Greensboro
Raleigh
Charlotte
VIRGINIA
Richmond
Roanoke
Newport News
Norfolk
WEST VIRGINIA
Charleston
MARYLAND
Baltimore
Annapolis
Washington, D.C.
DELAWARE
Wilmington
Dover
PENNSYLVANIA
Harrisburg
Pittsburgh
Philadelphia
NEW JERSEY
Trenton
Newark
NEW YORK
Buffalo
Rochester
Syracuse
Albany
New York City
CONNECTICUT
Hartford
Bridgeport
RHODE ISLAND
Providence
MASSACHUSETTS
Boston
Worcester
VERMONT
Burlington
Montpelier
NEW HAMPSHIRE
Manchester
Concord
MAINE
Augusta
Portland
OKLAHOMA
Tulsa
Oklahoma City
TEXAS
Amarillo
Lubbock
Odessa
Abilene
Fort Worth
Dallas
Austin
Beaumont
Houston
San Antonio
Laredo
Corpus Christi

# ATLAS

## UNITED STATES: PHYSICAL

100°W
90°W
80°W
70°W
50°N
40°N
30°N
CANADA
Lake of the Woods
Upper Red Lake
Lower Red Lake
Leech Lake
Mesabi Range
Mille Lacs Lake
Isle Royale
Lake Superior
Keweenaw Peninsula
Upper Peninsula
Lake Michigan
Lower Peninsula
Lake Huron
Lake St. Clair
Lake Erie
Lake Ontario
Niagara Falls
St. Lawrence River
Lake Champlain
Adirondack Mountains
Green Mts.
White Mts.
Connecticut R.
Hudson R.
Finger Lakes
ME
Mt. Katahdin 5,267 ft. (1,605 m)
Mt. Washington 6,288 ft. (1,917 m)
VT
NH
NY
MA
CT
RI
Cape Ann
Cape Cod
Long Island
NJ
PA
MD
DE
Delaware Bay
Cape Charles
Chesapeake Bay
Albemarle Sound
Cape Hatteras
Cape Fear
ND
SD
NE
KS
OK
TX
MN
WI
IA
MO
AR
LA
MI
IL
IN
OH
KY
TN
MS
AL
GA
SC
NC
VA
WV
FL
GREAT PLAINS
Black Hills
Lake Oahe
Missouri River
Sand Hills
North Platte R.
South Platte R.
Platte River
INTERIOR PLAINS
Smoky Hills
Red Hills
Missouri River
Lake of the Ozarks
Harry S. Truman Reservoir
Ozark Plateau
Arkansas River
Canadian River
Ouachita Mountains
Red River
Llano Estacado
Edwards Plateau
Pecos River
Brazos River
Colorado River
Sabine River
Toledo Bend Reservoir
Sam Rayburn Reservoir
Galveston Bay
COASTAL PLAIN
Mississippi River
Wisconsin River
Lake Winnebago
Illinois River
Wabash River
CENTRAL PLAINS
Ohio River
Lake Barkley
Cumberland Gap
Cumberland R.
Tennessee R.
Mt. Mitchell 6,684 ft. (2,037 m)
Allegheny Mts.
APPALACHIAN MOUNTAINS
Potomac R.
James R.
Roanoke R.
PIEDMONT
Cape Fear River
Savannah River
Stone Mountain
Chattahoochee R.
Ocmulgee R.
Oconee R.
Altamaha R.
Alabama R.
Tombigbee R.
Okefenokee Swamp
St. Johns River
Lake Pontchartrain
Mississippi Delta
Mobile Bay
Cape Canaveral
Tampa Bay
Lake Okeechobee
Everglades
Cape Sable
Florida Keys
Straits of Florida
ATLANTIC OCEAN
Gulf of Mexico
BAHAMAS
CUBA

# ATLAS

## TEXAS: CITIES AND HIGHWAYS

## TEXAS: LAND AND WATER

# ATLAS

## GEOGRAPHY TERMS

**basin** bowl-shaped area of land surrounded by higher land

**bay** body of water that is part of a sea or ocean and is partly enclosed by land

**bluff** high, steep face of rock or earth

**canyon** deep, narrow valley with steep sides

**cape** point of land that extends into water

**channel** deepest part of a body of water

**cliff** high, steep face of rock or earth

**coast** land along a sea or ocean

**coastal plain** area of flat land along a sea or ocean

**delta** triangle-shaped area of land at the mouth of a river

**desert** dry land with few plants

**dune** hill of sand piled up by the wind

**fall line** area along which rivers form waterfalls or rapids as the rivers drop to lower land

**fjord** deep, narrow part of a sea or ocean, between high, steep banks

**floodplain** flat land that is near the edges of a river and is formed by the silt deposited by floods

**foothills** hilly area at the base of a mountain

**glacier** large ice mass that moves slowly down a mountain or across land

**gulf** body of water that is partly enclosed by land but is larger than a bay

**harbor** area of water where ships can dock safely near land

**hill** land that rises above the land around it

**island** land that has water on all sides

**isthmus** narrow strip of land connecting two larger areas of land

**lake** body of water with land on all sides

**marsh** lowland with moist soil and tall grasses

**mesa** flat-topped mountain with steep sides

**mountain** highest kind of land

**mountain pass** low place between mountains

**mountain range** row of mountains

**mouth of river** place where a river empties into another body of water

**oasis** area of water and fertile land in a desert

**ocean** body of salt water larger than a sea

**peak** top of a mountain

**peninsula** land that is almost completely surrounded by water

**plain** flat land

**plateau** area of high, flat land with steep sides

**reef** ridge of sand, rock, or coral that lies at or near the surface of a sea or ocean

**river** large stream of water that flows across the land

**riverbank** land along a river

**sea** body of salt water smaller than an ocean

**sea level** the level that is even with the surface of an ocean or sea

**slope** side of a hill or mountain

**source of river** place where a river begins

**strait** narrow channel of water connecting two larger bodies of water

**swamp** area of low, wet land with trees

**timberline** line on a mountain above which it is too cold for trees to grow

**tributary** stream or river that empties into a larger river

**valley** low land between hills or mountains

**volcano** opening in the Earth, often raised, through which lava, rock, ashes, and gases are forced out

**waterfall** steep drop from a high place to a lower place in a stream or river

INTRODUCTION

# Why Study SOCIAL STUDIES?

“Every one of you already holds the important office of citizen. Over time you will become more and more involved in your community. You will need to know more about what being a citizen means. Social studies will help you learn about citizenship. That is why social studies is important in your life.”

The authors of *Stories in Time*

# THE POWERFUL IDEAS OF SOCIAL STUDIES

Think about the many groups of which you are a part. Your family, your class, and your community are each a different kind of group, and you are a member of each one. You are also a member—or **citizen**—of your town, your state, and your country. Citizens work to improve the many groups to which they belong and to make the whole world a better place.

To help you think, feel, and act as a citizen, *Stories in Time* begins every lesson with a question. That question connects you with one or more of five powerful ideas that citizens need to understand in order to make decisions. Each question also links you to the lesson's story, helping you see how the story relates to your own life. The lesson helps you understand about being a citizen by letting you see how people from many places and times have thought, felt, and acted.

Each lesson will help you organize your thinking around one or more of the five powerful ideas of social studies.

POWERFUL IDEA NUMBER 1

## COMMONALITY AND DIVERSITY

In some ways people everywhere are alike. We all have basic needs for things such as food, clothing, and shelter. We all laugh, get angry, and have our feelings hurt. These are examples of our commonality, or what we all share. At the same time we need to understand that each person is different from everyone else. We each have our own ways of thinking, feeling, and acting. That is our diversity. An understanding of commonality and diversity can help you see that every person deserves respect.

POWERFUL IDEA NUMBER 2

## CONFLICT AND COOPERATION

Because all people are not exactly alike, they may have conflicts, or disagreements. People can often overcome their conflicts by cooperating, or working together. In social

In this painting, Texas leaders are gathered to write the Texas Declaration of Independence. Taking part in government is one way these leaders were carrying out the office of citizen.

studies you will learn about the disagreements people have had throughout time and about many of the ways people in Texas have found to settle their disagreements. You will also learn ways to cooperate and to resolve conflict in your own life.

POWERFUL IDEA NUMBER 3

## Continuity and Change

While some things change over time, other things stay the same. Many things have stayed the same for years and will probably stay the same in the future. This means that they have continuity. Understanding continuity and change can help you see how things in the world came to be as they are. You will learn that past events have shaped your life and that present events can help you make better decisions about the future.

POWERFUL IDEA NUMBER 4

## Individualism and Interdependence

Citizens can act by themselves to make a difference in the world. Their actions as individuals may be helpful, or they may be harmful to other citizens. But much of the time, people do not act alone. They depend on others to help them. People depend on their families, their schools, their churches, their governments, and other groups and organizations. Such interdependence connects citizens with one another and affects their lives.

POWERFUL IDEA NUMBER 5

## Interaction Within Different Environments

People behave in ways that affect other people. People's actions also affect their surroundings, or **environment**. This is true of their home environment, their school environment, and any other environments of which they may be a part. Understanding such interactions is important to understanding why things happened in the past and why things happen today.

When you take part in student government, you are also carrying out the office of citizen.

Understanding interaction is also key to understanding social studies. The subjects that make up social studies are all interconnected. You will learn, for example, that history (the study of people's past) is related to geography (the study of the Earth's surface and its people). Civics and government (the study of how people live together in a community) is related to economics (the study of how people use resources). All of these subjects are related to the study of culture (people's ways of life, including customs, ideas, and practices). And they interact with one another to tell a story. Together they tell a story of how people have lived over time and how they made contributions as citizens. Understanding the story will help you learn how to hold the office of citizen.

**What are the five powerful ideas of social studies?**

SKILLS

# HOW TO Read Social Studies

## Why Is This Skill Important?

Social studies is made up of many different stories about people and places. Sometimes you read these stories in library books. Other times you read them in textbooks, like this one. Knowing how to read social studies can make it easier to study and do your homework. It will help you identify main ideas and important people, places, and events.

## Understand the Process

Follow these steps when reading any lesson in this textbook:

**1.** Preview the whole lesson.
- Look at the title and headings to find out the topic of the lesson.
- Look at the pictures, captions, and questions for clues about what is in the lesson.
- Answer the Link to Our World question at the beginning of the lesson to find out how the lesson relates to your life today.
- Read the Focus on the Main Idea statement. It gives you the key idea that the lesson teaches.
- Look at the Preview Vocabulary list to see what new terms will be introduced.

**2.** Read the lesson for information on the main idea. As you read, you will come to a number of checkpoint questions. Be sure to find the answers to these questions before you continue reading the lesson.

**3.** When you finish reading the lesson, say in your own words what you have learned.

**4.** Look back over the lesson. Then answer the review questions–from memory if possible. The lesson review will help guide you in checking your understanding, thinking critically, and showing what you know.

## Think and Apply

Use the four steps in Understand the Process each time you are asked to read a lesson in *Stories in Time*.

BUILDING CITIZENSHIP

# HISTORY

Studying history helps you see the links between the past and the present. It also helps you better understand how the events of today can affect the events of the future. **History** is about what happened last month and last year as well as what happened in the long-ago past.

As you read about the past, ask yourself the following questions. They will help you think like a historian, a person who studies the past.

- **What happened?**
- **When did it happen?**
- **Who took part in it?**
- **How and why did it happen?**

## WHAT HAPPENED?

To find out what really happened in the past, you need proof that it happened. You can find proof by studying what people have written or said about the past. Some records of the past are made by people who saw or took part in an event, or something that happened. They might have written down their thoughts in a journal. They might have told their story in a letter or a poem. They may have taken a photograph, made a film, or drawn a picture. Each of these records gives the people of today a direct link to a past event.

Other records of the past do not directly link to an event. They were recorded by someone who was not there at the time. A magazine article, a newspaper story, or a book might be written at a later time by someone who did not take part in an event.

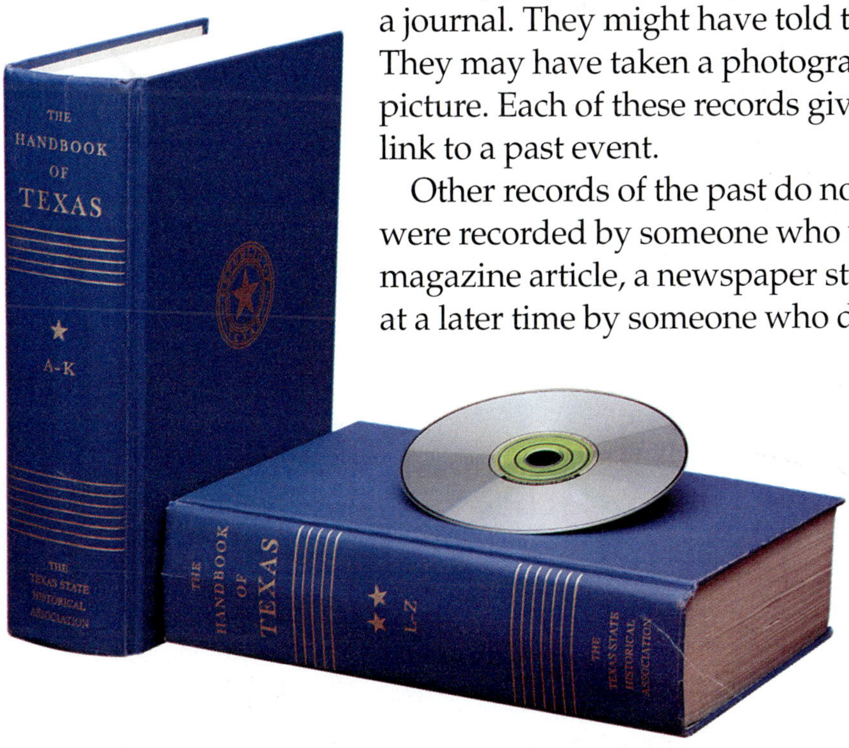


You can learn about the past by reading reference materials.

This old photograph gives the people of today a direct link to the past. What can you tell about the past from this photograph and the photograph on the next page?

Records of history do not have to be old. Students in the future can watch the video this man is filming to learn about the past.

When you read this book, you will read many kinds of records of the past. The stories told in each lesson contain the words and pictures of people in the past as well as descriptions by historians. Maps and graphs also help tell the story.

## When Did It Happen?

One way to build a story of the past is to put events related to the story in the order in which they happened. When you read this textbook, you will notice that the events described at the beginning of a chapter happened before those described at the end of a chapter.

You will see time lines in this textbook. A time line is a diagram that shows the events that took place during a certain period of time. Some time lines show a period of a month or a year. Other time lines show a period of 10 years, 100 years, or 1,000 years. Time lines can help you understand how one event may have led to another.

## Who Took Part in It?

To understand the stories of the past, you need to know about the people in the stories and the times in which they lived. By learning more about these people, you can understand the actions and feelings of people from other times and other places.

By reading the words of people of the past, you can come to understand their point of view. A person's **point of view** is his or her set of beliefs that have been shaped by factors such as whether that person is old or young, male or female, rich or poor. A person's point of view is also shaped by a person's culture and race. Your understanding of history will grow when you study the many different points of view of the people who took part in the story. This also will help you see that other people, even those living in other places and other times, are a lot like you.

## How and Why Did It Happen?

Many events in history are linked to other events. To find the links between events, you will need to identify causes and effects. A **cause** is any action that makes something happen. What happens because of that action is an **effect**.

To understand an event, you need to analyze its causes and effects. **Analyzing** is a way of thinking in which you break something down into its parts and look closely at how those parts connect with each other. When you analyze an event, you look at things such as who was there and what the time period was like. Then you can summarize or form a conclusion about how or why it happened.

**What questions can you ask yourself when you read about the past?**

This family that lived in Texas long ago was like your family in many ways.

# GEOGRAPHY

The stories you will read in this book all have a setting. The setting of a story includes the place where it happens. **Geography** is the study of the many different settings around the world. Studying geography helps you answer these questions about a place:

- **Where is it? (location)**
- **What is it like there? (place)**
- **Who lives there? (human-environment interactions)**
- **How did they get there? (movement)**
- **How is the place like other places? How is it different? (regions)**

The answers to these questions tell you what you need to know to understand a setting. The five questions are so important that many people call them the five themes, or key topics, of geography.

## 1. Location

Everything on the Earth has its own location. A **location** is where something can be found. Location can be described in many ways. For example, you live in Texas. Texas is located among the 50 states that make up the United States. The United States is located on the continent of North America. North America is located in the Western Hemisphere, or the western half of the planet Earth.

## 2. Place

Every location on the Earth is made up of unique features that make it different from all other places. Features of a place can include landforms, bodies of water, climate, soil, plant and animal life, and other natural resources. Many places also have features made by people, such as buildings, bridges, farms, and roads. People also help make one place different from another.

### TEXAS WITHIN THE WESTERN HEMISPHERE

**LEARNING FROM DIAGRAMS**
Texas is a unique state in the United States. It is also a part of both the North American continent and the Western Hemisphere.

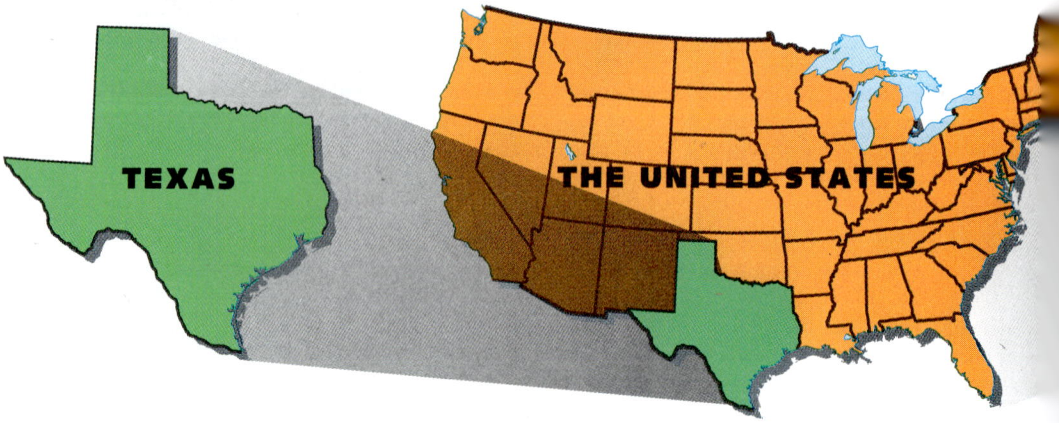

## 3. Human-Environment Interactions

Humans and the environment interact, or behave in ways that affect each other. People interact with their environment in different ways. Sometimes they change it. For example, they clear land to grow crops or build cities. They sometimes pollute the environment. The environment can also cause people to change the way they act. For example, people who live in cold places wear warm clothing. Sometimes things that happen in nature, such as hurricanes and tornadoes, cause great changes in people's lives.

## 4. Movement

Each day, people in different parts of Texas, the United States, and the world interact with one another. These kinds of interactions involve movement. People and products move by transportation. Ideas move through the different forms of communication. Studying geography can help you understand how people, products, and ideas got to where they are.

## 5. Regions

Areas on the Earth whose features make them different from other areas can be called **regions**. A region can be described by such things as the landforms or the plant life that exist there. A region can be mountainous, or it can be covered by thick rain forests. Big areas, such as the state of Texas, are sometimes divided into regions that are easier to compare and contrast. Texas is often divided into North Texas, South Texas, East Texas, West Texas, and Central Texas.

**What are the five themes of geography?**

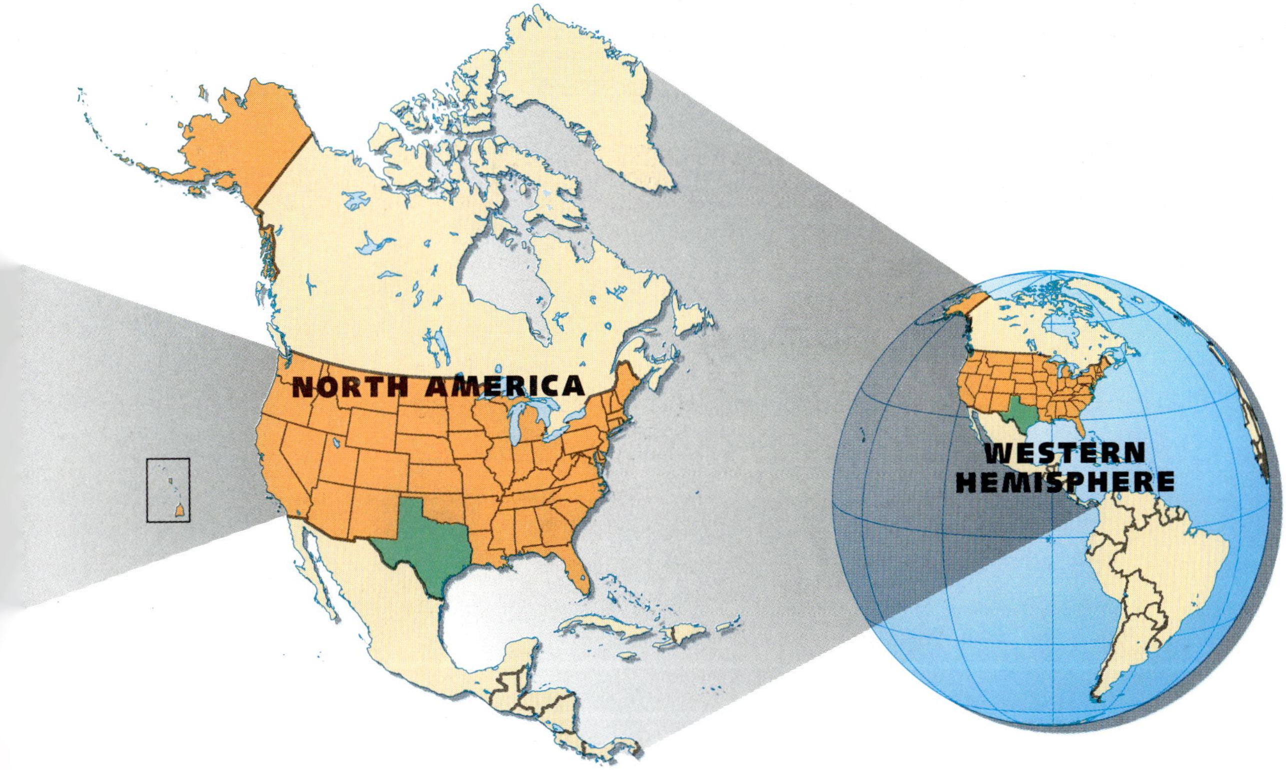

S·K·I·L·L·S

# How To Read a Map

## Why Is This Skill Important?

Knowing how to read maps is important for learning social studies and for taking action as a citizen. Maps tell you about the world around you through the five themes of geography: location, place, human-environment interactions, movement, and regions.

## Understand the Process

Maps are drawings of places on the Earth. Mapmakers include certain elements on most. These elements include the title; the key, or legend; the compass rose; the scale; and sometimes an inset map. Mapmakers often add a grid of numbered lines to help people locate places more easily.

1. The **map title** tells you the subject of the map. The title may also help you understand what kind of map it is. Physical maps show landforms and bodies of water. Political maps show cities and state and national borders. Many of the maps in this

### THE UNITED STATES

book are historical maps that show Texas as it was in the past.

2. The **map key**, or map legend, explains what the symbols used on the map stand for. Symbols may be colors, patterns, lines, or other special marks, such as circles, triangles, or squares. According to the map key for the map on this page, dots are used to show large cities. A star stands for the state capital of Texas, Austin.

3. The **compass rose**, or direction marker, shows the main, or cardinal, directions—north, south, east, and west. It also helps you find the intermediate directions, which are between the cardinal directions. Intermediate directions are northeast, southeast, southwest, and northwest.

4. The **map scale** compares a distance on a map with a distance in the real world. A map scale helps you find the real distance between places on a map.

A small map within a larger map is called an **inset map**. Inset maps have their own scales. Inset maps make it possible to show places in greater detail or to show places that are beyond the area covered on the main map.

5. The lines on some maps that cross each other to form a pattern of squares are called a **grid**. One set of lines crosses the map from left to right, or west to east. These are called lines of latitude. Another set of lines crosses the map from top to bottom, or north to south. These are called lines of longitude. The location of a place can be described by the spot where a line of latitude and a line of longitude cross.

## Think and Apply

Map Skill

Look at the maps on pages 28 and 29. Identify the parts of the maps. Discuss with a partner what information you find.

# Civics and Government

In studying **civics** and **government** you learn about citizenship and the ways in which citizens govern themselves. A government is the system that helps people in a community live together in order and safety. In Texas and other communities, citizens have an important part in making the government work. The laws that guide the actions of people are written and carried out by citizens. In *Stories in Time* you will learn how the Texas government works today. You will also learn about the people and events that shaped the government of Texas in the past.

# Economics

The **economy** of a country or state is the way its people use its resources to meet their needs. The study of how people do this is called economics. In *Stories in Time* you will read about how people in Texas in the past made, bought, sold, and traded goods to get what they needed or wanted. You will learn how the economy of Texas came to be what it is today.

# Culture

In this book you will learn about people of the past who have made Texas what it is today. You will learn who these people were, what they looked like, and how they spoke and acted. You will explore their customs and beliefs and their ways of thinking and expressing ideas. You will look at their families and communities. All these things make up their **culture**. Each human group has a culture. In *Stories in Time* you will discover the many cultures in Texas's story, past and present.

✓ **What kinds of things do you learn when you study civics and government, economics, and culture?**

S·K·I·L·L·S

# HOW TO

# Work Together in Groups

## Why Is This Skill Important?

Learning social studies is sometimes easier when you work with a partner or in a group. Many projects you will do in class would be difficult for one person to do. If you work with other students, each of you can work on part of a project. For a group project to succeed, each member needs to cooperate with the others. Knowing how to work together is an important skill for students and for all citizens.

## Understand the Process

Suppose your group was asked to do a project, such as presenting a short play about the Battle of the Alamo. You might find it helpful to follow a set of steps.

1. Organize and plan together.
   - Set your goal as a group.
   - Share your ideas.
   - Cooperate with others to plan your work.
   - Make sure everyone has a job.
2. Act on your plan together.
   - Take responsibility for your jobs.
   - Help one another.
   - If there are conflicts, take time to talk about them.
   - Show your group's finished work to the class.
3. Talk about your work.
   - Discuss what you learned by working together.

## Think and Apply

Follow these steps for working together as you take part in the activities in *Stories in Time*.

BUILDING CITIZENSHIP

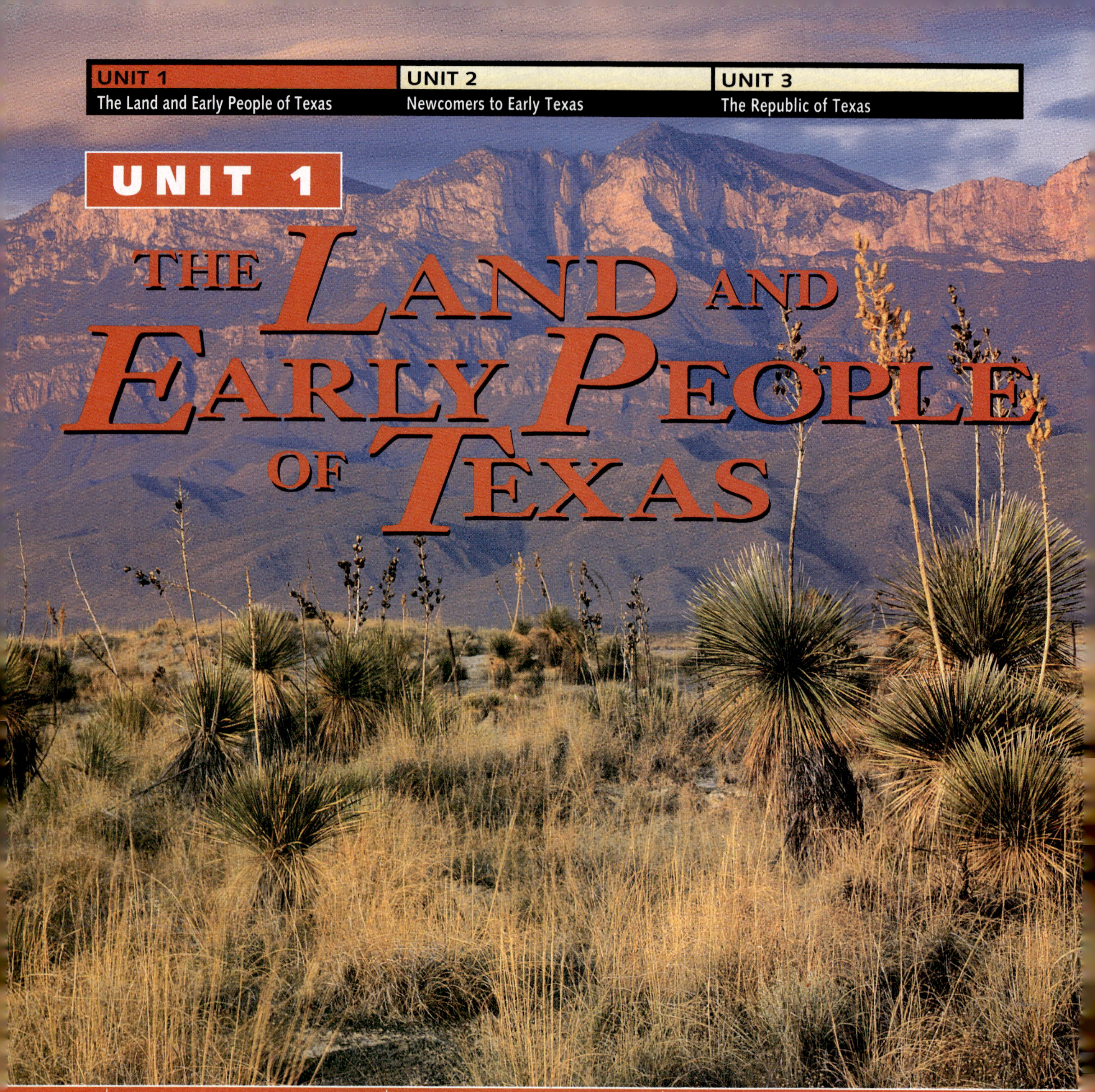

# UNIT 1

# THE LAND AND EARLY PEOPLE OF TEXAS

**14,000 years ago**

**12,000 years ago**

**By 12,000 years ago**
Earliest people follow herds of animals into what is now Texas

**10,000 years ago**

**10,000 years ago**
Giant animals die out and many people leave

**8,000 years ago**

**7,000 years ago**
New groups of people arrive

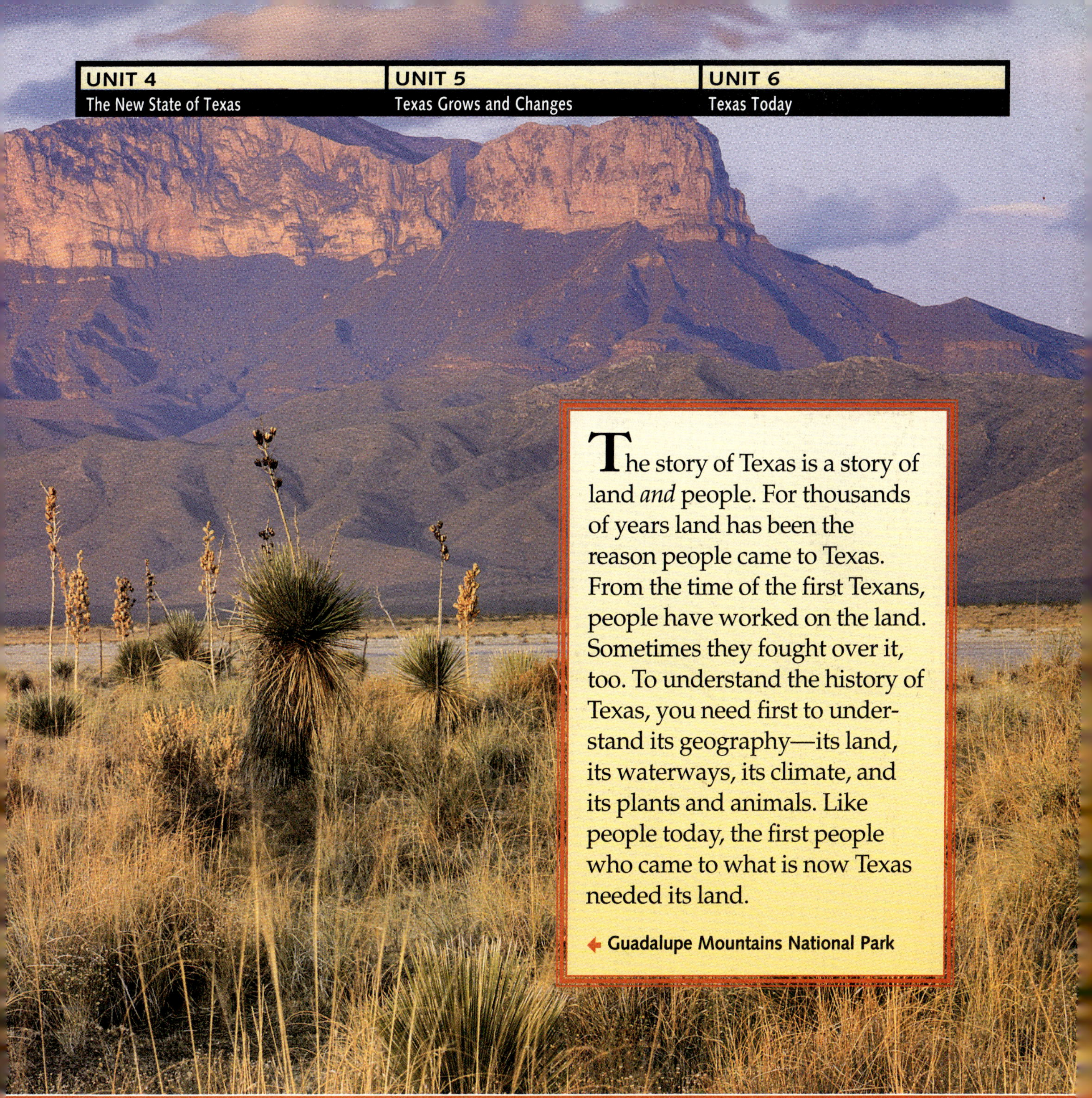

The story of Texas is a story of land *and* people. For thousands of years land has been the reason people came to Texas. From the time of the first Texans, people have worked on the land. Sometimes they fought over it, too. To understand the history of Texas, you need first to understand its geography—its land, its waterways, its climate, and its plants and animals. Like people today, the first people who came to what is now Texas needed its land.

**Guadalupe Mountains National Park**

**6,000 years ago** | **4,000 years ago** | **2,000 years ago** | **Present**

**2,000 years ago**
People begin farming in what is now Texas

**300 years ago**
Indians in North America begin riding horses to hunt buffalo

*Set the Scene with Literature*

# THE ARMADILLO FROM AMARILLO

WRITTEN AND ILLUSTRATED BY
LYNNE CHERRY

**Sasparillo Armadillo (sas•puh•RIH•loh ar•muh•DIH•loh) wants to know where in the world he is. Beginning in South Texas, Armadillo travels across the state. Read about the different kinds of land he sees and the places he visits on his journey.**

An armadillo from Texas wondered,
"Where in the world am I?
What's out beyond these tangled woods?
What's out beyond the sky?"

So Armadillo packed up his things
and left his home behind.
He headed off on a northeast course
to seek what he could find.

He traveled to the nearby city
of San Antonio,
and from the top of the highest tower,
he saw where he might go.

But Armadillo still wondered, "Where?
Where in the world am I?
What's out beyond the prairie grass?
What's out beyond the sky?"

He followed the river past twisted oaks,
through ancient juniper trees
shared by warblers and vireos
and Carolina chickadees.

**vireos** (VIR•ee•ohz)
small, colorful birds

The landscape changed dramatically
through woodland, towns, and plains.
Armadillo explored canyons
and walked through heavy rains.

He walked for weeks and came to Austin,
continued west and north
to Abilene and Lubbock,
he hiked and sallied forth.

**sallied** (SA•leed)
traveled

Armadillo often along the way
climbed up to higher ground.
He scurried up the canyon walls
and stopped to look around.

How different were the plains above—
flowers went on for a mile!
Armadillo decided to settle down
and stay there for a while.

But Armadillo still wondered, "Where?
Where in the world *am* I?
Perhaps I'd have a better idea
if I could somehow fly."

One day he asked the golden eagle
as she came breezing by,
"What can I do for a bird's-eye view
from up in the big blue sky?"

"Hop on my back," said the eagle.
"I'll fly you wide and far.
And then you'll see, eventually,
where in the world we are."

Upward and upward the eagle flew.
Armadillo held on tight.
"With my tail-tip curled I'll explore the world
from morning until night!"

Armadillo looked down below and asked,
"Where in the world *are* we?"
"We're over a prairie, and in the distance,
that's Amarillo you see.

"We've flown over the prairie.
We've flown over a town.
Amarillo means yellow, my dear little fellow,
and the prairie's all yellow and brown!"

"I see Amarillo," said Armadillo.
"Could we see all Texas, though?
And if we fly *higher* up into the sky,
could we see New Mexico?

"Or if we fly *higher* up into the sky,
could we see the entire earth?"
"Well, certainly, surely, if you hold on securely,
we'll try!" cried the eagle with mirth.

"*Amarillo's* a *city*?" asked Armadillo.
To this the eagle replied,
"Yes, Amarillo's a city in *Texas,*
the *state* where we reside.

"And Texas is in the *United States*,
our *country* wide and dear,
on the *North American continent,*
which is on the *earth,* a sphere."

CHAPTER 1

# THE TEXAS LANDSCAPE

> “Texas is an endless vista of changing landscapes . . . coastal plains and arid desert; and, of course, the coast, washed by the warm waters of the Gulf of Mexico. . . . Texas was always exciting to me.”
>
> Lady Bird Johnson, wife of former President Lyndon Baines Johnson

LESSON 1

# THE SHAPE OF THE LAND

## Link to Our World

**What does the land look like where you live?**

***Focus on the Main Idea***
**Read to find out what makes each of the four land regions of Texas different.**

***Preview Vocabulary***
**natural region**
**coastal plain**
**inland**
**sea level**
**elevation**
**panhandle**
**escarpment**
**plateau**
**basin**

When Claudia Alta Taylor was only two years old, people started to call her Lady Bird. They said she was "as pretty as a lady bird." After Lady Bird grew up and married Texas leader Lyndon Baines Johnson, her travels became a geography lesson of her home state. As the wife of a state leader, she visited much of Texas and learned about her state's natural regions. A **natural region** is a part of the Earth that has one major kind of natural feature, such as mountains or plains.

## THE GULF COASTAL PLAIN

Lady Bird grew up in the East Texas town of Karnack. Karnack is about 150 miles (241 km) east of Dallas on a broad, tree-filled coastal plain. A **coastal plain** is low, mostly flat land that lies alongside an ocean.

The Coastal Plain region of the United States lies along the Atlantic Ocean and the Gulf of Mexico. The part of the Coastal Plain that is in Texas is called the Gulf Coastal Plain. This region stretches along the Gulf of Mexico from Port Arthur, near the Louisiana border, to Brownsville in South Texas. The Gulf Coastal Plain reaches nearly 200 miles (322 km) inland from the Gulf. **Inland** means "away from the coast." The Gulf Coastal Plain covers much of East and South Texas—almost one-third of the state.

The land of the Gulf Coastal Plain is lowest near the Gulf of Mexico, where it is at sea level. Land no higher

You might find a starfish somewhere along the 367 miles (591 km) of shoreline in Texas.

Map Skill **REGIONS** Texas is a large state with four different natural regions.
■ Which natural region extends the farthest east?

than the surface of an ocean is said to be at **sea level**. As you move inland, however, the land begins to rise. By the time you reach Austin, the **elevation**, or height of the land, is about 550 feet (168 m) above sea level.

**What does the land on the Gulf Coastal Plain look like?**

## The Central Plains

Lady Bird and Lyndon Johnson lived on a ranch west of Austin, the capital of Texas. Austin is on the edge of the Gulf Coastal Plain. Not far north of the city is another region of plains, called the Central Plains.

Rolling hills cover much of the Central Plains in Texas. In many places rivers and streams have cut steep-sided hills and valleys into the land.

The elevation of the Central Plains is higher than that of the Gulf Coastal Plain. Here the land rises from about 600 feet (183 m) above sea level in the east to about 2,000 feet (610 m) above sea level at the western edge.

**What land features make up the Central Plains region of Texas?**

## The High Plains

To the west of the Central Plains lie the Great Plains, or High Plains. This natural region is higher and more level than the land to the east. The Great Plains of North America reach from Central Texas north into Canada.

Most of the Texas Panhandle lies on the High Plains. A **panhandle** is a narrow strip of land that is joined to a bigger piece of land. On a map this land looks like the handle of a pan.

In the Texas Panhandle the border between the Central Plains and the High Plains is marked by a landform called the Cap Rock Escarpment. An **escarpment** is a long wall of steep cliffs where the elevation of the land changes. At Cap Rock the rolling Central Plains meet the high, flat land of the High Plains. When the Spanish explorers first saw this land, they were surprised at what seemed to be an "ocean of land."

In the southern part of the High Plains region of Texas is a landform called the Edwards Plateau. Like any other **plateau** (pla•TOH), part of the land of the Edwards Plateau is high and flat, like a table. The southern and eastern parts of the Edwards Plateau, however, have many hills. In fact, this land west of Austin is so hilly that it is often called the Hill Country. Lyndon Baines Johnson grew up in the Hill Country, and he and Lady Bird lived on a ranch there.

The southern High Plains region in Texas is marked by another escarpment, the Balcones Escarpment. The word *balcones* (bal•KOH•nays) is Spanish for "balconies," which is what the escarpment looks like. South and east of the Balcones Escarpment lies the lower land of the Gulf Coastal Plain.

**What landforms mark the High Plains region in Texas?**

Cap Rock Canyons State Park

**PLACE** The state of Texas has a variety of landforms.

- How do the landforms in East Texas differ from those in West Texas?

## THE MOUNTAINS AND BASINS

The most western region of Texas is the Mountains and Basins region. It is the highest and the driest part of Texas. Lady Bird Johnson once said this land was like "great soaring cliffs that rose up on each side like giant pipe organs."

The mountains here are part of the Rocky Mountains, which stretch through the western United States from Mexico to

Texas has 91 mountains that are 5,280 feet (1,609 m) or higher. The highest of these is Guadalupe Peak.

## LANDFORMS ACROSS TEXAS

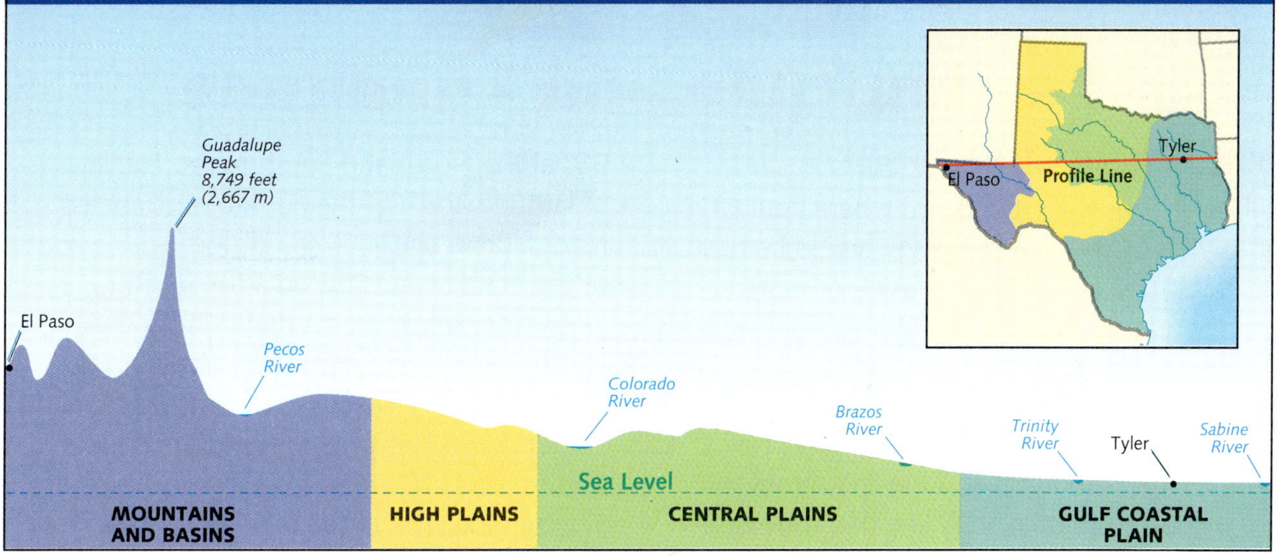


**LEARNING FROM DIAGRAMS** If you were to drive from Tyler to El Paso, you would cross all four natural regions in Texas.

■ What natural region would you be in once you crossed the Colorado River?

Canada. In Texas the Rocky Mountains are made up of many small mountain ranges. The Davis Mountains are about in the center of the Mountains and Basins region. The Chisos Mountains are to the south, and the Guadalupe (gwah•dah•LOO•pay) Mountains lie to the north. Guadalupe Peak is the highest point in Texas at 8,749 feet (2,667 m) above sea level.

Between the mountains are large, dry basins. A **basin** is low, bowl-shaped land with higher ground all around it. The basins in this Texas region are deserts. The largest is the Chihuahuan (chee•WAH•wahn) Desert.

**✓ What landforms make the Mountains and Basins region different from the plains regions?**

## LESSON 1 REVIEW

### Check Understanding

1. **Recall the Facts** What are the four natural regions of Texas?
2. **Focus on the Main Idea** How is each natural region in Texas different from the others?

### Think Critically

3. **Link to You** Which region of Texas do you live in? Describe the land where you live.
4. **Think More About It** More people live in the Gulf Coastal Plain region than in the other regions. Why do you think this is so?

### Show What You Know

**Map Activity** Use clay to make a landform map of Texas. Model the land features of each of the four natural regions. Display your map in the classroom.

SKILLS

# HOW TO

# Use Latitude and Longitude

## Why Is This Skill Important?

Has anyone ever asked you where your city or town is? One correct answer would be to say it is in Texas. But there is another more specific way to tell where a place is.

## Latitude and Longitude

To help you find places, mapmakers draw lines on maps and globes. One line shows the **equator**, an imaginary line that runs east and west around the middle of the Earth. The equator is a line of **latitude**, or a parallel. Other lines of latitude also run east and west around the globe, above and below the equator.

Lines of latitude are measured in degrees (°). They are measured from 0° at the equator to 90° at the North and South poles. The lines of latitude north of the equator are labeled *N* for North. The lines of latitude located south of the equator are labeled *S* for South.

Another set of lines is drawn from the North Pole to the South Pole. These north-south lines are called lines of **longitude**, or meridians. The **prime meridian** is the starting point for measuring all the other lines of longitude. The prime meridian passes near London, England.

Lines of longitude are measured from 0° at the prime meridian to 180°. Lines of longitude west of the prime meridian are labeled *W* for West. Those lines east of the prime meridian are labeled *E* for East.

**LATITUDE AND LONGITUDE**

**LATITUDE**

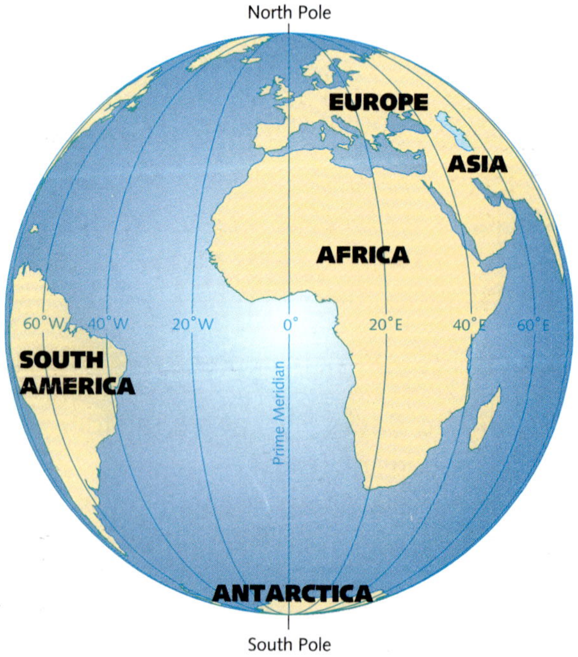


**LONGITUDE**

TEXAS LATITUDE AND LONGITUDE

## Understand the Process

When lines of latitude and longitude are drawn on a map or globe, they form a pattern called a grid. These lines make it easy to find **location**, where a place is. You can give the location of a place by naming the lines of latitude and longitude that lie closest to that place.

- What line of latitude is closest to the southern tip of Texas?
- What line of longitude is closest to the eastern border of Texas?
- Find Midland on the map of Texas. On what line of latitude is Midland? On what line of longitude is Midland? To tell where Midland is located, name its latitude first and then its longitude. Midland is near 32°N latitude and 102°W longitude.
- Look at the map of Texas again. Find Austin. Which line of latitude is closest to it? Which line of longitude is closest? Austin is near 30°N latitude and 98°W longitude.
- How can you explain where Beaumont and Lubbock are on the map? Beaumont is near 30°N latitude and 94°W longitude. Lubbock is near 34°N latitude and 102°W longitude.
- What lines of latitude and longitude are best for describing the location of Wichita Falls?

## Think and Apply

Map Skill Use latitude and longitude to tell where you live in Texas. Write a paragraph to describe to a friend how you found your location on the map.

# Lesson 2

# Rivers and Streams

## Link to Our World

**How do rivers and streams change the land?**

***Focus on the Main Idea***
**Read to find out how rivers can both wear down and build up land.**

***Preview Vocabulary***

| | |
|---|---|
| **aquifer** | **erosion** |
| **channel** | **canyon** |
| **tributary** | **floodplain** |
| **river system** | **dam** |

There are more than 40 rivers and 11,000 streams in Texas. Some of these waterways are wide and deep. Others are narrow and shallow. Some are always full of water, while others have just a little water for much of the year. Yet all rivers and streams change the land of Texas.

The Rio Grande flows through Santa Elena Canyon.

### Water on the Land and in the Land

What happens to the water that falls on the land when it rains? Some water dries up. Some sinks into the ground. The rest runs down the land's surface and becomes part of a river or stream.

The place where a river or stream begins is its source, or starting place. The Rio Grande is the longest river in Texas. It marks the border between Texas and Mexico. The Rio Grande starts in the Rocky Mountains, where melting snow forms a small stream.

Not all rivers start in mountains, though. Many Texas rivers have their source in the High Plains. Some of these rivers begin where lakes spill over their shores. Others are formed where water pours out of springs under the ground. These springs get their water from underground pools between layers of rock and sand. These unseen pools of water are called **aquifers** (A•kwuh•ferz). Aquifers fill with water when rain soaks into the ground.

No matter where or how they start, all rivers and streams flow from higher to lower ground. Along the way each carves a **channel**, or path, through the land.

At the end of a river or stream is its mouth. The mouth of a river or stream is the place where it flows into a larger body of water. Most of the rivers and streams in Texas flow into the Gulf of Mexico.

**What are the three main parts of a river or stream?**

## DRAINING THE LAND

The Rio Grande flows 1,885 miles (3,034 km) from its source in the Rocky Mountains to its mouth at the Gulf of Mexico. On the river's long journey, it is joined by other bodies of water,

Rivers in Texas range from the Rio Grande (right), at 1,885 miles (3,034 km) long, to the Comal River, which is just 2.5 miles (4 km) long.

**LOCATION** There are three groups of rivers in Texas. The rivers of one group flow into the Mississippi River valley. The rivers of another group flow directly into the Gulf of Mexico. A third group includes the Rio Grande and its tributaries.

- Which major rivers on this map do not flow directly into the Gulf of Mexico?

or tributaries (TRIH•byuh•tair•eez). A **tributary** is a river or stream that flows into a larger river or stream. Tributaries are sometimes called branches.

Together a river and its tributaries make up a **river system**. All river systems drain, or carry water away from, the land around them.

Sooner or later the water in most Texas rivers and streams reaches the Gulf of Mexico. Rivers in the northern part of the state, such as the Red River, are tributaries of the Mississippi River, which flows east of Texas. The Mississippi River flows into the Gulf of Mexico.

Not all Texas rivers drain into the Gulf of Mexico, however. In basins, like those in West Texas, rivers drain into low, bowl-shaped land. In a basin there is no place for water to go. Rivers that flow down from the Texas Mountains and Basins region do not flow into the Gulf. Most flow into desert lands and dry up.

**What are some ways rivers drain the land?**

## WEARING DOWN THE LAND

Rivers have great power to shape the land. As one scientist has said, "There is no force on this planet more powerful than water flowing over time." In Texas the erosion (ih•ROH•zhuhn) caused by flowing water has formed many of the state's land features. **Erosion** is the wearing away of the land's surface.

> ***"THERE IS NO FORCE ON THIS PLANET more powerful than water flowing over time."***
>
> Rod Nash, scientist

Over time, flowing water has cut many deep canyons in Texas. A **canyon** is a narrow valley with steep sides. Canyons are formed as water erodes the land.

The moving water sweeps rocks and sand down the river channel. It also carries soil that has been washed into the river by rain. As the rocks, sand, and soil are bounced and tumbled in the moving water, they scrape along the river bottom and sides. This helps the flowing water carve an even deeper and wider path.

**How does a river shape a canyon?**

Millions of years ago the Rio Grande cut this deep canyon into the land of Texas.

Flooding can be a serious problem in some parts of Texas. What kinds of damage can a flood cause?

## FLOODS AND PEOPLE

Flowing water tears down the land, but it can also build it up. A river may add new soil to its floodplain. A **floodplain** is the low, flat land along a river. When a river floods, water spreads out over the floodplain. As the floodwaters flow back into the river's channel, silt is left behind. Silt is fine sand and soil. After many floods, this silt builds up into rich soil.

At one time or another, most rivers flood. Floods can do much more than just cover the ground with muddy water. They can destroy homes and farms and people's lives. Texans know how quickly a dry river bottom can become a wild, rushing river. People in some parts of Texas have built walls, or **dams**, across many rivers and streams to help control flooding. A dam can protect against flooding by not letting too much water flow through the river at one time.

**What have some people in Texas done to control flooding on the rivers?**

## LESSON 2 REVIEW

### Check Understanding

1. **Recall the Facts** How do rivers in Texas get their start?
2. **Focus on the Main Idea** In what ways do rivers and streams wear down and build up the land?

### Think Critically

3. **Personally Speaking** Do you think people should choose to live on floodplains? Explain your answer.

### Show What You Know

**Observation Activity** Flowing water is always eroding the land. Look around your home, your school, or your neighborhood. What kinds of erosion do you see? Describe each kind. Then compare your findings with those of a classmate.

LESSON 3

# WEATHER AND CLIMATE

## Link to Our World

**What gives the place where you live a climate all its own?**

***Focus on the Main Idea***

**Read to find out why different places in Texas have different climates.**

***Preview Vocabulary***

| | |
|---|---|
| **climate** | **precipitation** |
| **temperature** | **drought** |
| **humid** | **tornado** |
| **norther** | **hurricane** |

A writer named Michael Grant once described the weather of Texas with the words "hot, dry, dust, wind, cold, sleet, thunder, puddles, drama." What words might you use to describe the weather where you live?

The kind of weather a place has most often, year after year, makes up its **climate**. Climate has three main parts. They are temperature (TEM•per•choor), wind, and precipitation (prih•sih•puh•TAY•shuhn).

The Panhandle of Texas receives more than 24 inches (61 cm) of snow a year.

### TEMPERATURE

**Temperature** is the measure of how warm or cold a place is. Often the temperature of a place depends on its location.

Texas is located far to the south in the United States. Its southern border is only about 26 degrees north of the equator. Places that are near the equator generally have a warm climate. The line of latitude that passes between San Antonio and Houston also passes through the deserts of North Africa!

Because of its location, Texas is very hot in the summer. Temperatures in some places are often above 100°F (38°C). The highest temperatures are found in the southern part of Texas along the Rio Grande.

Temperature also depends on elevation. Land that is higher above sea level has lower temperature. Temperatures there might drop as much as 3 degrees Fahrenheit for every 1,000 feet (305 m) in elevation. So it is no surprise that the coolest temperatures in Texas are found in the mountains of West Texas.

**How do location and elevation affect climate?**

## Wind

Because East Texas is close to the Gulf of Mexico, it gets lots of humid air. **Humid** air has a lot of moisture, or water, in it.

In summer the water of the Gulf is cooler than the land. So winds blowing across the Gulf help keep the land near the coast cooler than places farther inland. In winter the Gulf water is warmer than the land. Winds blowing warm, humid air help keep the coastal areas warm in winter.

Unlike the humid air in East Texas, the air in southwestern Texas is dry. Winds blowing dry air come from northern Mexico. Because these winds cross land, they carry little moisture.

Different still are the winds in the Panhandle of North Texas. They blow into Texas from the north. In winter great blasts of cold air called **northers** may suddenly sweep into the region.

Frederick Law Olmsted, who visited Texas in the 1850s, described a norther this way:

> "First a chilly whiff, then a puff . . . and bang, it is upon us."

Northers may bring snow, ice, and freezing winds. Temperatures drop quickly when a norther hits, and its chill may be felt from the High Plains to the Gulf Coastal Plain.

**How do winds blowing over land and over water affect climate in Texas?**

## Precipitation

Precipitation is another important part of climate. **Precipitation** can be rain, sleet, hail, or snow. Precipitation is most often measured as rainfall.

Some places in Texas get very little precipitation. Other places get a lot—sometimes all at one time! More than 20 inches (51 cm) fell around Houston during four days in 1994. It caused the San Jacinto (SAN jah•SIN•toh) River to flood, and 13,000 people living on the floodplain had to leave their homes. In most years Houston gets 45 inches (114 cm) of precipitation for the whole year.

Cloudbursts, like this one, sometimes soak the normally dry land of West Texas.

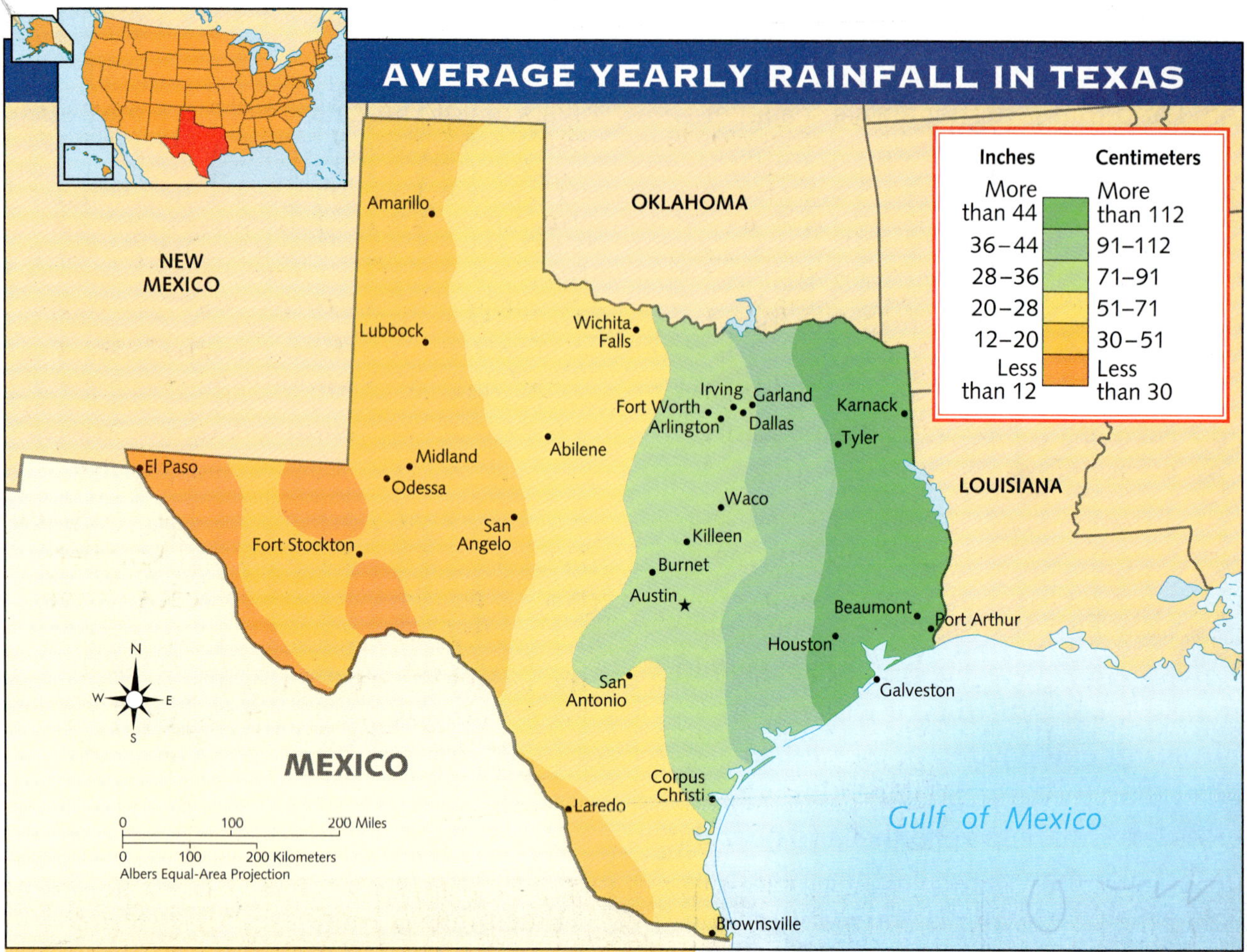


Map Skill **PLACES** The amount of rain Texas receives varies greatly in different parts of the state.

- Which city receives more rain, Lubbock or Killeen?

There is less rainfall in Texas as you move from east to west across the state. East Texas receives between 40 and 50 inches (between 102 and 127 cm) of precipitation a year. West Texas gets only 8 to 15 inches (20 to 38 cm) of precipitation each year.

Even with the dry climate, floods are still a problem in the Mountains and Basins region of West Texas. When it does rain there, sometimes it really pours! The sky may suddenly get dark. Then a cloudburst, or sudden hard rain, may quickly flood the land.

One Texas writer said that rain comes up in almost every conversation. "Did you get any, how much, where, hope you do."

A long period of very little or no rain is called a **drought**. Droughts can be serious. If the weather gets too dry, the soil can blow away and the rivers and streams can dry up.

**How is precipitation different in East and West Texas?**

Lack of rain has caused this land to crack. Many parts of West Texas often experience drought conditions like this.

## Stormy Weather

The "drama" in Michael Grant's words about Texas is for the state's strong, and often sudden, storms. Texas seems to have more kinds of storms than any other state. At times, these storms damage property and hurt people.

Besides the northers sweeping through North Texas in the winter, huge thunderstorms often form there in spring and fall. When cold air from the north meets warm air from the south, these storms may drop hail, or pieces of ice, along with rain.

In the spring, North Texas also has tornadoes (tawr•NAY•dohz). A **tornado**, also called a twister, is a funnel-shaped storm with swirling winds. The narrowest part of the tornado travels near the ground. When the tornado touches the ground, its strong winds can blow apart buildings and overturn cars and trucks.

Every few years a hurricane roars in from the Gulf of Mexico. A **hurricane** is a very strong storm that brings high winds and heavy rains. Storm clouds whirl around the eye, or center, of the hurricane at speeds up to 150 miles (241 km) per hour. The strong winds can cause huge waves. When a hurricane hits the coast, the waves can cause flooding over the land and damage to buildings.

On April 10, 1979, a tornado devastated the city of Wichita Falls.

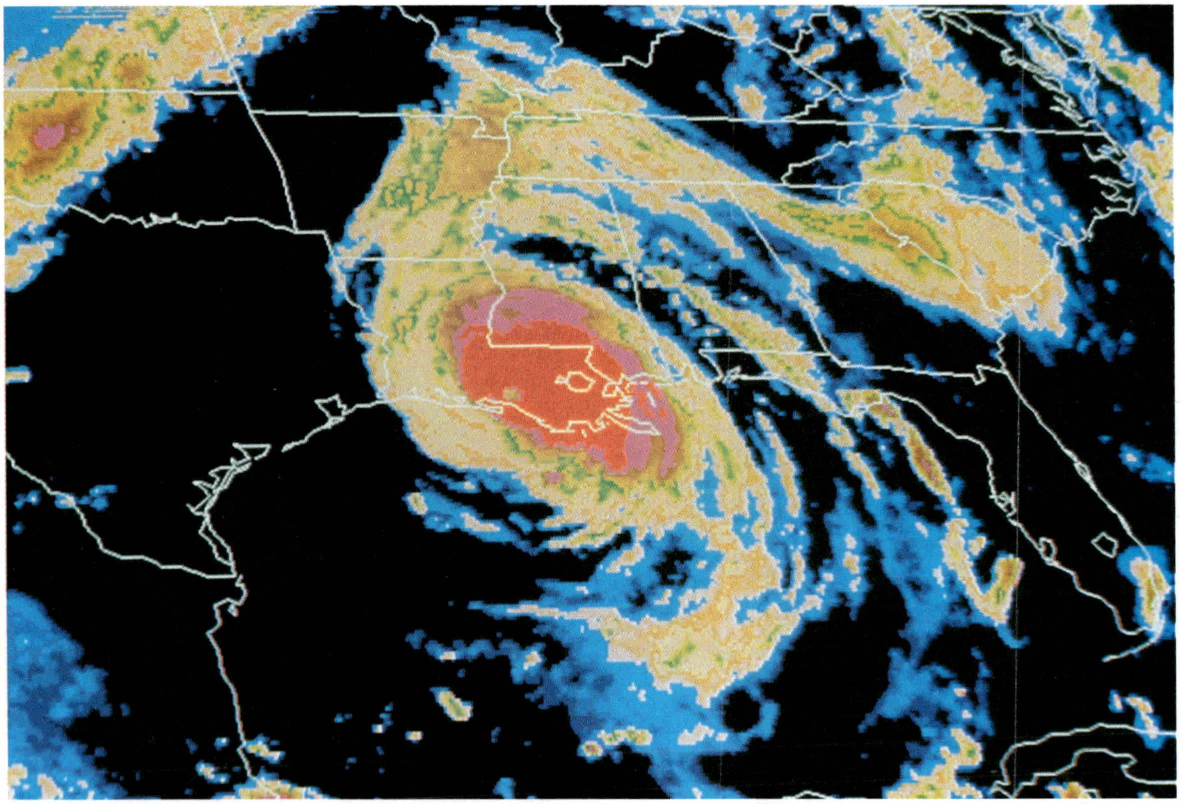

This photo, taken from space, shows the shape of a hurricane near Texas. How might a hurricane affect the people who live in the Gulf Coastal Plain region of Texas?

On September 8, 1900, the worst hurricane in the history of Texas hit the city of Galveston. Winds of 120 miles (193 km) per hour and a wall of water 15 feet (4.5 m) high destroyed much of the city. More than 2,600 buildings were destroyed, and more than 6,000 people drowned in the flooding.

After the big hurricane of 1900, the people of Galveston built a seawall 17 feet (5 m) high for protection against hurricanes. When another hurricane struck Galveston, in 1915, the seawall kept waves from flooding the city, and few people lost their lives.

**What kinds of strong storms happen in Texas?**

## LESSON 3 REVIEW

### Check Understanding

1. **Recall the Facts** What is climate?
2. **Focus on the Main Idea** Why do different parts of Texas have different climates?

### Think Critically

3. **Think More About It** How might climate affect the way people live?
4. **Link to You** What affects the climate where you live?

### Show What You Know

**Planning Activity** Write down the steps your family might take if a storm should hit your area. Identify safe spots in your home, and make a list of supplies you might need for the storm. Share your plan with your family.

# Lesson 4
# Plant and Animal Life

## Link to Our World

**What kinds of plants and animals live in your part of Texas?**

***Focus on the Main Idea***
**Read to find out about the plants and animals in the different kinds of land in Texas.**

***Preview Vocabulary***
**vegetation**
**prairie**
**desert**
**mesquite**
**marsh**

When you know the climate of a place, you can understand the **vegetation**, or plant life, that grows there. Places with humid climates have some kinds of plants that do not grow in dry climates. Grasses can grow in dry climates as well as in warm, humid climates. Most trees, however, need a lot of moisture. Only places with a lot of precipitation have thick forests.

Once you know about the vegetation of a place, you can understand its animal life. The woodlands, grasslands, drylands, and wetlands of Texas are the homes of many kinds of animals.

## Woodlands

Thick grasses, bushes, and large trees grow in the eastern parts of the Gulf Coastal Plain. Forests, or woodlands, of pine trees cover much of the land. This part of East Texas came to be known as the Piney Woods. The Piney Woods covers more than 16 million acres—a region about the size of West Virginia!

"The best childhood you could possibly have was where I had mine, in the Piney Woods of East Texas," says one woman. "That soft, sandy land is good for going barefooted, and the woods are full of wild animals and things to eat."

Rabbits, squirrels, and deer eat the fruits and nuts of the many trees in the Piney Woods. Smaller plants, such as blackberry bushes and violets, cover the forest floor.

There are more than 500 varieties of violets. Some types are common in the woodlands of Texas.

South of the Piney Woods, near Beaumont, lies a woodland and swamp area called the Big Thicket. This region has been set aside as a national forest because of its interesting plant and animal life. Cypress trees grow out of the water, and pitcher plants eat insects. More than 300 kinds of birds live in the deep forest of the Big Thicket.

**What are the two woodland areas in East Texas?**

## GRASSLANDS

West of the Piney Woods are **prairies**, or flat grasslands. Farther west, in the Central Plains and High Plains, there is less yearly rainfall. Low bushes, cactus plants, and short grasses cover most of this land.

One fact about this area seems strange. Two narrow strips of forest cross through the prairies, forming an area called the Cross Timbers. Cedar, elm, oak, and many other trees grow in the Cross Timbers.

Horned lizards, sometimes called horned toads, live on the grasslands. To scare off other animals, these lizards sometimes shoot a tiny stream of blood from the corners of their eyes. Because they look so scary, horned lizards have been used as monsters in movies.

Prairie dogs also live on the grasslands in burrows, or holes. They dig their burrows close together, and some burrows are connected. Large groups of burrows, called prairie dog towns, are still found in some parts of the High Plains.

**Why does the Cross Timbers region seem strange?**

Horned lizards (above) and prairie dogs (below) are some of the Texas prairie's most interesting animals. Prairie dogs live in large groups that may include more than 500 members.

In dry desert regions of Texas, you might come face-to-face with a snake like this gray-banded king snake.

## DRYLANDS

In the basins of West Texas, the land is dry, with few plants. Most kinds of plants cannot live in this **desert**. Short grasses, low bushes, and cactuses grow here. So does the treelike bush called **mesquite** (muh•SKEET). The long roots of the mesquite search for underground water. Some mesquite roots may reach down 60 feet (18 m).

Snakes, lizards, rabbits, and mice are some of the animals that live in the drylands of West Texas. During the day they stay cool in holes and under plants. At night they come out to eat insects, plants, and other animals.

Small desert animals get water from the food they eat. These small animals are eaten by larger desert animals such as coyotes (ky•OH•teez) and foxes. Coyotes and foxes must get water from springs or water holes. Some deer and antelope live in the desert also.

**What plants and animals live in the Texas drylands?**

## What?

### Mesquite

Mesquite needs little water to grow. When it does get plenty of water, it grows into a large tree. Some mesquite trees grow as high as 60 feet (18 m). Tree trunks may be as wide as 3 feet (91 cm) across. Mesquite grows pods that look like green beans. People long ago often ate the pods. Today the pods are used as food for cattle and horses. People use mesquite wood for fuel, to make fence posts, and to build shelters.

The Aransas National Wildlife Refuge is an important wetlands area in Texas. Wildlife refuges protect species of animals that are in danger of becoming extinct.

## WETLANDS

Along the coast of the Gulf of Mexico are many shallow bays and flat, low wetlands called **marshes**. Marshes are areas of land that are often covered with water because the land is low.

Sea grasses grow in the water, and their seeds feed many kinds of birds. Other birds feed on the small animals that live in the shallow waters. From October to April the coastal marshes near Rockport are the home of one of the largest birds on Earth—the whooping crane. Whooping cranes are also called "whoopers," because their loud calls sound like blasts blown on a trumpet. Their wings measure more than 7 feet (2 m) from tip to tip. They stand about 5 feet (1.5 m) tall, which makes them the tallest birds in North America.

There are not many whooping cranes left in the world today. Scientists are trying to help them survive. Each year whooping cranes fly from as far away as Canada to spend the winter in the Aransas (uh•RAN•zuhs) National Wildlife Refuge. This refuge is known across the United States as one of the last homes of the whooping cranes.

✓ **Why do whooping cranes and other birds come to the Texas wetlands?**

## LESSON 4 REVIEW

### Check Understanding

1. **Recall the Facts** What are four kinds of land in Texas that have different types of plant and animal life?
2. **Focus on the Main Idea** How are the plants and animals different in the four kinds of land in Texas?

### Think Critically

3. **Think More About It** In what ways do the animals in different kinds of land depend on the plants there?
4. **Link to You** Name one kind of plant that can be found where you live, but not in some other places.

### Show What You Know

**Map Activity** Make a picture map, using plant and animal pictures cut from magazines. With your classmates, paste the pictures on an outline map of Texas to show where each kind of plant or animal lives.

S·K·I·L·L·S

# How To

## Use a Table to Group Information

### Why Is This Skill Important?

Have you made any comparisons lately? To make a comparison, you look at what is the same and what is different about two or more things. A table like the one below can help you group the information you are comparing.

### Remember What You Have Read

You have read about the vegetation and the animal life in the different kinds of land in Texas. The table below lists the things you learned in the lesson and shows you how to organize that information. Look at the table and think again about what you have read.

### Understand the Process

You can group many kinds of information by using the same kind of table. Use the following steps to set up your table.

1. Think about what you want to compare. This table compares plant and animal life in the different kinds of land in Texas.
2. Think about the best way to look at what is to be compared. This table groups the plants and animals by where they live—woodlands, grasslands, drylands, or wetlands.
3. What is the same and what is different about the plants and animals in different kinds of land?

### Think and Apply

Think about the first lesson in this chapter. Create a table for the four natural regions of Texas. Then compare the landforms in the different regions of the state.

Prickly-pear cactus

**SOME TEXAS PLANT AND ANIMAL LIFE**

| KINDS OF LAND | PLANT LIFE | ANIMAL LIFE |
|---|---|---|
| **Woodlands** | thick grasses<br>bushes<br>large trees<br>pitcher plants | rabbits<br>squirrels<br>deer<br>birds |
| **Grasslands** | low bushes<br>cactus plants<br>short grasses | horned lizards<br>prairie dogs |
| **Drylands** | short grasses<br>low bushes<br>cactus plants<br>mesquite | snakes<br>lizards<br>rabbits<br>mice<br>coyotes<br>foxes<br>deer<br>antelope |
| **Wetlands** | sea grasses | small water birds<br>whooping cranes |

Whooping cranes

# CHAPTER 1 REVIEW

## CONNECT MAIN IDEAS

Use this organizer to show that you understand how the chapter's main ideas are connected. First copy the organizer onto a separate sheet of paper. Then complete it by writing one or two sentences to summarize each lesson.

**The Texas Landscape**

**Lesson 1**
The Shape of the Land

**Lesson 2**
Rivers and Streams

**Lesson 3**
Weather and Climate

**Lesson 4**
Plant and Animal Life

## WRITE MORE ABOUT IT

1. **Write a Descriptive Paragraph** Describe what you might see, hear, feel, and smell if you took a walk through a forest, field, or other natural area near where you live.

2. **Design a Bumper Sticker** Write a saying about a natural feature, animal, or plant found in Texas. Then write your saying on a strip of paper to make a bumper sticker. Illustrate your work.

## USE VOCABULARY

Use each vocabulary word in a sentence that helps explain its meaning.

1. elevation
2. plateau
3. river system
4. erosion
5. floodplain
6. precipitation
7. drought
8. tornado
9. vegetation
10. marsh

## CHECK UNDERSTANDING

1. Name the four natural regions of Texas. What landforms can be found in each region?
2. What is the driest region of Texas?
3. Describe the three parts of a river.
4. What is the longest river in Texas?
5. How is an aquifer filled?
6. How do river systems drain the land?
7. How have rivers shaped the land features of Texas?
8. How does the Gulf of Mexico affect climate in East Texas?
9. Name two woodland areas found in East Texas.
10. Name some plants and animals that can be found on the prairies of Texas.
11. Why is mesquite well suited to the drylands of Texas?

## THINK CRITICALLY

1. **Think More About It** How are tornadoes and hurricanes alike?
2. **Cause and Effect** Explain how flooding can help build rich soil over time.
3. **Explore Viewpoints** Why might some people not want to put a dam across a river?
4. **Think More About It** How is temperature related to climate?
5. **Cause and Effect** Two people are visiting the same mountain in the Chisos Mountains. One is standing at the bottom of the mountain. The other is at the top. Which person is more likely to need a sweater? Give a reason for your answer.
6. **Think More About It** Why are the animals that live in the woodlands different from those that live in the wetlands?

## APPLY SKILLS

Map Skill

**How to Use Latitude and Longitude** Look at the map of Texas on page 45. What is the longitude of the point farthest east in Texas? What is the longitude of the point farthest west? What is the latitude of the point farthest north in Texas? What is the latitude of the point farthest south?

**How to Use a Table to Group Information** Make a table to compare the temperature and precipitation in the four natural regions of Texas.

## READ MORE ABOUT IT

*Alamo Across Texas* by Jill Stover. Lothrop, Lee & Shepard. This book tells the story of an alligator's trip across Texas.

*Desert Voices* by Byrd Baylor and Peter Parnall. Aladdin. Ten creatures use poetry to describe their lives in the desert.

CHAPTER 2

# THE EARLIEST TEXANS

“We are of the soil and the soil is of us. We love the birds and beasts that grew with us on this soil. They drank the same water we did and breathed the same air. We are all one in nature.”

From a description of Native Americans by Chief Luther Standing Bear

Ancestors of today's Pueblo Indians once lived in West Texas.

LESSON 1

# Early People of Texas

## Link to Our World

**How do people today change as the world around them changes?**

***Focus on the Main Idea***
**Read to find out how life changed for the early people of Texas as their land and the climate changed.**

***Preview Vocabulary***

| | |
|---|---|
| **band** | **tribe** |
| **environment** | **specialize** |
| **scarce** | **culture** |
| **fertile** | **civilization** |

The very first people who lived in Texas used spear points like this to hunt large animals.

The earliest people to come to the land that is now Texas arrived thousands of years ago. Long before that time, a piece of land connected the continents of Asia and North America. People may have traveled on this land into North America. For thousands of years, these people's children and their children's children spread over the continent. They may have reached present-day Texas as early as 12,000 years ago.

## Land and People Long Ago

When the first people arrived, the land was very different from the Texas of today. Rainfall was greater. Moist prairies and forests covered much of the land.

The plant life fed many large animals. Some of these animals weighed thousands of pounds. Herds of giant deer, camels, buffalo, and huge mammoths—large, elephant-like animals—grazed on the prairies. Mastodons, which also looked like elephants, roamed the woodlands. They used their trunks to reach for leaves and tear off tree bark. Giant armadillos, some the size of a small car, searched for roots and insects to eat.

The first people to come to Texas were most likely hunters looking for food. They traveled in **bands**, or small groups of families that lived and worked together. Because they were always on the move, these people used shelters made of animal skins. The shelters could be set up and taken down quickly. At night the people camped near rivers or streams. During the day they followed the great herds and hunted.

Imagine how hard it was for these people to kill a giant mammoth! The animal stood 14 feet (4 m) tall and had tusks 14 to 16 feet (4 to 5 m) long. The hunters had nothing but spears with stone tips. To do their job they had to work as a team.

From just one mammoth a band got enough meat to last for months. The hide was used to make clothing and shelters. The bones became tools and weapons.

**✓ Why did the first people come to what is now Texas?**

**ROUTES OF EARLY PEOPLE**

**Map Skill** **MOVEMENT** Thousands of years ago early people began to move into what is now North America and South America.

■ What continents did the early people cross before reaching South America?

Early hunters used a spear-throwing stick called an atlatl. This tool made the spear travel with great speed and force.

## FOOD GATHERERS

Over hundreds and hundreds of years, the land slowly changed. The climate became hotter and drier. Lakes and rivers dried up. Many of the plants that the animals ate could no longer grow.

By about 10,000 years ago, most of the mammoths and other giant animals had died out, or become extinct.

Some people moved away as the **environment**, or the land and climate around them, changed. Other people changed their ways of life. Since they could no longer hunt giant animals for food, clothing, and shelter, they had to fish and to hunt for smaller animals. They also began to gather different kinds of plants for food.

Some early people lived in places where food was **scarce**, or hard to find.

In time they learned where certain plants grew best. They learned at what times of the year nuts, berries, and other plant parts would become ripe enough to eat. The people traveled each season to the places where they could gather food.

**What changes did early people make when the giant animals they hunted became extinct?**

## Early Farmers

By about 7,000 years ago, new groups of people had begun moving into the lands that are now Texas. These people's children and their children's children went on hunting and gathering food for thousands of years. About 2,000 years ago, however, some groups found that if they planted seeds, they could grow their own food. They began to farm.

Not all people became farmers, because not every place was good for farming. The first farms in the region were in what is now East Texas and along the Rio Grande. These places had plenty of water, and the soil was **fertile**, or rich.

### What?

#### Maize

Early people learned how to grow more maize, a kind of corn, by keeping the soil moist. One way they did this was by building small mud walls around each plant. When it rained, water stayed around the plant longer. When there was little rain, farmers poured water onto each plant. Some Native Americans still do these things in their gardens today.

This is a scene from a mural painted by the Mexican artist Diego Rivera. The scene shows how ancient American cultures grew maize.

Tulum, on the Yucatán Peninsula of Mexico, was once a great Mayan city.

The earliest farmers still hunted and gathered food. But many early farmers did not move from place to place for hunting and gathering. They settled in one place, cleared fields, and built shelters that would last. With more food, people lived longer and their numbers grew. Some formed **tribes**, or groups of many bands that share land and a way of life.

In some farming tribes, people began to **specialize**, or work on one job they could do well. Some people in a tribe specialized in making pots or weaving. Others became traders.

The tribes soon had their own cultures. Ways of dressing, speaking, behaving, and believing make up a **culture**. A tribe's culture sets it apart from other tribes.

**How did farming change the way some early people lived?**

## The Great Civilizations

People in Central and South America were among the first farmers in the Western Hemisphere, or western half of the Earth. Between 7,000 and 4,700 years ago, the earliest farmers learned how to grow beans, squash, and maize (MAYZ). Later the farmers grew other plants they could eat, such as tomatoes, pumpkins, peanuts, potatoes, and sweet potatoes.

Between 2,500 and 500 years ago, people near what is now Texas had developed great civilizations. A **civilization** (sih•vuh•luh•ZAY•shuhn) is a culture that usually has large cities and highly developed arts and sciences. To the south, in Mexico and Central America, the Mayas and Aztecs had formed great civilizations. To the east the Mound Builders of the Mississippi River valley and to the west the Pueblos of the Mountains and Basins region had great civilizations, too.

Each of the civilizations of North America was known for its art, music, and religion. To support people in cities, each civilization had to have highly developed ways to grow food.

Scientists believe that early people of present-day Texas may have met or been related to people from these great civilizations. Early people of Texas may have traded goods and ideas with those people.

**What four great civilizations grew near present-day Texas?**

## When?

### 600 Years Ago

About the same time the Aztecs had their civilization in Mexico, the Incas had a great civilization in South America. The land of the Incas stretched 2,500 miles (about 4,000 km) along the Andes Mountains, from present-day Colombia far into Chile. More than 7 million Incas lived and worked in cities and on farms. About this same time, Inuits hunted and gathered food in the Arctic region of North America. Ways of life for people in the Western Hemisphere were very different from one another.

An example of Inca pottery

## LESSON 1 REVIEW

### Check Understanding

1. **Recall the Facts** Why did mammoths and other giant animals die out in Texas?
2. **Focus on the Main Idea** How did life change for the early people when their environment changed?

### Think Critically

3. **Personally Speaking** Would you rather have lived as a hunter and gatherer or as a farmer? Explain your answer.
4. **Cause and Effect** How did farming affect the other kinds of work people did?

### Show What You Know

**Art Activity** Suppose you have written a book called *Early People of Texas.* Draw a cover for your book. Show the lives of hunters, gatherers, and farmers. Add your book cover to a bulletin board display in your classroom.

# LESSON 2 INDIANS OF THE GULF COASTAL PLAIN

## Link to Our World

**How do Texans today use the land and its resources?**

***Focus on the Main Idea***
**As you read, look for ways the early people of Texas used the land and its resources.**

***Preview Vocabulary***
**temple**
**exchange**
**confederation**
**nomad**
**shaman**

The early people of the Western Hemisphere are known as Native Americans or American Indians. By the year 1500, more than 30,000 Indians lived in what is now Texas. Most of these people lived on the Gulf Coastal Plain. Among these groups were the Caddos (KAD•ohz) in the Piney Woods, the Karankawas (kuh•RANG•kuh•wawz) in the wetlands along the coast, and the Coahuiltecans (koh•uh•WEEL•teh•kuhnz) in South Texas. Like people today, these people had to provide food, clothing, and shelter for themselves and their families.

Copy of a ceremonial pipe used by the Caddo Indians

### THE CADDOS

The largest and most developed group of Native Americans in Texas was the Caddos. About 25 separate bands of Caddos lived in the Piney Woods region. Each group had its own village.

The Caddos lived where there was fertile soil and plenty of rain. They lived by farming as well as by hunting and gathering. Maize was the most important food that they grew, but they also grew others. Most scientists believe the Caddos were related to the Mound Builders. The Mound Builders got their name because of the large mounds, or hills of earth, that the people built.

The Caddos lived in large, round houses with grass roofs. The houses looked like beehives. Some Caddo houses were as large as 30 feet (9 m) across. Inside was

The Caddos lived by farming as well as by hunting and gathering.

space for sleeping, storing food, grinding maize, and keeping a fire.

A group of 20 or more Caddo houses made up a village. In each village was a **temple**, a place to pray. A leader ruled each village. In some villages either men or women could become leaders.

The Caddos carved wood, wove cloth, and made pottery. They traded these goods mostly to people who lived on the Central Plains, to the west. The Caddos **exchanged**, or traded, wooden tools, cloth, and clay pots for buffalo skins.

Some of their neighbors attacked the Caddo villages, stealing goods and destroying shelters. To defend themselves, several groups of Caddo villages joined in a confederation. A **confederation** is a group made up of different, smaller groups who join to help one another.

**How did the land and climate of the Piney Woods help the Caddos?**

## What?

### The Name of Texas

Texas got its name from the Caddos. Members of the Caddo confederation called each other *tayshas,* which means "friends." When the Spanish explorers first met the Caddos, they tried to say *tayshas* in their own language. The word became *Tejas* (TAY•hahs). In English, *Tejas* became *Texas.* In time *Tejas* and *Texas* became the names for a land much larger than that of the region of the Caddos. Today the Texas state motto is *Friendship*.

## THE KARANKAWAS

South of the Caddos lived the Karankawas and other smaller Indian groups. These groups lived along the Gulf of Mexico, between present-day Galveston and Corpus Christi. The climate there is hot and humid, and the soil is sandy and wet. The Karankawas did not farm, but like the Caddos, they made the best use they could of their natural resources.

Map Skill **REGIONS** Indian groups settled in each of the four natural regions of Texas.

- Which Indian group lived in the region of Texas with the highest elevation?

The Karankawas lived in small bands, and they all shared the work of finding food. They were **nomads**, or people who move from place to place. They built their shelters not to last but to be easy to move. The Karankawas first stuck a pole into the ground or bent a small tree. Then they stretched animal skins or grass mats over the pole or tree. In warm weather they left the shelter only partly covered so that the wind could blow through it.

Much of what the Karankawas ate came from the sea and the wetlands. They used arrows and long, powerful bows to catch fish near the shore. They gathered oysters, turtles, and some plants. They also hunted alligators. The Karankawas often rubbed alligator fat or shark oil on their bodies to keep mosquitoes away.

The Karankawas spent much of their time hunting and gathering. They did not have time to specialize in jobs as the Caddos did. The tools that the Karankawas made were simple ones. They fished with bows and arrows because they did not make fishhooks. Their canoes, which were just tree trunks with the middle dug out, could not travel far without tipping.

**What natural resources did the Karankawas use?**

## THE COAHUILTECANS

The Coahuiltecans lived inland on the Gulf Coastal Plain to the west of the Karankawas. Like the Karankawas, the Coahuiltecans spent much of their time searching for food.

Food was scarce on the dry grasslands. The Coahuiltecans ate almost anything they could hunt or gather. They ate the fruit of prickly-pear cactuses and the beans of mesquite trees. They dug up the roots of the agave (ah•GAH•vay) plant and drank its sap. They used traps to catch rabbits, birds, wild pigs, and even deer. The Coahuiltecans also ate insects, worms, and snakes.

In this dry region, there was not enough food for large groups of people. So instead of living in villages as the Caddos did, the Coahuiltecans lived in small bands as the Karankawas did. Many of the bands, however, spoke a common language.

The members of a band were most often members of the same family. Some older group members were religious leaders called **shamans** (SHAH•muhnz). Shamans took care of people who were ill and kept the group's traditions alive.

Hundreds of small bands of Coahuiltecans spread over much of what is now South Texas. They lived there for a very long time and later mixed with other people. Like the other Indians of the Gulf Coastal Plains, the Coahuiltecans made the most of the natural resources they found.

Coahuiltecans were nomads, searching for their food rather than growing it themselves.

**In what ways were the Coahuiltecans and Karankawas alike?**

## LESSON 2 REVIEW

### Check Understanding

1. **Recall the Facts** What Native American groups lived on the Gulf Coastal Plain?
2. **Focus on the Main Idea** How did the early people of Texas use the land and its natural resources?

### Think Critically

3. **Past to Present** The early people of Texas had to meet their needs with few natural resources. How do Texans today handle the same problem?
4. **Personally Speaking** In what part of Texas would you choose to live if your family depended on hunting and gathering for food? Why?

### Show What You Know

**Storytelling Activity** Suppose you were an early Indian who lived on the Gulf Coastal Plain. Write a story to tell about one day in your life. Share your story with a group of classmates.

LESSON 3

# INDIANS OF THE CENTRAL AND HIGH PLAINS

## Link to Our World

**How might using new resources change people's way of life today?**

***Focus on the Main Idea***
**Read to find out how the buffalo and the horse changed life for the Indians of the Central Plains and the High Plains.**

***Preview Vocabulary***
**crop**
**tepee**
**council**

At the time of the early Indians, many buffalo, or American bison, as scientists call them, lived in North America. Millions of these hairy, cowlike beasts roamed the land. The herds were so large that they were said to blacken the horizon.

Buffalo roamed in four great herds over the middle of the continent. Scientists today call one of these herds the Texas herd. It covered the southern part of the High Plains of North America and the western edge of the Central Plains. The different groups of Indians in these regions hunted and used the buffalo in many ways.

Buffalo were an important resource to Indians of the High Plains and the Central Plains of Texas.

### THE TONKAWAS

The Tonkawas (TAHN•kuh•wuhz) lived on the Edwards Plateau near present-day Austin. Some of the tribe, however, used lands along the rivers and streams of the Central Plains to the east. The Tonkawas were nomads. They roamed the area that is now Central Texas, gathering nuts, fruits, and berries. They also hunted deer, rabbits, turtles, birds, and even snakes.

Living south of the great Texas herd, the Tonkawas did not see as many buffalo as other Plains Indians did. Yet the buffalo became important to the Tonkawas' way of life.

The Tonkawas ate almost every part of the animal, often eating the meat raw. To prepare for times when there were no buffalo to hunt, the Tonkawas dried some of the meat. The dried meat, which we know as jerky, could be kept for many months.

Almost everything the Tonkawas used was made from parts of the buffalo. They carried water in bags made from buffalo stomachs. They made tools from horns, rope from hair, and clothing from hides. They built shelters using buffalo hides and bones as well as other animal skins.

The Tonkawas used buffalo skins to make much of their clothing, such as moccasins (above).

Because the Tonkawas could not always find buffalo for food, they lived in small bands. Finding enough food for everyone was easier for a small band than for a large one.

**In what ways did the Tonkawas use the buffalo?**

## The Lipan Apaches

The Lipan Apaches (lee•PAHN uh•PACH•eez) lived in small groups and farmed. Their farms were small, more like gardens. Their **crops**, or plants grown for food, were maize, beans, and squash. The women of the tribe grew the crops.

This painting, by the artist Theodore Gentilz, shows a typical Lipan Apache camp.

The Lipan Apaches also hunted and gathered. The men hunted for food, roaming on foot from the Hill Country of Central Texas north to the Red River.

To get food and other materials, the Lipan Apaches often attacked the villages of the Caddos and other Indian groups. The Lipan Apaches were very good hunters. They became even better after they learned to ride horses.

**LEARNING FROM DIAGRAMS** The Plains Indians often communicated with one another through sign language.

- Why do you think the Indians raised their hands to the sides of the head to make the sign for buffalo?

Along with giant mammoths and other animals, horses had died out in North America long before—about 10,000 years ago. When the Spanish first came to North America in the 1500s, they brought horses with them from Europe. Some of the horses ran away and lived wild. During the 1600s some Indians began catching wild horses and learning to ride them. On horses the Indians could travel a long way to hunt buffalo. A group of Indians on horseback could kill as many animals as they needed.

Because the Lipan Apaches followed the buffalo herds, they built shelters that were easy to move. One kind was the **tepee**. The Lipan Apaches made tepees from buffalo hides. They stretched the hides over a circle of poles that were tied together at the top. A hole at the top of the tepee let out smoke from a campfire. Inside the tepee the ground was covered with hides. The Lipan Apaches also used hides for their beds.

Like the Tonkawas, the Lipan Apaches used the buffalo for many of their needs. However, after they got horses, the Lipan Apaches could depend on the buffalo for much of their food. They spent less time farming.

**✓ How did using the horse change the way the Lipan Apaches lived?**

The Comanches learned to tame wild horses and became excellent riders.

## The Comanches

The horse also changed life for the Comanches (kuh•MAN•cheez). The Comanches lived on the High Plains in what is today the Texas Panhandle. Before they had horses to ride, the Comanches lived in small bands as nomads. They gathered wild plants and hunted on foot.

With the horse the Comanches became fine buffalo hunters. With a steady supply of food, the Comanches were able to begin living in larger groups. Each group had one chief to lead its warriors and one chief to lead its hunters. A **council**, or group of leaders, helped the chiefs make decisions both in times of war and in times of peace.

Hunting and fighting were at the center of Comanche life. Fine riders and fierce warriors, the Comanches soon spread across much of Central Texas. The spread of the Comanches affected many of the other tribes. The Comanches pushed out the Tonkawas and the Lipan Apaches. These people in turn pushed other Indian groups from their lands.

**How were the Lipan Apaches and the Comanches alike?**

## Lesson 3 Review

### Check Understanding

1. **Recall the Facts** What three groups of Indians lived on the Central Plains and the High Plains of Texas?
2. **Focus on the Main Idea** How did the buffalo and the horse affect the lives of the Indian people?

### Think Critically

3. **Think More About It** Why was it important for Indian hunters to learn to ride a horse?
4. **Past to Present** The horse changed the way some Indians lived. What new things today are changing the way Texans live?

### Show What You Know

**Speaking Activity** Imagine that you are a young Indian who has caught a wild horse and learned to ride it. You think your group's members all should do the same. Plan a speech to give to the council. Explain how useful the horse would be for hunting and travel. Present your speech to a group of classmates.

S·K·I·L·L·S

# How To

# Read a Time Line

## Why Is This Skill Important?

Because time is hard to picture, people often use time lines to help them see when events happened. A **time line** is a graph that shows the order in which events took place and the amount of time that passed between them. To understand the early history of Texas, you need to know when important events happened.

## Understand the Process

The time line on this page shows when important events happened in the early history of Texas. The marks on the line show the units of time. Like a map, a time line has a scale. But the scale on a time line measures time, not distance. On the time line below, the space between two marks stands for one **century**, or 100 years. Just as days and years are units of time, so is a century. The dates near the left end of the time line came first. The dates near the right end of the time line came later.

The first event on this time line is the bringing of horses to North America by the Spanish. This happened in the sixteenth century, or between the years 1501 and 1600. Look to the right of that event to see the next important event. That was the first use of horses by the Plains Indians. This happened in the seventeenth century, or between the years 1601 and 1700. What was the next important event after that? Between which years did it take place? In which century was that?

## Think and Apply

Think about some of the important dates in your life, in the past and in the time to come. Make a time line that shows the twentieth and twenty-first centuries. Label the centuries and mark the year you were born, the year you will graduate from high school, and other important years for you in this and the next century. Add pictures to your time line and then display it on a bulletin board.

### HISTORICAL EVENTS IN THE EARLY HISTORY OF TEXAS

1501 | 1601 | 1701 | 1801

**16TH CENTURY**
The Spanish bring horses to North America

**17TH CENTURY**
Indians living on the plains begin to ride horses

**18TH CENTURY**
Comanches move through Texas on horses

# Lesson 4

# Indians of the Mountains and Basins

## Link to Our World

**How do people today solve the problems of living in very hot or very cold climates?**

***Focus on the Main Idea***

**Read to learn how the Jumanos and other desert peoples solved the problems of living in a hot, dry climate.**

***Preview Vocabulary***

| | |
|---|---|
| **adapt** | **ally** |
| **irrigate** | **government** |
| **adobe** | **ancestor** |

Early Indians were able to **adapt**, or fit their ways, to living in every region of Texas. The land and its resources affected where they lived and the kinds of shelters they built. Indians ate what they could grow, gather, or catch. They made their clothing from what they could find.

### The Jumanos

The Jumanos (hoo•MAH•nohs) lived in the far western part of what is now Texas. This part of the Mountains and Basins region is mostly desert. The Jumanos were able to live on this hot, dry land because they **irrigated** their crops. They moved water from nearby rivers and streams to their fields of maize, beans, squash, and cotton.

Most Jumanos farmed and lived in villages, but some were nomads. They gathered plants in the desert. They also hunted buffalo on the plains to the east. As they followed the herds, they traded with the people they met along the way. The Jumanos may have traded goods with the Caddos as far away as the Piney Woods.

Most Jumano villages in what is now West Texas were built close to the Rio Grande. Some were near the present-day city of El Paso. Their shelters were built of stone and **adobe** (ah•DOH•bay), or clay. Stone and adobe shelters were cool in summer and warm in winter.

This stone mask was made by Jumano Indians living in what is now New Mexico.

From time to time Apaches and Comanches attacked Jumano villages. They stole crops and the cotton cloth made by the Jumanos. Later the Jumanos became allies of the Apaches. An **ally** is a partner. These allies tried to fight off the Comanches, who were pushing out other Indian groups all over Texas.

**What did the Jumanos use to build their shelters?**

Hundreds of years ago there might have been a Jumano village on this land in West Texas.

## The Pueblo Civilization

The Jumanos may have learned many of their ways of living from the Pueblo Indians. The two groups were probably related to each other. The Pueblos lived in a great civilization in what is now the southwestern United States. They were located mostly in present-day New Mexico and Arizona.

Like their ancestors, some Pueblo Indians still live in adobe shelters. This Pueblo building is in Taos, New Mexico.

The word *pueblo* is the Spanish word for *town*. The Spanish used the word to describe both the villages of adobe shelters and the people who lived there. The shelters of the Pueblos looked like apartment buildings. Many were four stories high.

Each Pueblo village had its own government. A **government** is a group of people who lead a village, city, state, or country. Religious leaders ruled the Pueblo villages. Religion was important to the Pueblos because they believed their gods helped bring rain for their crops.

Most Pueblos were farmers. Because they lived in dry basins, the people irrigated their crops, using water from nearby rivers and streams. The Jumanos most likely learned how to irrigate from their Pueblo **ancestors**, family members of long ago.

**Why was religion important to the Pueblos?**

Pueblo Indians lived in parts of Texas long ago. Now they live primarily in New Mexico and Arizona.

## LESSON 4 REVIEW

### Check Understanding

1. **Recall the Facts** Which early Indian tribe most likely learned its way of life from Pueblo ancestors?
2. **Focus on the Main Idea** How did the Jumanos solve the problems of living and farming in a hot, dry climate?

### Think Critically

3. **Think More About It** How were Jumano and Pueblo shelters different from other Indian shelters?
4. **Past to Present** West Texas has the same hot, dry climate it had when the Jumanos lived there. How do Texans today solve the problems of living in such a climate?

### Show What You Know

**Art and Writing Activity** Imagine that you are a travel writer. Create a brochure telling why people should visit the lands of the Jumanos and the Pueblos. Make your brochure part of a class display.

# CHAPTER 2 REVIEW

## CONNECT MAIN IDEAS

Use this organizer to show that you understand how the chapter's main ideas are connected. First copy the organizer onto a separate sheet of paper. Then complete it by writing one or two sentences that tell how each group used the land and other resources.

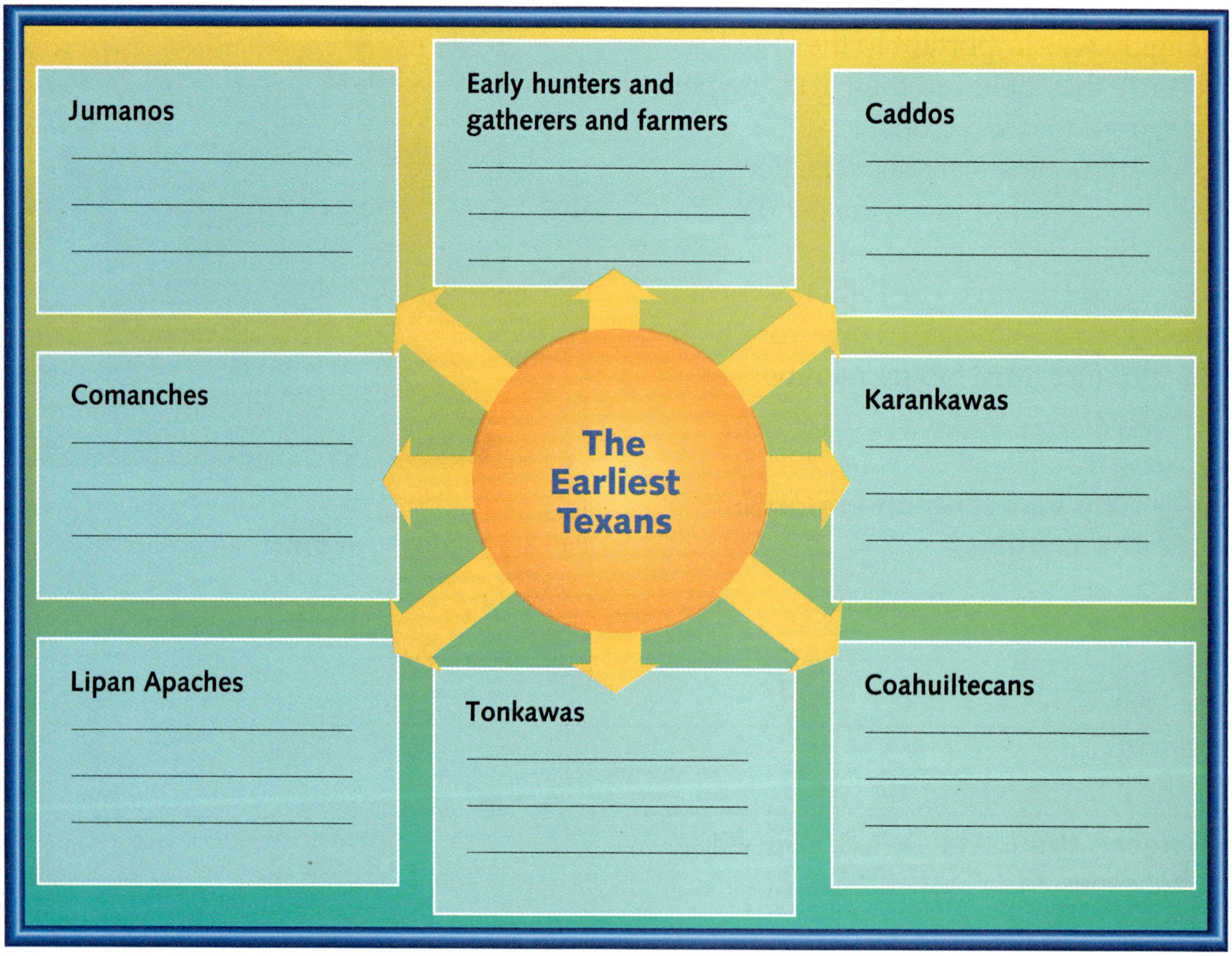


## WRITE MORE ABOUT IT

1. **Write a Persuasive Speech** Imagine that you are a leader of a Caddo village. Write a persuasive speech telling why you think your village should or should not join the confederation.

2. **Write a Set of Instructions** Write instructions for a friend that explain how to make a tepee. List the materials that your friend will need. Tell what to do first. Then list the other steps in order.

## USE VOCABULARY

For each pair of vocabulary words, write a sentence or two explaining how the words are related.

1. scarce, fertile
2. specialize, crop
3. culture, civilization
4. band, shaman
5. nomad, tepee
6. council, government
7. adapt, irrigate

## CHECK UNDERSTANDING

1. Why did the first people come to what is now Texas?
2. How did a change in climate affect the plants and animals that lived about 10,000 years ago?
3. How did farming change life for the early people of Texas?
4. What are the Aztecs and Mayas best known for?
5. How did the Caddos get food?
6. In what natural region of present-day Texas did the Karankawas live?
7. Who brought horses to North America in the 1500s?
8. How did using horses change the lives of Indian groups such as the Comanches and the Lipan Apaches?
9. Why was adobe a good material for Jumano homes?
10. Who were the leaders of Pueblo villages?

## THINK CRITICALLY

1. **Link to You** How might a change in the environment affect people's lives today?
2. **Personally Speaking** Would you rather have been part of a large civilization or a small band? Why?
3. **Think More About It** How did the ways early people lived affect the kinds of homes they built?
4. **Cause and Effect** What might have happened to the early Indians of the High Plains if the buffalo had become scarce?
5. **Think More About It** Why do you think the Plains Indians often communicated with one another through sign language?

## APPLY SKILLS

**How to Read a Time Line** Draw a time line to show the twentieth century through the twenty-fifth century. What is the first year shown on your time line? Is the year 2300 in the twenty-third century or the twenty-fourth century? In what century is the year 2150? What is the last year in the twenty-fifth century?

## READ MORE ABOUT IT

*Buffalo and Indians on the Great Plains* by Noel Grisham. Eakin. This book describes how Indians of the Great Plains hunted and used the buffalo.

*Indians Who Lived in Texas* by Betsy Warren. Hendrick-Long. The details in this book paint a picture of ten Indian tribes that lived in Texas.

## Making Social Studies Relevant

# American Indians in Texas Today

Pat Lester Peterson was nine years old in 1957 when she and her family arrived in Dallas. She felt like an immigrant, or a person who moves to a new country. The big city was strange to her, but her heart was filled with hope. However, Pat and her family were not immigrants from a faraway place. They were not from Europe, Africa, Asia, or South America. They were Choctaw (CHOCK•taw) Indians from Oklahoma.

Hundreds of years ago tens of thousands of American Indians lived in Texas. But by 1900 fewer than 500 American Indians lived there. Over time white settlers forced most of them to leave Texas. Slowly, however, Indians began to return. Today more than 66,000 American Indians live in Texas. They have come from as near as Oklahoma and as far away as Alaska.

Some groups, such as the Alabamas and the Coushattas (koo•SHAH•tuhz) from Louisiana, the Tiguas (TEE•wuhz) from New Mexico, and the Kickapoos (KICK•uh•pooz) from the Great Lakes region, live on reservations. On this land, which was set aside for Indians by the state and federal governments, they raise cattle, grow crops, and work in the lumber and oil businesses. They rely on natural resources, much as the Caddos, Jumanos, and other early Indian groups did long ago. The largest reservation in Texas is the Alabama-Coushatta Reservation near Livingston, in East Texas.

Many American Indians living in Texas, however, do not live on reservations. Most, like Pat Lester Peterson, live in big cities, where they work as doctors, artists, teachers, business owners, and laborers. The Dallas-Fort Worth area has more American Indians than any other place in Texas—more than 20,000 from 79 different tribes from all over North America.

**Pat Lester Peterson stands in front of a mosaic that depicts the Dallas skyline as it was when her family moved to the city in 1957.**

## Think and Apply

Think about the American Indians who live in your community or in another area of Texas today. Identify some of the Indian groups to which they belong. Then find out how these groups have contributed to local communities, to Texas, and to the United States. Also research reservations in Texas. What do they show about the life of American Indians in Texas?

Dallas school children learn about Native American culture.

UNIT 1

# Story Cloth

A story cloth uses pictures instead of words to tell a story. Follow the pictures shown in this story cloth to help you review the things you read about in Unit 1.

## Summarize the Main Ideas

1. The Caddos lived in the Piney Woods of the Gulf Coastal Plain. They lived by farming maize and other vegetables, as well as by hunting and gathering.
2. The Karankawas were nomads. Most of what they ate came from the sea and the wetlands along the Gulf coast.
3. The Coahuiltecans were also nomads who spent most of their time searching for food on the dry grasslands of the Gulf Coastal Plain.
4. The Jumanos lived in the Mountains and Basins region in shelters built of adobe. They farmed by irrigating their crops.
5. On the Central Plains of Texas, the Lipan Apaches used the buffalo for many of their needs.
6. With the horse the Comanches became fine hunters and fierce warriors on the High Plains.

**Draw Another Scene** Choose one of the Indian groups described in Unit 1 but not shown in this story cloth. Draw a picture that shows a scene of daily life for the group you chose. Tell where your scene should be placed in the story cloth.

# UNIT 1 REVIEW

## COOPERATIVE LEARNING WORKSHOP

**Remember**

- Share your ideas.
- Cooperate with others to plan your work.
- Take responsibility for your work.
- Show your group's work to the class.
- Discuss what you learned by working together.

**Activity 1**

### Publish a Magazine

As a class, list the different kinds of homes the early people of Texas built. Then work in small groups to write magazine articles, with each group writing about a different kind of home. Each magazine article should have an illustration and a description of how the home was built. Collect the articles in a class magazine called *Homes of Early People in Texas.* Share your magazine with other students who might want to learn about the earliest Texans.

**Activity 2**

### Perform a Simulation

Role-play a scene about a buffalo hunt. Think about all the preparations and activities that would be part of the hunt. Use some of the vocabulary words from this unit as you act out your scene for the class. Part of the scene should show how the buffalo is used after the hunt.

**Activity 3**

### Make a Weather Table

Draw a table with four columns. As a class, name the different kinds of weather found in Texas. List the kinds of weather in the first column of the table. In the second column, write words that describe each kind of weather. In the third column, list the regions where each type of weather might be found in Texas. In the fourth column, draw a picture of the weather. Be sure to give the table a title.

**Activity 4**

### Build a Model

With a group of your classmates, make a model of the home you wrote about in Activity 1. Draw a large map of Texas for a classroom table display. Place your model on the map, in the region where that kind of home would have been built.

## USE VOCABULARY

Choose a word from the first column that is related to a word in the second column. Tell how each pair of words is related.

| | |
|---|---|
| **1.** tribe | **a.** climate |
| **2.** vegetation | **b.** river system |
| **3.** canyon | **c.** culture |
| **4.** government | **d.** council |

## CHECK UNDERSTANDING

**1.** How did the lives of early people change after the mammoths died out?

**2.** Where does the water go after it rains?

**3.** How does elevation change from the Gulf Coastal Plain to the Mountains and Basins region?

**4.** Name the plants and animals that can be found in each of the four kinds of land in Texas.

**5.** Why did some Caddo villages join a confederation?

**6.** In what ways were the Lipan Apaches and the Comanches alike?

**7.** Why was irrigation important to groups like the Jumanos and the Pueblos?

## THINK CRITICALLY

**1. Link to You** How do natural land features affect how and where people live today?

**2. Think More About It** Why do you think religious leaders were the rulers in Pueblo villages?

**3. Cause and Effect** How do you think the use of the horse helped trade between the different American Indian tribes?

## APPLY GEOGRAPHY SKILLS

Map Skill

**How to Use Latitude and Longitude** The Aztecs, Mayas, and Incas had different cultures. The location of each group affected its way of life. Use the map to answer the questions that follow.

**GREAT CIVILIZATIONS OF NORTH AND SOUTH AMERICA**

**1.** What are the lines of latitude and longitude that give the location of the Aztecs?

**2.** Which group lived the farthest north? Which group lived the farthest south?

**3.** Which group lived to the west of the Mayas? Which groups lived east of the Aztecs?

**4.** Imagine that you are a member of an Indian group that lives near latitude 60° N. What would you need to do to adapt to life in that climate?

UNIT 2

# Newcomers to Early Texas

1500 — 1550 — 1600 — 1650

**1521**
The Spanish conquer the Aztecs and take control of their lands

**1528**
Europeans explore what is now Texas

**1598**
The Spanish claim lands north of Mexico, including present-day Texas

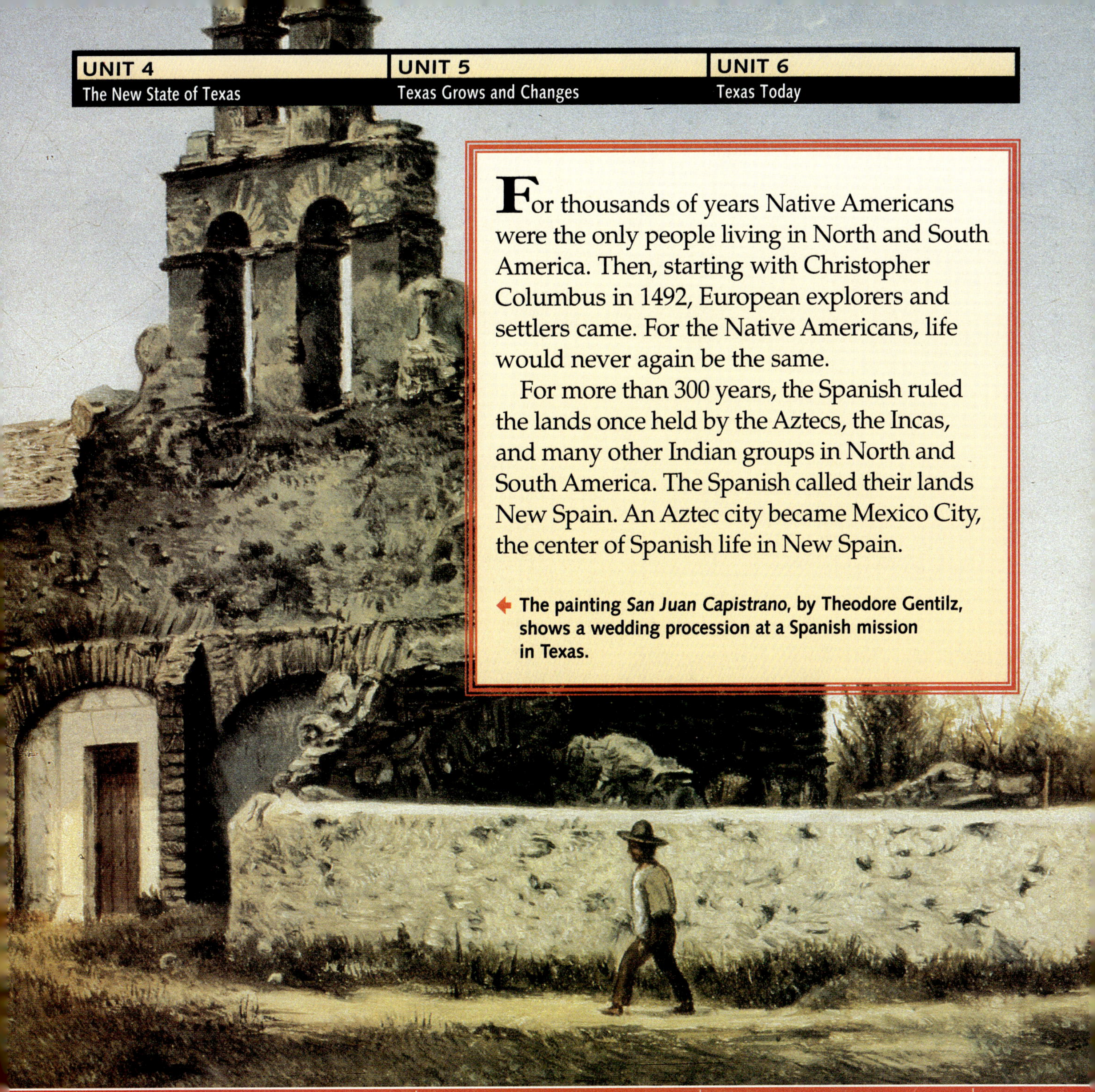

For thousands of years Native Americans were the only people living in North and South America. Then, starting with Christopher Columbus in 1492, European explorers and settlers came. For the Native Americans, life would never again be the same.

For more than 300 years, the Spanish ruled the lands once held by the Aztecs, the Incas, and many other Indian groups in North and South America. The Spanish called their lands New Spain. An Aztec city became Mexico City, the center of Spanish life in New Spain.

**The painting *San Juan Capistrano*, by Theodore Gentilz, shows a wedding procession at a Spanish mission in Texas.**

**1700**

**1682** The first Spanish mission is built in West Texas

**1750**

**1776** The United States breaks away from Britain and becomes a country

**1800**

**1821** Mexico breaks away from Spain and becomes a country

Austin colony is settled

**1830** Mexico tries to stop new settlers from the United States from coming to Texas

**1850**

*Set the Scene with Literature*

# Cabeza de Vaca

***by Gertrude Kerman***

**The first European to land on Texas soil may have been Alonzo Álvarez de Piñeda (pin•YAY•dah), a Spanish sea captain. In 1519, the year in which Hernando Cortés began his conquest of the Aztecs in Mexico, Álvarez sailed along the Texas coast. He camped near what is now Brownsville. Nine years passed before other Europeans returned.**

**In 1528 the Spanish government sent explorers to Florida. The explorers had been trying to return to Mexico City when a storm sank their ships off the Florida coast. Pánfilo de Narváez, the leader of the explorers, ordered that five rafts be built. The explorers would try to sail to Mexico on these rafts. Narváez led one group. Álvar Núñez Cabeza de Vaca led another. Now read their story.**

Narváez turned to his crew. "Row toward land!" he ordered. There was nothing Cabeza could do but follow his commander.

Unhappily, Cabeza's oarsmen were too weak to keep up with the other raft, and the distance between the two vessels grew steadily. "Harder! Row harder!" Cabeza pleaded, but the exhausted rowers fell over their oars. He shouted to Narváez. "Throw us a rope! My men cannot hold their oars." For answer, Narváez waved his crew onward. "Señor, if you do not pull us, we shall be separated forever!" Cabeza implored again.

But Narváez was like a man turned to stone. Only once again did he speak. It was before his raft fell below the horizon. "Save yourself! Save yourself—if you can!"

"If you can . . ." the waves murmured as they lapped the sides of Cabeza's raft. For a day and a night now, the tides had pushed it along aimlessly. Then a cool breeze

had sprung up and some of the men had recovered enough to swing the heavy oars.

Suddenly the breeze turned into a gale which sent the crew sprawling. By the fourth day the men were seasick and half-drowned. Only Cabeza remained on his feet. Then he, too, flopped down and let himself drift into forgetfulness.

He awoke with a start. Some object had struck the raft and made it quiver. He raised his head just as a huge wave lifted the raft and knocked it down with a great force. He found himself tumbling, head over heels, into the water. His men spilled out around him, like so many ears of corn. Then he came up, half-blinded and gasping for breath.

"We are saved! We are saved!" Cabeza gasped. The huge wave had dashed the raft against a beach. And he laughed and cried in turn.

It was November 6, 1528. The raft had traveled one thousand miles since it had left Florida forty-six days earlier. Now it lay shattered on the sands of an unknown island [most likely Galveston Island, Texas].

Cabeza de Vaca stood on the beach and looked around him. The raft that had brought him to this island lay smashed at the water's edge. Everything the Spaniards had owned—clothing, muskets, water bags—was lost. . . . "Worse, we have no boat. We shall have to depend on our legs to get us home."

**For eight years Cabeza de Vaca and three others walked all over present-day Texas, parts of New Mexico, and Mexico. One of these explorers was an African named Estêban (ehs•TAY•bahn), also known as Estevanico. For much of the time, the explorers were prisoners of the Karankawas and other Indian groups. From the Indians, they heard stories of great cities of gold. When the explorers finally got back to Mexico City, they told these stories to the Spanish government leaders. The promise of gold and other riches caused great excitement.**

CHAPTER 3

# SPANISH TEXAS

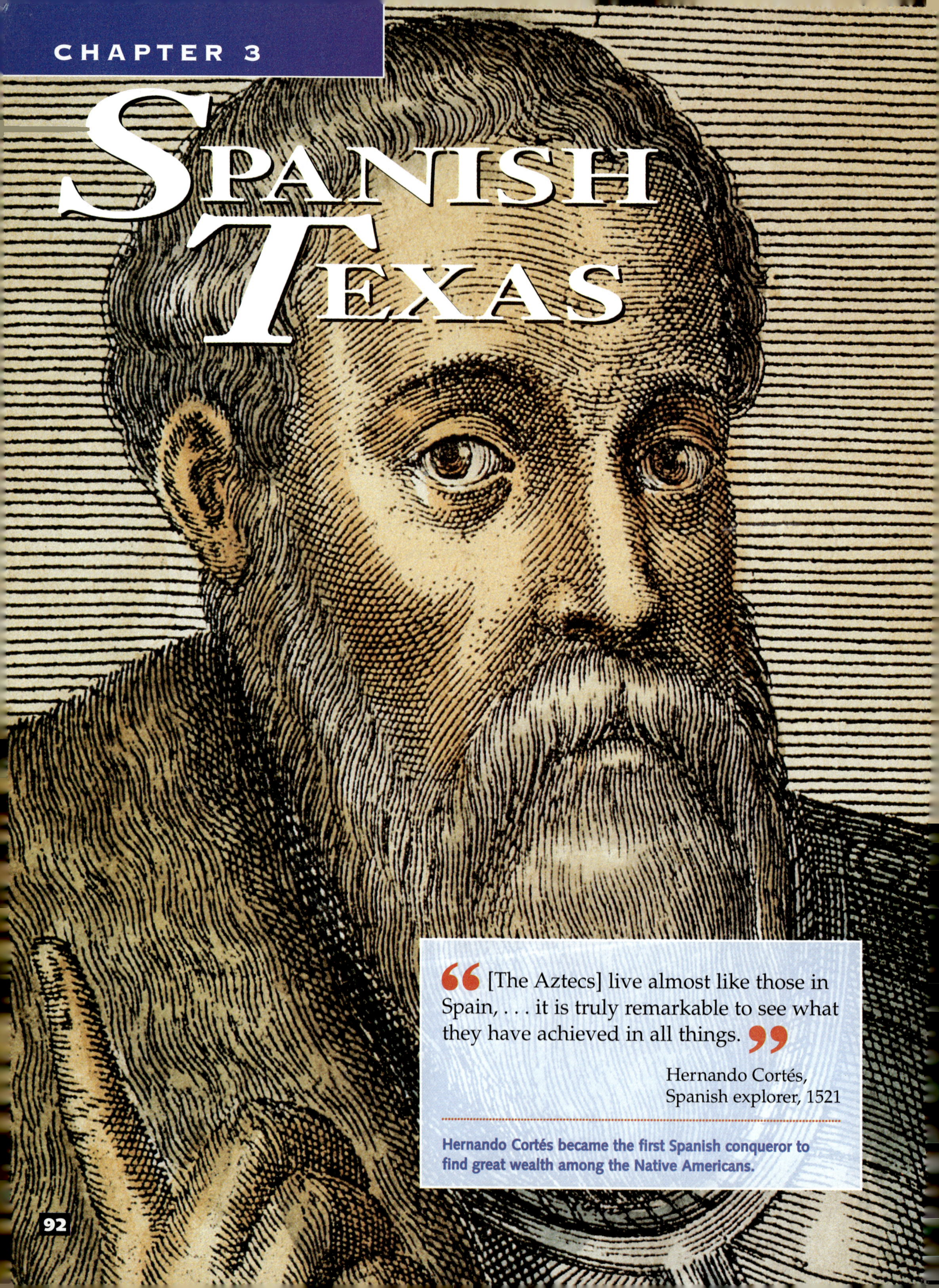

"[The Aztecs] live almost like those in Spain, . . . it is truly remarkable to see what they have achieved in all things."

Hernando Cortés,
Spanish explorer, 1521

**Hernando Cortés became the first Spanish conqueror to find great wealth among the Native Americans.**

LESSON 1

# Spanish Explorers

## Link to Our World

**Why do people go exploring today?**

***Focus on the Main Idea***
**Read to find out why the Spanish wanted to explore the lands north of Mexico.**

***Preview Vocabulary***
**conquistador**
**expedition**
**missionary**
**colony**

Once Cabeza de Vaca and the other explorers returned to Mexico City, the Spanish were excited to hear their stories. The explorers told of seeing huge herds of "humpbacked cows," or buffalo. Their most interesting stories, however, were about the Seven Cities of Cíbola (SEE•boh•lah), a group of great Indian cities said to be filled with gold and riches.

This gold ornament is an example of the great wealth found among the Aztecs.

## The Seven Cities of Gold

The Spanish heard that some Indian people living north of the Aztecs had great wealth and riches. Spanish **conquistadors** (kahn•KEES•tah•doors), or conquerors, had found great riches among the Aztecs in Mexico and the Incas in South America. The Spanish hoped to find such wealth among the Pueblos and other Indian peoples in North America, too.

The Spanish government sent Estéban and Marcos de Niza, a Franciscan priest, back to the lands north of Mexico to search for the golden cities. They led a small group of explorers to somewhere in present-day New Mexico or Arizona. Then Estéban told his group to stay behind. He set out for the golden cities alone, but he never returned.

The waiting explorers became afraid and decided to return to Mexico. But having come so far, they wanted to see the golden cities first. So for a short time, they followed the path Estéban had taken. From far off they saw a pueblo that seemed to shine like gold in the sunset. After seeing this, the explorers hurried back to Mexico and told everyone that the stories about the golden cities were true. Then the Spanish were really excited!

**What were the Spanish explorers looking for at Cíbola?**

## THE CORONADO EXPEDITION

In 1540 the Spanish decided to send a large expedition to Cíbola. An **expedition** is a journey into an area to learn more about it. The Spanish chose Francisco Coronado (kawr•oh•NAH•doh) to go to Cíbola and bring back gold. The Spanish government spent a lot of money on Coronado's expedition. They were sure the riches of Cíbola would repay them many times over.

Coronado set out in 1540 with a huge army of soldiers and Catholic **missionaries**,

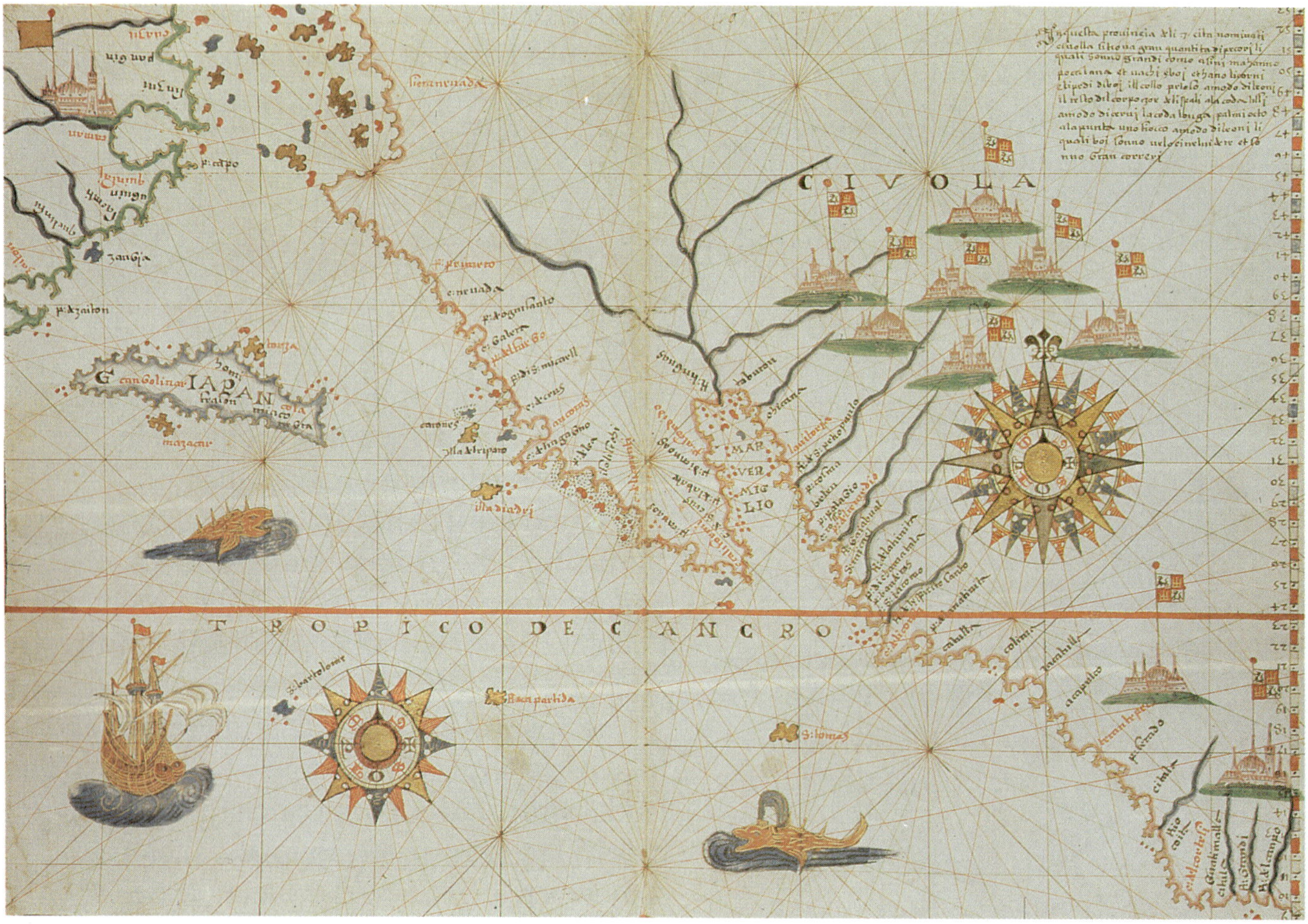


This Spanish map from the sixteenth century shows the supposed location of the fabled Seven Cities of Cíbola. How does this map differ from most present-day maps?

Coronado's expedition included more than 1,000 soldiers and Indians, 1,500 horses and mules, and thousands of cattle and sheep.

or religious workers. They followed an Indian trail north to where Cíbola was said to be. But when they got there, they could find no gold. When the first explorers had seen the Indian pueblo from far off, it had seemed to be made of gold. Actually, the sunset had made the light-colored adobe buildings only look like gold.

Coronado and his fellow explorers went on exploring, however. They met an Indian who told them about a place called Quivira (kee•VIR•ah). Quivira, he said, was a land of great riches, where people ate from dishes made of gold. Remembering what had happened at Cíbola, Coronado did not know if he should believe the Indian's story. In the end he decided to look for Quivira.

Coronado and his fellow explorers crossed much of the Texas Panhandle in search of Quivira. They may have been the first to see Palo Duro Canyon. The Spanish had never seen a land so vast with "no trees except at the rivers." They were amazed at the "sea of grass" that seemed to have no end. They saw the humpbacked cows that Cabeza de Vaca

## Who?

### Conquistadors

The typical Spanish conquistador was about 30 years old and uneducated. Like most, he came from a poor family and grew up in the western part of Spain, near the border of Portugal. After some conquistadors—like Cortés—became rich and famous, others from the same part of Spain decided to try to make their own fortunes in the Americas. Most conquistadors also wanted to bring Christianity to the Americas. It was said they came for gold, glory, and God.

This Native American rock painting shows the arrival of Spanish settlers in the lands north of Mexico.

had seen. Coronado and his group also saw the Cap Rock Escarpment. They may have been the ones who named the Llano Estacado, or Staked Plain.

After months of travel the Spanish reached Quivira, in the center of what is now Kansas. It turned out to be just another Indian village! The Coronado expedition sadly returned to Mexico. The explorers had not found any gold.

**What did Coronado find out about Cíbola and Quivira?**

## Thanksgiving in Texas

The Spanish stopped exploring for a time. The next expedition did not take place until 1598. That year a conquistador named Juan de Oñate (ohn•YAH•tay) led a group of 400 soldiers and settlers, along with 7,000 or more head of cattle, into the lands north of Mexico. His goal was to build a settlement there, but he also wanted to find gold.

It took Oñate's expedition nearly three months to cross the harsh desert south of

## Where?

### Llano Estacado

In Texas, the Llano Estacado (YAH•noh es•tah•KAH•doh), or Staked Plain, is part of the High Plains. Why this landform is called the Staked Plain is not really known. One story says that early Spanish explorers marked their trails by using stakes, or wooden posts. A different story tells that the Spanish explorers tied their horses to stakes because there were no trees. Yet another story explains that when people looked east from the Pecos River Valley, the edge of the High Plains looked like a stockade—a fort fenced with stakes.

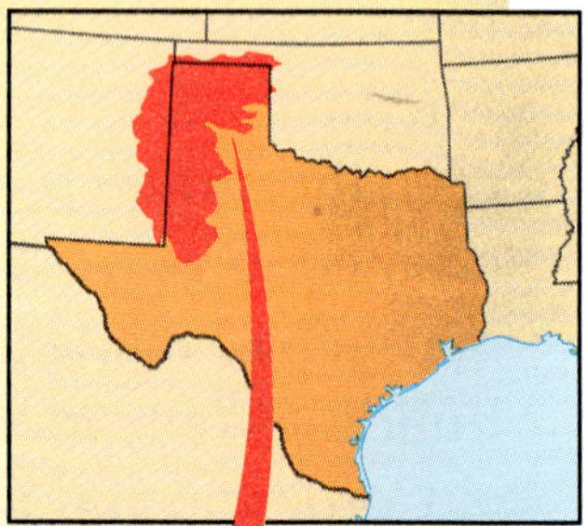

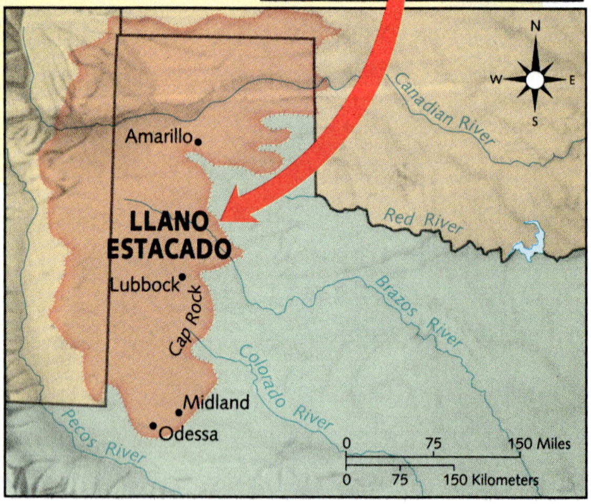

the Rio Grande. On April 20, 1598, the group crossed the river into Texas. They named the crossing El Paso del Norte. This means "the pass to the North."

Oñate was very happy that the expedition had reached the river. He asked that all the expedition members put on their best clothes and gather for a thanksgiving. One settler wrote,

> "We were happy our trials were over; as happy as were the passengers in the Ark when they saw the dove returning with the olive branch."

Ten days later, Oñate called everyone together for another ceremony. In it he claimed the lands north of the Rio Grande for the king of Spain.

Oñate's expedition went on into what is now northern New Mexico. There, along the Chama River, he started a group of settlements. Then he and some of his soldiers searched for gold in the land that is now Texas.

Like Coronado before him, Oñate did not find gold. The Spanish decided that there was not a wealth of gold in the lands north of Mexico. For more than 75 years, they stopped sending expeditions there.

**What were the two goals of Oñate's expedition?**

**REGIONS** By the 1700s three European countries had claimed most of the land in North America.

■ Which country would have built a settlement along the Mississippi River?

## France Claims Texas

Juan de Oñate had claimed the land north of the Rio Grande for the Spanish. However, in 1685 the French came to take it away. That year French explorer René-Robert Cavelier (ka•vuhl•YAY), known as Sieur de La Salle (luh SAL), brought soldiers and settlers to set up a colony. A **colony** is a settlement ruled by a faraway country. The colony the French set up was called Fort St. Louis. It was on Matagorda Bay on the Texas coast between present-day Galveston and Corpus Christi.

French explorer Sieur de La Salle explored a large part of North America. He traveled north into what is now Canada and was honored on a Canadian postage stamp.

Fort St. Louis had suffered many problems. Crops grew poorly, and food ran out. Many settlers became sick and died. A few of the settlers, who blamed La Salle for the colony's problems, killed the French leader. After his death a group of Karankawas attacked the colony and burned down its shelters.

Word of the French colony reached Mexico. The Spanish leaders did not want their new lands settled by another country. The government sent soldiers to make the French leave. However, the colony was already destroyed by the time the Spanish soldiers got there.

The Spanish then decided to keep a closer watch on their new lands. They wanted to make sure that neither the French nor any other European people would try to take their land.

✓ **Why did the Spanish government send soldiers to the French colony?**

## Lesson 1 Review

### Check Understanding

1. **Recall the Facts** In what year did Coronado's expedition leave for Cíbola?
2. **Focus on the Main Idea** Why did the Spanish send explorers to the lands north of Mexico?

### Think Critically

3. **Cause and Effect** What caused the Spanish to stop exploring the lands north of Mexico?
4. **Think More About It** What did the Spanish gain from their expeditions?
5. **Personally Speaking** Would you like to have been a member of an expedition that explored the lands north of Mexico? Why or why not?

### Show What You Know

**Letter-Writing Activity** Imagine that you are on an expedition in the 1500s to the area in Texas where you live. Write a letter to a friend in Mexico, telling what you are doing and what you have seen. Share your letter with a classmate.

S·K·I·L·L·S

# HOW TO

## Follow Routes on a Map

### Why Is This Skill Important?

How do you get from home to school? You follow a route. **Routes** on maps show the paths people follow.

### Understand the Process

This map shows the routes Spanish and French explorers took. First, read the map key to learn which explorers the symbols stand for.

- The red line shows Cabeza de Vaca's route.
- The blue line shows Coronado's route.
- What does the green line show?

Now trace each route with your finger. Use the map and the map key to answer these questions.

1. Which explorer passed near Palo Duro Canyon?
2. Which explorer landed at Fort St. Louis?
3. To which city did Cabeza de Vaca travel?

### Think and Apply

Map Skill

Write a paragraph describing the route you follow to get from home to school. Have a partner read your paragraph and draw a map that shows your route.

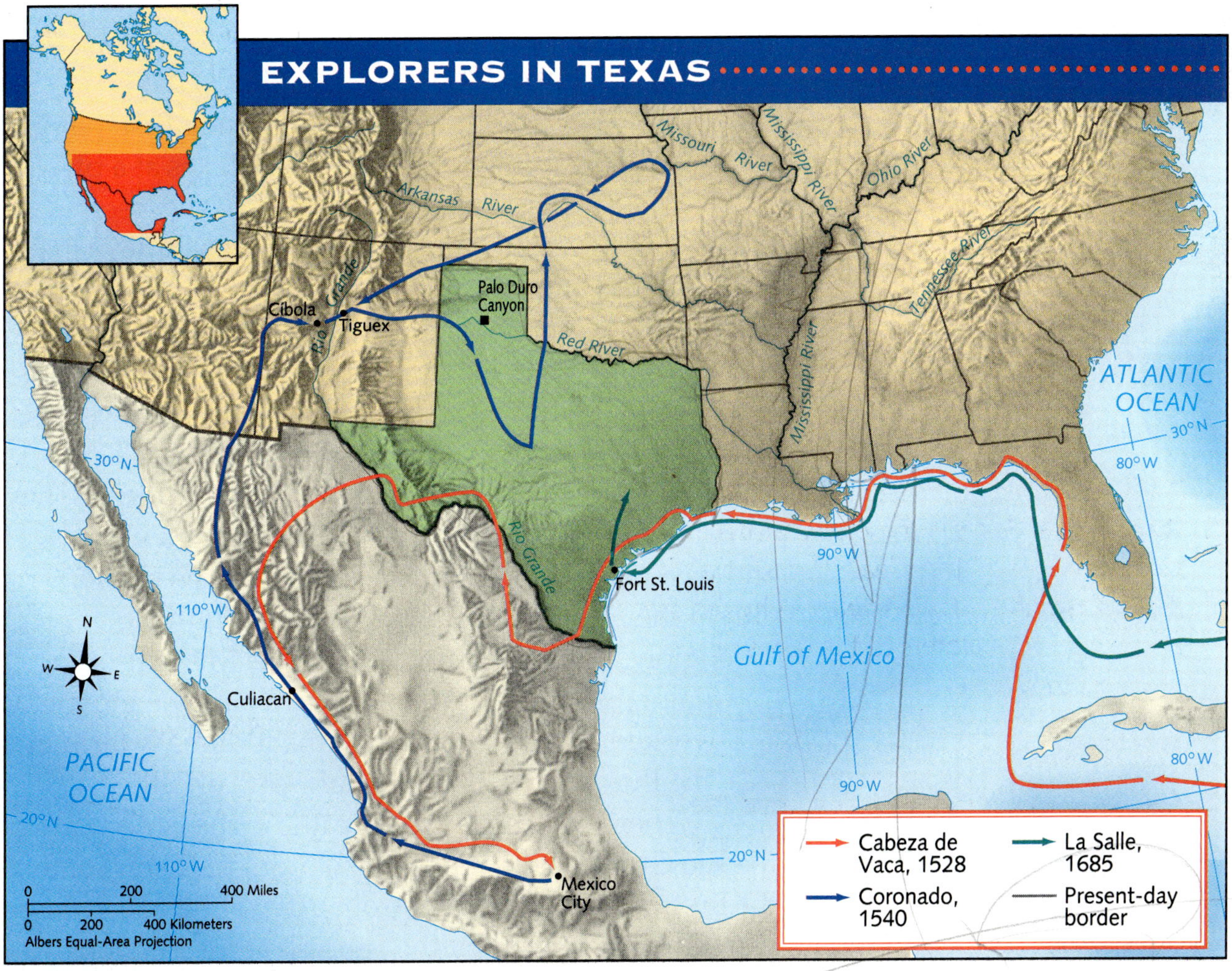

# Spain Settles Texas

Lesson 2

## Link to Our World

**Why do people today start settlements in new places?**

***Focus on the Main Idea***

**As you read, look for reasons why the Spanish started settlements in what is now Texas.**

***Preview Vocabulary***

| | |
|---|---|
| **mission** | **plaza** |
| **vaquero** | **mestizo** |
| **presidio** | **heritage** |

Wanting to make sure that they could hold on to their new lands, the Spanish decided to build their own settlements there. In the late 1600s and early 1700s, they built **missions**, or religious settlements. They also built forts to protect the missions. Later the Spanish built towns to attract more settlers.

## The Missions

In 1682 the Spanish built their first mission. It was in what is now West Texas at a place called Ysleta (ees•LAY•tah), near present-day El Paso. This was the land of the Jumanos. In 1690 the Spanish built another mission in the land of the Caddos, in what is now East Texas. It was built near the present-day town of Weches. Over the next 60 years, the Spanish built 20 more missions in their new lands. The missions were where most of the Indians first met Europeans.

The missions were towns run by Catholic priests. They contained homes, workplaces, churches, and schools, and were usually surrounded by a wall. The priests taught the Indian men and women the Catholic religion and the Spanish way of life. Missions also maintained farms and ranches, where the Indians worked. The priests trained the Indians to farm in the European way and to take care of cattle.

There were no horses or cattle in the lands north of the Rio Grande until the Spanish brought them. Some of the first **vaqueros** (bah•KAY•rohs), or cowhands, in Texas were Indians trained by the Spanish at the missions.

San Juan Capistrano in San Antonio was one of the many Spanish missions built in Texas during the late 1600s and early 1700s.

Some Indians did not like living at the missions or working for the Spanish. The missions did not change the way of life of all the Indians. However, they did help Spain maintain its hold on the lands north of the Rio Grande.

**✓ Why did the Spanish build missions in Texas?**

## Presidios

Spanish soldiers came with the Catholic priests to Texas. Their job was to protect the people in the missions and people traveling from mission to mission. The soldiers built **presidios** (pray•SEE•dee•ohs), or forts, where the people could go to escape an attack.

Presidios were built strong enough to protect the Spanish from any attackers. They were made mostly of wood, stone, or adobe. Inside were various buildings. Soldiers lived in some of the buildings. Weapons and supplies were stored in others. Surrounding each presidio was a wall on which the soldiers placed several cannons.

Most presidios had only a few soldiers, who were like present-day police officers. Their work was hard and dangerous. Like the missions, the presidios were important in helping Spain keep hold of their lands.

**✓ Why did the Spanish build presidios in Texas?**

## Towns

The best-known of the early Spanish settlements in what is now Texas was San Antonio de Bexar. It started in 1718 as a mission and presidio. Later the Spanish government decided to send more settlers to build a town nearby. The town was planned before the first settlers arrived.

It was to be built around a **plaza**, or town square. Streets were to run out from the plaza. An irrigation system would bring water from the San Antonio River to the settlers' homes and crops.

At the Spanish missions in Texas, priests taught the Indians the Catholic religion and the Spanish way of life.

Lively dances (above) were often held in the Spanish settlements. A musician might have played a Spanish guitar (right) at one of these celebrations.

When the plans were finished, the Spanish government asked families to come and live in the town. To get them to come, the government offered money, supplies, and free land.

Most of the settlers were **mestizos** (mes•TEE•zohs), people whose ancestors were Spanish and Indian. Settlers came from Spain's Canary Islands off the coast of Africa. Other settlers were from Africa.

The people called their town Villa de San Fernando. It later became known as San Antonio and was the center of Spanish life in Texas.

**How did San Antonio begin?**

## Problems in Settling

By 1800 only about 3,000 Spanish people lived in the missions and towns. About 1,000 soldiers lived in the presidios. Spanish settlement was slow because life was hard for settlers.

The Coahuiltecans were at war with the Lipan Apaches. The Lipan Apaches were at war with the Comanches. And the Comanches were at war with most other Indians of the region. Few Spanish settlers were willing to live in a place where they might be killed in an Indian war.

The early Spanish settlements faced other problems. Drought dried up many crops. Floods washed away other crops. Diseases killed large numbers of people. But most of these settlements survived.

**Why did so few Spanish settlers come to Texas?**

**MAJOR SPANISH SETTLEMENTS IN TEXAS, 1600s AND 1700s**

**HUMAN–ENVIRONMENT INTERACTIONS**

Map Skill
- Why do you think most of the first Spanish settlements were on the Gulf Coastal Plain?

San José Mission in San Antonio is an example of the rich Spanish heritage in Texas. Is there an example of the Spanish heritage near where you live?

## The Spanish Heritage

The early Spanish settlers were few, but their heritage is everywhere in Texas. **Heritage** is the culture people today have gained from people in the past. For example, there are old Spanish buildings, such as mission churches, in many parts of the state.

Some Texans today follow the Catholic religion, the form of Christianity brought by the Spanish missionaries long ago. The first schools in Texas were at Catholic missions set up by the Spanish.

The early Spanish brought the first horses and cattle to North America. The ranching they started helped the city of San Antonio and many South Texas towns grow and do well.

Today many Texans speak and write the Spanish language. The Spanish heritage also lives on in the names of Texas's rivers, cities, landforms, foods, and many everyday things.

**Where can the Spanish heritage be seen and heard in Texas today?**

## Lesson 2 Review

### Check Understanding

1. **Recall the Facts** What kinds of settlements did the Spanish start in the lands north of Mexico?
2. **Focus on the Main Idea** Why did the Spanish start settlements in what is now Texas?

### Think Critically

3. **Personally Speaking** Do you think the Spanish government tried hard to settle Texas in the 1600s and 1700s? Explain.
4. **Explore Viewpoints** Why did the Spanish missionaries try to change the Indians' way of life? Why did some Indians not want their way of life changed?

### Show What You Know

**Map Activity** Use a map of Texas to find some cities, landforms, and waterways with Spanish names. Study the map to see if some parts of Texas have more Spanish names than others. Write a paragraph to explain your findings. Share your paragraph with a classmate.

## CHAPTER 3
# REVIEW

## CONNECT MAIN IDEAS

Use this organizer to show that you understand how the chapter's main ideas are connected. First copy the organizer onto a separate sheet of paper. Then complete it by writing one or two sentences that answer each question.

**Spanish Texas**

| LESSON 1 | LESSON 2 |
|---|---|
| Who came to Texas? | Who came to Texas? |
| Why did they come? | Why did they come? |
| Where did they go? | Where did they go? |
| What did they do? | What did they do? |

## WRITE MORE ABOUT IT

1. **Write a Story** Imagine that you are a Native American who has just met Spanish explorers traveling across Texas. Write a story that you could tell your children. Describe some ways the explorers are different from people you have seen before.
2. **Write a Report** Write a short report that explains how the Spanish missions and presidios were started in Texas.
3. **Write a Journal Entry** Imagine that you are a member of Coronado's expedition. Write a journal entry about what one day was like.

## USE VOCABULARY

Match each Spanish word with its correct meaning.

| | |
|---|---|
| **conquistador** | **plaza** |
| **mestizo** | **presidio** |
| **missionary** | **vaquero** |

1. conqueror
2. religious worker
3. cowhand
4. fort
5. town square
6. person whose ancestors are Spanish and Indian

## CHECK UNDERSTANDING

1. What place was Coronado looking for when he and his fellow explorers crossed the Texas Panhandle?
2. What land did Oñate claim for the king of Spain?
3. Who set up Fort St. Louis?
4. What happened to La Salle's colony?
5. Where was the first Spanish mission in Texas?
6. What did Spanish mission priests want Indians to do?
7. What were the duties of the presidio soldiers?
8. How did the Spanish get families to move to San Antonio de Bexar?
9. Why did Spanish settlements in Texas grow slowly?
10. What parts of the Spanish heritage remain in Texas today?

## THINK CRITICALLY

1. **Personally Speaking** Imagine that you are a newcomer to Texas seeing a herd of buffalo for the first time. How would you describe them?
2. **Link to You** Where do people go exploring today? How is this exploration like the Spanish exploration of Texas? How is it different?
3. **Explore Viewpoints** Why do you think the French believed they could start a colony in Texas after the Spanish had claimed the land?
4. **Cause and Effect** How did the French colony at Fort St. Louis affect the Spanish settlement of Texas?
5. **Explore Viewpoints** Why do you think some Indians did not want to change their way of life?

## APPLY SKILLS

**How to Follow Routes on a Map** Look in newspapers or old magazines for a map that shows a route. Cut out the map and tape it to a sheet of paper. Below the map, describe the route shown. What places are along the route? What do you think the reason was for showing this route on a map?

## READ MORE ABOUT IT

*Cabeza de Vaca: Conquistador Who Cared* by Mary D. Wade. Colophon House. A biography of the Spanish explorer.

*With Domingo Leal in San Antonio—1734* by Marian L. Martinello and Samuel P. Nesmith. University of Texas. A true story, this book describes the life of a young boy who lived near a Spanish mission.

CHAPTER 4

# THE ANGLO-AMERICANS ARRIVE

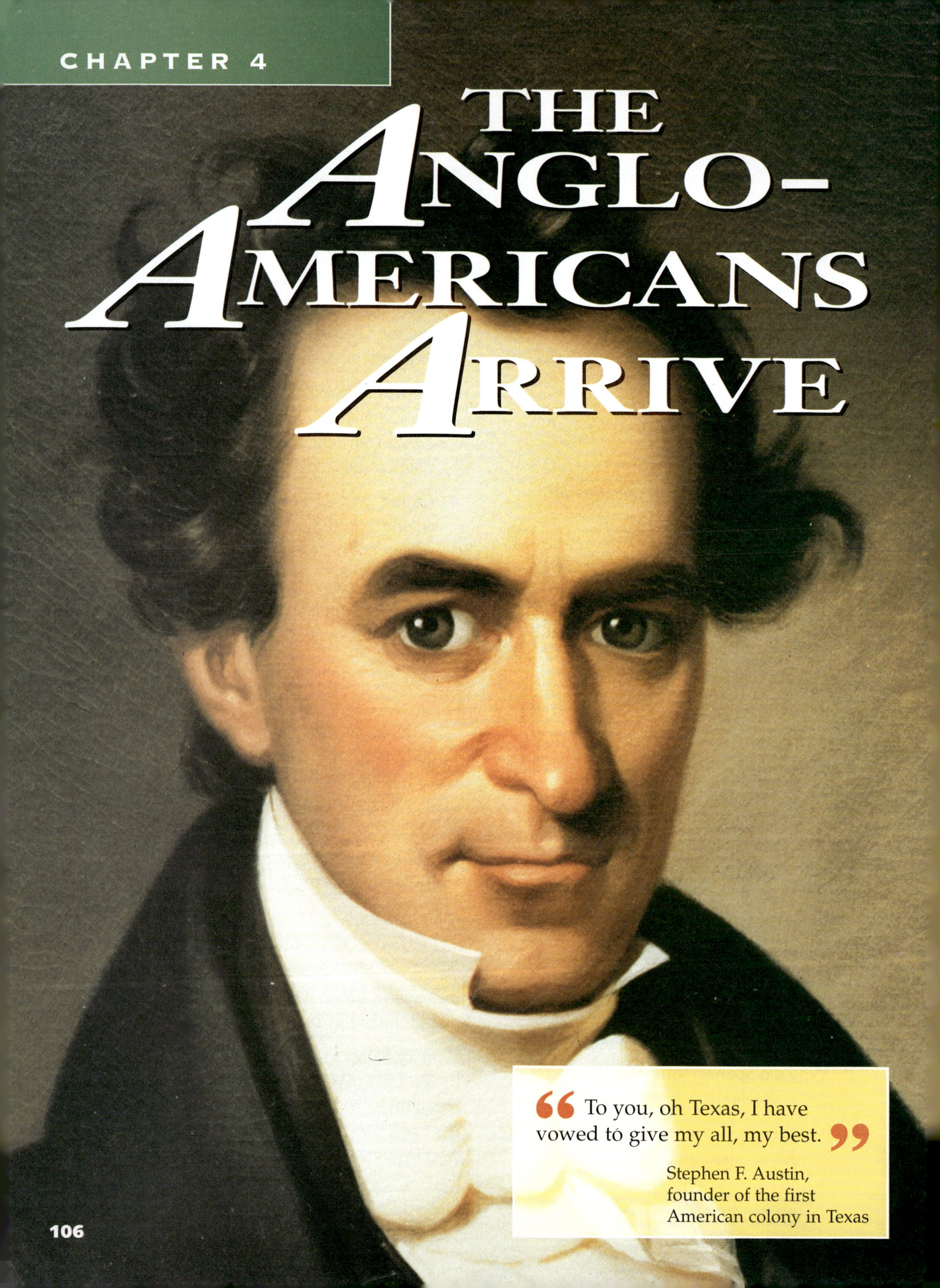

“To you, oh Texas, I have vowed to give my all, my best.”

Stephen F. Austin, founder of the first American colony in Texas

Lesson 1

# Texas Colonies

## Link to Our World

**How do events that happen in one place affect people's lives in other places today?**

***Focus on the Main Idea***

**Read to understand how events that happened in Mexico and the United States affected the settlement of Texas.**

***Preview Vocabulary***

**frontier**
**grant**
**militia**
**capital**
**Anglo**
**slave**
**filibuster**
**empresario**
**Tejano**

By the late 1700s Texas had a neighbor to the north—the United States of America. The United States broke away from Britain in 1776 and became a country. The new country included lands along the Atlantic coast, but the Americans kept pushing west. By the early 1800s they began pushing into Texas, looking for new lands to settle. Texas became an important frontier. The **frontier** was the place where settled land ended and wilderness began.

This map, drawn in the nineteenth century, shows the boundary between the United States and Mexico, along the Red and Sabine rivers.

## The Austins in Texas

In 1820 a Missouri business person named Moses Austin went to San Antonio to meet with the Spanish governor of Texas, Antonio Martínez. Austin had heard that the Spanish government was giving **grants**, or gifts, of land to people willing to set up colonies in Texas. Austin asked Governor Martínez for land. The governor said that Austin could settle 300 American families in Texas.

Moses Austin died not long after he returned to the United States. He was never able to start his plan. In a letter to their son, Mrs. Austin wrote that on the day Moses died, "he called me to his bedside and with much distress and difficulty of speech begged me to tell you to take his place."

# What?

## Revolution in Mexico

Father Miguel Hidalgo (ee•DAHL•goh) began a rebellion in Mexico against Spain in 1810. The Spanish government stopped the rebellion and then ordered that Father Hidalgo be shot. Soon events that happened in Europe weakened Spain's hold on Mexico and its other colonies in the Americas. The Mexican leaders saw this weakness as a chance to gain independence. In 1821 Mexico was at last able to break away from Spain.

Moses' son, Stephen F. Austin, went to Texas in 1821. He explored the region and decided that the land between the Colorado and Brazos (BRAH•zohs) rivers was a good place for a colony. The soil was fertile for growing crops, and the winters were not too cold. Plenty of water flowed in rivers and streams. There were many trees that could be used for building shelters. In Austin's words, this country was "as good in every respect as man could wish for."

Austin began gathering families for his colony. Then a problem came up. In 1821 there was a change in the government of Texas. Mexico broke away from Spain and became its own country. Texas now belonged to Mexico. Spain had allowed the Austins to bring settlers to Texas. Would Mexico allow the same?

Stephen F. Austin went to Mexico City to talk to the new leaders. Finally they said he could bring the Americans to Texas. The Mexican leaders trusted Austin. They appointed him as a judge for his colony. They also said he could set up a **militia**, or unpaid army, to protect his settlers.

**What was Moses Austin's plan for Texas?**

### The Austin Colony

Stephen F. Austin settled his people on the land he had explored. A few came in 1821, and a few more in 1822. In 1823 Stephen F. Austin set up a town to be the **capital**, or center of government, for the colony. He called the town San Felipe de Austin (SAN fay•LEEP•ay day AWS•tuhn).

There Austin built his home, a "dogtrot house." One settler, Noah Smithwick, described it as "a double log cabin with a passage through the center, a porch with dirt floor on the front with windows opening upon it, and a chimney at each end of the building." The opening in the center helped keep a dogtrot house cool in summer. It was just like the shelters built by the other settlers from the United States.

The first Americans to settle in the Austin colony had many problems. A ship from the United States bringing food, seeds, and farm tools to the colony sank. A drought the first year caused crops to fail, leaving people without enough food.

Stephen F. Austin drew this map of the colonies in Texas in 1822.

The Karankawas and Tonkawas did not like losing their lands to the new colony and tried to scare off some of the settlers.

Stephen F. Austin worked to solve these problems. He helped people get the land they wanted. He bought food for the settlers. He set up militias to protect the settlements from Indians. He worked with the Mexican government for the good of the settlers.

Stephen F. Austin's log cabin was typical of the homes built in the Austin colony by settlers from the United States.

**What problems did the first settlers of Austin's colony face?**

Jane Long (left) was one of the Old Three Hundred. Determined settlers like Long established many cities in Texas, such as Galveston (above).

## The Old Three Hundred

To bring in settlers, Austin described the colony in newspapers in cities from New Orleans to Boston. He visited friends and wrote them letters, asking them to move to Texas. He invited any honest, hard-working person to join him in Texas. He warned, however, that "no idler" would be welcome. Austin offered any family willing to come to Texas large areas of land at very low cost.

By 1825 there were 297 families living in the Austin colony. These first families became known as the Old Three Hundred, because of Moses Austin's land grant to settle 300 families. Most of the Old Three Hundred were from the southern part of the United States. Most were Anglo-Americans, or **Anglos**, people whose ancestors came from Britain. Those who owned slaves took them to Texas, too. A **slave** is a person who is owned by another person and made to work. About one in every five of these settlers was an African slave. Slaves had no freedom.

One of the best-known of the early settlers from the United States was Jane Long. Long came to Texas with James, her husband, a few years before Moses Austin received his grant. James Long was a **filibuster**, a soldier in a private army. He went with the army to try to conquer land in Texas from the Spanish. While her husband was fighting in Mexico, Jane Long spent the winter of 1821 with only her young daughter and a 12-year-old slave girl, Kian (KEE•uhn), also known as Kiamatia. They camped on the coast of Texas near Point Bolivar and hunted and fished for their own food. After learning that James Long had been killed, they joined the Austin colony. Jane Long and Kian showed the spirit of the early settlers of Texas.

**Who were the Old Three Hundred?**

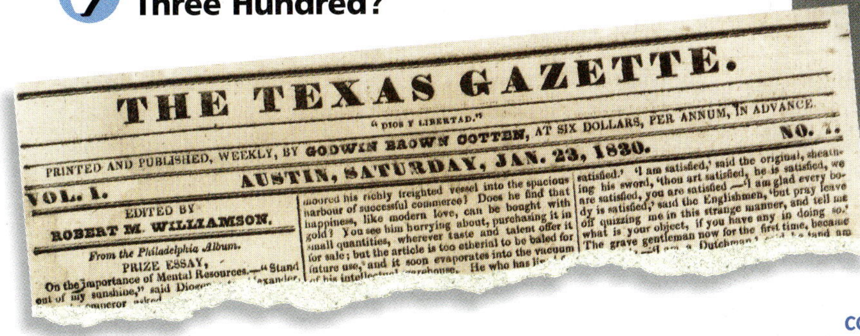

THE TEXAS GAZETTE.

"DIOS Y LIBERTAD."

PRINTED AND PUBLISHED, WEEKLY, BY GODWIN BROWN COTTEN, AT SIX DOLLARS, PER ANNUM, IN ADVANCE.

VOL. I. AUSTIN, SATURDAY, JAN. 23, 1830. NO. 1.

EDITED BY ROBERT M. WILLIAMSON.

From the Philadelphia Album.

PRIZE ESSAY,

On the importance of Mental Resources.—"Stand out of my sunshine," said Dioge...

moored his richly freighted vessel into the spacious harbour of successful commerce? Does he find that happiness, like modern love, can be bought with gold? You see him hurrying about, purchasing it in small quantities, wherever taste and talent offer it for sale; but the article is too etherial to be baled for future use, and it soon evaporates into the vacuum ...

satisfied.' 'I am satisfied,' said the original, sheathing his sword, 'thou art satisfied, he is satisfied, we are satisfied, you are satisfied —I am glad every body is satisfied,' said the Englishmen, 'but pray leave off quizzing me in this strange manner, and tell me what is your object, if you have any in doing so.' The grave gentleman now for the first time, became ...

By 1823 San Felipe de Austin was a busy community with its own newspaper. *The Texas Gazette* (left) was the first newspaper published in the Austin colony. Robert M. Williamson (above) was the newspaper's editor.

## "Gone to Texas"

By 1823 San Felipe de Austin had two hotels, a blacksmith shop, a number of stores, and more than 30 houses. It also had a newspaper, *The Texas Gazette.* Seeing the success of this settlement, the Mexican government let other people do what Stephen F. Austin had done. It gave these other people land grants and the right to sell the land at low cost. These people, called **empresarios** (ehm•pray•SAH•ree•ohs), helped bring more settlers to Texas.

Eager for cheap land, thousands of people started for Texas. The letters *GTT*—for "gone to Texas"—appeared on the doors of empty cabins and city apartments in the United States. Europeans also came to Texas with the hope of making a better life in a new land.

Empresario Green DeWitt brought 100 families from Missouri and started a settlement between the Guadalupe and Lavaca rivers. The settlement did well as a ranching and farming colony around present-day Gonzales (gohn•ZAH•lays).

John McMullen and James McGloin brought settlers from Ireland to land south of San Antonio. Another Irish colony settled along the Gulf coast near the present-day city of Refugio.

**What did the letters *GTT* mean?**

## THE TEJANOS

Many Mexicans also moved to Texas to start new lives. These settlers from Mexico came to be called **Tejanos** (tay•HAH•nohs). Mexican empresario Martín de León (mar•TEEN day lay•OHN) started a colony of some 200 families. Many of these families settled in Victoria, the town founded by de León.

Most of the Tejanos lived in South Texas near the Rio Grande. Some also settled in towns farther north, such as San Antonio and present-day Goliad (GOH•lee•ad).

Like the settlers from the United States, the Tejanos started farms and ranches. One of the Tejano ranchers who did well was Erasmo Seguín (ay•RAHS•moh say•GEEN). The Seguín ranch, La Mora, or The Mulberry Tree, was along the San Antonio River near present-day Karnes City.

Erasmo Seguín was a close friend of Stephen F. Austin. He worked hard to help Austin's settlers. Juan Seguín, his son, was also a friend to the "Texians," as some of the Americans began to call themselves. Other well-known Tejanos were José Antonio Navarro, Placido Benavides, and Juan Antonio Padilla.

Martín de León was an important empresario in Texas. He brought nearly 200 families from Mexico to Texas.

The Mexican government had hoped that many more of its own citizens would move to Texas, but the number of Tejanos was never great. Settlers from the United States, however, kept coming to Texas in great numbers. By the 1830s there were more than four times as many settlers from the United States as from Mexico.

**Who were the Tejanos?**

**LEARNING FROM DOCUMENTS**
This land-grant certificate gave a settler permission to join an empresario's colony.
- What was the name of the company that issued this certificate?

# LESSON 1 REVIEW

## Check Understanding

1. **Recall the Facts** Why did Stephen F. Austin set up his colony where he did?
2. **Focus on the Main Idea** How did events that happened in Mexico and the United States affect settlement in Texas?

## Think Critically

3. **Think More About It** Why did people from both Mexico and the United States settle in Texas?
4. **Personally Speaking** If you were starting a colony, what things would you consider in choosing a location?
5. **Explore Viewpoints** Why do you think the Tonkawas and Karankawas wanted the settlers to move?

## Show What You Know

**Simulation Activity** Imagine that you are helping Stephen F. Austin persuade more people to move to Texas. Role-play a conversation with a partner, telling your partner why he or she should move to the Austin colony. Be sure to tell about what settlers would find in their new town.

S·K·I·L·L·S

HOW TO

# Use a Line Graph to See Change

### Why Is This Skill Important?

A line graph is a good way to show information and how that information changes over a period of time. This line graph shows how the population of settlers in Texas grew in the eighteenth and nineteenth centuries. **Population** is the number of people who live in a place.

### Understand the Process

The numbers on the side of the graph stand for the population. The periods of time from 1745 to 1835 are spaced across the bottom of the graph.

There is a dot on the line above some of the years. Find the year 1745. Trace the line up until you reach the dot. Then move your finger to the left to find the population number. This number is an estimate, or close guess, of the population in 1745. In 1745 there were about 1,500 settlers in what is now Texas.

Now find the year 1825. What was the population in that year? If you connected the dots with a line, you could see clearly how the population changed from the time of the Spanish settlements to the time after Mexico broke away from Spain.

### Think and Apply

Think about the change shown on this graph. Compare and contrast the growth in population from 1745 to 1825 with the growth in population from 1825 to 1835. Write a paragraph that might explain this change.

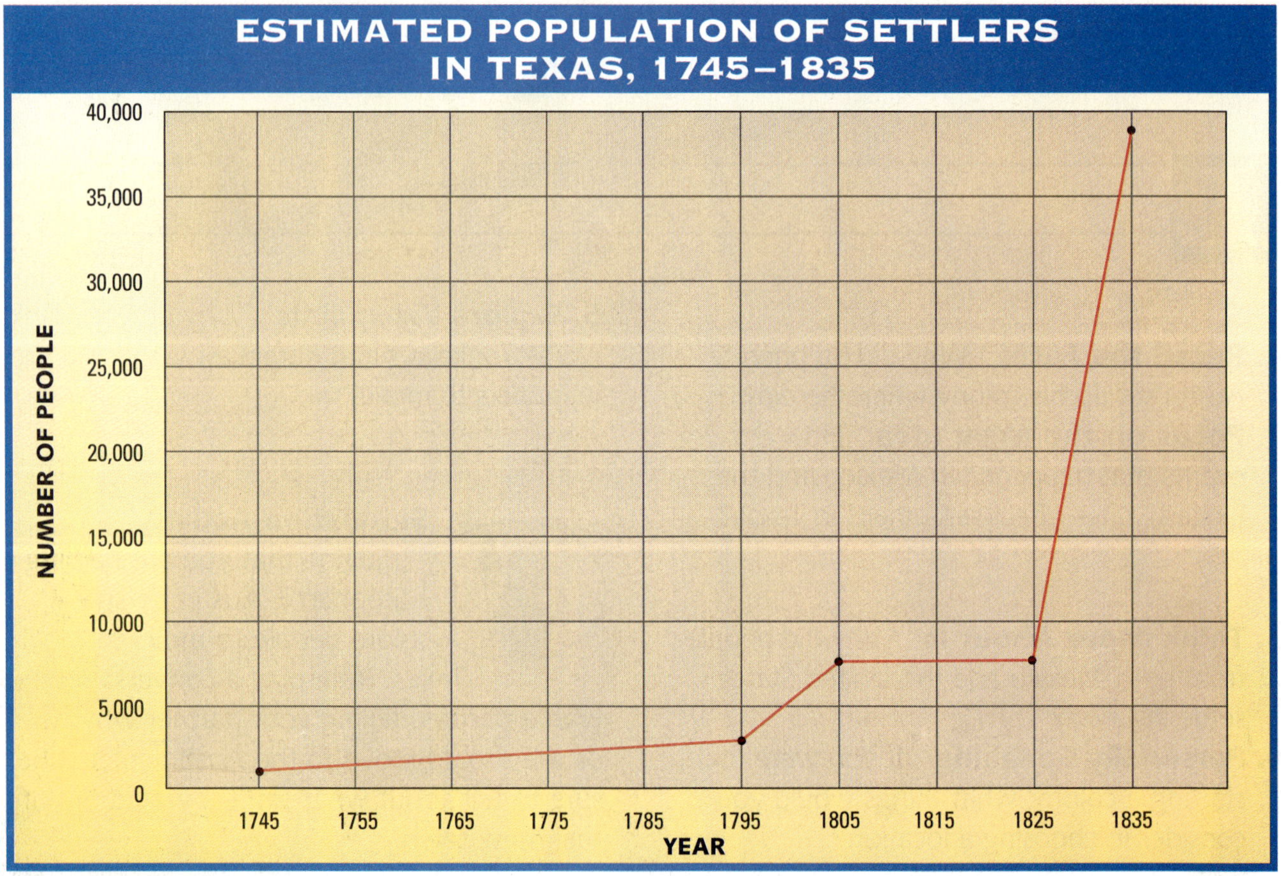

LESSON 2

LEARN *with* LITERATURE

Focus on Colonial Life

# TEXAS FOOTPRINTS

***by Rita Kerr***

**Among the Old Three Hundred, the first settlers in Austin's colony, was the Pryor family. In 1821 William and Beth Pryor and their children, Mary, Harriet, and Elizabeth, left their home in Alabama to make themselves a new life in the rich lands of Texas. As an adult, Harriet Pryor allowed her mind to drift back to her family's last days in Alabama and to their difficult journey to their new home in Texas. Read now about one person's memories of moving to Texas.**

Back in 1821, Papa had heard folks talking about Stephen Austin. Austin had received a grant from the Mexican government to take 300 families to Texas to start a colony. Harriet remembered her father saying to her mother, "Life has not been easy. It was bad when we lived in Tennessee with Mary and little Harriet. We had hoped life would be better here in Alabama, but now we are having trouble scratching out a living."

Harriet's mother had said, "These are just hard times, William."

"I know, but we have to think of the girls. Perhaps we should join Austin's group going to Texas, Beth. I understand there's plenty of good, rich land and beautiful streams of water. They say herds of buffalo and horses run wild on the broad prairies. Texas might be just the place for us. You know it won't be many years before the girls will be settling down with their own families. We have to plan for the future, Beth."

They had talked and talked about Texas. Finally, Papa settled the matter. They were moving! They loaded the covered wagon with all it would hold and joined the other settlers.

Harriet had nothing but unhappy memories of that journey. It was awful. The weather turned cold. The rains came. The trails were knee-deep in mud. More than once their heavy wagon got stuck. Everyone had worked to get it out. Several other wagons had to be unpacked to get them unstuck.

With the heavy rains, many of the rivers overflowed their banks. When Harriet closed her eyes, she could still see little Elizabeth clinging to her mother

Many settlers journeyed to Texas during the 1820s and 1830s in covered wagons.

when the wagons were carried across the rushing waters on rafts or flat-bottom barges.

A number of people got sick. Harriet's mother was one of them. Before they reached Texas, she came down with chills and a high fever. Harriet had nightmares of the dreadful night Ma took a turn for the worse. She and her sisters spent the night in another wagon while some of the women tried to help Ma. There was nothing they could do.

The next morning, an eerie silence fell upon the camp. Everyone spoke in hushed whispers and, with downcast eyes, walked around shaking their heads. Harriet knew something was wrong before Papa took her into his arms and told them the awful news. Their mother had died. Harriet would never forget that day. They buried their mother beside the trail.

The rest of the journey was like a bad dream. Mary tried to take her mother's place, but no one could. After the wagons rolled into Texas it seemed they would never stop. But they did. Someone said the town of San Felipe de Austin would be built on that very spot.

Harriet's father was not concerned about a town. He wanted to find a piece of land that would suit their needs. He picked a site on the east side of the Brazos River next to Stephen Austin's land and went to work. Chopping trees and notching the logs for a house was not easy. Harriet and her sisters tried to help, but there was not much they could do.

The one-room house they built had no windows or floor. Papa said those would come later. Crude as it was, the cabin was more comfortable than living in the crowded wagon. Harriet hated that wagon. It would always remind her of her mother's death.

Mosquitoes and gnats came in through the cracks between the logs of the house. The girls tried to fill the cracks with mud, but it did not keep out the bugs. The mosquitoes were bad in the daytime. At night they were awful. Papa put up netting to keep the insects from eating them alive during the night.

Once the cabin was finished, it was time to plant the corn. Corn was their main food. Like the other settlers, they ate it boiled and fried and roasted. Mary made mush, hominy, grits, and bread with corn. When the girls complained, their father said, "Remember, anything will taste good if you are hungry. We should thank the good Lord we've got it. And, of course, give thanks for the cow that gives us milk for this butter."

Some of the settlers had brought slaves to Texas. They also brought cotton. And they soon learned that cotton grew well in Texas.

Harriet was concerned because her father worked so hard. He was in the field from dawn until dusk. When he came home in the evenings, he had blisters on his hands from chopping trees and pulling weeds. Mary sometimes worked at her father's side. She wore a wide-brimmed bonnet and a long-sleeved dress to protect her skin from the blistering sun. But she turned brown and freckled anyway. The other women who worked in the fields got sunburned too.

Scratching out a living on the Texas frontier was hard work. Settlers would have to clear their land to make room for their farms.

At mealtime the Pryor family might have used kitchen utensils like the ones pictured (far right).

Mary insisted that her younger sisters learn to sew and cook the way their mother had taught her. She kept saying, "Someday you will get married and have girls you will have to teach."

With so much work to be done, everyone had a job. Papa made sure there was plenty of wood for the fireplace. Elizabeth was to help with the dishes and churn the butter. Harriet filled the buckets with water and helped Mary with the cooking.

Every Monday, Papa built a fire in the yard and brought water for the washing. The girls had to keep the fire going to get the water hot enough to wash the clothes. They took turns sloshing them up and down with a long stick to loosen the dirt. Once everything was clean and rinsed, the clothes were spread over the bushes to dry. Tuesday was the day they ironed. It was a chore they did not enjoy. The flat iron was heavy and had to be reheated many times. The girls looked forward to Wednesday. They would not have to wash and iron for a whole week!

One day Mary found a precious treasure in the family trunk. It was a small bundle of garden seeds that had been tucked in the folds of her mother's wedding dress. With their father's help, the girls dug holes in the ground and buried the tiny seeds. What fun they had watching the plants shoot up! Harriet had wonderful memories of their first delicious meal of turnips and peas from that garden.

## Literature Review

1. Why did the Pryor family move to Texas?
2. After reading Harriet Pryor's story, do you think you would have enjoyed moving to Texas in the 1820s? Explain your answer.
3. Imagine that your family was one of the Old Three Hundred. Use the information in the story to help you write journal entries about the things you did during one week in the Austin colony.

LESSON 3

# THE START OF TROUBLE

## Link to Our World

**How can different views cause problems for people today?**

***Focus on the Main Idea***
**Read to understand how different views caused problems between the Mexican government and the Texas settlers.**

***Preview Vocabulary***
**rights**
**conflict**
**treason**
**democracy**
**dictator**

Most of the more than 20,000 settlers in Texas by 1830 were Anglo-Americans from the United States. In the 10 years since the start of the Austin colony, the United States had sent more people to Texas than Spain and Mexico had sent in the 150 years before that!

## DIFFERENT VIEWS

At first the newcomers got along well with the Mexican government. After a few years, however, Anglo-Americans saw that they had different **rights**, or freedoms, under Mexican laws than they had had under the laws of the United States.

The Anglo-American settlers had become Mexican citizens, but they knew little about Mexico or Mexican culture. Most Anglo-Americans did not learn to speak Spanish, which was the language of the Mexican government. It was therefore hard for the Mexican leaders and the Anglo-Americans to discuss their problems.

Another problem for the Anglo-Americans in Texas was religion. The Mexican government did not allow Protestants to practice their religion. Many Protestants from the United States had said they would become Catholics so they could

1830 Mexican military uniform

The Old Stone Fort at Nacogdoches served briefly as the capital of Fredonia. The fort continued to be important to the Republic of Texas long after the Fredonia Rebellion.

move to Texas. However, most of them had not kept this promise.

The Mexican government also passed a law against owning slaves in Mexico. Many Texans who came from the southern United States owned slaves. They were afraid that Mexico would soon pass a law against owning slaves in Texas, too. The Texas settlers believed they had a right to keep their enslaved people.

The Mexican government felt as if it was losing control over the Anglo-American colonies in Texas. Instead of fitting in with Mexico, Texas began to look like a part of the United States. The Anglo-American settlers kept their own culture, rather than accepting or adapting to Mexican culture. The Anglo-American settlers traded freely with the United States. Such trade did not help Mexico.

**On what issues did the Anglo-Americans in Texas and the Mexican government have different views?**

## The Fredonia Rebellion

One of the first **conflicts**, or disagreements, between the Mexican government and the Anglo-American settlers occurred in East Texas as the result of a misunderstanding. In 1825 the Mexican government gave two American brothers, Haden and Benjamin Edwards, a land grant for 800 families near Nacogdoches (nah•koh•DOH•ches). When the Edwards brothers arrived, however, they found other settlers already living on some of this land.

The Edwards brothers asked the Mexican government for help in getting their land back, but the government took the side of the earlier settlers. While Haden was in the United States on business, Benjamin decided to fight for their claim to the land. He and a small group of settlers rode into Nacogdoches waving a red-and-white flag. On it were the words *Independence, Liberty,* and *Justice.* Benjamin said they were breaking away from Mexico and starting their own country. They called it Fredonia.

For a month Benjamin Edwards and his followers stayed in the Old Stone Fort at Nacogdoches. It was the capital of their new country. When Mexican soldiers went to Nacogdoches to end the rebellion, Benjamin crossed the Sabine River to the United States. Some of his followers were put in jail. Because of the Fredonia Rebellion, Mexican leaders worried that other Anglo-Americans in Texas might decide to break away from Mexico.

**What was the effect of the Fredonia Rebellion on Mexican leaders?**

## The Laws of 1830

In 1830 the Mexican leaders changed their laws for settling Texas. They no longer gave land grants to people from the United States. They let only people from Mexico and from Europe settle there. The Anglo-Americans in Texas who had families that were still in the United States were angry. Now the rest of their families could not join them in Texas.

The Mexican leaders also put a tax on goods made in the United States and sold in Texas. The tax made American goods cost more. The Mexican government wanted Texans to buy goods from Mexico instead of from the United States. The leaders hoped that this tax would weaken the ties between Texans and Americans.

The new laws of 1830 made many Anglo-Americans in Texas angrier than ever. In 1833 Stephen F. Austin went to Mexico City, planning to ask President Antonio López de Santa Anna to change the laws about who could move to Texas.

For the most part, the Mexican soldiers sent to Texas to enforce the laws of 1830 did very little to stop the angry feelings among the Texans.

**Map Skill**

**HUMAN-ENVIRONMENT INTERACTIONS**

**By 1836 there were many fast-growing settlements in Texas.**

- **What settlements shown on this map were built along the Colorado River?**

Austin also wanted to ask Santa Anna to make Texas a separate state of Mexico. That way, Texans could elect their own state leaders.

After Austin arrived in Mexico City, he had to wait for months to talk to someone in the government. Meanwhile, he wrote a letter to some Texans in San Antonio, telling them to start the state government without waiting for word from Mexico. Mexican leaders read the letter and put Austin in jail for **treason**, or working against his country. He did not see Texas again until 1835.

✓ **What new laws for Texas did the Mexican government make in 1830?**

## Santa Anna Comes to Power

While Stephen F. Austin was in jail, the Mexican government went through some changes. Many Mexicans wanted their government to be a democracy. A **democracy** is a government in which the people rule by making decisions themselves or by electing leaders to make decisions for them. However, in 1835 President Santa Anna took control of the government of Mexico and became a dictator. The **dictator** of a government is the leader who makes all the important decisions for an entire country.

This change in government made many Mexicans angry. Some Tejanos and other

Mexicans were against Santa Anna. One of these was Stephen F. Austin's friend Erasmo Seguín. Another was Lorenzo de Zavala. De Zavala had once worked for Santa Anna. When Santa Anna became a dictator, De Zavala quit his government job, moved to Texas, and worked against Santa Anna.

Under Santa Anna's rule the Mexican government sent soldiers to Texas to collect taxes and to make people obey Mexican laws. Once again there was conflict. Some Texans tried to stop the soldiers from collecting taxes. The government sent 1,000 soldiers to Texas to arrest the Texas leaders. Fighting broke out between Texans and Mexican soldiers.

When he became dictator of Mexico in 1835, Antonio López de Santa Anna made it clear that he would not give Texans their freedom.

The Mexican government finally freed Stephen F. Austin in July 1835. By that time Austin felt that a peaceful solution to the problems between Texas and the Mexican government was not possible. Texans would have to fight for their rights. Three months later Texas and Mexico were at war.

**Why were many Texans and other Mexicans angry about the way Santa Anna ruled?**

## LESSON 3 REVIEW

### Check Understanding

1. **Recall the Facts** Which leader became a dictator of Mexico in 1835?
2. **Focus on the Main Idea** How did different views about Texas cause problems between Anglo-American settlers and the Mexican government?

### Think Critically

3. **Cause and Effect** What caused the Mexican government to change its laws for Texas? How did the change affect the lives of the Anglo-Americans in Texas and their families in the United States?
4. **Think More About It** How did Stephen F. Austin and the Anglo-American settlers try to solve their problems with the Mexican government? What other ways might they have tried?

### Show What You Know

**Writing Activity** Imagine that you are a reporter for *The Texas Gazette* in 1830. Write an article giving your views on the changes in Mexico's laws. Share your article by making it part of a bulletin board display.

S·K·I·L·L·S

# HOW TO

# Identify Cause and Effect

## Why Is This Skill Important?

Suppose that you are waiting for your ride to school. You discover that you have forgotten your homework. You run back home to get it, and you miss your ride.

Something that makes something else happen is a **cause**. What happens is the **effect**. Running back for your homework is the cause of your missing your ride. Missing your ride is the effect of running back for your homework.

Life is full of causes and effects. Because history is about life in the past, history, too, is full of causes and effects. So are history books!

## Remember What You Have Read

Do you remember reading the following sentence in the last lesson?

> Because of the Fredonia Rebellion, Mexican leaders worried that other Anglo-Americans in Texas might decide to break away from Mexico.

## Understand the Process

Often word clues help you find causes or effects. The cause in the sentence is the Fredonia Rebellion. What is the effect of the Fredonia Rebellion?

Sometimes things that happen in history have more than one cause. The chart below shows the causes that led to the jailing of Stephen F. Austin. You will see that sometimes the effect of one thing that happens becomes the cause of the next thing that happens.

## Think and Apply

BUILDING CITIZENSHIP

Think about the causes and effects of things that happen in people's lives. What might be some causes of a family's moving away from a community? What might be some effects for the family that is moving? What might be some of the effects for the community they are leaving or for the community they are moving to?

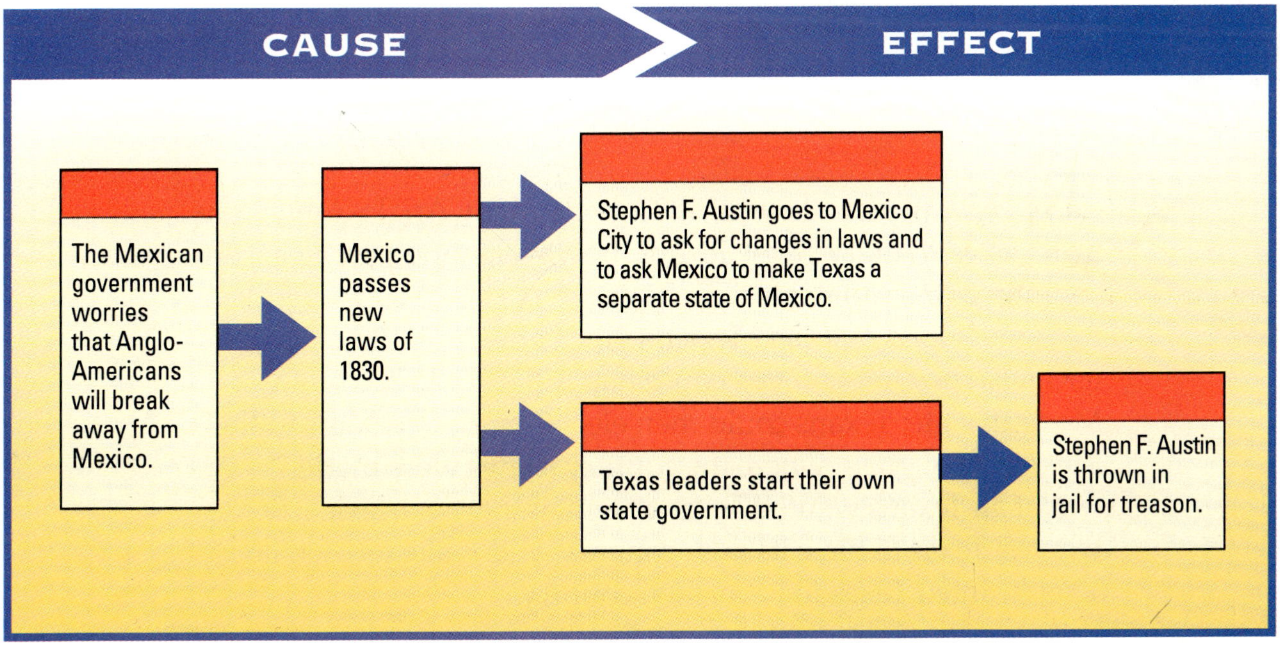

COUNTERPOINTS

# MEXICAN STATE OR NEW COUNTRY?

The new Mexican laws of 1830 made many Anglo-Americans in Texas very angry. Most Texans, however, hoped for a peaceful solution to the problems with Mexico.

Some hoped that the Mexican government would change its laws. They felt that this could happen if Texas became a Mexican state. Texans could then elect their own leaders to the Mexican Congress, where the country's laws were made.

Not all Texans wanted Texas to remain part of Mexico. Some wanted Texas to have its own congress and make its own laws. They wanted Texas to be its own country.

Two Texans who made their feelings clear about this issue were Stephen F. Austin and William B. Travis. Austin had started the first Anglo-American colony in Texas. Travis was a lawyer from the United States. He came to Texas in 1831, when it was against the law for Americans to move to Texas. Read the following words from the two men. What were their views on whether Texas should remain part of Mexico or become its own country?

**Stephen F. Austin**

"If things can be kept quiet in the colony all will end right and prosperously, of this I have no doubt. What is needed there is a *dead calm.* All reflecting men will become convinced that the true interest of Texas is never to separate from Mexico, and that it is the true interest of this nation to encourage the population of Texas and make a state of it."

**William B. Travis**

"The rumor of troops coming to Texas in great number must be false. Such a measure would kindle a flame in Texas that would burn in twain the slender cords that connect us to the ill-fated Mexican Confederation. I am more and more convinced every day of the utter futility of our friend Austin's favorite plan of hanging on to Mexico."

## COMPARE VIEWPOINTS

1. What did Stephen F. Austin think about Texas staying with Mexico? How do you know?
2. What did William B. Travis think about Texas staying with Mexico? How do you know?
3. What other views might Texans have had? Read the following words from Isaac Holman, a farmer from San Augustine. "In relation to matters of Government we are perfectly at peace. . . . Society is much better here than perhaps you might imagine." What did Holman think about Texas staying with Mexico? How is Holman's view different from the views of Austin and Travis?

## THINK -AND- APPLY

People often have different views about certain subjects. You have read that three Texans each had a different view about Texas staying with Mexico. On what subjects do you think Texans today might have different views?

# CHAPTER 4 REVIEW

## CONNECT MAIN IDEAS

Use this organizer to show that you understand how the chapter's main ideas are connected. First copy the organizer onto a separate sheet of paper. Then complete it by writing one or two sentences that explain how each item affected the Anglo-American settlers in Texas.

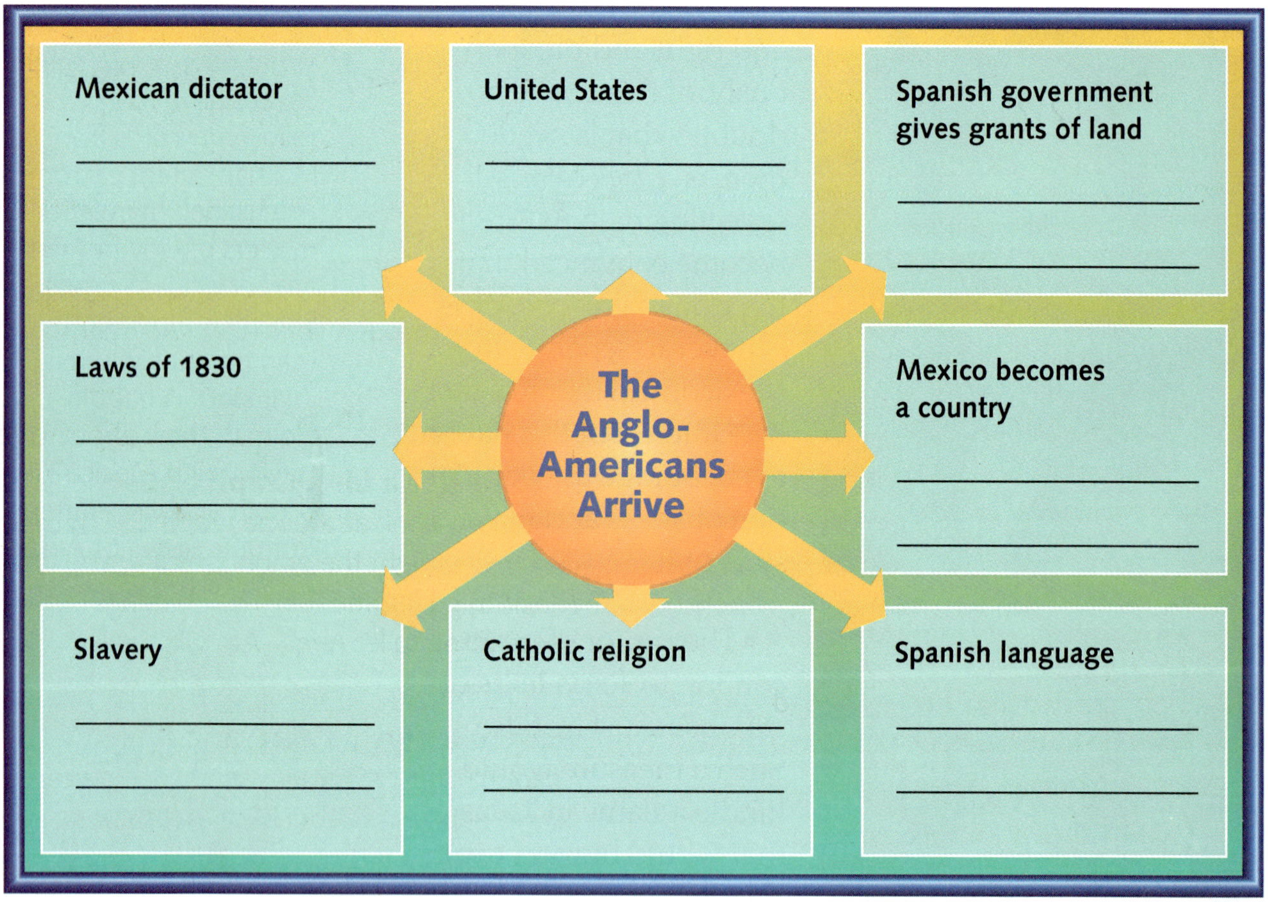


## WRITE MORE ABOUT IT

1. **Write a Letter** Imagine that you are living in the Austin colony in 1821. Write a letter to friends in the United States, telling them what to bring when they move to Texas. Describe what their life might be like the first year.

2. **Write a News Report** Imagine that you are a newspaper reporter for *The Texas Gazette* in 1825. Write a short report that describes an interview you had with Benjamin Edwards about the start of the Fredonia Rebellion.

## USE VOCABULARY

Use each vocabulary word in a sentence that helps explain its meaning.

1. frontier
2. capital
3. slave
4. rights
5. conflict
6. democracy

## CHECK UNDERSTANDING

1. Why did Stephen F. Austin go to Mexico City in 1821?
2. What town was the capital of the Austin colony?
3. What did Stephen F. Austin offer to the settlers willing to move to Texas?
4. What kinds of things did empresarios do?
5. Who were some famous Tejanos?
6. What difficulties did settlers face as they journeyed to Texas?
7. How was language a problem for the Anglo-American settlers in Texas and for the people in the Mexican government?
8. Why were many Texans worried about the Mexican law against owning slaves?
9. How did Mexican leaders try to force Texans to buy Mexican goods?
10. What did Lorenzo de Zavala do when Santa Anna took over the Mexican government?

## THINK CRITICALLY

1. **Think More About It** Why do you think both the Spanish and Mexican leaders in Mexico allowed Anglo-Americans to settle in Texas?
2. **Link to You** Some events that took place in Mexico affected settlers in Texas. What events in other places in the world have affected you and your family in the United States?
3. **Personally Speaking** If you were a Tejano settler, how do you think you would have felt when Santa Anna took over the Mexican government as a dictator?
4. **Cause and Effect** How did the issue of religion affect relations between the Mexican government and Anglo-American settlers in Texas?
5. **Explore Viewpoints** Why might ties between Texas and the United States have weakened if Texans had stopped buying goods from the United States?

## APPLY SKILLS

**How to Use a Line Graph to See Change** Look at the line graph on page 114. How might the graph look if the Mexican government in 1821 had not been willing to let Anglo-Americans settle in Texas?

**How to Identify Cause and Effect** Read the *Different Views* section on pages 120–121. What examples of cause and effect can you find in this section?

## READ MORE ABOUT IT

*Jane Long: A Child's Pictorial History* by Elizabeth Dearing Morgan. Eakin. With many photographs and maps, this book describes the events in Jane Long's life.

*Stephen F. Austin: The Father of Texas* by Jean Flynn. Eakin. This book presents a picture of Stephen F. Austin's life.

## Making Social Studies Relevant

# Then & Now

Have you ever been to Buenos Aires? Mexico City? New Orleans? If you go to any of these places, you will notice that buildings there look like buildings in Texas cities such as San Antonio and El Paso. In all these cities you can find churches and other buildings that have the same Spanish or French styles. You can also see many of the same customs practiced in these and other places. For example, many African Americans living in Texas practice some of the same customs and traditions as Africans now living in places such as the Caribbean and Brazil.

You can see these similarities because many of the same groups of Europeans and Africans who came to Texas long ago settled also in other places in the Western Hemisphere. These people were the ancestors of many Texans, and they left a heritage that has lasted. You can see it in the buildings, customs, and in the faces of many present-day Texans.

People and places throughout the Western Hemisphere are different in their own ways, but they share parts of a common past.

New Orleans, Louisiana

Buenos Aires, Argentina

San Antonio, Texas

New Orleans, Louisiana

## THINK AND APPLY

BUILDING CITIZENSHIP

Think about the ways the buildings and people of a place tell you about that place's past. Explore your own community to find links to its history and links to other places in the Western Hemisphere. Draw a poster showing these links to the past and to other places. Display your poster with those of your classmates.

Mexico City, Mexico

UNIT 2

# STORY CLOTH

Follow the pictures shown in this story cloth to help you review the events in Unit 2.

## Summarize the Main Ideas

1. In 1540 Coronado led an expedition of Spanish soldiers across the Texas Panhandle. They may have been the first to see Palo Duro Canyon.
2. An Indian told Coronado of a land of great riches, called Quivira. However, Quivira turned out to be like any other Indian village.
3. The Spanish built missions in Texas. Catholic priests taught the Indians the Catholic religion and the Spanish way of life.
4. Stephen F. Austin offered large areas of land to settlers who would help start the Austin colony.
5. In 1830 the Mexican leaders changed their laws for settling Texas. Santa Anna became a dictator and sent soldiers to Texas to see that the new laws were obeyed.
6. Many people in Texas became angry enough with the Mexican government to fight for their rights.

**Write a Newspaper Article** Imagine that you are taking part in one of the events shown in this story cloth. Write a short newspaper article about the event. Include your article in a class newspaper.

**Write About the Story** Write captions, or descriptive sentences, for each of the scenes shown in this story cloth.

FREEMEN OF TEXAS
To Arms!!! To Arms!!!!
"Now's the day, & now's the hour."

UNIT 2
# REVIEW

## COOPERATIVE LEARNING WORKSHOP

**Remember**

- Share your ideas.
- Cooperate with others to plan your work.
- Take responsibility for your work.
- Show your group's work to the class.
- Discuss what you learned by working together.

**Activity 1**

### Draw a Mural

Work with a group of classmates to draw a mural on a large sheet of paper. Create scenes based on the events that you learned about in this unit. Write captions that tell about the explorers or settlers as they were described in the text. Hang the mural on a wall, and ask other groups in your class to identify each scene.

**Activity 2**

### Plan a Spanish Heritage Day

With your class, plan a "Spanish Heritage" day. Bring to class samples of food, art, clothing, and music that are part of the Spanish heritage found in Texas today. Invite classmates or guest speakers to discuss Spanish traditions that they practice at home.

**Activity 3**

### Make a Class Scrapbook

Bring pictures to class that show the Spanish heritage in Texas today. You might bring in postcards of the old missions, pictures of clothing, pictures of musicians or dancers, recipes, or a list of places with Spanish names. Show your classmates what you bring, and then add your items to a class scrapbook.

**Activity 4**

### Perform a Skit

With a group of classmates, write a short skit about Stephen F. Austin's trip to Mexico City in 1833. One of you can be Austin. Others can be members of the Mexican government. Be sure to discuss some of the problems that troubled Anglo-Americans and Mexicans.

## USE VOCABULARY

Use each vocabulary word in a sentence that helps explain its meaning.

1. colony
2. dictator
3. expedition
4. grant
5. mission
6. treason

## CHECK UNDERSTANDING

1. What reports led the Spanish to explore the lands north of Mexico?
2. How did Stephen F. Austin try to get settlers to come to his colony?
3. What were the laws Mexico made for Texas in 1830?
4. Why did the Mexican government send soldiers to arrest Texas leaders in 1835?
5. How did Stephen F. Austin think the problems between the Mexican government and the Anglo-Americans would have to be settled?

## THINK CRITICALLY

1. **Cause and Effect** How did the Indians affect some of the settlements in Texas?
2. **Think More About It** What did Stephen F. Austin mean when he said that "no idler" would be welcome in the Austin colony?
3. **Link to You** Why is it important that leaders who have different views meet and talk about problems?
4. **Explore Viewpoints** In 1830, why might the settlers from Mexico and the settlers from the United States have had different views about the Anglo-American colonies in Texas?

## APPLY GEOGRAPHY SKILLS

### How to Follow Routes on a Map

Map Skill

More than 250 years after Coronado's expedition, another group set out to explore the High Plains of the United States. An American named Zebulon Pike led a group of American soldiers to the country's western frontier in 1806. Spanish officers arrested Pike and his men after they crossed into land claimed by Spain. The party was sent, unharmed but under guard, back to United States territory. Use the map below to answer the questions that follow.

**PIKE'S ROUTE, 1806–1807**

1. What places did Pike visit along his route?
2. What part of Texas did Pike travel through?
3. What was the direction of Pike's route after he left San Antonio and headed toward United States territory?

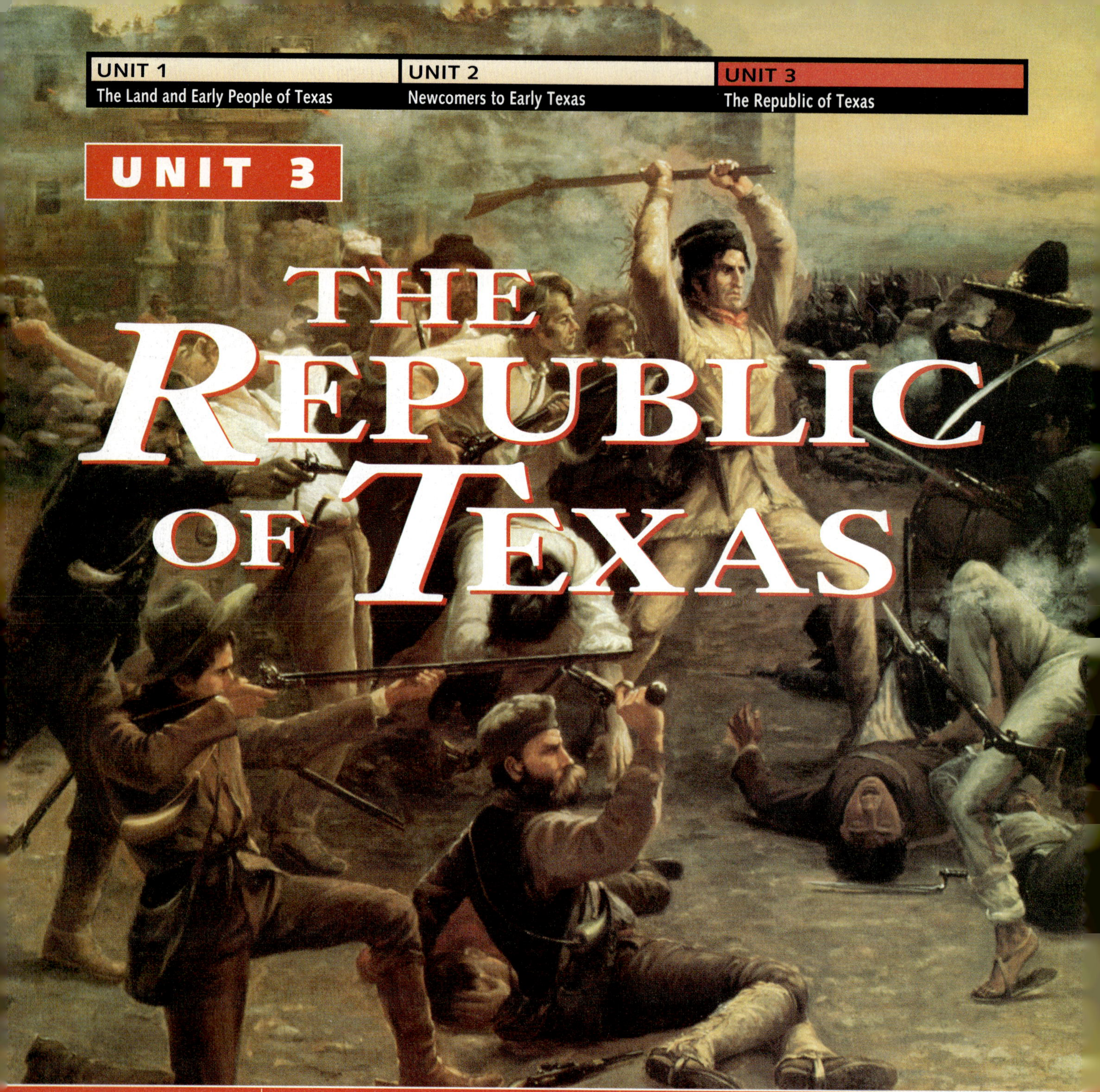

UNIT 3

# THE REPUBLIC OF TEXAS

1835

**1835**
Battle of Gonzales starts Texas Revolution

**1836**
The Alamo falls

Texans win at San Jacinto

Texas wins its independence from Mexico

Sam Houston is elected president of the Republic of Texas

**1838**
Mirabeau Lamar is elected president of the Republic of Texas

1840

**1839**
Austin becomes the capital of the Republic of Texas

Lone Star flag becomes the national flag of the Republic of Texas

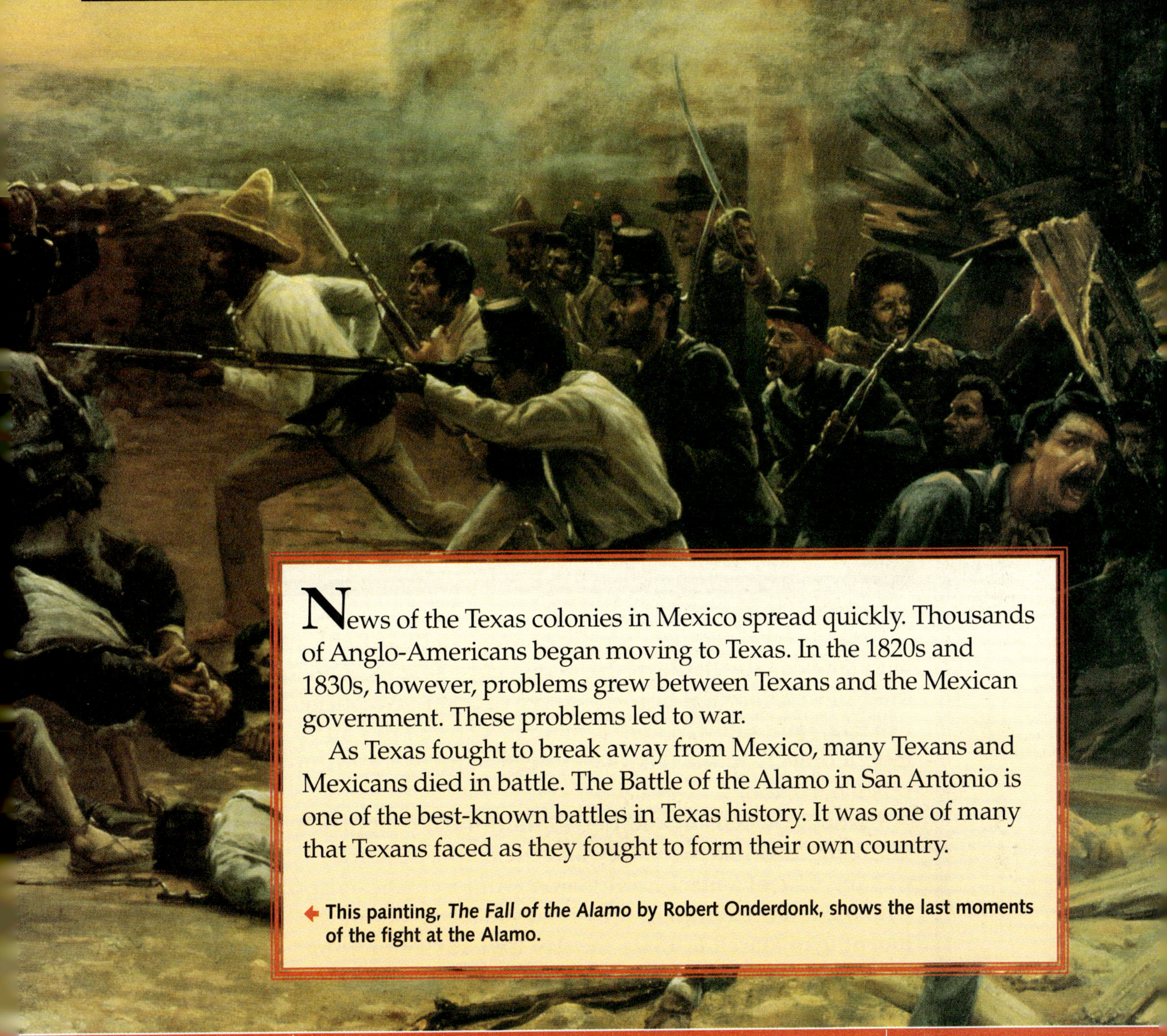

News of the Texas colonies in Mexico spread quickly. Thousands of Anglo-Americans began moving to Texas. In the 1820s and 1830s, however, problems grew between Texans and the Mexican government. These problems led to war.

As Texas fought to break away from Mexico, many Texans and Mexicans died in battle. The Battle of the Alamo in San Antonio is one of the best-known battles in Texas history. It was one of many that Texans faced as they fought to form their own country.

**This painting, *The Fall of the Alamo* by Robert Onderdonk, shows the last moments of the fight at the Alamo.**

**1845**

**1845**
**Texas joins the United States**

**1846**
**The United States and Mexico go to war**

**1850**

**1850**
**Present-day Texas borders set**

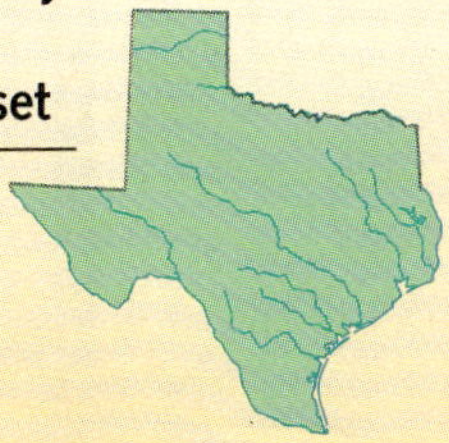

*Set the Scene with Literature*

# SUSANNA OF THE ALAMO

## *A True Story*

***written by John Jakes***
***illustrated by Paul Bacon***

**Texans yelled "Remember the Alamo!" in their fight with Mexico. The Battle of the Alamo gave Texans some of their most important heroes—Davy Crockett, Gregorio Esparza, James Bowie, and William B. Travis. They all fought bravely in the terrible battle. Susanna Dickenson was a hero, too.**

**Susanna Dickenson and her 15-month-old daughter, Elizabeth Angelina, lived through the battle. Susanna was the wife of a blacksmith named Almeron Dickenson, who died in the fighting. Now read the true story of the morning of March 6, 1836, the day General Santa Anna led his Mexican soldiers in the final attack on the Alamo.**

Ten days passed.
Eleven.
Twelve . . .

Gunfire from both sides remained steady. Santa Anna's military bands played during the night, so the Texans lost sleep. The Mexican army kept growing . . . to two thousand, then three.

Eating a supper of fried beans with Susanna, Almeron, exhausted, shook his head. "Sometimes I wonder why we're holding out, Sue. Killing isn't right, or good. Those soldiers out there don't want to die any more than we do."

"I know," she said softly. "But maybe we want to be free more than they do."

Gazing at her with love, he reached out and squeezed her hand. And nodded.

Before dawn on Sunday, March 6, Santa Anna's armies were stirring. Dozing in an old damp blanket with Angelina in her arms, Susanna woke suddenly.

"What is that music?" she whispered.

Guns were crackling outside the chapel. Artillery matches glowed near the cannon on the walls. Susanna stared into the horrified face of her friend Señora Esparza.

**artillery** mounted guns, like cannons

"You know what the bugle call means, Señora. Please tell me."

"Santa Anna is tormenting us. It is the *deguello.* It means the same thing as the big red flag. Show no mercy. Kill everyone."

**bugle** horn

Sharp as knives, the bugle notes flew through the air. Susanna clutched her baby. She heard shouting, ladders thumping against the Alamo walls.

She rushed into the plaza as the first enemy rocket lit the paling sky. She saw Travis running toward the north wall, carrying a sword and shotgun. Before Crockett and others pushed Susanna back inside to safety, she heard Travis cry, *"The Mexicans are upon us—!"*

Susanna's heart beat fast. With the other women and children, she huddled in the sacristy, a small room off the chapel. Hers was the only American face. But all the faces shared a common look. It seemed to say:

*We are frightened. But we stayed here to show what we're made of. Now it's time.*

In the sacristy, Susanna never saw the final brief battle, only heard it:

Booming cannon.

Shouts of attackers and defenders.

Cries of wounded and dying.

Almeron calling orders to his cannoneers . . .

Angelina fretted, clutching her mother's apron. Susanna knew that the Texans were losing.

Suddenly, powder-stained, Almeron was there.

"Great God, Sue, the Mexicans . . ."

All of Santa Anna's bands were playing the *deguello* together, so everyone could hear it above the gunfire.

". . . they're inside the north wall. Hear them?"

*"Viva Santa Anna! Viva Santa Anna!"*

"If they spare you, save our child."

And he was gone.

Forever.

**Viva Santa Anna** Long live Santa Anna

# THE TEXAS REVOLUTION

"I ask all of you here today to unite in our cause for a free Texas."

Lorenzo de Zavala,
Texas leader, 1835

Lorenzo de Zavala supported the Texans in their struggle against the Mexican government. He later served as vice president of the Republic of Texas.

LESSON 1

# THE REVOLUTION BEGINS

## Link to Our World

**When is it important to stand up for what you believe?**

***Focus on the Main Idea***
**Read to find out why Texans were willing to fight for what they believed.**

***Preview Vocabulary***
**revolution**
**volunteer**
**surrender**

Stephen F. Austin was angry when he returned to Texas from Mexico in 1835. Before his time in jail, Austin had been a loyal citizen of Mexico. He had wanted the settlers to be loyal, too. But his meeting with Santa Anna had changed his mind. Austin now said, "We must defend our rights, ourselves, and our country." Texas must be free!

### FIRST BATTLES

The Texas Revolution began on October 2, 1835. A **revolution** is a change of government made by force, usually through a war. The first battle in the Texans' fight to break free from Mexican rule was fought at the town of Gonzales on the Guadalupe River. It was a small fight, but it set off a war that changed Texas and its people forever.

This mosaic depicting the Battle of Gonzales is displayed at the Municipal Building in Gonzales.

The Battle of Gonzales began when Mexican soldiers were sent to the town to take back a small brass cannon. The cannon had been given to the Texans years before to fight the Indians. The Texans had refused to return it. Instead, they had hung a flag on it with the words *Come and Take It*. When the Mexicans tried to do that, a crowd of 160 Texans beat back the Mexican soldiers. The Mexicans returned to San Antonio without the cannon.

Because of the trouble at Gonzales, Mexican general Martín Perfecto de Cós (mar•TEEN pair•FEK•toh day KOHS) decided to bring more soldiers to Goliad and

San Antonio. Cós was the leader in charge of the Mexican lands in Texas and was married to Santa Anna's sister.

On October 9, 1835, after their victory at Gonzales, 50 Texans attacked 30 Mexican soldiers at Goliad. In the short battle one Mexican soldier was killed. The only Texas soldier wounded was Samuel McCulloch, a free African living in Texas. Meanwhile, there were several hundred Texans marching to San Antonio.

On December 5, 1835, the Texans attacked San Antonio. Many Tejanos, including Erasmo Seguín and his son Juan, joined the Anglo-Americans in the fight. After four days the Texans captured San Antonio and made General Cós and his army go back to Mexico. Texas was free of Mexican soldiers.

**✓ Where were the first battles of the Texas Revolution?**

## Who?

### Juan Seguín, 1806–1889

Juan Seguín was a Tejano defender of the Alamo, but he did not die in the fighting. He was sent through the Mexican lines to try to get help. After the Alamo, Seguín went on fighting for the rights of all Texans. He later helped make laws for Texas, and he worked to have them printed in Spanish as well as English. He was also mayor of San Antonio.The present-day town of Seguin, between Houston and San Antonio, is named for this Tejano hero of the Texas Revolution.

## Defenders of the Alamo

After the victory at San Antonio, many Texans believed the war might be over, so they left the city. However, an army of 5,000 Mexican soldiers was on its way to San Antonio to take back the city, and only about 100 Texans were there to defend it.

More Texans were needed, and soon some arrived. Many were **volunteers**—people who offer their help, usually without pay. They came from the United States and even from Europe to help the Texans fight for freedom.

William B. Travis and 30 soldiers rode in from San Felipe de Austin. Travis was a 26-year-old lawyer from Alabama. James Butler Bonham, also from Alabama, and a group from Gonzales joined the Texas army. Juan Seguín and ten other Tejanos also came.

Davy Crockett came from Tennessee with 12 other Tennessee volunteers. "I have come to aid you all that I can in your noble cause," Crockett said to the Texans.

James Bowie had lived in Louisiana before he moved to Texas in 1828. Bowie was to lead the Texans, but he became ill. So William B. Travis took charge.

The Mexican army was near San Antonio now, and the Texans had only about 190 fighters. The Texans gathered at the Alamo, an old church. On February 23, 1836, General Santa Anna arrived with part of the Mexican army. Soon the Alamo was surrounded.

**✓ Who were three defenders of the Alamo?**

## THE ALAMO FORTRESS

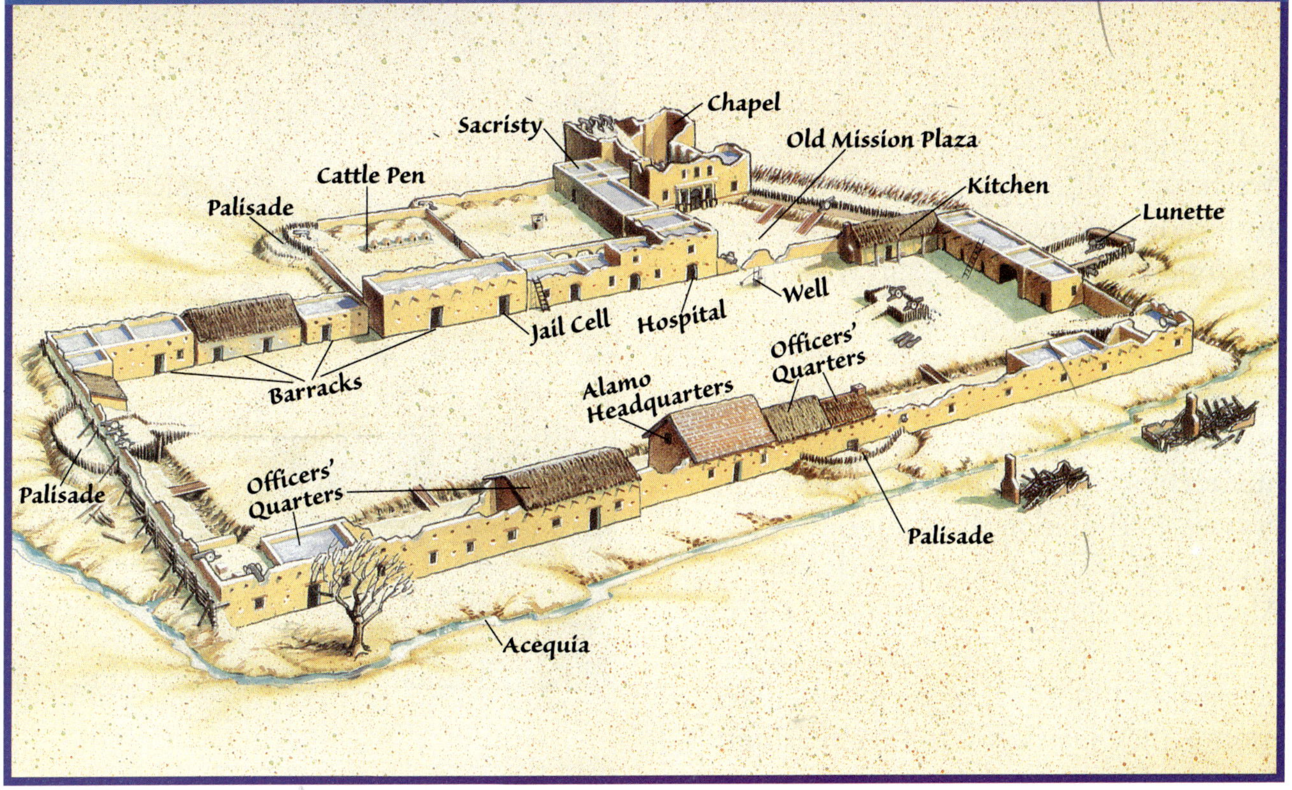


**LEARNING FROM DIAGRAMS** This diagram shows what the Alamo probably looked like the night before the Mexican attack.

- If you were a Texas military leader at the Alamo, where in the fort would you place a lookout to watch for the Mexican army?

## TEXANS TAKE A STAND

The small group of Texans knew that they could not defeat the huge Mexican army. On February 24, William B. Travis sent out several letters asking for help. In one letter he promised never to **surrender**, or give up. He wrote,

> "I am determined to sustain myself as long as possible & die like a soldier who never forgets what is due to his own honor & that of his country—VICTORY OR DEATH."

For 13 days the Mexican army fired cannons at the Alamo walls. From the tops of the walls, the defenders of the Alamo shot back with rifles. They knew that Santa Anna was making plans for an all-out attack.

The final attack came before sunrise on March 6. When the order to attack was given, nearly 2,000 Mexican soldiers ran toward the Alamo. They shouted, *"Viva Santa Anna!"* The Mexican soldiers quickly reached the Alamo's walls and raised ladders so they could climb over.

The Texans fought off the first line of attackers. But more Mexican soldiers were soon climbing over the walls. Hand-to-hand fighting raged all through the Alamo. One Mexican soldier later wrote, "The Texans defended . . . every inch of the fort."

When the smoke cleared at the Alamo, at least 182 Texans and as many as 1,600 Mexicans lay dead.

The fighting was over in less than two hours. Almost all of the Texans and hundreds of Mexicans died in the battle. Susanna Dickenson, a Texan who had survived the fighting, was sent by Santa Anna to tell the Texas leaders that the Alamo had fallen. She reached Gonzales on March 13. Her story kept alive the memory of the Texans who had fought bravely and died at the Alamo.

News of what had happened at the Alamo soon spread to every part of Texas and to the United States. When people heard about those who had fought at the Alamo, they wanted to fight, too. Santa Anna had failed to end the Texas Revolution. "Remember the Alamo!" yelled the Texas soldiers as they gathered at Gonzales. The Texans were ready to fight on.

**How did Texans learn about the fall of the Alamo?**

The Alamo has a special meaning in both Texas and United States history. To many, it stands for the high price people sometimes have to pay for freedom.

## LESSON 1 REVIEW

### Check Understanding

1. **Recall the Facts** What happened at the Battle of Gonzales?
2. **Focus on the Main Idea** Why were Texans so willing to fight in the Texas Revolution?

### Think Critically

3. **Link to You** How did the Battle of the Alamo give Texans a heritage of courage?
4. **Think More About It** How did a defeat—the fall of the Alamo—help the Texans in their revolution?

### Show What You Know

**Writing Activity** Imagine that you are a reporter for *The Texas Gazette* in March 1836. Write the first paragraph for an article on what happened at the Alamo. Display your paragraph.

# LESSON 2 TEXAS DECLARES ITS INDEPENDENCE

## Link to Our World

**How do people today organize new groups?**

***Focus on the Main Idea***
**Read to find out how Texans worked to set up their new country.**

***Preview Vocabulary***
**independence** **abolish**
**declaration** **republic**
**congress** **constitution**

While the Texans at the Alamo were getting ready for Santa Anna's attack, another group of Texans were meeting at the town of Washington-on-the-Brazos. The Texans were now ready to organize their fight because they knew that Santa Anna would not give up his control of Texas. Now the war was to be a fight for **independence**, or freedom.

### TEXAS IS FREE

The 59 Texans who met at Washington-on-the-Brazos decided that Texas had to have independence from Mexico. In order to defend their rights, they would have to start their own country.

On March 2, 1836, these Texans signed the Texas Declaration of Independence. A **declaration** announces a fact. The Texas Declaration of Independence said that Texas was now a free country and was no longer under Mexican rule.

Among the signers was Lorenzo de Zavala. Before he moved to Texas, De Zavala had been a member of the Mexican Congress. A **congress** is a law-making branch of a national government. Two other Tejanos, or Mexicans living in Texas, joined De Zavala. Their names were José Antonio Navarro (hoh•SAY ahn•TOH•nee•oh nah•VAR•roh) and José Francisco Ruiz (hoh•SAY frahn•SEES•koh roo•EES). Both of these men had been born in San Antonio.

George Childress was head of the committee that wrote the Texas Declaration of Independence.

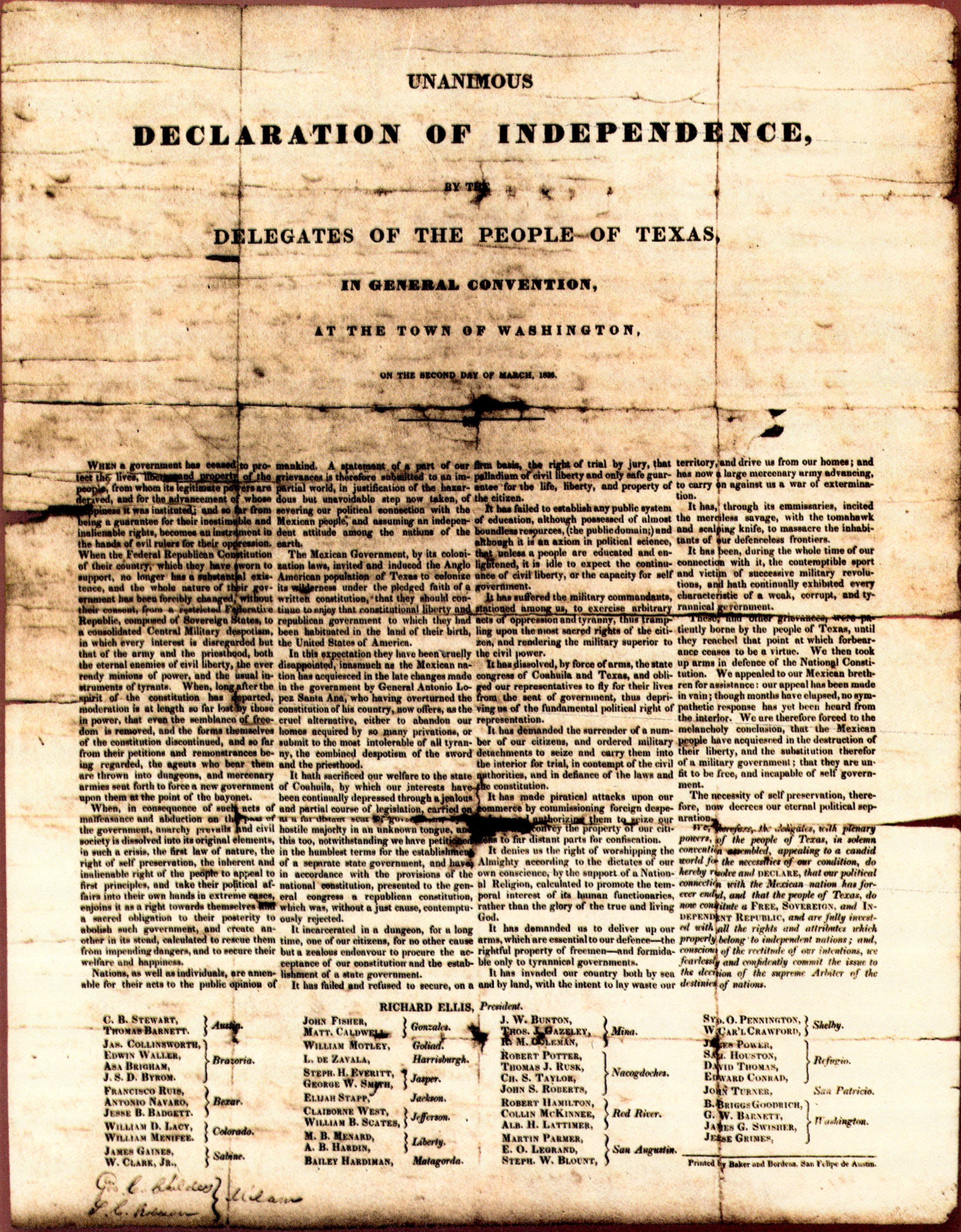

UNANIMOUS

# DECLARATION OF INDEPENDENCE,

BY THE

## DELEGATES OF THE PEOPLE OF TEXAS,

IN GENERAL CONVENTION,

AT THE TOWN OF WASHINGTON,

ON THE SECOND DAY OF MARCH, 1836.

WHEN a government has ceased to protect the lives, liberty and property of the people, from whom its legitimate powers are derived, and for the advancement of whose happiness it was instituted; and so far from being a guarantee for their inestimable and inalienable rights, becomes an instrument in the hands of evil rulers for their oppression. When the Federal Republican Constitution of their country, which they have sworn to support, no longer has a substantial existence, and the whole nature of their government has been forcibly changed, without their consent, from a restricted Federative Republic, composed of Sovereign States, to a consolidated Central Military despotism, in which every interest is disregarded but that of the army and the priesthood, both the eternal enemies of civil liberty, the ever ready minions of power, and the usual instruments of tyrants. When, long after the spirit of the constitution has departed, moderation is at length so far lost by those in power, that even the semblance of freedom is removed, and the forms themselves of the constitution discontinued, and so far from their petitions and remonstrances being regarded, the agents who bear them are thrown into dungeons, and mercenary armies sent forth to force a new government upon them at the point of the bayonet.

When, in consequence of such acts of malfeasance and abduction on the part of the government, anarchy prevails and civil society is dissolved into its original elements, in such a crisis, the first law of nature, the right of self preservation, the inherent and inalienable right of the people to appeal to first principles, and take their political affairs into their own hands in extreme cases, enjoins it as a right towards themselves and a sacred obligation to their posterity to abolish such government, and create another in its stead, calculated to rescue them from impending dangers, and to secure their welfare and happiness.

Nations, as well as individuals, are amenable for their acts to the public opinion of mankind. A statement of a part of our grievances is therefore submitted to an impartial world, in justification of the hazardous but unavoidable step now taken, of severing our political connection with the Mexican people, and assuming an independent attitude among the nations of the earth.

The Mexican Government, by its colonization laws, invited and induced the Anglo American population of Texas to colonize its wilderness under the pledged faith of a written constitution, that they should continue to enjoy that constitutional liberty and republican government to which they had been habituated in the land of their birth, the United States of America.

In this expectation they have been cruelly disappointed, inasmuch as the Mexican nation has acquiesced in the late changes made in the government by General Antonio Lopez Santa Ana, who having overturned the constitution of his country, now offers, as the cruel alternative, either to abandon our homes acquired by so many privations, or submit to the most intolerable of all tyranny, the combined despotism of the sword and the priesthood.

It hath sacrificed our welfare to the state of Coahuila, by which our interests have been continually depressed through a jealous and partial course of legislation, carried on at a far distant seat of government, by a hostile majority in an unknown tongue, and this too, notwithstanding we have petitioned in the humblest terms for the establishment of a separate state government, and have, in accordance with the provisions of the national constitution, presented to the general congress a republican constitution, which was, without a just cause, contemptuously rejected.

It incarcerated in a dungeon, for a long time, one of our citizens, for no other cause but a zealous endeavour to procure the acceptance of our constitution and the establishment of a state government.

It has failed and refused to secure, on a firm basis, the right of trial by jury, that palladium of civil liberty and only safe guarantee for the life, liberty, and property of the citizen.

It has failed to establish any public system of education, although possessed of almost boundless resources, (the public domain;) and although it is an axiom in political science, that unless a people are educated and enlightened, it is idle to expect the continuance of civil liberty, or the capacity for self government.

It has suffered the military commandants, stationed among us, to exercise arbitrary acts of oppression and tyranny, thus trampling upon the most sacred rights of the citizen, and rendering the military superior to the civil power.

It has dissolved, by force of arms, the state congress of Coahuila and Texas, and obliged our representatives to fly for their lives from the seat of government, thus depriving us of the fundamental political right of representation.

It has demanded the surrender of a number of our citizens, and ordered military detachments to seize and carry them into the interior for trial, in contempt of the civil authorities, and in defiance of the laws and the constitution.

It has made piratical attacks upon our commerce by commissioning foreign desperadoes, and authorizing them to seize our vessels, and convey the property of our citizens to far distant parts for confiscation.

It denies us the right of worshipping the Almighty according to the dictates of our own conscience, by the support of a National Religion, calculated to promote the temporal interest of its human functionaries, rather than the glory of the true and living God.

It has demanded us to deliver up our arms, which are essential to our defence—the rightful property of freemen—and formidable only to tyrannical governments.

It has invaded our country both by sea and by land, with the intent to lay waste our territory, and drive us from our homes; and has now a large mercenary army advancing, to carry on against us a war of extermination.

It has, through its emmissaries, incited the merciless savage, with the tomahawk and scalping knife, to massacre the inhabitants of our defenceless frontiers.

It has been, during the whole time of our connection with it, the contemptible sport and victim of successive military revolutions, and hath continually exhibited every characteristic of a weak, corrupt, and tyrannical government.

These, and other grievances, were patiently borne by the people of Texas, until they reached that point at which forbearance ceases to be a virtue. We then took up arms in defence of the National Constitution. We appealed to our Mexican brethren for assistance: our appeal has been made in vain; though months have elapsed, no sympathetic response has yet been heard from the interior. We are therefore forced to the melancholy conclusion, that the Mexican people have acquiesced in the destruction of their liberty, and the substitution therefor of a military government; that they are unfit to be free, and incapable of self government.

The necessity of self preservation, therefore, now decrees our eternal political separation.

*We, therefore, the delegates, with plenary powers, of the people of Texas, in solemn convention assembled, appealing to a candid world for the necessities of our condition, do hereby resolve and* DECLARE, *that our political connection with the Mexican nation has forever ended, and that the people of Texas, do now constitute a* FREE, SOVEREIGN, *and* INDEPENDENT REPUBLIC, *and are fully invested with all the rights and attributes which properly belong to independent nations; and, conscious of the rectitude of our intentions, we fearlessly and confidently commit the issue to the decision of the supreme Arbiter of the destinies of nations.*

RICHARD ELLIS, *President.*

C. B. STEWART, THOMAS BARNETT. — *Austin.*
JAS. COLLINSWORTH, EDWIN WALLER, ASA BRIGHAM, J. S. D. BYROM. — *Brazoria.*
FRANCISCO RUIS, ANTONIO NAVARO, JESSE B. BADGETT. — *Bexar.*
WILLIAM D. LACY, WILLIAM MENIFEE. — *Colorado.*
JAMES GAINES, W. CLARK, JR. — *Sabine.*
JOHN FISHER, MATT. CALDWELL — *Gonzales.*
WILLIAM MOTLEY, — *Goliad.*
L. DE ZAVALA, — *Harrisburgh.*
STEPH. H. EVERITT, GEORGE W. SMYTH, — *Jasper.*
ELIJAH STAPP, — *Jackson.*
CLAIBORNE WEST, WILLIAM B. SCATES, — *Jefferson.*
M. B. MENARD, A. B. HARDIN, — *Liberty.*
BAILEY HARDIMAN, — *Matagorda.*
J. W. BUNTON, THOS. J. GAZELEY, R. M. COLEMAN, — *Mina.*
ROBERT POTTER, THOMAS J. RUSK, CH. S. TAYLOR, JOHN S. ROBERTS, — *Nacogdoches.*
ROBERT HAMILTON, COLLIN MCKINNEE, ALB. H. LATTIMER, — *Red River.*
MARTIN PARMER, E. O. LEGRAND, STEPH. W. BLOUNT, — *San Augustin.*
SYD. O. PENNINGTON, W. CAR'L CRAWFORD, — *Shelby.*
JAMES POWER, SAM. HOUSTON, DAVID THOMAS, EDWARD CONRAD, — *Refugio.*
JOHN TURNER, — *San Patricio.*
B. BRIGGS GOODRICH, G. W. BARNETT, JAMES G. SWISHER, JESSE GRIMES, — *Washington.*

Printed by Baker and Bordens, San Felipe de Austin.

**LEARNING FROM DOCUMENTS** The Texas Declaration of Independence is based on the United States Declaration of Independence.

- What people were represented by the delegates who signed the Texas Declaration of Independence?

To write the Declaration and the Constitution, the delegates met at Washington-on-the-Brazos in an unfinished building belonging to a blacksmith.

Most of the other signers of the Declaration came from the United States. Before moving to Texas, one of the signers, Sam Houston (HYOOS•tuhn), had lived for years with the Cherokees in Tennessee. He had fought in the War of 1812 and served as a member of the United States Congress and as governor of Tennessee.

Other Anglo-American signers of the Texas Declaration of Independence were Richard Ellis, Robert Potter, Martin Parmer, and Samuel P. Carson. George Childress headed the group that wrote the declaration.

**Who were three signers of the Texas Declaration of Independence?**

## The Texas Declaration of Independence

The declaration that was signed in Texas on March 2, 1836, was much like the United States Declaration of Independence of July 4, 1776. Even some of the wording was the same. However, the Texans had changed the words *Great Britain* to *Mexico*.

Both declarations said that the duty of the government was to protect lives, liberty, and property. When a government fails to do this, the people have the right to abolish such a government and create another. To **abolish** is to put an end to.

Like the United States Declaration of Independence, the Texas Declaration of Independence lists the reasons for breaking away from the ruling country. The most important reason Texans wanted to break away from Mexico was that Santa Anna had abolished democracy in Mexico and had become a dictator.

The Texans gave other reasons. One was that the new laws of 1830 no longer allowed people from the United States to move to Texas. Another was that the Mexican government did not protect the rights of its citizens. The Texans were also angry that Stephen F. Austin had been kept in jail for nearly two years without a trial.

**What reasons did Texans give for breaking away from Mexico?**

## The New Texas Government

After declaring Texas's independence, the Texas leaders made a plan of government for the new country, the Republic of Texas. A **republic** is a government in which the people are free to choose their leaders. The leaders carry out the programs that most of the citizens want.

The plan of government, or **constitution**, was written using the United States Constitution as a model. There was to be a congress to make the laws, a president and a vice president to carry out the laws, and a court system to settle important issues and to make sure that the laws were fair.

Because Texas was at war, the government planners chose leaders to serve until the time when the people could vote for their own officials. David Burnet was chosen as the first president of the Texas Republic. Burnet was a rancher and sawmill owner. Lorenzo de Zavala became vice president. The first goal of the new government was to win the war against Santa Anna's army. Sam Houston was chosen to lead the Texas army.

**✓ What kind of government did the Texans set up for their new country?**

### Where?

### Washington-on-the-Brazos

Washington-on-the-Brazos, also known as Old Washington, was set up in 1834 near a crossing on the Brazos River. The town was named by its settlers for Washington, Georgia, not Washington, D.C. Washington-on-the-Brazos is best known for the meeting of Texas leaders that was held there in 1836, when the Texas Declaration of Independence and the Texas Constitution were written. The town is still there today, southeast of College Station.

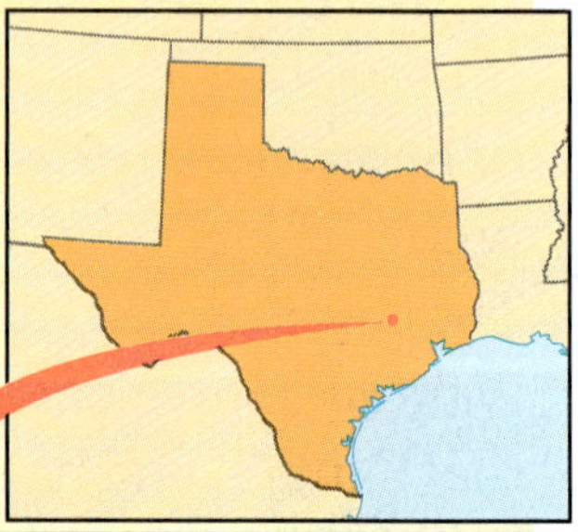

## Lesson 2 Review

### Check Understanding

1. **Recall the Facts** Who were the first leaders of the Republic of Texas?
2. **Focus on the Main Idea** What did the Texas leaders do to get their new country started?

### Think Critically

3. **Think More About It** Why do you think some people might have wanted Texas to remain a part of Mexico?

### Show What You Know

**Simulation Activity** Suppose you were at the meeting at Washington-on-the-Brazos in March 1836. With a classmate, role-play a conversation you might have had with someone before the signing of the Texas Declaration of Independence.

SKILLS

# How To

## Make a Thoughtful Decision

### Why Is This Skill Important?

Everyone must make decisions. You make many of them each day. Some decisions are easy. Others are harder, but they may be more important. You can learn how to make thoughtful and informed decisions.

### Remember What You Have Read

You have read about the hard decisions people had to make during the Texas Revolution. Some had to choose between fighting and not fighting. The defenders of the Alamo chose to fight. People also had to decide whether they would stay in Texas or return to the United States. The most important and hardest thing for them to decide was whether to fight for independence or to continue living under Mexican rule.

### Understand the Process

You can use the following steps to make a thoughtful decision.

- Find out what your choices are.
- Think about the possible results of each choice.
- Make what seems to be the best choice based on these outcomes.
- Think about what might happen as a result of your choice.

### Think and Apply

Now, think about a choice you have made in school. What steps did you follow? What choice did you make? Do you think you made a thoughtful decision? Explain.

BUILDING CITIZENSHIP

Davy Crockett (left), James Bowie (center), and William B. Travis (right) all made the hard decision to fight for Texas's independence. Do you think you would have decided to fight for independence if you had lived in Texas during the revolution?

LESSON 3

# On to Victory

## Link to Our World

**What might help bring a conflict to an end?**

***Focus on the Main Idea***
**Read to find out what helped bring the Texas Revolution to an end.**

***Preview Vocabulary***
**scout**
**retreat**
**massacre**

The meeting at Washington-on-the-Brazos ended on March 18, 1836. Now the Texans faced their hardest task. In order to keep their independence and their new government, the Texans had to win the war against Santa Anna's army.

### Houston and His Army

To begin command of the Texas army, Sam Houston left the meeting at Washington-on-the-Brazos before it ended. On March 11 he reached Gonzales to get his soldiers ready to fight. There were fewer than 400 of them. They were a ragged-looking group of volunteers. They carried guns they had brought from home. They had no uniforms, so they dressed in their everyday clothes.

Houston sent his scouts ahead to look for Santa Anna's army. His **scouts** explored areas to gather information about the land and the enemy. Houston's best scout was Erastus Smith, or "Deaf Smith." Smith could not hear well, but people said he could "read footprints like handwriting" and "smell an enemy ten miles away."

Sam Houston fearlessly led the Texas troops into battle and to final victory. What qualities do you think a good leader needs to have?

**MOVEMENT** Two of the largest Mexican armies that moved into Texas were commanded by Santa Anna and Urrea.
■ Whose army traveled near Laredo?

Houston waited at Gonzales for the news from Smith. Then, on the night of March 13, Smith returned with Susanna Dickenson and the few others who had lived through the attack on the Alamo. Houston heard their terrible story and learned that Santa Anna's army had left San Antonio. It was marching toward Gonzales!

**Why did Sam Houston go to Gonzales?**

## The Runaway Scrape

Houston ordered everyone to leave Gonzales right away. He did not feel that his army was ready to fight. The troops needed more time to train for battle. The people of the town and the nearby farms took everything they could carry. Near midnight on March 13, the Texans burned Gonzales so there would be nothing for Santa Anna's army to capture.

Houston's army and the people of Gonzales hurried away in the darkness. For more than a month they traveled east toward Louisiana to escape Santa Anna's army. Their journey came to be known as the Runaway Scrape. A scrape is a fight. Along the way more Texans joined the group. They, too, burned their towns behind them.

The victims at Goliad were marched unknowingly to their death.

Dilue Rose Harris and her family were among those caught up in the Runaway Scrape. She was 11 years old at the time. She later remembered it as a time of heavy rains, floods, and confusion.

> “Our hardships began at the Trinity. The river was rising and there was a struggle to see who should cross first. Measles, sore eyes, whooping cough, and every other disease that man, woman, or child is heir to, broke out among us.”

The hardest thing for the Texans to accept, however, was knowing that they were running from a fight. They were not getting back at Santa Anna's army for the deaths of the Alamo's defenders. They were not fighting for their freedom. They were **retreating**, or pulling back. At this time, though, the Texans could do nothing else. They needed more soldiers with better training.

**✓ What did Sam Houston do when he learned that Santa Anna's army was marching toward Gonzales?**

## “Remember Goliad!”

As the Texans retreated, another terrible thing happened. On March 14, 1836, between 300 and 400 Texas fighters led by Colonel James Fannin were near the town of Goliad. Sam Houston knew the larger Mexican army might attack Goliad, so he ordered Fannin to retreat to Victoria.

Fannin moved too slowly. As the Texans left Goliad, they were met by Mexican soldiers led by General José Urrea (hoh•SAY oor•RAY•ah). The Mexicans took the Texans back to Goliad as prisoners and held them in the old Spanish presidio.

This pocket watch belonged to Colonel James Fannin.

This painting, by William Huddle, depicts Santa Anna's surrender to Sam Houston.

A few days later Santa Anna ordered General Urrea to shoot his prisoners. On March 27, 1836, more than 300 Texans were **massacred**, or killed without a chance to fight back.

A number of the Texans had run away from the Mexicans before the shooting took place. Francisca Alvarez, a nurse with the Mexican army, hid some of these Texans. She later became known to Texans as the Angel of Goliad. After the killing, "Remember Goliad!" became a battle cry for the Texas army.

**What happened to the Texan prisoners at Goliad?**

## Victory at San Jacinto

After hearing about what happened at Goliad, some Anglo-American settlers in Texas were worried. Many left their homes to go back to the United States. General Sam Houston, however, called his army together.

Houston knew that he would need more soldiers with better training. He built an army of 1,600 volunteers, some of them Tejanos, led by Juan Seguín. Houston taught his soldiers how to fight. They learned how to work together as an army. The Texans were ready when they finally met Santa Anna's army again.

Houston's scouts discovered Santa Anna's soldiers camped near the

Santa Anna wore these spurs at the Battle at San Jacinto.

## Where?

### San Jacinto Battleground

The place where Texas won its independence is on the east side of the city of Houston. The San Jacinto Monument that stands there today rises high above the flat Gulf Coastal Plain for all to see. The monument was built in 1936 on the one-hundredth birthday of Texas's independence.

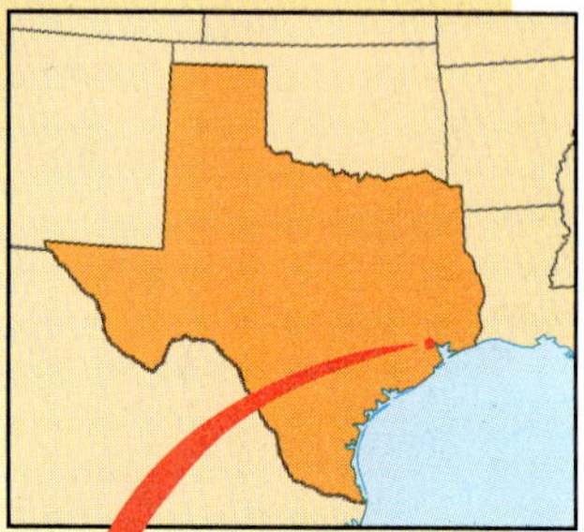

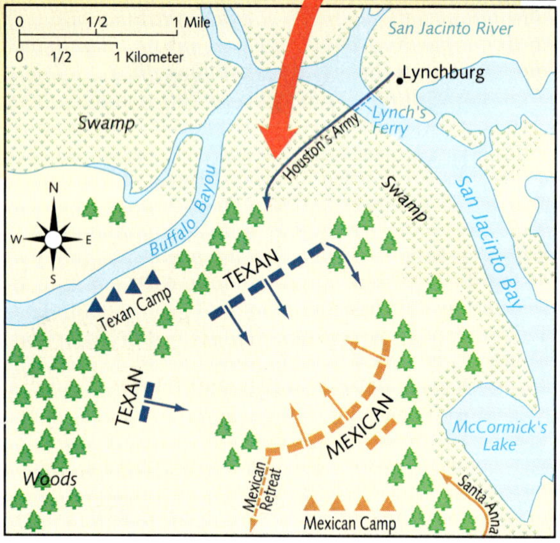


San Jacinto River. Shouting "Remember the Alamo!" and "Remember Goliad!," the Texans attacked on the afternoon of April 21, 1836.

The attack came as a surprise to the Mexican soldiers. Many were sleeping when the Texans charged. The battle was over in minutes, and the Mexicans retreated. Some of the Texans followed them, killing hundreds to pay back the Mexican army for the deaths at the Alamo and Goliad. In the end they killed about 630 Mexican soldiers and captured 730. Only 9 Texans died in the battle, and only about 30 were wounded. Houston was wounded when a rifle ball shattered his ankle.

The next day the Texans found Santa Anna hiding in the woods. Many of them wanted to shoot him. However, they took Santa Anna to Sam Houston, who was sitting under a tree caring for his wounded ankle. Houston did not let the Texans hurt the Mexican leader. Instead, he treated him with respect and later let him return to Mexico. Victory at San Jacinto had helped Texas win its independence from Mexico. Texas was now its own country.

**How were the Texans able to win the Battle of San Jacinto so easily?**

## LESSON 3 REVIEW

### Check Understanding

1. **Recall the Facts** What was the Runaway Scrape?
2. **Focus on the Main Idea** What helped end the Texas Revolution?

### Think Critically

3. **Personally Speaking** Do you think Sam Houston showed that he was a good leader? Explain your answer.
4. **Think More About It** How did individual Texans help during the war? How did Texans work together to win the war?

### Show What You Know

**Poster Activity** Make a poster to show one of the events that happened in this lesson. Take turns with a partner telling about the story you have shown.

S·K·I·L·L·S

HOW TO

# Read a Vertical Time Line

## Why Is This Skill Important?

You have already learned that a time line shows events that happened over certain periods of time. But you have seen only one kind of time line. There are different ways of listing the events on time lines—**horizontally**, from left to right, or **vertically**, from top to bottom.

## Understand the Process

The events on the time line on this page are marked in the order in which they took place. Instead of being listed from left to right, the events on this time line are listed from top to bottom. The dates near the top came first. The dates closer to the bottom came later.

Time lines can show different periods of time. Some time lines you have seen in this book show hundreds of years. This time line shows seven months in the fight for Texas independence. The space between two marks stands for one month.

- The time line begins at the top with the month of October 1835. Look at the bottom of the time line. What is the last month listed?
- Dates of specific events are listed on the right-hand side of the time line. When did the first event happen?
- What happened in December 1835?
- Which event happened first, the Battle of the Alamo or the Battle of San Jacinto?

## Think and Apply

Research some important dates in the history of your town. In what year was the town founded? When was your school built? When was the biggest building in your town built? When was the present mayor elected? Make a vertical time line that shows some of these important events. Add pictures to your time line if you like, and then display it on a bulletin board. Compare this time line with the one you made in Chapter 2.

**EVENTS OF THE TEXAS REVOLUTION**

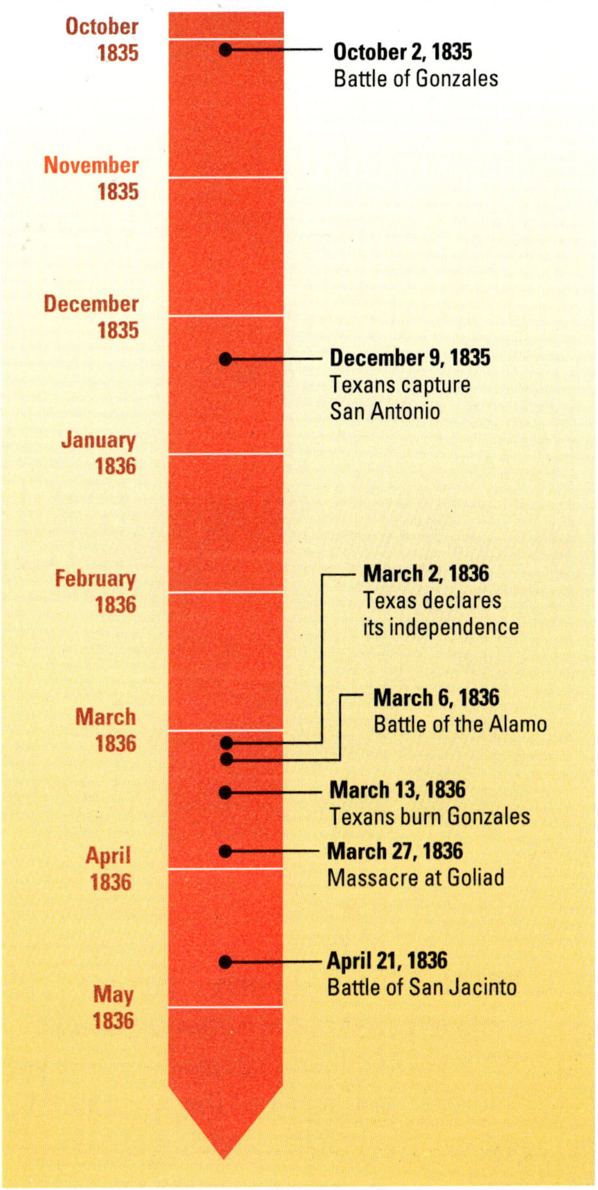

# CHAPTER 5 REVIEW

## CONNECT MAIN IDEAS

Use this organizer to show that you understand how the chapter's main ideas are connected. First copy the organizer onto a separate sheet of paper. Then complete it by filling in the missing information.

### The Texas Revolution

**Cause:** ______________________________

**Effect:** Texans hope to change their government.

**Cause:** Texas leaders decide to start a new country.

**Effect:** ______________________________

**Cause:** ______________________________

**Effect:** Texans win the revolution.

## WRITE MORE ABOUT IT

1. **Write a Journal Entry** Imagine that you were part of the Runaway Scrape. Write a journal entry explaining how you felt when you received the news about the events at Goliad and San Jacinto.

2. **Write a Persuasive Letter** Write a letter to persuade others to join the Texas Revolution. List three reasons why you feel the fight for independence is the best choice for the settlers of Texas.

## USE VOCABULARY

For each group of vocabulary words, write a sentence or two explaining how the words are related.

1. revolution, declaration, independence
2. republic, constitution, congress
3. scout, surrender, retreat

## CHECK UNDERSTANDING

1. How did the battle over a small cannon at Gonzales set off a war?
2. Name some of the heroes at the Alamo.
3. Why did William B. Travis send for help at the Alamo?
4. How did Texans show courage at the Alamo?
5. Who were some of the people that signed the Texas Declaration of Independence?
6. What does it mean when something is abolished?
7. What did Sam Houston do to prepare for battle with Santa Anna?
8. Who was the Angel of Goliad?
9. What did the victory at San Jacinto mean for Texas?
10. What did many Texans want to do to Santa Anna after they found him?

## THINK CRITICALLY

1. **Cause and Effect** Why did the Texans declare their independence from Mexico?
2. **Past to Present** How do people today defend their rights? How are their methods similar to or different from the ones used during the Texas Revolution?
3. **Think More About It** Why did Santa Anna send Susanna Dickenson to tell Texans about the fall of the Alamo?
4. **Personally Speaking** Do you think it was necessary for the Texans to burn their towns behind them during the Runaway Scrape? Explain your answer.
5. **Think More About It** How did remembering the Alamo and Goliad help Texans win the battle at San Jacinto?
6. **Explore Viewpoints** Why do you think Sam Houston protected Santa Anna after the battle at San Jacinto?

## APPLY SKILLS

**How to Make a Thoughtful Decision**
Imagine that a friend has asked you to leave your family and join the Texas army to fight for freedom. What steps might you follow to decide whether to fight?

**How to Read a Vertical Time Line**
Draw a vertical time line, and write the days of the week along the left-hand side. On the right-hand side, record several things that you did in the past week.

## READ MORE ABOUT IT

*Davy Crockett* by Felicity Trotman and Shirley Greenway. Raintree. This book tells the life story of Davy Crockett, from his childhood in the woods of Tennessee through his heroic fight at the Alamo.

*The Great Texas Scare: A Story of the Runaway Scrape* by Martha Tannery Jones. Hendrick-Long. This story of two families from Nacogdoches relates the panic of the Runaway Scrape.

CHAPTER 6

# A Country Called Texas

"Texas must be free, that her citizens may be happy."

Sam Houston,
in a letter to
Colonel John Forbes, 1836

# LESSON 1 GETTING STARTED

## Link to Our World

**How do people today get new groups working?**

***Focus on the Main Idea***
**Read to learn how the Texans got their new government working after the revolution.**

***Preview Vocabulary***
**treaty**
**election**
**cabinet**
**recognize**
**archives**

After the Battle of San Jacinto, the Texans held Santa Anna as their prisoner at the town of Velasco (vay•LAS•koh), near the mouth of the Brazos River. There, Santa Anna signed a **treaty**, or written agreement, with the Texans. The Treaty of Velasco ended the Texas Revolution. Now it was time for Texans to get their new country started.

### ELECTING A NEW GOVERNMENT

David Burnet, president of the temporary government, called for an election to be held on September 5, 1836. In an **election**, citizens make choices by voting. More than 6,000 Texas men voted to choose people for the new government. At that time, women were not allowed to vote either in Texas or in the United States.

Sam Houston, a hero of the war, was chosen president of the Republic of Texas. Mirabeau Lamar (MIR•uh•boh luh•MAR) became vice president. Like the United States president, Houston chose a **cabinet**, or group of people, to help run the country.

The job of the Texas Rangers (right) was to protect the people of the newly founded Republic of Texas. Rangers could be identified by the badges they wore (above).

Houston gave Stephen F. Austin the job of secretary of state. Austin would help by talking and working with other countries. When Austin died less than two months after taking the job, people all over Texas were sad. Houston told his fellow Texans, "The first pioneer of the wilderness has departed."

Voters in the election of 1836 also approved the Texas Constitution. This was the plan of government written by the Texas leaders in March at the town of Washington-on-the-Brazos. It had set up the Republic of Texas.

**Who was elected president of the Republic of Texas in 1836?**

## What?

### The Texas Navy

As the Texas Rangers protected Texans on land, the Texas navy kept the coastal towns safe from naval attacks by Mexico. In 1836 the navy had four ships—*Independence*, *Liberty*, *Brutus*, and *Invincible.* Despite the importance of the navy, Sam Houston had problems with its commanders. By late 1837 Houston did away with the navy. The Texas Congress, however, restored the navy in 1839. The *San Antonio* (shown here) was among the new ships.

## Protecting Texans

The Texas Revolution was over, but the danger of attack from Mexico was not. Mexico did not **recognize**, or agree to, the Treaty of Velasco. This was the treaty that Santa Anna had signed in order to end the fighting. Several times after the war, Mexican soldiers had marched into Texas and attacked towns.

Attacks by Comanches and other Indian groups were another danger to Texans. One of the first jobs of the new government was to find a way to protect the Texans.

A line of forts was built on the frontier to separate Mexico and the Indian lands from the rest of Texas. Law officers known as the Texas Rangers protected the frontier. The Texas government also asked towns to form their own militias. The volunteer soldiers would defend their towns if they were attacked by Mexican troops or Indians. During peaceful times the volunteers would go about their own work.

**Who were the Texas Rangers?**

## Choosing a Capital

The first elected congress of the republic met at Columbia on October 3, 1836. The congress soon found that Columbia, which is in present-day Brazoria County, was too small. So the capital was moved to the town of Houston.

Houston was only a little larger than Columbia in 1836. It grew quickly, however, as more people came to work for the new government. Houston was the capital of Texas from 1836 to 1839.

Some leaders thought the town of Houston was too far east to serve all of Texas. They wanted the capital to be closer to the center of the country. In 1839 the congress chose a new place for the capital. It was the settlement of Waterloo on the Colorado River. The town was given the new name Austin to honor Stephen F. Austin, who had given Texas its start.

**What three towns have served as the capital of Texas?**

This woodcut shows Austin in about 1840. At the time, fewer than a thousand people lived in the frontier town. The large house on the hill belonged to the republic's second president, Mirabeau Lamar.

Texas Rangers were successful in loading the government archives onto wagons. Fearing the capital was to be moved, angry citizens, led by Angelina Eberly, persuaded Texas leaders to keep the archives in Austin.

## THE ARCHIVES WAR

In 1842, Mexican soldiers once again entered Texas. They got as far north as San Antonio, and it looked as if they might reach Austin. President Houston decided to move the government **archives**, or records, from Austin to keep them safe.

Because Houston wanted to move the archives, some people worried that he also wanted to move the capital. The citizens of Austin did not want the capital to be moved. A small group of Austin citizens, led by Angelina Eberly, gathered around the government workers as they loaded the archives onto wagons. All of a sudden, shots were fired. This short fight came to be known as the Archives War. In the end the archives stayed in Austin.

**What caused the Archives War?**

## LESSON 1 REVIEW

### Check Understanding

1. **Recall the Facts** How were Texans protected in the new republic?
2. **Focus on the Main Idea** What did Texans do to get their new government working after the revolution?

### Think Critically

3. **Personally Speaking** If you were the president of the Republic of Texas, what kind of people would you choose for your cabinet?
4. **Explore Viewpoints** Why do you think Mexico would not recognize the Treaty of Velasco and end the fighting?

### Show What You Know

**Map Activity** Think about the reasons the capital of the Republic of Texas was moved several times. Suppose it was your job to choose a place for the Texas capital today. Using a map of Texas, decide whether you will choose a new town or keep Austin as the capital. Share with a partner your reasons for your choice.

LESSON 2

LEARN *with* LITERATURE

Focus on Texas Pride

# Sarah's Flag for Texas

***by Jane Alexander Knapik***

The same year Austin was chosen as the capital of Texas, the republic chose a national flag. It was the same flag you see today as the state flag. The Texas flag looks much like one made by Sarah Dodson in 1835. Dodson made a Lone Star flag for her husband, Archie Dodson, and other fighters from Harrisburg, Texas. They carried the flag into battle at Gonzales and San Antonio. Later, a flag almost like it flew over the building in Washington-on-the-Brazos, where Texas leaders signed the Texas Declaration of Independence.

Now read about a time in Texas history, after the revolution, when many Texans were filled with pride in their new country. The year is 1839, and Archie Dodson has just returned to Harrisburg from the new Texas capital at Austin. He brings exciting news for Sarah and her brother's wife, Liza.

"I saw your flag, Sarah!" he told her as she and the two children greeted him at the front gate.

At first Sarah didn't know what he meant. She was so busy with her home and family that she had not thought about the little flag in several years.

"I saw the new flag of the Republic of Texas," Archie said again, with excitement in his voice. "It's so much like your flag that I think someone must have copied yours. I drew a sketch of it for you," he said, handing her a piece of paper. "You see the white star? It's set on a blue background, just like yours was. The only differences are that this official flag is larger than yours, and the red and white stripes are horizontal."

Sarah asked Archie to hold baby Milton while she studied the sketch. As was her way, she said very little except to thank Archie for the news.

"You're the amazin' woman who set them all to thinking about a Lone Star design," he said, trying to get her to show the same excitement he felt. "Just don't forget your part in making that flag!"

Enjoying his words and looking very pleased with everything, Sarah went into the cabin to tuck the sketch inside her special box of keepsakes.

After supper and after the children went to bed, Sarah brought the sketch out again for Liza to see. "I wonder what James Ferguson knows about the new flag," she said to Archie. "He probably had something to do with the fact that the new flag of the Republic of Texas looks so much like the Harrisburg flag. Or maybe Mr. De Zavala remembered seeing my flag."

Soon after that, the Dodsons went to a patriotic gathering in the nearby town of Richmond, in Fort Bend County. Sarah hoped that someone would bring a new Texas flag. Sure enough, she was excited to see a Lone Star flag, waving freely in the breeze. Its staff was positioned near the speaker's stand, where Sam Houston and other Texas heroes would be honored that day.

**In 1965 the state of Texas made these words the pledge to the Texas flag.**

**"Honor the Texas Flag;
I pledge allegiance to thee,
Texas, one and indivisible."**

**patriotic** feeling pride for one's country

Everything about the patriotic gathering was a wonderful experience for Sarah and her family. Many Texas babies were being named in honor of General Houston that year, and the Dodsons hoped their next baby would be a son they could name Houston Dodson. When the baby born in 1841 turned out to be a daughter, however, no one was surprised about the choice of names for her: Harriet Houston Dodson.

The Texas flag (left) that flew over the first capitol building in Austin in 1839 (below) looked similar to the one designed by Sarah Dodson.

## Literature Review

1. What does it mean to be "patriotic" or to celebrate at a "patriotic gathering"?
2. After the Texas Revolution many people named their children to honor the heroes of the war. In what other ways do people of today show their pride in a group or a country?
3. Read Archie Dodson's comparison of the new Texas flag to Sarah Dodson's flag. Draw what you think Sarah Dodson's flag looked like.

S·K·I·L·L·S

# How To

# Understand National Symbols

## Why Is This Skill Important?

You know that a flag stands for a country or a state. Did you know that through the years, flags of six different countries have flown over Texas? You have already read about four of the countries that ruled or claimed Texas.

## Understand the Process

Countries and states choose symbols to show on their flags. **Symbols** are signs that stand for something else. Some symbols are colors. On the Texas state flag, blue is for loyalty. Red is for bravery or courage. White is for freedom and purity.

Symbols can also be shapes. On the United States flag, the 13 stripes stand for the first 13 colonies. There is a star for each of today's 50 states. The Texas state flag has a single star—the Lone Star.

Some symbols are designs or drawings. On the Mexican flag, the bird on a cactus, holding a snake, stands for a sign that showed the Aztecs where to build their settlement. The flags of Spain and France have symbols used by rulers of those countries in the 1500s and 1600s. Both flags were later changed after changes were made in their governments.

## Think and Apply

Suppose you were asked to design a flag for your class. What would it look like? Draw your flag, or write a paragraph to describe it.

Texas under Spain
1519–1685;
1690–1821

Texas under France
1685–1690

Texas under Mexico
1821–1836

Texas as a Republic
1836–1845
Texas as a State
1845–present

Texas in the Confederacy
1861–1865

Texas in the United States
1845–1861;
1865–present

LESSON 3

# PROBLEMS OF THE NEW COUNTRY

## Link to Our World

**How do leaders today work to solve the problems of their community, state, or country?**

***Focus on the Main Idea***

**Read to learn how Texas leaders worked to solve the problems of the republic.**

***Preview Vocabulary***

| | |
|---|---|
| **term** | **redback** |
| **policy** | **immigrant** |
| **title** | **plantation** |

Sam Houston's first **term**, or period of time, as president of the Republic of Texas was from 1836 to 1838. The Texas Constitution stated that a person could not serve as the president two terms in a row. In 1838 Mirabeau Lamar was elected president and served a three-year term. In 1841 Houston was again elected president. The two leaders had different ideas about how to solve the new republic's problems.

## WARS BETWEEN SETTLERS AND INDIANS

Because so many Texans came to settle on or near Indian lands, the republic needed a **policy**, or plan, for living among the Indians.

The Cherokees came to East Texas in 1820, when white settlers began driving them off their lands in the southeastern United States. The Cherokees wanted to live in peace in Texas. During the Texas Revolution, Sam Houston and an African businessperson named William Goyens had worked out a treaty that gave the Cherokees **title** to, or ownership of, this land. When Houston became president of the republic, he would not let settlers take the Cherokees' land.

Sam Houston, shown here in a Cherokee headdress, was called "the Raven" by the Cherokees.

William Goyens and Sam Houston were trusted by the Cherokees. Why do you think the Cherokees trusted them?

When Mirabeau Lamar became president in 1838, however, he said the Cherokees had no right to their land. He ordered them to leave Texas. When they refused, he sent 500 Texas soldiers to make them leave.

For two days the soldiers and the Cherokees fought. Hundreds of Cherokees were killed, and their towns and fields were burned. When the fighting was over, the body of Chief Bowles, the Cherokees' leader, was found. In his hand was a tin box. It contained the peace treaty made with Houston and Goyens.

## Who?

### William Goyens 1794–1856

About 9 out of 10 of the Africans who lived in the Texas colonies and later the Republic of Texas were enslaved people. Of the small group of free Africans, William Goyens was the best known. Goyens was an important citizen of Nacogdoches, where he owned a blacksmith shop. He was trusted by Tejanos, Indians, and Anglo-Americans. Goyens and Houston worked out a treaty with the Cherokees during the Texas Revolution. The treaty kept the Indians from taking sides in the fight between Texans and Mexicans.

In West Texas the bitter fighting between the settlers and the Comanches grew worse during Lamar's term as president. When settlers moved onto Comanche lands, the Indians attacked the settlements and destroyed them. Lamar then sent more soldiers west.

**What caused the problems between the republic and the Indians?**

## Money Problems

Years of fighting the Indians had cost the Republic of Texas millions of dollars. Also, the destruction of crops and towns during the revolution and the Indian wars had left many people poor. One Texan of that time wrote,

> "The country has been completely ravaged by the armies. Houses have been robbed, provisions taken, cattle have been driven out, and the game frightened off."

Many people were not able to pay their taxes. Texas had to borrow money from other countries to buy supplies for its soldiers. To repay this money, the republic had to keep borrowing more money. Soon the country owed millions of dollars.

The new government decided to print more of its own money. These new dollar bills were called **redbacks** because of their color. However, this did not solve the money problem. By 1841 the Texas dollar was worth only about two cents compared with the United States dollar.

**✓ Why did the Texas government have money problems?**

## German Immigrants Help Solve the Money Problem

Texans thought of another way to solve their money problems. Texas had plenty of land. The republic needed more citizens who would pay taxes, so the Texas government gave away land to get people to move to Texas. A family received 1,280 acres. A single settler got half that amount. Just as in the days of the Texas colonies, the offer of free land brought a great rush of **immigrants**, people who move into a country from another country.

Most of the new settlers came from the southern United States, but people also came from other countries. The largest European immigrant group during this time came from Germany. In 1842 a group of Germans set up the Society for the Protection of German Immigrants in Texas. Led by John Meusebach (MOY•zuh•bahk), the society brought thousands of Germans to Central Texas. They built the towns of Fredericksburg, New Braunfels (BRAWN•fuhlz), and others in the region.

The German settlers got along well with the Indians. They even signed a treaty with the Comanches. In return for sharing their lands with the Germans, the Comanches received $3,000 in gifts. Today the treaty is remembered as one that helped both the settlers and the native peoples.

**✓ How did Texans use land to solve their money problem?**

To pay its bills, the Republic of Texas printed paper money—dollar bills called redbacks. The Texas government promised to exchange them for gold later.

## SETTLEMENT PATTERNS

The number of people in Texas increased from about 38,000 in 1836 to more than 140,000 ten years later. Most of the settlers earned their living by farming and ranching.

Many new small farms were started in the woodlands of East Texas, where the Caddos had first farmed. The fertile land along the rivers on the Gulf Coastal Plain was good for growing cotton. Very large farms called **plantations** used slaves to do the work. They grew about 300 pounds (136 kg) of cotton per acre.

Cattle ranching became an important business when ranchers bred their cows with an unusual type of cattle called Texas longhorns. Longhorns had been brought many years earlier to the Spanish missions. One of the best-known ranchers in Texas in the 1840s was James Taylor White. He arrived in Texas from Louisiana in about 1820 with just three cows. By the 1840s White owned 30,000 head of cattle and more than 40,000 acres of ranch land.

Most Texans in the 1840s lived on farms and ranches. However, people were steadily moving to the cities. As a result, several cities in Texas began to grow. San Antonio remained the largest city in Texas. Houston kept growing even though the capital was moved from there to Austin. Galveston became a busy port from which Texas cotton was shipped around the world.

**✓ What did most Texans do for a living during the years of the republic?**

Tejanos helped build the Republic of Texas. Many Mexicans had been against Santa Anna and had fought alongside the Texans. By 1846 some of them were among the 140,000 people living in Texas.

## LESSON 3 REVIEW

### Check Understanding

1. **Recall the Facts** What were some of the problems Texas leaders faced after the revolution?
2. **Focus on the Main Idea** How did Texas leaders work to solve the problems of the republic?

### Think Critically

3. **Explore Viewpoints** How were Houston's and Lamar's policies toward the Indians different?
4. **Think More About It** Why do you think the German settlers were able to make peace with the Comanches?

### Show What You Know

**Current Events Activity** Look in newspapers and magazines, or listen to the news on radio or television. List some of the problems the leaders of the United States or Texas are facing. With a partner, compare and contrast today's problems with some of those the leaders of the Republic of Texas faced.

LESSON 4

# TEXAS JOINS THE UNITED STATES

## Link to Our World

**How can some issues change a government's plans?**

***Focus on the Main Idea***
**Read to learn why it took several years for Texas to become part of the United States.**

***Preview Vocabulary***
**majority**
**slave state**
**free state**
**annex**
**boundary**

For nine years, from 1836 to 1845, the Republic of Texas was an independent country. From its beginning, the **majority**, or greater part, of the republic's citizens hoped their country would one day become a state of the United States. However, two issues during this period kept Texas from becoming a state. The first was the issue of slavery. The second was the United States government's fear of making trouble with Mexico.

During the time of slavery in the United States, some slaves in the South tried to escape to the free states in the North.

### THE SLAVERY ISSUE

Today people believe that slavery was wrong. During the mid-1800s many Americans believed they had a right to own slaves, and many were willing to fight and even die for that right. Disagreements over slavery began to tear the United States apart.

At the time, the United States was divided equally between **slave states**, in which people could own slaves, and **free states**, in which all people were free. The free states were in the North. The slave states were in the South. The southern states wanted Texas to join them because another slave state would add to their power in the United States Congress. The northern states, however, did not want Texas to become a state. Because of the disagreement

On October 13, 1845, Texas voters approved annexation by a vote of 4,254 to 257. On February 19, 1846, Texas president Anson Jones (right) lowered the Lone Star flag at the capitol building (above) and turned over the power of government to Texas's first governor, James P. Henderson.

between the northern and southern states, the United States Congress kept delaying making Texas a part of the United States.

Texas president Sam Houston said that if the United States did not **annex**, or add on, Texas, Texas might become an ally of Great Britain or France. France was the first European government to recognize Texas as a country. It recognized Texas about a year after the United States did. In 1840 France built the French Legation, or government office, in Austin. It still stands today. Later, Great Britain and the Netherlands also recognized the Republic of Texas.

Houston and other Texas leaders did not really want to join with any European countries. However, the idea of Europeans as allies of Texas on the United States' western borders worried the members of the United States Congress. By 1843 leaders from both sides were making plans for the United States to annex Texas.

Slavery still made annexing Texas a problem for the United States, but many Americans now wanted Texas to become part of the country. Early in 1845 the United States Congress voted to annex Texas, and later the Texas voters agreed to annexation. On December 29, 1845, Texas became the twenty-eighth state of the United States.

On February 19, 1846, people from all over Texas came to Austin to celebrate. Bands played and people cheered. At the capitol building the republic's Lone Star flag was taken down and the United States flag, the Stars and Stripes, was raised. As Anson Jones, the republic's final president, lowered the Lone Star flag for the last time, he said, "The Republic of Texas is no more."

**Why did slavery make annexing Texas a problem for the United States?**

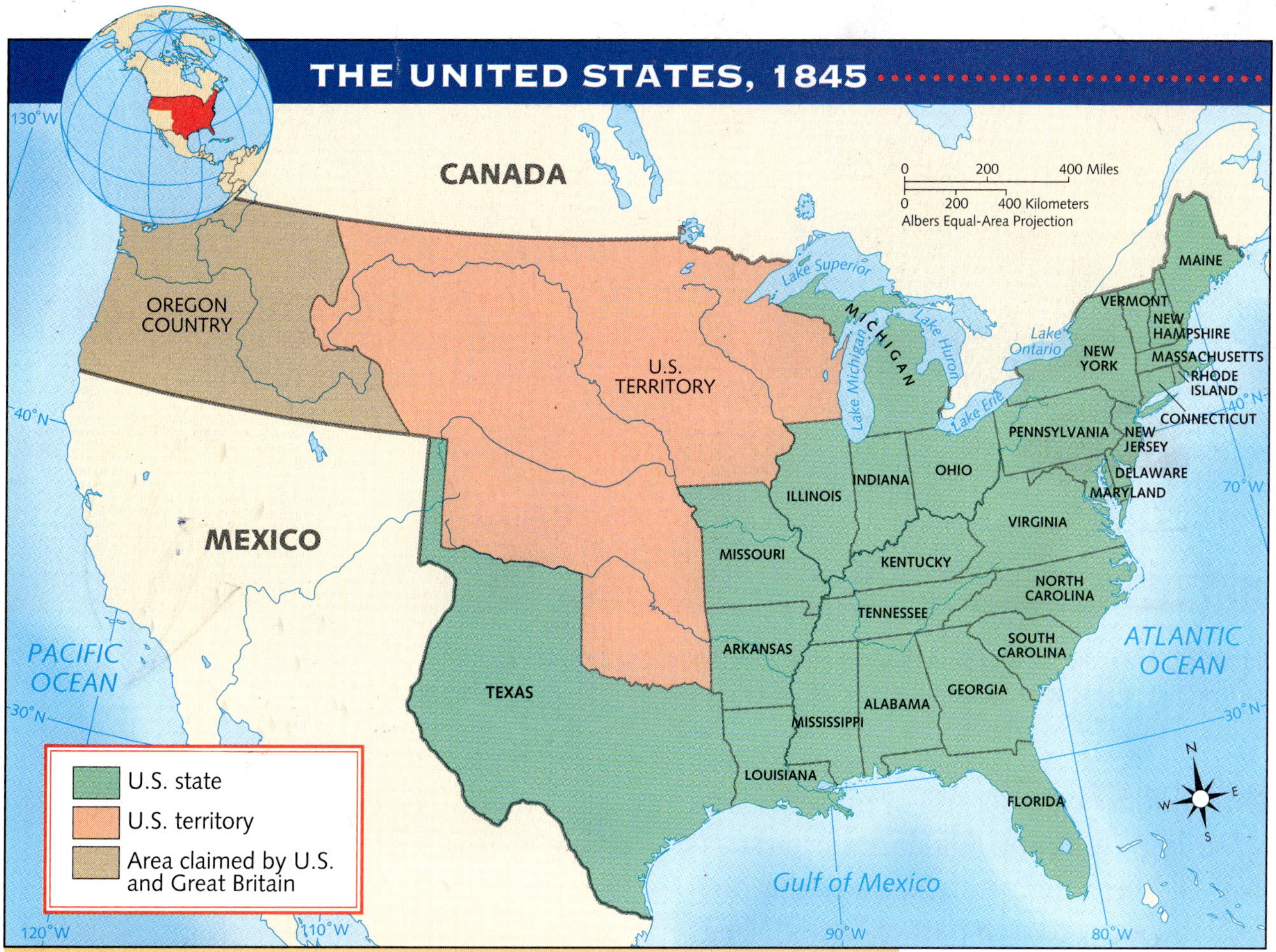


Map Skill

**REGIONS** When Texas became a state in 1845, it was much larger than it is now.

■ The northern tip of Texas was once near which line of latitude?

## War with Mexico

As the United States had expected, the Mexican government was very angry about losing Texas. To Mexican leaders, Texas was still a rebelling colony. They had never agreed to the Treaty of Velasco, which Santa Anna had signed in 1836.

Mexico and the United States also disagreed on the boundaries of Texas. A **boundary** is the border, or edge, around a place. In 1846 Mexican and American soldiers fought over a boundary between the Nueces (noo•AY•says) River and the Rio Grande. This led to war between the two countries, beginning on May 13, 1846.

For almost two years, more than 8,000 Texans, among them the Texas Rangers, fought in the Mexican-American War. The war ended when the United States Army captured Mexico City. A treaty was signed in the small town of Guadalupe Hidalgo (gwah•dah•LOO•pay ee•DAHL•goh). The treaty ended the war on February 2, 1848.

In the treaty, the United States and Mexico agreed that the Rio Grande was to be the southern boundary of Texas. Texas said, however, that the Rio Grande formed both its southern and its western boundaries. This would have given Texas half of present-day New Mexico, with the

The Mexican-American War ended when General Winfield Scott and the United States Army captured Mexico City.

city of Santa Fe, and parts of present-day Wyoming, Colorado, Oklahoma, and Kansas. Many people in Santa Fe did not want their city to be a part of Texas. Most spoke Spanish and wanted to form their own state.

Texas and the United States Congress argued about the boundaries of Texas for two years. In 1850 they finally reached an agreement. The United States paid the state of Texas $10 million for its lands in present-day New Mexico, Wyoming, Colorado, Oklahoma, and Kansas. Today Texas still has the northern and western boundaries that were agreed on in 1850.

**Why did Mexico and the United States go to war in 1846?**

## LESSON 4 REVIEW

### Check Understanding

1. **Recall the Facts** What were two causes of the Mexican-American War?
2. **Focus on the Main Idea** Why did it take so long for Texas to become a state?

### Think Critically

3. **Cause and Effect** What were the effects of the Mexican-American War?
4. **Think More About It** How might Texas history have been different if Texas had remained its own country?

### Show What You Know

**Writing Activity** Imagine that you are living in Texas in 1845. You have been asked to write a column for your community's newspaper. Write two headlines giving the news that Texas has become a state. One of the headlines should show that you are pleased about this. The other should show that you had wanted Texas to remain a republic. Display your headlines on a bulletin board.

S·K·I·L·L·S

HOW TO

# Use a Historical Map

## Why Is This Skill Important?

Colors are important map symbols. Sometimes colors help you tell water from land on a map. Colors and patterns on a map can also show how a place has changed over time.

## Understand the Process

On the map below, color has two meanings. First, it shows the size of a **political region**, the area occupied by a city, state, or nation. Second, it stands for a certain period of time. The solid green shows the boundaries of present-day Texas. The pattern of green stripes shows an area that was a part of Texas before 1850.

Use the colors and patterns on the map and the map key to answer these questions.

1. Did Texas gain or lose land in 1850? What symbol helped you find the answer?
2. What natural feature forms much of the southern boundary of present-day Texas?
3. The lands that Texas sold to the United States are now in what states?

## Think and Apply

Map Skill

Think about other ways colors and patterns might be used on a map. Draw another map or write a paragraph to show or describe these ways.

# COUNTERPOINTS

# BECOME A STATE OR BUILD AN EMPIRE?

Houston

Lamar

"My great desire is that our country Texas shall be annexed to the United States. . . . It is policy to hold out the idea that we are very able to sustain ourselves against any power . . . , yet I am free to say *to you* that we cannot do it."

"I shall feel that the blood of our martyred heroes had been shed in vain."

Texans did not agree on the future of Texas in the early 1840s any more than they had in the early 1830s. In the 1830s the question had been whether Texas should join Mexico as a state or become its own country. In the 1840s the question was whether Texas should join the United States as a state or remain an independent country and build its own empire. An **empire** is a country that has other lands under its rule.

The republic's two most important leaders had different views. Sam Houston wanted Texas to become a part of the United States. Mirabeau Lamar wanted Texas to remain a republic. As president of Texas, Lamar sent expeditions west to claim more land. He wanted the republic to build an empire.

Smithwick

When Texas finally became a state, some Texans still were not sure if this was a good idea. Now read the words of a Texan named Noah Smithwick. His words describe how he felt at the moment when Texas president Anson Jones lowered the Lone Star flag and said, "The Republic of Texas is no more."

> "Many a head bowed, many a broad chest heaved, and many a manly cheek was wet with tears when that broad field of blue in the center of which, like a signal light, glowed the lone star . . . was laid away among the relics of the dead republic. But we were most of us natives of the United States, and when the stars and stripes, the flag of our fathers, was run up and catching the breeze unrolled its heaven-born colors to the light, cheer after cheer rent [tore] the air. Methinks the star in the lower left-hand corner should have been especially dedicated to Texas."

## COMPARE VIEWPOINTS

1. Which side did Sam Houston take in the question of whether Texas should become a state or build an empire?
2. Which side did Mirabeau Lamar take in the question of whether Texas should become a state or build an empire?
3. Did Noah Smithwick agree with Sam Houston or Mirabeau Lamar? How do you know?
4. What reason did Noah Smithwick give for his view?
5. If you had been a Texan at that time, which side would you have taken? Give at least two reasons for your answer.

## THINK -AND- APPLY

People may agree or disagree with the views their leaders have on certain issues. On what issues today might Texans have different views from those of their leaders?

CHAPTER 6

# REVIEW

## CONNECT MAIN IDEAS

Use this organizer to show that you understand how the chapter's main ideas are connected. First copy the organizer onto a separate sheet of paper. Then complete it by writing three details to support each main idea.

### A Country Called Texas

Texas sets up a new government.

______________________________

______________________________

______________________________

Leaders work to solve the problems of the new Republic of Texas.

______________________________

______________________________

______________________________

Texas joins the United States.

______________________________

______________________________

______________________________

## WRITE MORE ABOUT IT

1. **Write a Report** Write a short report that explains how the Republic of Texas was annexed by the United States.

2. **Write a Speech** Write a speech to make people want to move from Europe to the Republic of Texas.

## USE VOCABULARY

Use each vocabulary word in a sentence that helps explain its meaning.

1. treaty
2. election
3. immigrant
4. plantation
5. majority
6. boundary

## CHECK UNDERSTANDING

1. Who was the first elected president of the Republic of Texas?
2. Why was Texas in danger of attack by Mexico even though the Texas Revolution was over?
3. Why has Texas had three capitals?
4. Why did citizens in Austin want the government archives to stay there?
5. Who was William Goyens?
6. Why did the Republic of Texas give away land to immigrants?
7. How did most Texans make a living in the republic?
8. Why was Texas not annexed by the United States earlier? Give two reasons.
9. What caused the war between Mexico and the United States in 1846?
10. Why did Texas and the United States argue about the boundaries of Texas after the Mexican-American War?

## THINK CRITICALLY

1. **Think More About It** What is the difference between a dictator and a president?
2. **Personally Speaking** What qualities do you think a Texas Ranger needed?
3. **Cause and Effect** How do you think the growth of the Republic of Texas added to conflicts with the Indians?
4. **Cause and Effect** How might things have been different for the Cherokees if President Houston had served his second term right after his first term?
5. **Explore Viewpoints** Why do you think most Texans wanted Texas to join the United States?

## APPLY SKILLS

**How to Understand National Symbols**
Some people have their own flags. The President and Vice President of the United States have their own flags. Design your own flag, with symbols that have special meaning to you. Then write a paragraph explaining what each symbol stands for.

Map Skill

**How to Use a Historical Map**
Compare the map on page 175 with the map on page 177. How would you change the map on page 177 to show the lands that Mexico once claimed?

## READ MORE ABOUT IT

*The Story of the Lone Star Republic of Texas* by R. Conrad Stein. Childrens Press. A story of Texas that begins with the Austin colony and ends with statehood.

*The Texas Rangers* by Mike Cox. Eakin. Ten action-packed stories give young readers a glimpse into the colorful history of the Texas Rangers.

## MAKING SOCIAL STUDIES RELEVANT

# DON'T MESS WITH TEXAS

A writer named John Steinbeck once said that Texas is not only a state but also a state of mind. Texans have long been known all over the world for the great pride they have in their state. It is a pride based on the state's size as well as its history.

Texans fought and won a war for independence, and for almost a decade the Republic of Texas was an independent nation. This feeling of independence lives on in the state today. Texans see themselves as tough, self-reliant people. You can see this spirit in many ways.

In 1985 Texas leaders decided that the state needed a slogan that would make people stop littering along its highways. The leaders wanted the slogan to show the pride Texans have for their state and to tell newcomers and visitors about Texas. The slogan they decided on is "Don't mess with Texas."

## Think and Apply

With a partner, brainstorm other phrases or slogans you think show pride in Texas and its past. Hold a class election to vote for the best slogan, and then write it on a banner. Display the banner in your school.

Coming up with a slogan (above) is just one of the creative ways Texans have been known to show pride for their state. Hand-made boots (left), a giant mascot (center), and parades (right) tell the world just how proud Texans are of the Lone Star State.

UNIT 3

# STORY CLOTH

Follow the pictures shown in this story cloth to help you review the events in Unit 3.

## Summarize the Main Ideas

1. The Texas Revolution began on October 2, 1835, when Texans and Mexican soldiers fought over a cannon in Gonzales.
2. On March 2, 1836, the Texas Declaration of Independence was signed at Washington-on-the-Brazos. The declaration stated that Texas was now an independent country.
3. The Alamo fell to the Mexicans on March 6, 1836. "Remember the Alamo!" became a battle cry for the Texas army.
4. Santa Anna surrendered to Sam Houston on April 22, 1836, after Texas won the battle of San Jacinto. Texas had won its independence from Mexico.
5. Sam Houston was elected president of the Republic of Texas on September 5, 1836. The Lone Star flag became the national flag.
6. Hundreds of Cherokees and Comanches were killed fighting for their land. The years of fighting between the settlers and the Indians cost the republic millions of dollars.
7. Texas became the 28th state of the United States on December 29, 1845.

**Write a Time Capsule Entry** Choose one of the events shown in this story cloth. Write a paragraph or draw a picture with a caption to help someone in the future understand what the event was about. Place your entry in a container with those of your classmates and bury it somewhere near your school.

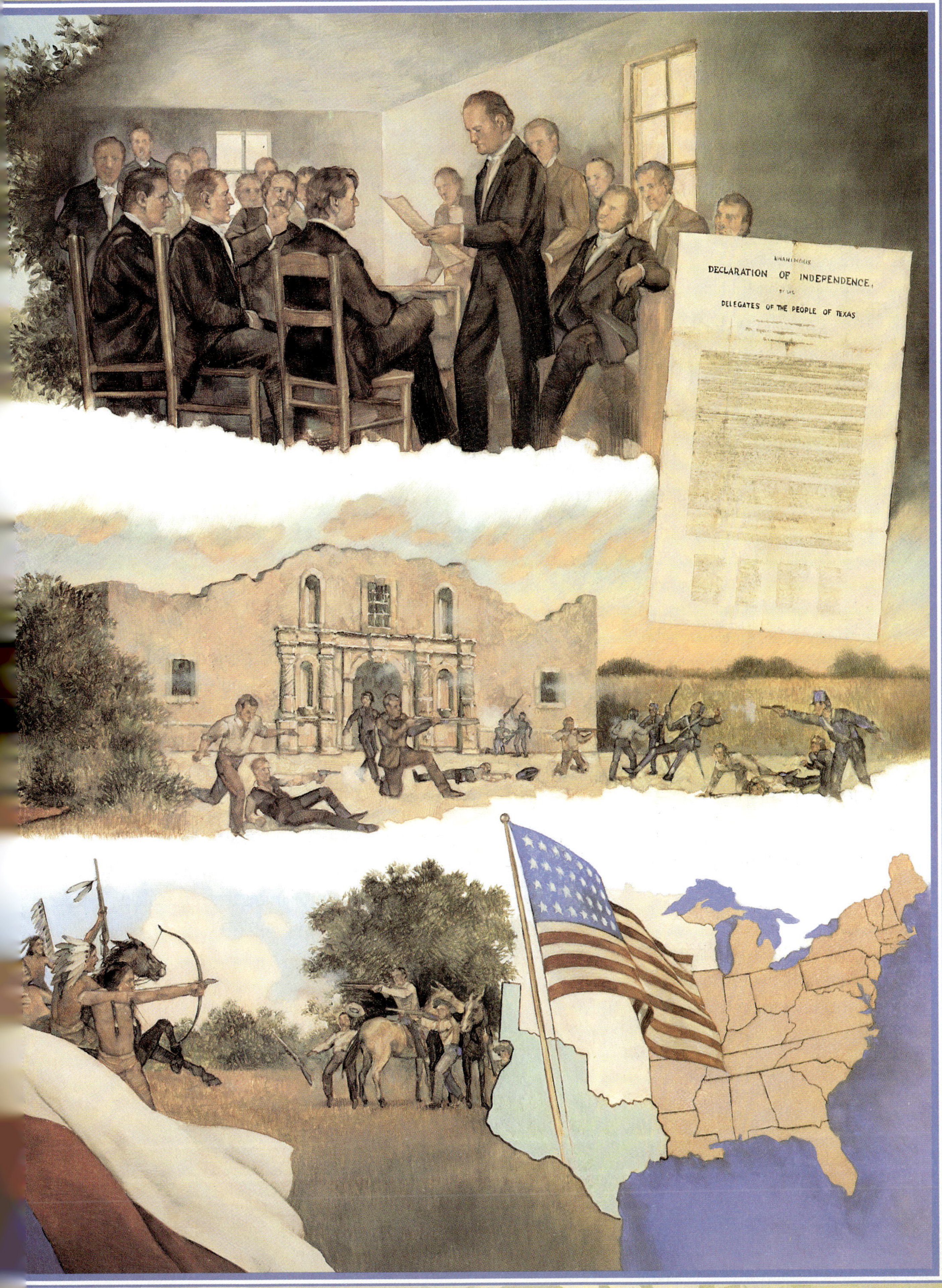
DECLARATION OF INDEPENDENCE,
DELEGATES OF THE PEOPLE OF TEXAS

# UNIT 3 REVIEW

## COOPERATIVE LEARNING WORKSHOP

**Remember**

- Share your ideas.
- Cooperate with others to plan your work.
- Take responsibility for your work.
- Show your group's work to the class.
- Discuss what you learned by working together.

**Activity 1**

### Honor Your Hero

With a group of classmates, choose one person that you admire from the Texas Revolution to be the subject for a poster. Each student should do a special job to help produce the poster. Some can work on drawing a scene showing the person in action. Other students can write words or phrases around the picture that tell why that person should be honored. Add your poster to a class display called "Heroes of the Texas Revolution."

**Activity 2**

### Perform a Simulation

Role-play a conversation that might have taken place between Santa Anna and Sam Houston after the battle at San Jacinto. Use words from the lesson to help make your scene seem realistic.

**Activity 3**

### Conduct a Class Debate

Sam Houston and Mirabeau Lamar had very different opinions on whether Texas should join the United States or build its own empire. With your classmates, brainstorm a list of reasons why Texas should join the United States. Then list reasons why Texas should remain a separate country. Conduct a class debate using this information.

**Activity 4**

### Make a Diorama

With a group of classmates, use a cardboard box to make a diorama that shows one of the events in this unit. First, cut the short edges of the box, fold them back so that the box is flat, and draw the background scene. Then draw the figures on construction paper and cut them out. Paste the figures to a base made of heavy paper. Tape the edges of the shoe box back in place, and set up the figures in the diorama. Present your diorama to the rest of the class, with each member of your group telling part of the story you have shown.

## USE VOCABULARY

For each group of vocabulary words, write a sentence or two that explains how the words are related.

1. revolution, volunteer
2. independence, republic
3. election, cabinet
4. immigrant, plantation

## CHECK UNDERSTANDING

1. How did the Battle of the Alamo affect the Texas Revolution?
2. According to the Constitution of the Republic of Texas, how were Texans to be governed?
3. What was the Treaty of Velasco?
4. What steps did the new government take to protect Texans?
5. Why did some leaders want the state capital to be moved from Houston?
6. Who was Angelina Eberly?
7. How did slavery affect the decision of the United States Congress to annex the Republic of Texas?

## THINK CRITICALLY

1. **Explore Viewpoints** How do you think most Texans felt when Santa Anna was captured after the victory at San Jacinto?
2. **Think More About It** Why did most immigrants to Texas in the 1800s settle in East Texas?
3. **Cause and Effect** In what ways did the history and government of the United States affect the Texas Revolution?
4. **Explore Viewpoints** As a young man, Sam Houston lived with the Cherokees. How do you think this affected his policy toward American Indians in Texas?
5. **Past to Present** The Republic of Texas printed dollar bills that some people called redbacks. Why do you think some people today call dollar bills greenbacks?

## APPLY GEOGRAPHY SKILLS

Map Skill

**How to Use a Historical Map** In 1850 the United States was divided between states that allowed slavery and those that did not. Use the colors on the map and the map key to answer the questions that follow.

**THE UNITED STATES, 1850**

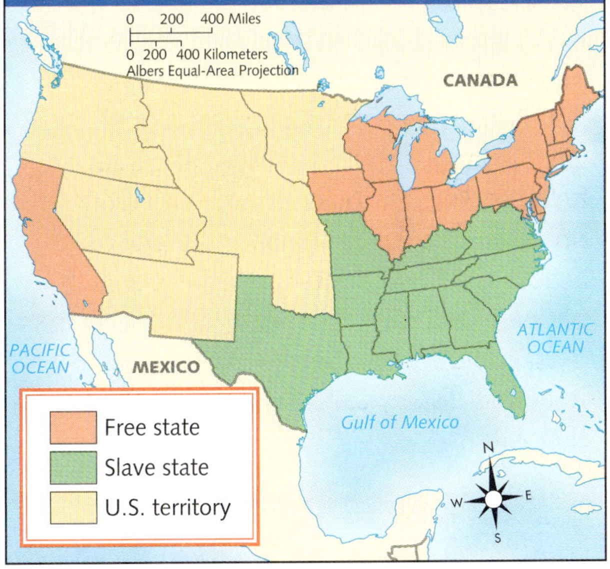


1. What color shows free states? What color shows slave states?
2. What does the color tan stand for?
3. Were there more free states or slave states in 1850?
4. How would this map be different if Texas had been a free state?

UNIT 4

# THE NEW STATE OF TEXAS

**1850**

**1852**
Czech immigrants settle in Central Texas

King Ranch is founded

**1855**

**1854**
Polish immigrants build the settlement of Panna Maria

**1860**

**1861**

Texas secedes from the United States and joins the Confederacy

The Civil War begins

**1863**
President Lincoln signs the Emancipation Proclamation

The Confederates win the Battle of Sabine Pass

**1865**

**1865**
The Civil War ends

The new state of Texas faced many problems. One of the biggest had to do with slavery. Most Texans did not own slaves. Even so, slavery affected almost everyone in the state. After a time, slavery led Texans and the rest of the nation into a terrible war.

Other problems led to other kinds of wars. There were wars over the land. Some were between Texans and Native Americans. Others were between the farmers who claimed the land and the ranchers who grazed cattle on it.

In 1880 Texans began laying thousands of miles of railroad track. The railroads linked Texans with one another and with people in Mexico and in other parts of the United States.

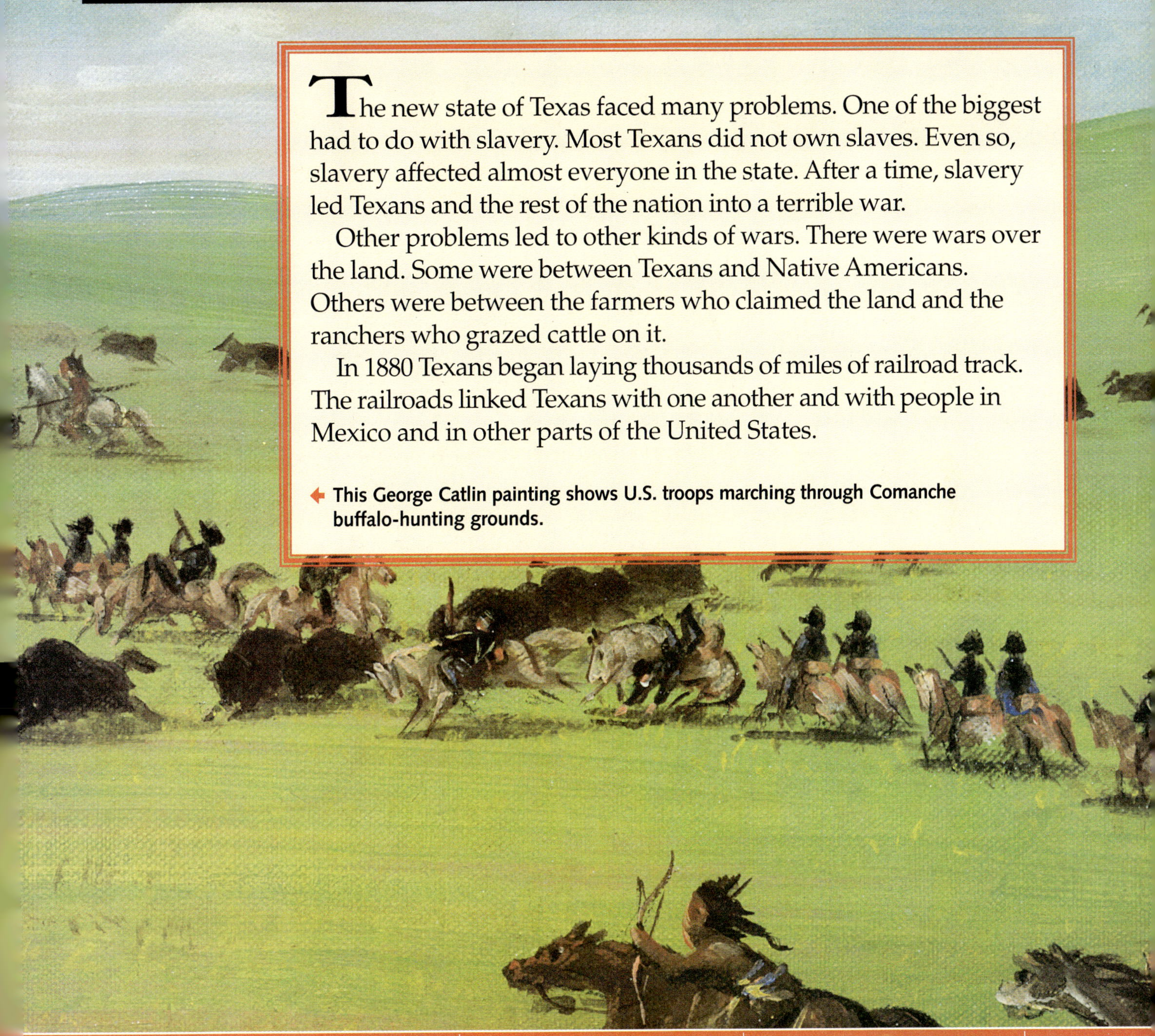

**This George Catlin painting shows U.S. troops marching through Comanche buffalo-hunting grounds.**

**1870** **1875** **1880** **1885**

**1870** Texas rejoins the United States

**1872** Trains come to Dallas

**1874** Battle of Palo Duro Canyon

**1875** Quanah Parker and the Comanches surrender at Fort Sill

**1876** Texas approves a new constitution

Charles Goodnight starts his ranch

*Set the Scene with Literature*

# Johnny Texas

written by Carol Hoff illustrated by Fred Willingham

**Johann (YOH•hahn) came to Harrisburg, Texas, from Leipzig (LYP•sig), Germany, when he was about ten years old. A man told him that he would be called Johnny in Texas. Johann repeated "Johnny Texas." From then on, that was what his friends and family called him.**

**Coming to Texas was a big change for Johnny and his family. In the very old city of Leipzig, tall stone buildings stood side by side along stone streets. Towers topped many of the buildings. When Johnny and his family reached Harrisburg, they saw a wide dirt road with a few one-story wooden buildings along it. The little town seemed very small to them.**

**But Texas gave Johnny and his family the chance to have their own land and a better life. They learned new ways of living in Texas. However, one thing they learned about in Texas—slavery—caused conflict in the family.**

Now that it was getting to be autumn there was more work to be done on the farm. One of their cows had a calf; hens were stealing nests in the brush, and weeks later coming proudly out with broods of fluffy yellow chicks; and Papa had bought three more young pigs to fatten for winter ham and bacon and sausage. Besides there was the fall garden to plant and the fall plowing to do, so Papa was looking for someone to help

**broods** groups of young animals

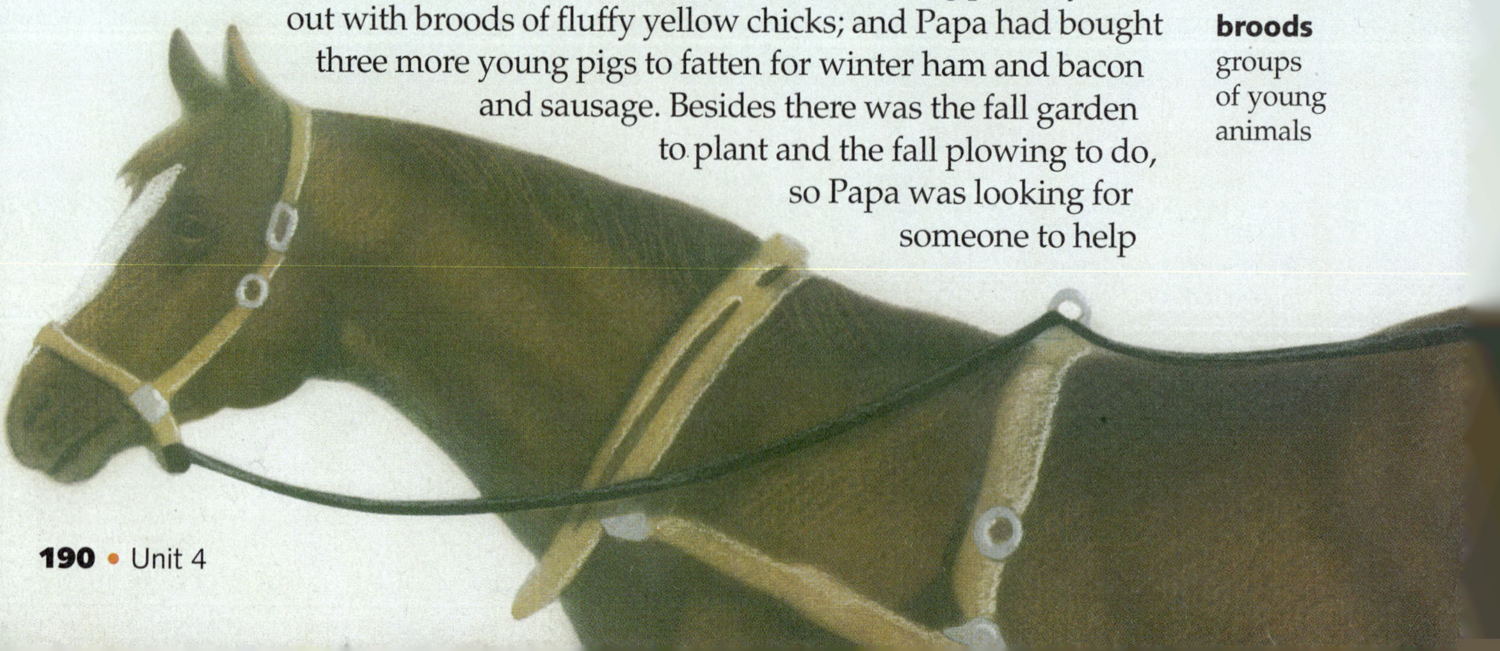

him with the work. And one Saturday evening he came riding home from Harrisburg with Tobias on the seat beside him.

Tobias was a tall, lanky, very black boy of nineteen, with sad, patient eyes in an unsmiling face. He moved in queer, jerky movements like a funny toy man whose joints were worked by a string. But even that first evening you could tell that he was a good worker.

After supper when Tobias had gone to the little shed next to the barn that was to be his room, Papa explained to Mama. "How do you like this Saturday surprise?" he asked. "I got him at a real bargain. I traded the new calf for him."

"Traded?" echoed Mama. "You mean that you bought Tobias?"

"Yes," said Papa.

"But why?"

"Jim Forman had inherited him from an uncle of his—Tobias and five other slaves. He didn't need all of them, so he was glad to get rid of him. And a lucky day for us it was."

**inherited** passed down from family members

"Is Tobias a slave?" asked Johnny, shocked.

"A human being traded for an animal?" said Mama, very low and quiet. "Oh, no!"

"It is the custom of the country," said Papa. "Many people have slaves."

"But it is not right," said Mama, still quietly but firmly, and Johnny's heart agreed.

"We will treat him well. He will have a good home. We will not be cruel to him."

"But he will not be free." Mama was standing, little but straight, and not a bit afraid now. Johnny felt a thrill of pride as he watched her. She still spoke quietly, but there was something in her words strong and fierce, like fire and a sword. "Freedom is a precious thing, Robert. It is why we came to Texas, why we are enduring a hard life, so that our children and our children's children will be free. And we can never be free when we hold another in slavery. It is not right or just. We must give Tobias his freedom tomorrow."

"But the calf?" Papa objected. "I have promised the calf."

"Better we should lose the calf," said Mama, "than lose our own self-respect."

But Papa was a stubborn man and would not admit that he was wrong. And for a week a heaviness hung over the household, not sorrow exactly, or anger, but a vague uncomfortable feeling. Mama went around very straight and quiet and gentle and never mentioned the matter of slavery. Papa tried hard to be bluff and hearty, but kept Tobias busy away from the house as much as possible. Johnny spent a great deal of time thinking about freedom.

**bluff and hearty**
sincere and friendly

He lay in the grass and looked up into the branches of an oak and tried to imagine what it was like to be a slave. Somebody gave you a place to sleep, and food and clothes. You could work and eat and sleep and sing and play just like other people, but you couldn't choose when you could work or play, and nothing you had was really yours. You couldn't speak just what you wanted to. You couldn't choose the kind of work you liked best, or the food you ate or the clothes you wore. You couldn't come and go as you pleased.

Once he asked Tobias about it. "Do you mind being a slave?" he asked as they rested in the shade at noon.

Tobias looked at him quickly and then lowered his eyes. "I was born in slavery," he said. "Don't make no diff'ence how I feels 'bout it. Can't do nothin' 'bout it." But he picked up a pebble and hurled it fiercely.

Finally one evening at bedtime Papa went over to Mama and put his arms around her. "You win," he said smiling. "Little Clara, you win. Tomorrow I will give Tobias his bill of sale. I have never felt comfortable about it, even on the drive home with him."

Mama smiled back at him and kissed him, and suddenly Johnny felt free again too.

Tobias did not leave them but stayed to work for wages. From a deerskin that he had tanned he made a little flat leather wallet to keep his bill of sale, which proclaimed him to be a freed man. He wore it constantly, tied around his neck with a leather thong, like a huge locket. Sometimes when he worked in the sun without his shirt, the wallet would swing against his black skin, shining with sweat, and always Johnny could see the flash of pleasure this reminder of his freedom gave him.

**thong** strap

CHAPTER 7

# THE LONE STAR STATE

“I am convinced that in time slavery will be abolished either by gentle means or by force, because . . . injustice cannot survive.”

Elise Waerenskjold, a Norwegian immigrant and Texas community leader, around 1850

LESSON 1

# AFRICANS, FREE AND SLAVE

## Link to Our World

**How do laws affect people today?**

***Focus on the Main Idea***
**Read to find out how laws passed in Texas after 1845 changed life for the Africans living there.**

***Preview Vocabulary***
**auction**
**cotton gin**
**textile mill**

African people lived in what is now Texas long before most Anglo-Americans came. An African named Estéban was with the Spanish in the 1500s when they explored the area. Africans lived in Texas when the area belonged to Spain. A few had their own land and cattle. Some worked for other settlers on farms and ranches.

This quilt is an example of the rich African heritage that slaves contributed to the culture of Texas.

### FREE AFRICANS

When Texas was a part of Mexico in the 1820s, a small number of free Africans moved there from the United States. Many had been slaves who had run away or been given their freedom. They came to Texas hoping that life there would be better than it was in the United States.

Then Texans broke away from Mexico in 1836 and formed the Republic of Texas. The new government passed laws saying that free Africans could no longer move to Texas. Those already there could not vote or buy land.

The Texas government did let a few Africans keep land they already owned. One of the richest, William Goyens, owned more than 12,000 acres. The Ashworth family owned ranchland and thousands of cattle in Jefferson County. Other free Africans worked as barbers, painters, tailors, carpenters, laundry workers, and blacksmiths.

When Texas became a state, more laws were passed that took away some of the freedoms of Africans. Free Africans could not own guns. They could not have meetings unless white people were present. Free Africans lived in fear of one day being made slaves.

**Why did free Africans come to Texas in the early 1820s?**

In Texas, slave auctions were held in Galveston and Houston. The average price for a slave was around $1,000.

## ENSLAVED AFRICANS

After Texas became a republic and then a state, more and more people moved there from the United States. Many settlers from the southern states brought their slaves. The number of enslaved people in Texas grew quickly. By 1860 there were more than 182,000 enslaved Africans in Texas, almost one-third of the people in the state.

Most slave owners had small farms and owned fewer than five slaves. People in towns sometimes owned slaves who worked as house servants, doing cooking, cleaning, and sewing.

Slaves were bought and sold, often from one neighbor to another. There were also slave **auctions**, or public sales, in Houston and Galveston. At auctions slaves were sold to the person who would pay the most money. This kind of sale often broke up families, sending a husband and wife or a mother and child to different slave owners.

**In what ways were slaves bought and sold?**

## COTTON PLANTATIONS

Most of the slaves in Texas lived on plantations in the eastern part of the state. There the fertile soil and good rainfall were just right for growing cotton. Cotton was the main crop for most East Texas farmers.

These farmers sold much of their cotton to textile mills in the northern states and in Europe. **Textile mills** are factories where cotton is made into cloth, or textiles. Mill owners paid high prices for Texas cotton.

It took a lot of work to grow cotton. Workers planted the cotton seeds and weeded the fields. They picked the cotton and ran the **cotton gin**, a machine that separates seeds from cotton fibers. Small plantations had 20 or 30 slaves. The largest plantations had more than 100. The work of enslaved people helped make the plantation owners rich.

**Where were most cotton plantations in Texas?**

## SLAVE LIFE

Slaves working on the cotton plantations had little free time. The workday began at dawn and ended at sunset, or as the slaves said, "from can see to can't see." When enslaved men and women were not working in the cotton fields, they did other jobs on the plantation. They did such things as clear land, build fences and roads, dig wells, and cut firewood. Some slaves worked in the plantation owner's home. They cooked, cleaned, sewed, and washed clothes.

Enslaved children worked, too. Young children gathered firewood, helped in the gardens and kitchens, and looked after the animals. Older enslaved children worked in the cotton fields with the adults.

Even slaves who were treated well by their owners were still not free. They were not allowed to choose where they lived. They could not choose what work they did. Some slaves could not even choose the person they married.

Some slaves tried to escape. Alone or in small groups, slaves who escaped often went to Mexico. They did this even though they knew they faced a terrible beating if they were caught.

**What work did enslaved children do?**

Baling cotton was just one step in getting it from the field to the market.

## LESSON 1 REVIEW

### Check Understanding

1. **Recall the Facts** What were some jobs held by free Africans in Texas?
2. **Focus on the Main Idea** How did life change for Africans after Texas became a republic and then a state?

### Think Critically

3. **Cause and Effect** How did the cotton industry affect slavery?
4. **Think More About It** Why do you think the Texas government wanted to limit the freedoms of Africans?

### Show What You Know

**Writing Activity** In a paragraph, describe the life of a slave in Texas. Add your paragraph to a class notebook titled "Slavery in Texas."

# LESSON 2 GROWTH AND IMMIGRATION

## Link to Our World

**What immigrant groups come to Texas today?**

***Focus on the Main Idea***
**Read to find out what immigrant groups came to live in the new state of Texas in the 1850s.**

***Preview Vocabulary***
**prosperity**

*Geh* (GAY) *mit ins Texas*, the poster in Germany said, "Go with us to Texas." To people in crowded Europe, the idea of acres of open land was too good to pass up. By the 1850s more than 35,000 Germans had moved to Texas. They had built the towns of Fredericksburg, New Braunfels, and others. The Germans were by far the largest group of immigrants to come to Texas from Europe. During the 1850s thousands of other Europeans came as well.

## CZECH IMMIGRANTS

A family from Germany brought these household items to their new home in Texas. What items from home would you take if you were moving to a new country?

In 1852 a group of 16 Czech (CHEK) families from eastern Europe landed at Galveston. They came from parts of what are now Austria, Hungary, Poland, and the Czech Republic. These Czech families followed other Czechs, who had first come to Texas in 1828. More had come in the 1840s. Now Czechs began moving to Texas in greater numbers.

Mostly farmers, the Czechs settled in Central Texas in what is now Fayette County. Not long after they arrived, they built their first school.

The Czechs believed in the saying "A sound mind in a sound body." To build strong bodies, they formed *sokols*, or exercise clubs, like the ones popular in Europe. *Sokol* is the Czech word for *falcon*, a bird that is a strong flyer. The Czechs made their bodies strong by exercising on bars and rings and other gymnastic equipment.

The Czechs also believed it was important to keep informed. They started reading clubs and shared books written in Czech. They also started newspapers. The *Texan* was the first Czech newspaper published in Texas.

**How did the Czech people keep their culture alive in Texas?**

## Polish Immigrants

The first of several hundred families from what is now Poland came to Texas in 1854. They had heard about Texas from a young priest named Father Leopold Moczygemba (moh•sheh•GEM•bah). Father Leopold had lived for a time in Castroville and New Braunfels. He served the German Catholics who had settled there. Father Leopold saw how well the Germans did in Texas and wrote letters to his family in Europe, telling good things about Texas.

Father Leopold knew life was not good in Europe. Food was scarce because of a war in Russia. The Russians had stopped shipping grain to Poland and other parts of Europe because their soldiers needed bread. The Polish people were also very unhappy because, living under Russian rule, they were made to fight for Russia in a war in Europe.

On December 3, 1854, a group of 150 Polish immigrants, including Father Leopold's father and brothers, arrived in Galveston after a two-month ocean journey. Several weeks later, they settled south of San Antonio, calling their village Panna Maria (PAHN•ah mah•REE•uh).

In the spring of 1855, the settlers planted their first crop. That summer, grasshoppers ate most of it. The following winter there was a drought, and more grasshoppers came in the spring. Instead of the **prosperity**, or success, promised by Father Leopold, the Polish settlers had found hardship in Texas. Some of them left, joining other Polish communities in the United States. Yet many stayed. Panna Maria is still a small village, very much the way it was in the 1850s.

**Where did Polish immigrants first settle in Texas?**

## Where?

### Panna Maria

On December 24, 1854, Polish immigrants settled on 300 acres of land along the San Antonio River. Only tall grasses and live oak trees greeted those first settlers. Under the largest tree, the people gathered to thank God for their new land. This was the location of the first Polish settlement in the United States. They named their settlement Panna Maria. Later the Polish settlers built a church next to the live oak tree. Both the church and the tree still stand today.

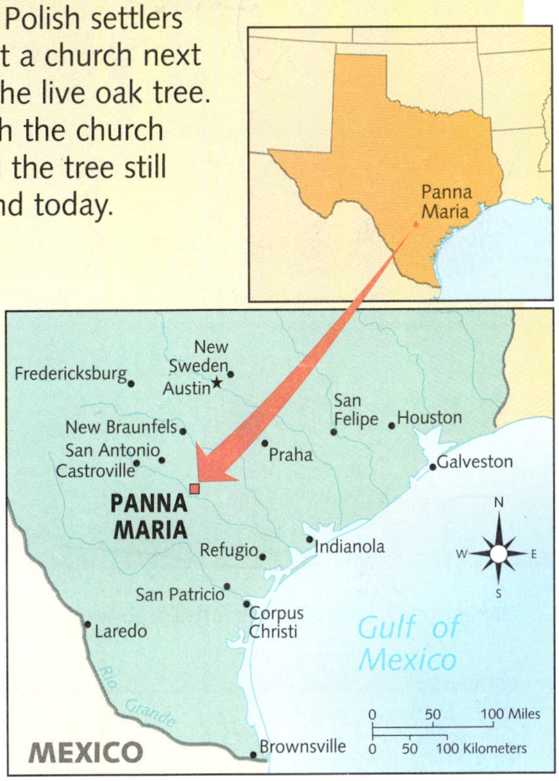

## OTHER EUROPEAN IMMIGRANTS

Thousands of people from other parts of Europe moved to Texas in the years after it became a state. Eastern European people known as Wends settled in Central Texas. There were Jewish settlers from Russia and other eastern European countries in many Texas towns. The first Norwegian settlement in Texas was in Henderson County. Settlers from Sweden, Italy, the Netherlands, Switzerland, and Belgium also came in large numbers.

The Europeans brought with them their music, arts, languages, literature, and traditions. They also brought their skills and crafts. All of these things became part of Texas culture, which was and still is a mix of customs from many lands.

These hopeful immigrants left Göteborg, Sweden, to sail to Texas.

By 1860 the population of Texas was four times larger than it had been in 1845. The European immigrants helped make the population grow. However, most new immigrants to Texas had come from the southern United States. Most were white farmers and their enslaved African workers.

**How did immigrants affect Texas in the years after it became a state?**

## LESSON 2 REVIEW

### Check Understanding

1. **Recall the Facts** Where did European immigrants settle in Texas?
2. **Focus on the Main Idea** What immigrant groups came to live in Texas in the 1850s?

### Think Critically

3. **Think More About It** For what reasons did people leave their countries to move to Texas?
4. **Cause and Effect** How did life in Europe make people want to move to Texas?

### Show What You Know

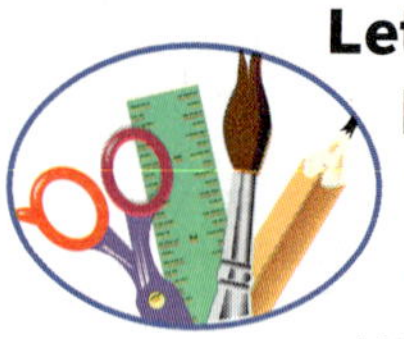

**Letter-Writing Activity** Imagine that you are writing a letter to someone in another country. Tell your pen pal why you think he or she might want to move to your community.

S·K·I·L·L·S

# How To

# Read a Bar Graph

## Why Is This Skill Important?

Graphs are one way to compare amounts. A bar graph compares amounts by using solid bars to stand for numbers. The bar graph on this page shows the populations of four groups of people living in Texas in 1860.

## Understand the Process

Along the bottom of the graph are the names of the four groups of people. The population numbers are shown on the left side of the graph. The numbers go from 0 to 400,000. Look at the graph, and tell which group had the largest population in 1860. Which group had the smallest population? The bar graph makes it easy to compare populations. However, it does not give exact numbers. Estimate the population of each of the four groups of people living in Texas in 1860.

## Think and Apply

In 1850 there were 58,500 Africans and 154,000 Anglo-Americans living in Texas. Make a bar graph comparing these two populations. Then write a paragraph that compares the populations of Anglo-Americans and Africans in 1850 with their populations in 1860.

POPULATIONS OF TEXAS, 1860

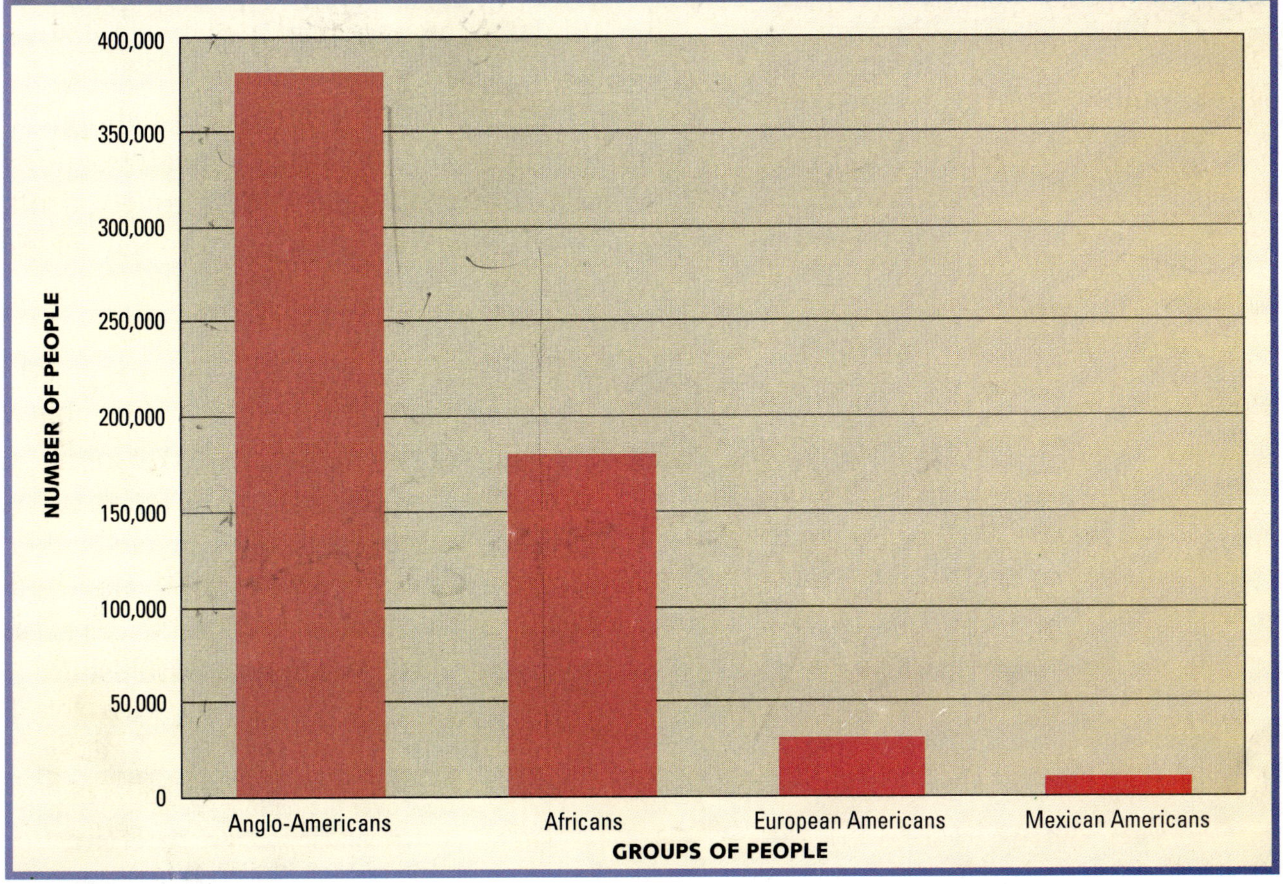

LESSON 3

# THE CIVIL WAR

## Link to Our World

**What can happen today when groups of people do not agree?**

***Focus on the Main Idea***
**Read to find out what happened in the early 1860s when Texans did not agree with the United States government.**

***Preview Vocabulary***
**civil war**
**federal**
**Union**
**secede**
**Confederacy**
**blockade**
**Juneteenth**
**Reconstruction**
**sharecropper**

From 1861 to 1865 the people of the United States fought a terrible war called the Civil War. A **civil war** is a fight between groups of citizens in the same country. The Civil War in the United States was between the states in the North and the states in the South. People in these two regions had failed to work out their disagreements.

## CAUSES OF THE WAR

In 1860 many people in the United States disagreed about the government. Some of the people felt that the **federal**, or national, government should be able to tell the states what to do. Others felt that state governments had the right to decide things for themselves. Much of this disagreement was over the issue of slavery.

People in the United States had disagreed about slavery for many years. The idea that slavery was wrong was not new. Yet in the southern states, including Texas, plantation owners depended on enslaved people as workers. Even some people who did not own slaves felt that the question of slavery should be decided by each state.

From 1861 to 1865 two separate flags flew over the nation when the northern states and the southern states fought each other in the Civil War.

Then, in 1860, Abraham Lincoln was elected President of the United States. Most Southerners did not want Lincoln to be President. They worried that he would end slavery. After Lincoln was elected, Southerners began to talk about not being a part of the **Union**, or the United States of America.

**What caused the Civil War?**

## A Nation Divided

South Carolina was the first state to **secede** (sih•SEED) from, or leave, the Union. Ten other states, Texas among them, followed. These states formed their own country. They called it the Confederate States of America, or the **Confederacy**.

The leaders of the Confederacy believed their states had the right to secede from the Union. They believed that the federal government of the United States did not care about their needs. President Lincoln felt that the states did not have the right to secede from the Union. Lincoln worried that if the United States were divided, then democracy would fail.

When Union soldiers refused to leave a fort that was now inside the Confederate border, the first battle of the Civil War took place. This happened in South Carolina on April 12, 1861.

**What country did the states of the South form?**

The Battle at Fort Sumter (left) was the first battle of the Civil War. During the war the Confederacy printed its own money (above).

On New Year's Day 1863, the Confederates recaptured the port of Galveston from Union forces.

## Texas in the Civil War

Earlier, in February 1861, Texas voters had to decide whether to secede from the Union. Not all Texans were for the Confederacy. Many German immigrants in Texas did not agree with the idea of slavery.

One Texas leader who stayed loyal to the Union was Governor Sam Houston. He had almost died fighting under the flags of the United States and Texas. Houston told Texas leaders,

> "I have served Texas under both of those flags for a long time. Gentlemen, you cannot forget those two flags—you cannot withdraw from the Union."

Texas did leave the Union. It joined the Confederacy in March 1861. Sam Houston was forced to give up being governor because he would not support the decision to secede from the Union.

Texas sent more than 60,000 soldiers to fight for the Confederacy, though about 2,000 Texans fought for the Union. Texas soldiers fought in important battles in many states. Texans at home grew food and made clothing and weapons for their soldiers.

**✓ Who were some Texans opposed to the Confederacy?**

## Battles in Texas

Most of the battles in the Civil War were fought in states other than Texas. Only a few battles took place in Texas. Some of these battles were fought in Texas ports. Union ships **blockaded**, or closed off, ports at Galveston, Sabine Pass, and Brownsville. The blockades made it hard to get goods and supplies into and out of Texas.

In October 1862, Union ships attacked Galveston. There were not enough Confederate soldiers there to defend the port, so Union soldiers were able to capture it. In January, though, the Confederate army took back Galveston.

The Battle of Sabine Pass was also fought in Texas. The battle took place near present-day Port Arthur on September 8, 1863. Union ships moving up the Sabine River were captured by the Confederates.

The last battle of the entire Civil War was fought at Palmito Ranch, near Brownsville, on May 13, 1865. This battle took place more than a month after General Robert E. Lee of the Confederacy had surrendered in Virginia. The news that the war was over had not yet reached Texas. The war went on in Texas until the end of May.

**✓ What Civil War battles were fought in Texas?**

## Life After the Civil War

The Civil War was still being fought when President Lincoln signed the Emancipation Proclamation in 1863. This important paper gave freedom to the enslaved people in the Confederacy.

Slaves in Texas did not become free until after the Civil War ended in Texas. On June 19, 1865, Union soldiers landed at Galveston. On that day General Gordon Granger of the Union army read a paper saying that all slaves were free. Since 1865, Texans have celebrated June 19, or **Juneteenth**, as a special day for freedom in Texas.

The period after the Civil War was called **Reconstruction**. People had to reconstruct, or rebuild, the way they lived now that slavery had ended. Texas state laws had to be changed. Texans who had been slaves had to find a new way of life.

Life in Texas after the Civil War was hard for everyone, but it was hardest for the people who had been enslaved. They owned no land. Without land, seeds, tools, work animals, and money, they could not start their own farms. Instead, many worked as sharecroppers, as did many poor white farmers. A **sharecropper** is a person who rents land to farm, paying the landowner with a share of the crops.

Juneteenth has been celebrated in Texas for more than 130 years. During the early part of this century, Juneteenth was one of the most popular social events for African Americans in Houston (above).

**LEARNING FROM DOCUMENTS** On June 19, 1865, General Gordon Granger issued orders freeing all slaves in Texas (right), but some areas of the state did not receive word until later that slaves were free.

- Who do you think "the Executive of the United States" refers to?

### GENERAL ORDERS, No. 3

The people of Texas are informed that in accordance with a Proclamation from the Executive of the United States, all slaves are free. This involves an absolute equality of rights and rights of property between former masters and slaves, and the connection heretofore existing between them becomes that between employer and free laborer. The freedmen are advised to remain at their present homes and work for wages. They are informed that they will not be allowed to collect at military posts, and that they will not be supported in idleness, either there or elsewhere. By order of

*G. Granger*
*Major General Commanding*

Many African American share-croppers in Texas led difficult lives. After giving a large portion of their crops to the landowner, many had very little money left.

The owner of the land gave each share-cropper a mule, a plow, and seeds. The owner then let the sharecropper use part of the land to raise crops. The landowner got one-third to one-half of the crop as a share. The sharecropper kept or sold the rest. Often, the sharecropper had barely enough to live on.

After the Civil War each seceded state could rejoin the Union if it did certain things. The state had to end slavery and write a new constitution that gave African American men the right to vote. No woman, regardless of color, could vote at that time. In 1870 Texas did these things and rejoined the United States.

Many white Texans became angry at the way the new state government was being run. They did not like the changes made during Reconstruction. In 1876 Texas leaders approved a new constitution to limit the power of the state government. This was the end of Reconstruction in Texas. Texas still uses the 1876 constitution today.

**What did a sharecropper do?**

## LESSON 3 REVIEW

### Check Understanding

1. **Recall the Facts** Why did most Southerners not want Abraham Lincoln to be elected President?
2. **Focus on the Main Idea** What happened in the early 1860s when Texans did not agree with the United States government?

### Think Critically

3. **Think More About It** Why is the Civil War sometimes called the War Between the States?
4. **Cause and Effect** Why do you think that a month passed before Texans learned that the war had ended?

### Show What You Know

**Writing Activity** Imagine that you are either a soldier in the Civil War or someone who has stayed at home in Texas. Write a page in a journal that describes what you did for one day.

S·K·I·L·L·S

# How To

# Read Symbols on a Map

## Why Is This Skill Important?

Maps use symbols to show where certain places are. Symbols can stand for cities and airports. They can also show where events took place, such as battles in the Civil War.

## Understand the Process

Look at the map key to see the symbols used on this map. Each symbol tells you something different about the place it is near.

The 🔥 symbol tells you there was a battle in that place. Find three places in Texas where Civil War battles were fought.

What city has the ★ symbol next to its name? What does that tell you?

Find the line of ships shown on the map. What do the ships stand for? In what body of water are they?

## Think and Apply

Map Skill

Draw a map of the neighborhood where you live. Use one symbol for your home. Use other symbols for buildings, roads, and places of interest. Include a map key to tell what each symbol stands for.

On your map, draw a line with arrows to show the route you follow to get from home to another place, such as a friend's house or the grocery store. Remember to add this symbol to the map key.

CHAPTER 7

# REVIEW

## CONNECT MAIN IDEAS

Use this organizer to show that you understand how the chapter's main ideas are connected. First copy the organizer onto a separate sheet of paper. Then complete it by writing one or two sentences to summarize each lesson.

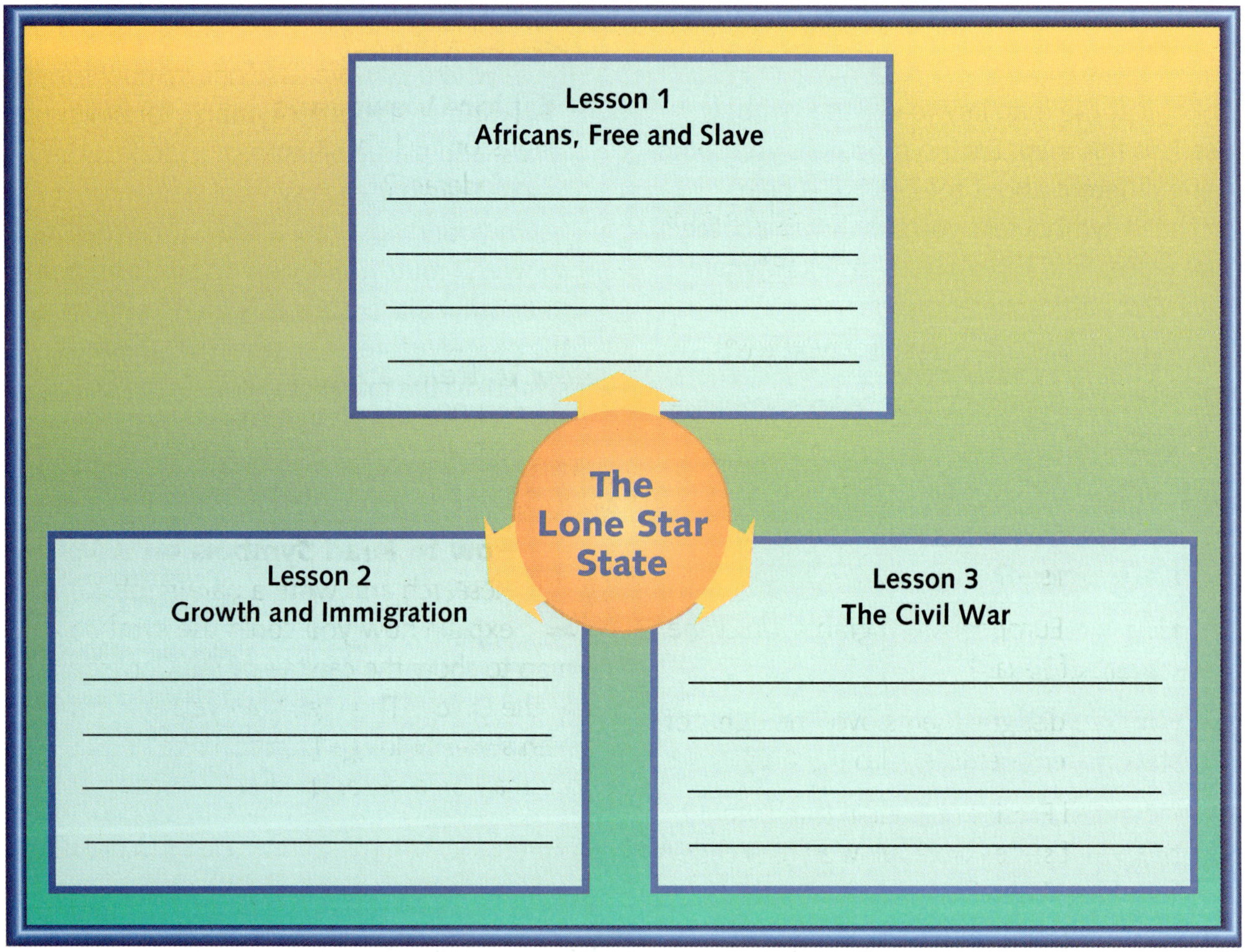


## WRITE MORE ABOUT IT

1. **Write a Comparison** Think about the lives of Africans in the new state of Texas. Then write a paragraph comparing their lives under slavery with their lives as free people after the Civil War. Share your paragraph with a classmate.

2. **Keep a Ship's Log** Imagine that you are traveling across the ocean from Europe to Texas. Keep a ship's log describing your journey. Tell why you left your old country and how you feel as you prepare to start a new life.

## USE VOCABULARY

For each pair of vocabulary words, write a sentence or two explaining how the words are related.

1. cotton gin, textile mill
2. secede, Confederacy
3. Reconstruction, sharecropper
4. civil war, Union

## CHECK UNDERSTANDING

1. Why did the number of enslaved Africans in Texas increase quickly after Texas became a state?
2. Where in Texas did most slaves live?
3. How did the Czech people keep informed in Texas?
4. In what way was life in Panna Maria different from what Father Leopold had promised?
5. How did European immigrants affect the culture of Texas?
6. How did disagreements over the rights of state governments lead to the Civil War?
7. What did President Lincoln think would happen if states were allowed to secede from the Union?
8. What did Texans do to help the Confederacy during the Civil War?
9. How did blockades affect Texas during the Civil War?
10. Where was the last battle of the Civil War fought?
11. When is Juneteenth celebrated in Texas?
12. How did sharecroppers pay landowners for the use of their land?

## THINK CRITICALLY

1. **Cause and Effect** In what way do you think the location of Texas made everyday life easier for Texans who stayed at home during the Civil War?
2. **Explore Viewpoints** Why do you think some European immigrants were against slavery but many people from the southern states were not?
3. **Explore Viewpoints** How did Sam Houston feel about Texas joining the Confederacy?

## APPLY SKILLS

**How to Read a Bar Graph** In 1850 there were 114,000 males and 99,000 females living in Texas. Make a bar graph comparing these two population numbers.

**How to Read Symbols on a Map** Research and write a paragraph to explain how you could use symbols on a map to show the capitals of the Confederacy and the Union. Then tell how you could show which states belonged to each one. Draw your map on a separate sheet of paper.

## READ MORE ABOUT IT

*Camels for Uncle Sam* by Diane Yancey. Hendrick-Long. This story describes how the United States Army experimented with using camels in the Southwest in the 1850s.

*A Paradise Called Texas* by Janice Jordan Shefelman. Eakin. Based on a true story, this book follows Mina and her parents in 1845 as they leave their home in Germany and move to Texas. Nominated for the Texas Bluebonnet Award in 1986.

CHAPTER 8

# THE YEARS AFTER THE CIVIL WAR

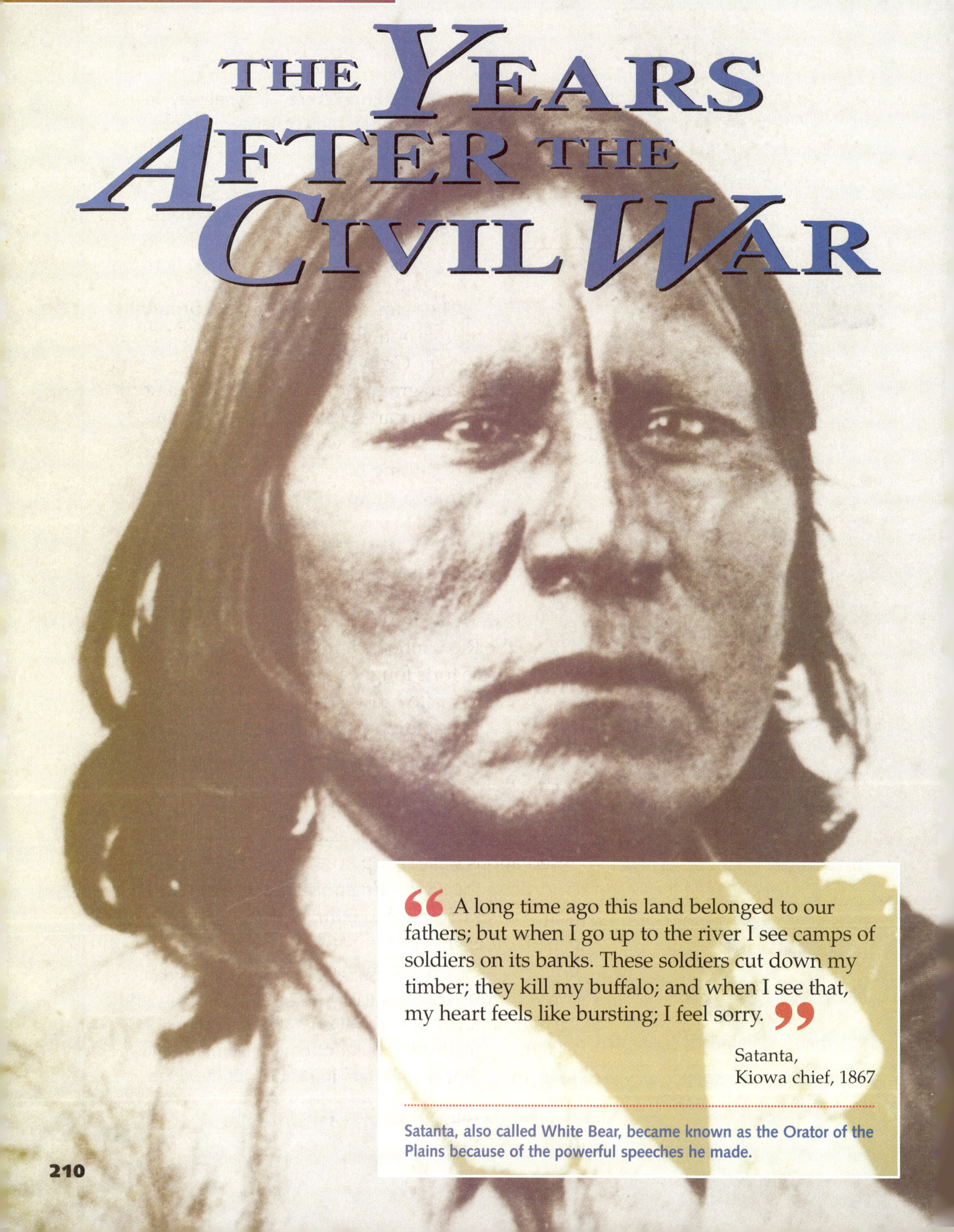

"A long time ago this land belonged to our fathers; but when I go up to the river I see camps of soldiers on its banks. These soldiers cut down my timber; they kill my buffalo; and when I see that, my heart feels like bursting; I feel sorry."

Satanta,
Kiowa chief, 1867

**Satanta, also called White Bear, became known as the Orator of the Plains because of the powerful speeches he made.**

LESSON 1

# WAR ON THE PLAINS

## Link to Our World

**What can cause a group's way of life to change?**

***Focus on the Main Idea***
**Read to find out what ended the way of life for Texas Indians in the late 1800s.**

***Preview Vocabulary***
**reservation**

Comanche horsehide shield

The years after the Civil War brought trouble both for Texas Indians and for Texas settlers. Growing settlements had pushed the Indian groups into the western and northwestern parts of Texas. As settlers began moving farther west, Indians became angry about losing their land.

### A New Government Plan

From 1849 to 1852 the United States government had built a line of forts in West Texas. The line stretched from the Red River to the Rio Grande. United States soldiers from these forts fought against the Comanches and Kiowas (KY•uh•wuhs).

The soldiers and Indians fought in other states in the West, too. The United States government decided to separate the Indians and the settlers. It planned to make the Indians move to **reservations**, land set aside only for them. Two reservations were set up in Texas in 1855 on unsettled land along the Brazos River. They covered more than 50,000 acres of land. More than 1,000 Caddos and members of other tribes were made to leave their lands and move to the reservations. Some Indians would not go.

Many Kiowas and Comanches did not agree to give up their land. They thought it was unfair for settlers to take their land and make them move to reservations. They fought back by attacking the settlers.

✓ **Why were Indian reservations set up?**

## TREATY OF MEDICINE LODGE CREEK

At Medicine Lodge Creek (above), the United States government gave the Indians sugar, coffee, and bread in addition to the nearly three million acres of land that was set aside for them. Comanche chief Ten Bears (right) refused to sign the treaty.

In 1867 the United States government held a meeting with the Indians to try to get them to stop fighting and move to the reservations. Chiefs from the Cheyenne (shy•AN), Arapaho, Kiowa, and Comanche people were among those at the meeting held at Medicine Lodge Creek in Kansas.

The government representatives offered the Native Americans land in the Indian Territory, which is now Oklahoma. To get the land, the Indians had to move within the boundaries of the reservation. The Indians also had to stop attacking white settlements.

The government said it would stop fighting with the Indians and keep its soldiers off the reservations. It would also provide food and other supplies for the tribes on the reservations. The government said it would treat the Indians kindly and fairly.

Some of the Indian leaders signed the treaty, but many did not. Comanche chief Ten Bears told why he did not.

> "If the Texans had kept out of my country there might have been peace. But that which you now say we must live on is too small. The Texans have taken away the places where the grass grew the thickest and the timber was the best. Had we kept that, we might have done the things you ask. But it is too late. The white man has the country which we loved, and we only wish to wander on the prairies until we die."

The buffalo was important to the Comanche way of life. The Comanches and other Plains Indians got almost everything they needed from the buffalo. On the reservations, there were not enough buffalo to meet the needs of all the Indians who lived there. Without the freedom to hunt buffalo off the reservations, the Comanches and other Plains Indians could not survive.

**✓ Why did the United States government hold a meeting with Indian leaders?**

## THE BUFFALO HUNTERS

In the early 1870s hunters began coming to Texas and the western United States to kill great numbers of buffalo. People had found a new way of making leather from buffalo skins, and the price of the skins had gone up. Buffalo hunting became an easy way to make money. A good hunter could kill hundreds of buffalo in a single day.

The hunters moved into the Texas Panhandle in 1873. Many Indians decided to fight to protect their way of life. They attacked settlers, soldiers, and hunters. In June 1874, Comanche, Cheyenne, and Kiowa leaders met to plan how to drive away the hunters. They decided to attack a camp in the Texas Panhandle.

The camp was at Adobe Walls on the Canadian River about 20 miles (32 km) northeast of present-day Borger. Adobe Walls was in the middle of one of the largest remaining grazing lands for the southern herd of buffalo, the Texas herd.

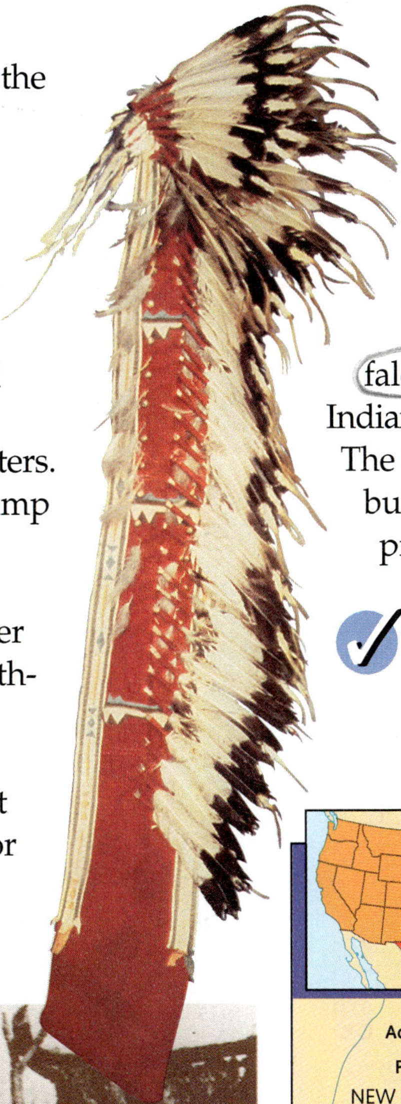

The Indians attacked in the early morning of June 27, 1874. But the hunters in the camp were able to hold off the Indians. Losing the fight at Adobe Walls made the Indians want even more to stop the buffalo hunters. In the next two months, Indians killed more settlers and hunters. The Indians felt that getting rid of the buffalo hunters was the only way to protect their way of life.

**Why did hunters kill so many buffalo?**

This buffalo hunters' camp on Evans Creek, Texas, was probably similar to the one attacked by Comanche, Cheyenne, and Kiowa Indians at Adobe Walls. The attacking Indians might have worn war bonnets like the one above.

## WAR ON THE PLAINS, 1871–1874

Map Skill

**REGIONS** The Comanches and the Kiowas were finally forced off their land after a series of battles in Texas between 1871 and 1874.

- In what part of the state were most of the battles fought?

Colonel Ranald S. Mackenzie (below) and about 500 soldiers followed a path to the bottom of Palo Duro Canyon (above) and surprised several villages of Indians. Many of the Indians escaped by climbing the steep cliffs of the canyon. A Kiowa artist later painted a tepee cover (center) with scenes of that attack.

## THE RED RIVER WAR

In August 1874 the United States government sent more than 3,000 soldiers to the source of the Red River in the Texas Panhandle. They were told to kill or remove all the Indians there. The battles that were fought between the soldiers and the Indians became known as the Red River War.

Colonel Ranald S. Mackenzie and his soldiers were sent to find the Indians who had attacked Adobe Walls. In late September Mackenzie learned that they were in Palo Duro Canyon, at the upper part of the Red River.

Palo Duro Canyon had been a safe place for Indians for hundreds of years. It had fresh water, and there were many animals for food. The high canyon walls kept them safe. Among the Indians in the canyon were the Quohada (kwoh•HAH•dah) Comanches, led by Quanah Parker; the Kiowas, led by Lone Wolf; and a few Cheyennes.

Just before dawn on September 28, 1874, Colonel Mackenzie led a surprise attack on the Indians at Palo Duro Canyon. Most of the Indians got away, but they had to leave their supplies and their horses. The soldiers burned the Indians' supplies and killed their horses.

The Indians faced a hard choice. They could try to live through the coming winter without food or shelter, or they could move to the reservations in the Indian Territory of present-day Oklahoma. All but a few gave up and moved to the reservations. Those who went on fighting, including Quanah Parker and his followers, finally gave up in June 1875. The Battle of Palo Duro Canyon was one of the last battles between the United States and the Texas Indians.

## Who?

### Buffalo Soldiers

Many of the soldiers who fought in the Red River War were African Americans. The Indians called them Buffalo Soldiers. The Indians thought that the soldiers' hair looked like that of a buffalo. The nickname was a sign of respect. The Indians saw the same fighting spirit in the Buffalo Soldiers that they saw in the buffalo.

**✓ Why was the Battle of Palo Duro Canyon important?**

## LESSON 1 REVIEW

### Check Understanding

1. **Recall the Facts** Why did the Indians attack the buffalo hunters at Adobe Walls?
2. **Focus on the Main Idea** What ended the way of life for Texas Indians in the late 1800s?

### Think Critically

3. **Think More About It** Why do you think some Indian leaders signed the treaty at Medicine Lodge Creek?
4. **Cause and Effect** Why would the Plains Indians not want other people to build settlements on the Great Plains?

### Show What You Know

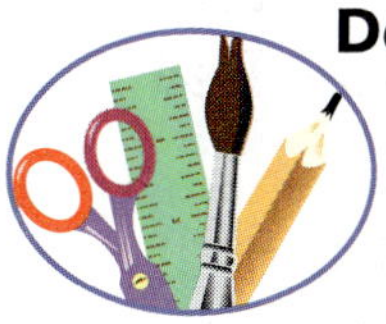

**Debate Activity** With your classmates, hold a debate on the question *Can people with different ways of life live together in peace?* Remember that a debate should show different points of view.

S·K·I·L·L·S

# HOW TO

## Predict Likely Outcomes

### Why Is This Skill Important?

You are careful when you cross a street because you know you could get hurt. You know what most likely will happen if you walk in front of a moving car. People make predictions every day. They look at the way things are and think about what will happen next.

### Remember What You Have Read

Think over what you have read about how the Plains Indians depended on the buffalo for their way of life. You can use this information to predict what you will learn next about how their life changed when they moved onto the reservations.

### Understand the Process

- Think about what you know.
- Make a prediction.
- Read or gather more information.
- Ask yourself some questions. Does the new information support my prediction? Do I need to change my prediction?
- Go through the steps again if your prediction does not seem to be correct.

### Think and Apply

BUILDING CITIZENSHIP

Predict what you will learn in the next lesson about the life of the Comanches on the reservations. Share your prediction with a classmate. As you read the next lesson, see if the new information supports your prediction.

*Land of Plenty* by John Clymer

LESSON 2

LEARN with LITERATURE

Focus on Reservation Life

# Quanah Parker

by Len Hilts

Quanah Parker was the last great war chief of the Comanches. After he and his followers moved to the Fort Sill reservation on June 2, 1875, Quanah Parker continued to lead his people in peace as he had in war. Some say he was able to bring peace between the two cultures because he had a Comanche father and an Anglo-American mother.

Cynthia Ann Parker was nine years old when she was taken from her home by Comanches in 1838. The Indians gave her the name Naduah, and she lived with them for the next 24 years. She married Peta Nocona, who became a chief, and had three children. Her first son was named Quanah.

Quanah Parker worked for peace on the reservation, but he knew how hard life was for his people there. Also, he was sad that the way of life he had grown up with was now gone.

The Comanche reservation at the edge of Fort Sill was a rectangle of wide, rolling plains, rich with grass and water. The purple-hazed Wichita Mountains stood behind it as a colorful backdrop. This land had been dear to the Comanches for centuries.

Even in this beautiful ancestral land, Quanah was sad and bitter at first. His people were full of discontent. His warriors, hunters for centuries, drew government rations every two weeks and could only dream of the days when they rode after buffalo across the plains.

**discontent** unhappiness

**rations** food and supplies in limited amounts

**coups** (KOOZ) daring moves showing how brave one is

They could not hunt, seek coups to build their fame, or tell of their deeds around the campfire. For them, there was no future. They lived, and yet they were dead.

No Comanche had ever planted a seed, and they could not bring themselves to do it now. They hated the cornmeal issued to them and fed it to their ponies. They were given beef, but preferred buffalo meat.

Not understanding their inner suffering, still the government tried to help. In 1876, the Indian Agent gave sheep to The People. The Indians had no taste for sheepherding and didn't like lamb chops or mutton.

Comanche lodges, once made of buffalo skins, now were of government-issue canvas. Colonel Mackenzie built houses for the leading chiefs, but they would not live in them. Accustomed to life in the prairie, they camped in the yards and let their dogs sleep inside. Quanah, just in from the plains, was not offered a house.

The Indian Agent tried simulated hunts. Each brave chose a steer in a corral, and the steer was turned out. Riding as his father once rode after buffalo, the brave shot the steer from his running horse. The women butchered the steer where it fell. It was an unsatisfying substitute for a real hunt.

Chief Mow-way said, "We are soaring eagles learning to live like barn owls." . . .

At age 18 Quanah Parker, whose name means "fragrance," became war chief of the Quohada Comanches, the tribe's largest band.

Mow-way was the head Comanche chief on the reservation. In 1878, he said to Quanah, "I am old. It is time for another to lead The People. The chiefs have chosen you, even though you are still a young man. Your white blood will be a bridge for us."...

Late in his life Quanah Parker built a house on the Fort Sill reservation so that his children could learn Anglo-American ways. He painted stars on the roof so that army generals who visited him could see that he had more stars than they had.

Quanah told Agent Haworth he thought a real buffalo hunt might ease the misery of The People. Haworth gave permission for an autumn hunt. As the leaves turned crisp, the whole tribe set out for the old hunting grounds.

The hunters ranged across the prairie for weeks but found no buffalo. The few antelope and deer they killed were barely enough to feed them. When the snow began to fall, they still had not seen one buffalo.

Quanah led The People sadly and in silence back to the reservation. They knew now that the old life was gone. Without buffalo, they could never live on the prairie again.

## Literature Review

1. Without hunting, how did the Comanches get their food on the reservations?
2. Chief Mow-way said, "We are soaring eagles learning to live like barn owls." What do you think he meant?
3. Use the information in the lesson to write a newspaper headline and an opening paragraph for a news article on the Indian reservation at Fort Sill, Oklahoma.

Partly because of his Anglo-American ancestry, Quanah Parker was able to bring peace between the Comanches and white settlers.

# LESSON 3 THE CATTLE KINGDOM

## Link to Our World

**How do people build businesses today?**

***Focus on the Main Idea***
**Read to find out how Texas ranchers built the Cattle Kingdom.**

***Preview Vocabulary***

| | |
|---|---|
| **longhorn** | **brand** |
| **cattle drive** | **stampede** |
| **long drive** | **barbed wire** |
| **breed** | |

Slavery had ended, but in the years after the Civil War, cotton continued to be a major product grown in Texas. New businesses, however, became important, too. During that time, Texans began to do more cattle ranching. From 1867 to the 1880s, cattle ranching was the main business and way of life in South and West Texas. Some people called these years the time of the Cattle Kingdom.

## THE BEGINNINGS OF RANCHING IN TEXAS

When Spanish soldiers and missionaries first came to Texas in the 1500s, they brought cattle with them for food. Some of the cattle got away and began to live in the wild. Different kinds of cattle bred with one another. The new calves were the first Texas longhorns.

**Longhorn** cattle were named for their unusually large horns. Sometimes the horns were more than 6 feet (2 m) from tip to tip. Longhorns had long legs and could run fast. If a longhorn was attacked by wolves or

Longhorns once numbered in the millions in Texas. The few that remain are kept for show rather than used for beef.

Mexican vaqueros were among those who worked the first large-scale ranches in Texas.

mountain lions, it could fight back with its horns or run away. Longhorns lived well in the dry brush country of South Texas.

During the 1700s and 1800s, the herds of longhorns in Texas grew. Many American and Mexican settlers who moved to Texas between 1800 and 1860 started ranches, catching longhorns to start their herds. These ranchers often chose land in South Texas along the Nueces and San Antonio rivers and along the Rio Grande. This land was too dry for most crops, but it was good grazing land for longhorns.

**Why were longhorns able to live well in the wild?**

## Early Texas Ranchers

One of the largest and best-known ranches in Texas was started by Richard King. King came to Texas during the Mexican-American War. He was a riverboat captain on the Rio Grande, and later he became a rancher. In 1852 King bought 75,000 acres of land in South Texas near Corpus Christi. After he died, Henrietta King, his wife, ran the ranch and bought more land. In time the King Ranch grew to more than 1 million acres. It was larger than the state of Rhode Island!

Richard King was only one of many early Texas ranchers. Aaron Ashworth, an African American, owned a large ranch in

Jefferson County in Southeast Texas. John Chisum set up one of the first ranches in North Texas. Manuel Músquiz started one of the first large ranches in West Texas.

Early Texas ranchers learned much from the Spanish and from Mexican vaqueros, who had been ranching for a long time. The Texas ranchers hired the vaqueros, who brought with them the skills, tools, and language of ranching.

The Mexican cowhands used a light rope called a lariat, from the Spanish words *la reata*. The lariat was also known as a lasso, from the Spanish word *lazo*. A contest of roping and riding took the name *rodeo*, from the Spanish word for *roundup*. Even the ranch itself got its name from the Spanish word *rancho*.

**From whom did early Texas ranchers learn how to run a ranch?**

## Rise of the Cattle Business

By the time of the Civil War, there were millions of longhorns in Texas. Because there were so many, they were not worth much money. In Texas, cattle sold for only about $4 each. Early ranchers raised cattle for leather and for tallow, or fat, which they used for making candles and soap.

In the years after the war, many people in northern cities wanted beef. The value of a longhorn rose from $4 to $40 in cities such as Chicago and New York. If Texas ranchers could get their cattle to northern markets, they could make more money.

There were no railroads from Texas to the cities in the north, so the only way to get cattle to market was by a cattle drive. It was called a **cattle drive** because the cowhands drove the cattle, or made them move, in the direction they wanted them to go. They drove them to railroad centers, first in Missouri

A lariat was an important tool. With this light rope, a cowhand could capture a 1,000-pound steer.

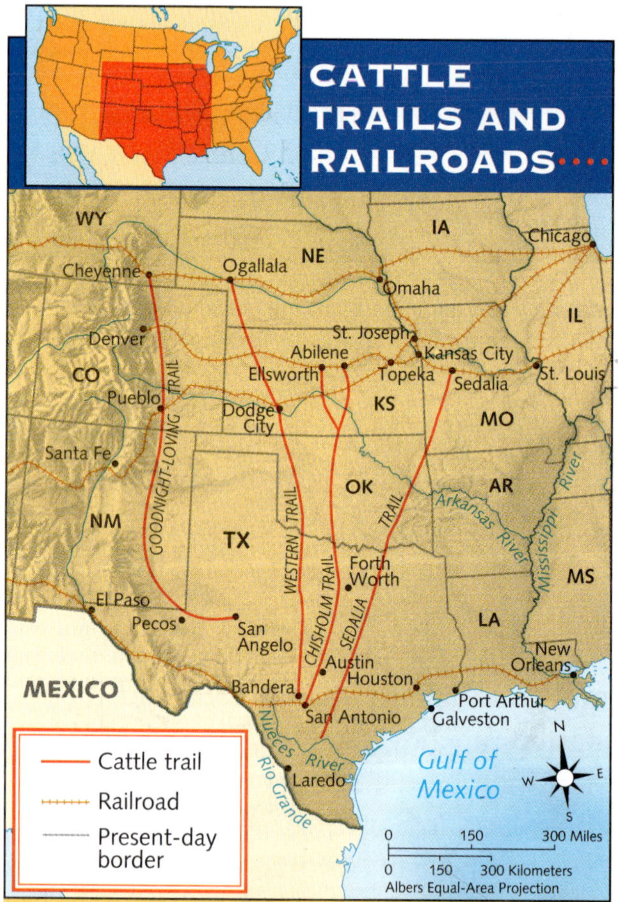


**MOVEMENT** Cattle trails extended farther north each year from 1866 until the late 1880s.

- Which trail would you take if you wanted to drive your cattle from Bandera, Texas, to Ogallala, Nebraska?

By the mid-1880s the J A Ranch, the ranch owned by Charles Goodnight and John Adair, covered more than 1.3 million acres of land in the Texas Panhandle and supported more than 100,000 head of cattle.

and later in Kansas, Nebraska, Colorado, and Wyoming. From there the cattle were transported by railroad to cities in the northern and northeastern United States.

The cattle drives followed several trails. One was the Chisholm (CHIH•zuhm) Trail. It was named for Jesse Chisholm, a rancher of Scottish and Cherokee ancestry. The Chisholm Trail started in South Texas, passed near San Antonio, Austin, and Fort Worth, and went on to Abilene, Kansas. When the cattle reached Abilene, they were sold and taken east by railroad.

Soon new trails went to other railroad towns, such as Dodge City, Kansas. Between 1870 and 1890, Texas ranchers drove about 10 million longhorns on the long trails north. These trips were called **long drives**.

**Why did Texas ranchers want to send their cattle to northern cities?**

## Famous Texas Ranchers

In 1876 Charles Goodnight started one of the first ranches in the Texas Panhandle. He used money from an Irish business partner, John Adair. Goodnight bred two different kinds of cattle, English Herefords and longhorns. Their calves were a new **breed**, or kind, that could stand the cold winters of the Panhandle. Goodnight's cattle also had more meat than the longhorns, so they could be sold for a higher price.

Another well-known Texas rancher was Daniel Webster Wallace. Wallace started working on long drives when he was 15 years old. He saved his money and

## What?

### Windmills

Windmills made it possible to start ranches in places far from water. Ranchers in areas where there were few rivers needed a way to use water from wells deep beneath the earth. Windmills provided the power to pump this water. Windmills have wide blades set in the shape of a wheel. When the wind strikes the blades, the wheel turns, which makes a pump work. As long as the wind blew—which it does much of the time on the High Plains—the pump would bring up a flow of groundwater from a well. Windmills made farming possible in West Texas.

bought a ranch near Colorado City. Like many African Americans of his time, Wallace had not been allowed to go to school as a child. To run a ranch, however, he knew that he needed to know how to read, write, and do mathematics. So when he was 25 years old, Wallace went to school.

Most ranchers were men, but some Texas women were also cattle ranchers. Margarita Villareal, Florencia Bonavide, and Paula Rodriguez owned ranches in Nueces County. Lizzie Johnson Williams and Margaret Heferman Borland also owned ranches. They even went on the long drives. Although women in Texas could own property, they still could not vote.

**Name two famous Texas ranchers.**

## Who?

### Nat Love (1854–1921)

Nat Love was one of the thousands of cowhands who worked in the great cattle drives from Texas. Love was born a slave in Tennessee, but he moved west to Dodge City, Kansas, after the Civil War. There he became an expert rider and roper. Love worked in cattle drives until 1889.

## COWHANDS AND THE LONG DRIVES

Cowhands helped drive the cattle north. One of every four cowhands on the long drives was Mexican or African American. Many African American cowhands were former slaves who had come to Texas after the Civil War. A cowhand's job was hard and often dangerous.

Work began with the spring roundup, when the cowhands gathered the cattle into pens. When the cattle were caught, they were marked with a **brand**, a symbol for the rancher who owned them. Most brands were the rancher's initials, but some were picture shapes, such as a rocking chair, a frying pan, or a bow and arrow. After the cattle were marked, the long drive began.

Each long drive took about 3 months. Cowhands spent 18 or 19 hours a day in the saddle, moving the cattle about 15 miles (24 km) a day. The cowhands worked in teams called trail outfits. Their leader was called the trail boss. Two cowhands led the way. Others rode beside and behind the cattle to keep the slowpokes moving.

At night the cowhands took turns staying awake. They had to be ready in case the cattle began to **stampede**, or

Cowhands took cooking equipment, such as funnels and matches, on the long drives. What do you think this funnel was used for?

run away. A sudden noise, like thunder, could scare them and start them running wildly across the plains.

**Why were cattle marked with brands?**

## The End of the Cattle Kingdom

The long drives, and the Cattle Kingdom itself, lasted only as long as there was plenty of land on the Great Plains available for grazing. By the 1870s ranchers began to lose their free grazing land. Farmers who shared the plains with the ranchers began fencing their land. They did not want thousands of longhorns running through their crops. Soon the ranchers, too, were fencing their land instead of letting their cattle roam free.

Before the 1870s most fences were built of rocks or wood. However, the plains of Texas did not have enough rocks or trees to build many fences. In 1873 Joseph Glidden of Illinois began to sell barbed wire. **Barbed wire** is twisted wire with sharp points, or barbs. A farmer or rancher could fence land by using only posts with this wire strung between them. A barbed-wire fence was easier and cheaper to build than a rock or wood fence.

Not all farmers and ranchers in Texas wanted the land to be fenced. Sometimes fences came between crops or cattle and the water they needed. Sometimes fences led to fighting.

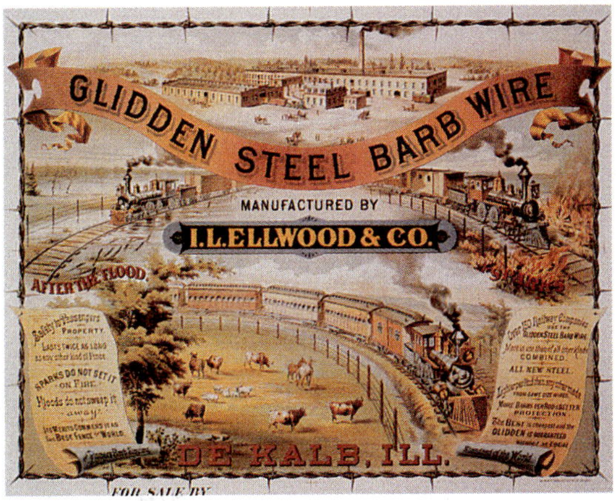


The invention of barbed wire forever changed the work of ranchers.

Barbed-wire fences made the long drives harder. Then the building of railroads into Texas ended the drives forever. By 1886 the state had more than 8,000 miles (12,874 km) of track linking it with the rest of the United States. Railroads now took the cattle to northern markets. They also brought more people to Texas.

**What caused the end of the Cattle Kingdom?**

## Lesson 3 Review

### Check Understanding

1. **Recall the Facts** Who were some of the best-known ranchers in Texas after the Civil War?
2. **Focus on the Main Idea** How did Texas ranchers build the Cattle Kingdom?

### Think Critically

3. **Think More About It** What do you think the ranchers had to think about when they made plans to send their cattle to market?
4. **Link to You** How does cattle ranching affect your life today?

### Show What You Know

**Poster Activity** Work with a partner to draw or find pictures of items the cowhands wore or took with them on a cattle drive. Write a caption for each item, telling how and why it was used.

LESSON 4

# THE RAILROADS COME TO TEXAS

## Link to Our World

**How does transportation help a place grow today?**

***Focus on the Main Idea***
**Read to find out how the railroads helped many Texas towns grow.**

***Preview Vocabulary***
**commission**

Most cowhands knew the tall tale of Pecos Bill. His parents lost him when he was a child, and he was raised by coyotes. As he got older, he did amazing things. He rode a tornado without a saddle. He roped longhorns with a rattlesnake. People said he knew everything about railroads. Railroads were important to Pecos Bill. They were even more important to the people of Texas.

A railroad conductor would often check a pocket watch to see if a train was on schedule.

## BUILDING RAILROADS IN TEXAS

When the Civil War ended in 1865, Texas had only a few railroads. There were only about 500 miles (805 km) of track in the entire state. All the track was built along the Gulf Coastal Plain. It connected port cities such as Galveston and Port Arthur with Houston and nearby farm areas. Trains were faster and less expensive than horse-drawn wagons for shipping goods.

In 1876 the state government began to give railroad companies land in return for laying track in Texas. In 1880 the Texas and Pacific Railway Company began laying track west of Fort Worth.

Railroads were important to the growth of many towns in Texas. People in North Texas towns such as Clarendon and Sweetwater moved their homes and businesses so they would be closer to the railroad. The Texas and Pacific was only one of many railroad companies laying track in Texas during the 1880s.

Railroads also linked Texas with Mexico. By 1900 Texas had nearly 10,000 miles (16,093 km) of railroad track, more than any other state.

**Why did railroad companies lay track in Texas?**

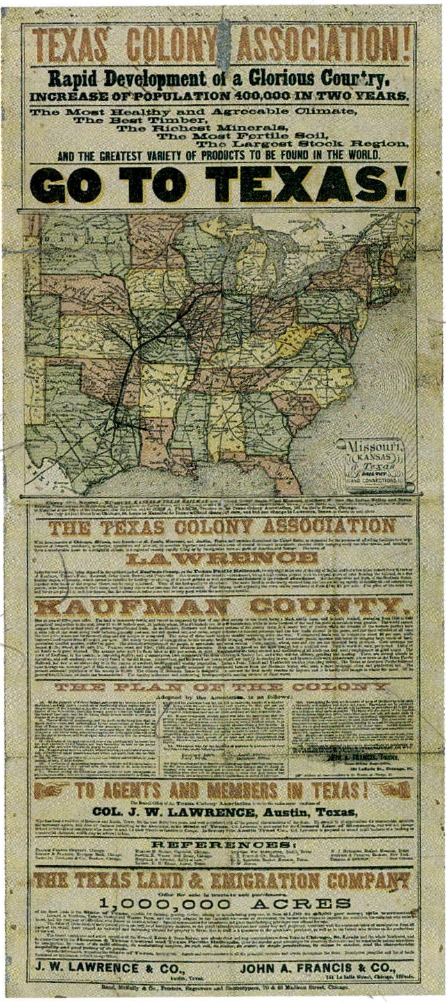


**LEARNING FROM DOCUMENTS** Railroad advertisements like this encouraged people to move to Texas.

- To what county in Texas does this company want people to move?

## The Railroad Changes Texas

Railroad owners wanted to sell the land they got from the state to new settlers. The railroads brought many of these people to West Texas.

As the railroads were built, West Texas changed very quickly. Farmers moved there in great numbers. New settlers built homes, schools, towns, and roads. The railroads carried the farmers' wheat and cotton crops and the ranchers' cattle to market. West Texas had been the home of the Plains Indians and the buffalo for hundreds of years. Now it was no longer the frontier it once was.

The railroads also helped Texas cities in the east grow

Providing rail service to some areas of West Texas was sometimes difficult. Do you think it was hard to build this railroad track near El Paso? Why or why not?

larger. One city that grew because of the railroads was Dallas. For many years it had been a small trading post. In 1860 only 750 people lived there. On July 16, 1872, the Houston and Texas Central Railroad Company brought the first train into Dallas. By 1873 the population of Dallas had grown to more than 7,000.

The railroads were both good and bad for Texans. Railroads helped settle West Texas and make East Texas cities grow. But the railroads also started charging higher prices for shipping goods. During the 1890s, when a drought hit Texas, life was hard for farmers and other business people who had to pay these high prices.

During his term as governor, James S. Hogg passed laws that required rail lines in Texas to properly maintain all their rail stations and other buildings.

To solve this problem, James S. Hogg, who was governor of Texas from 1891 to 1895, set up the Texas Railroad Commission. The **commission**, or special committee, made rules for all railroads in the state. It set prices and made sure that farmers and other business people were treated fairly.

Because Governor Hogg helped make laws that made many Texans happy, he became known as the People's Governor. He provided more money for the public school system and for the state colleges. He also improved the way the state prisons were run.

**Why did the railroad companies want people to move to Texas?**

## LESSON 4 REVIEW

### Check Understanding

1. **Recall the Facts** Name one city in Texas that grew because of the railroads.
2. **Focus on the Main Idea** How did the railroads help Texas towns grow?

### Think Critically

3. **Think More About It** How do you think giving land to the railroad companies helped the government of Texas? How did ... ange life for the Texans?

4. **Explore Viewpoints** What do you think was Governor Hogg's viewpoint on the importance of education?

### Show What You Know

**Research Activity** Research the railroads in Texas today. Find out which tracks are close to you and what services they provide. Share this information with your classmates.

SKILLS

# HOW TO

# Use a Time Zone Map

## Why Is This Skill Important?

A **time zone** is a region where people use the same time. A time zone map helps you find out what time it is in different time zones.

## Understand the Process

This map shows the time zones in the United States. You can see that most of Texas is in the Central Time Zone.

Look at the clock face that shows nine o'clock. It is above the Central Time Zone. Now find the clock face that shows eight o'clock. It is above the Mountain Time Zone. When it is nine o'clock in the Central Time Zone, it is eight o'clock in the Mountain Time Zone.

1. In which time zone is Dallas? El Paso?
2. When it is five o'clock in El Paso, what time is it in Dallas?

## Think and Apply

Map Skill

If you know the time in one time zone, you can figure out the time in another time zone. Write a paragraph that explains how to do this.

UNITED STATES TIME ZONES

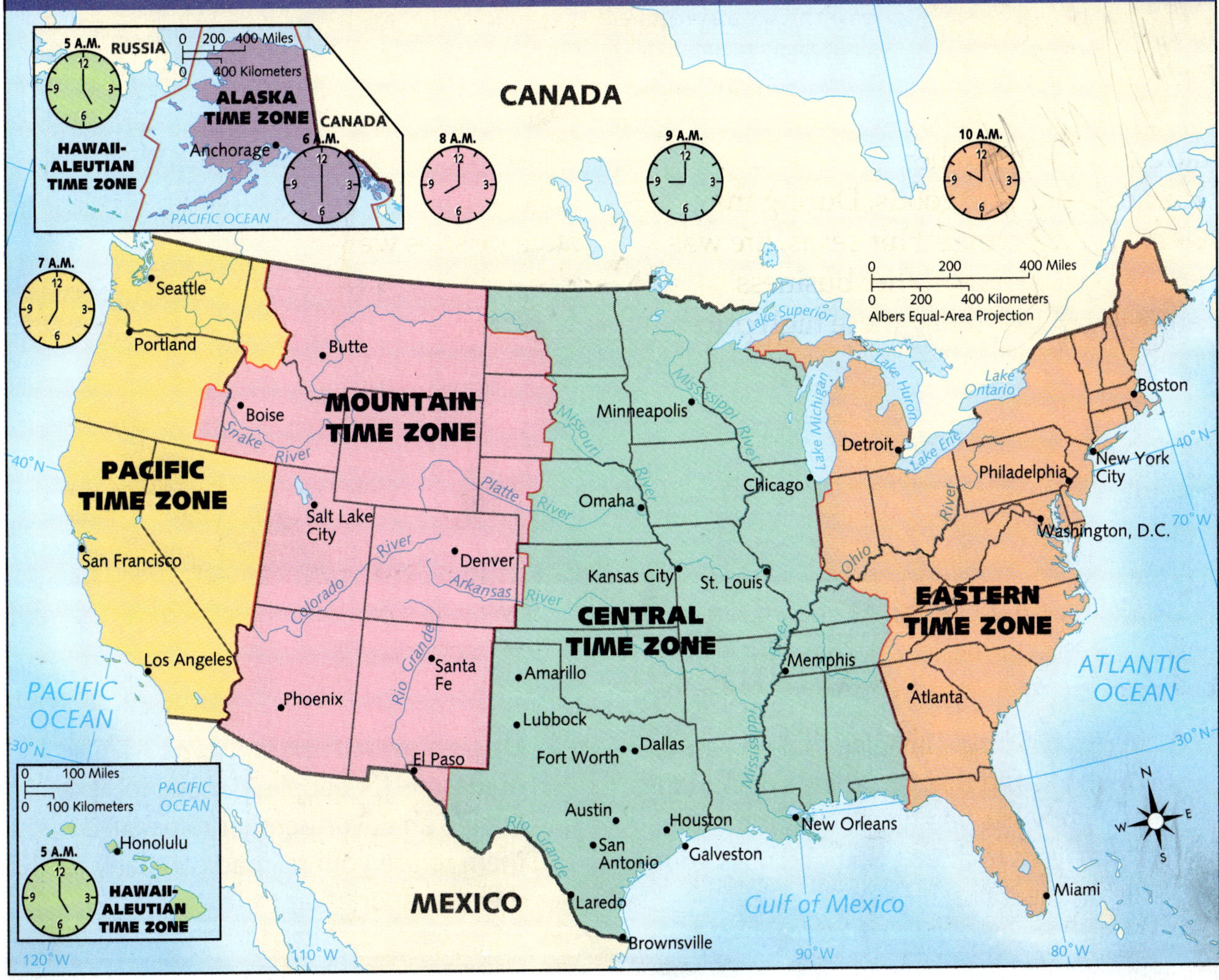

CHAPTER 8

# REVIEW

## CONNECT MAIN IDEAS

Use this organizer to show that you understand how the chapter's main ideas are connected. First copy the organizer onto a separate sheet of paper. Then complete it by writing a short phrase to summarize how each person, item, or event caused changes in Texas in the years after the Civil War.

**The Years After the Civil War**

**Lesson 1**

Reservations

______________________

______________________

Buffalo Hunters

______________________

______________________

Red River War

______________________

______________________

**Lesson 2**

Longhorns

______________________

______________________

Cattle Drives

______________________

______________________

Barbed Wire

______________________

______________________

**Lesson 3**

Railroads

______________________

______________________

Growth of Cities

______________________

______________________

Governor Hogg

______________________

______________________

## WRITE MORE ABOUT IT

1. **Write a Song** Imagine that you are a cowhand and that you enjoy singing songs at night while you watch over the cattle. Write lyrics to a song that describes your life on the trail.

2. **Design an Advertisement** Think of reasons for people to move to Texas. Design an advertisement to persuade them to use your railroad company for their transportation to Texas.

## USE VOCABULARY

Write a paragraph describing the cattle industry in Texas in the mid-1800s. Use each of the following vocabulary words in your paragraph.

1. longhorn
2. cattle drive
3. stampede
4. breed

## CHECK UNDERSTANDING

1. What did the United States government promise to do if the Indians would move onto reservations?
2. Why did buffalo hunters set up a camp at Adobe Walls?
3. Why was Palo Duro Canyon a safe place for the Indians?
4. What years were called the time of the Cattle Kingdom?
5. How did cattle get to markets in the northern and eastern parts of the United States?
6. Why did Charles Goodnight breed a new kind of cattle?
7. How did the Texas government attract railroad companies to the state?
8. What was the job of the Texas Railroad Commission?

## THINK CRITICALLY

1. **Link to You** What kinds of transportation link your town to the rest of the world, and how do they help your community grow?
2. **Explore Viewpoints** Why did Chief Ten Bears believe peace with the Texans was not possible?
3. **Think More About It** Why was the Battle of Palo Duro Canyon such a terrible defeat for the Indians even though most of them escaped?
4. **Cause and Effect** How did barbed wire make the cattle drives more difficult?
5. **Think More About It** In what ways did the railroads help farmers in Texas?

## APPLY SKILLS

**How to Predict Likely Outcomes** Think about the events that usually take place in your home on each day of the week. Predict the events that are likely to take place next week. What steps might you follow to make these predictions?

**How to Use a Time Zone Map** Imagine you are flying from New York City to Dallas. Your flight leaves at 7:00 A.M. and takes about 3 hours. Use the time zone map on page 229 to determine the time in Dallas when you land. Now imagine you are flying to Los Angeles. Your flight leaves Dallas at 12:00 noon and takes about 2 hours. What time is it in Los Angeles when you land?

## READ MORE ABOUT IT

*Charles Goodnight: Pioneer Cowman* by Sybil J. O'Rear. Eakin. Charles Goodnight led a life full of adventure as a cowhand, rancher, and Texas Ranger.

*Lizzie: Queen of the Cattle Trails* by Ann Fears Crawford. Benson. Lizzie Johnson started out teaching school and ended up driving her own herd of cattle.

Making Social Studies

# Relevant

## The Sounds of Texas Culture

People have come to Texas from all over the world—Africa, Asia, Europe, North America, and South America. Together all these people have given Texas a rich musical heritage.

Many of today's musicians continue the traditions that their ancestors brought to Texas. Mariachi (mar•ee•AH•chee) bands play the soulful popular music of Mexico. Blues, jazz, gospel, and spirituals are based on African traditional music. Country and western music comes from the music of European settlers in the rural American South.

Some musicians have combined these traditions to create new forms of popular music. Western swing music borrows from blues, country and western, and Mexican ballads. A style of music in Texas known as *conjunto* (KOHN•HUN•toh) combines forms of dance music—German polkas, Mexican waltzes, and Czech mazurkas. Tejano music, made popular by Texan singers such as Selena, combines *conjunto* with the rhythms of Latin American music.

Mexican dancers

## THINK AND APPLY

BUILDING CITIZENSHIP

Think of as many present-day Texas musicians, writers, and artists as you can. Identify the ways they have contributed to the state's cultural heritage. Create a classroom folder for the information you gather on present-day Texas culture.

Selena

Albert Collins

Mariachi musician

Stevie Ray Vaughan

Czech accordionist

UNIT 4

# STORY CLOTH

Follow the pictures shown in this story cloth to help you review the events in Unit 4.

## Summarize the Main Ideas

1. After Texas became a state, many settlers from the southern states moved to Texas. Many brought slaves with them. Most of the enslaved people in Texas lived and worked on cotton plantations.
2. Germans, Czechs, and Poles were some of the immigrants who moved to Texas from Europe.
3. Texas seceded from the United States, joined the Confederacy, and then fought in the Civil War.
4. Texans learned about the end of the war on June 19, 1865, as General Granger read a paper announcing that all slaves were free. In 1870 Texas rejoined the United States.
5. Disagreements over land led to battles between the Plains Indians in Texas and the United States government.
6. During the late 1800s, cattle ranching was the main business and way of life in South and West Texas. Ranchers would move their herds to northern markets on long drives.
7. Railroads brought many newcomers to Texas, moved cattle and goods, and helped Texas cities grow.

**Study the Pictures** Look carefully at the scenes in the story cloth. In a group, discuss how each scene shows a change in people's lives.

A Proclamation
905

UNIT 4

# REVIEW

## COOPERATIVE LEARNING WORKSHOP

**Remember**

- Share your ideas.
- Cooperate with others to plan your work.
- Take responsibility for your work.
- Show your group's work to the class.
- Discuss what you learned by working together.

Activity 1

### Create a Mural

Work in groups to create a mural about cotton. One group could study how cotton is farmed today. Another group could research the invention of the cotton gin. A third group could learn how textile mills spin cotton into cloth. Then work with classmates to create a mural that shows some of the steps in the process of growing cotton and making cotton products.

Activity 2

### Make Up a Game

Make up a game about the Texas railroads in the 1890s. The game should involve moving pieces on a game board that shows railroad tracks and cities in Texas. The object of the game is to reach the city of El Paso. Write a set of directions and rules for the game, and design a board and game pieces. Be sure to include on your game board things that would help or prevent travel. For example, your train gets rid of a heavy load and can now travel faster or an engine breakdown or broken track causes delays. Then form a team with a small group of classmates, and play the game against another team. See which team is the first to travel from Dallas to El Paso.

Activity 3

### Design a Postage Stamp

Work with a group of classmates to design a postage stamp that honors one of the people or events that you read about in Unit 4. Draw your design on a sheet of paper. Display your stamp with those of the other groups on a bulletin board for everyone to see. Write a paragraph explaining why you chose to honor that person or event.

## USE VOCABULARY

Fill in the blanks with the correct vocabulary word from the box.

| | |
|---|---|
| auctions | reservations |
| barbed wire | sharecropper |
| Juneteenth | stampede |

1. Enslaved people were often bought and sold at slave ________.
2. Texans celebrate ________ in honor of the Emancipation Proclamation.
3. The United States government wanted the Indians to move onto ________.
4. A crack of thunder might cause cattle to ________.

## CHECK UNDERSTANDING

1. What were some jobs held by free Africans in Texas before the Civil War?
2. Where in Texas did Civil War battles take place?
3. Why did the Kiowas and Comanches refuse to give up their land?
4. Why was South Texas well suited for ranching?
5. How did Governor Hogg help schools in Texas?

## THINK CRITICALLY

1. **Think More About It** How were the lives of sharecroppers and slaves alike? How were they different?
2. **Personally Speaking** If you had lived in Texas in 1861, how might you have felt about the state seceding from the Union?
3. **Cause and Effect** Which Indian group do you think would have found it easier to adjust to life on the reservations, the Caddos or the Tonkawas? Explain your answer.

## APPLY GEOGRAPHY SKILLS

### How to Read Symbols on a Map

European immigrants settled towns all over Texas. Use the map to answer the questions.

**EUROPEAN SETTLEMENTS IN TEXAS, 1865**

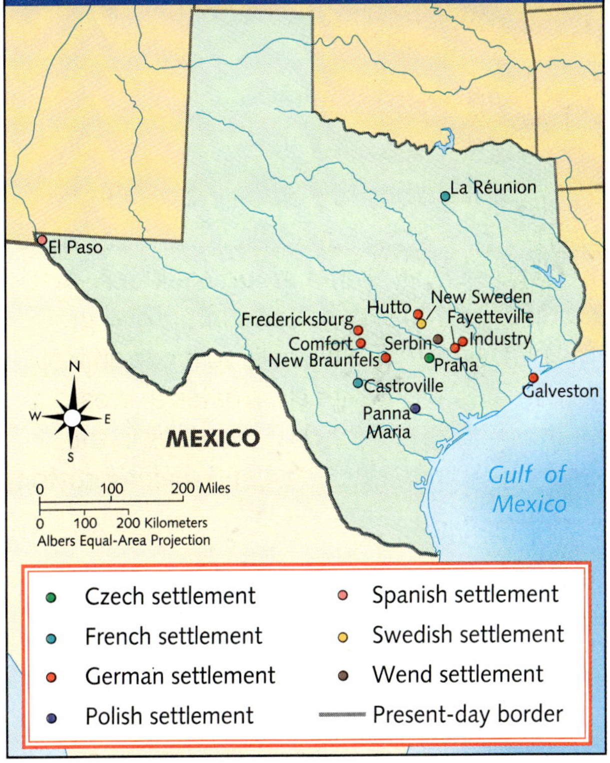


1. What is the color of the symbol for a Czech settlement?
2. Immigrants from which European country built the most settlements shown on this map?
3. Immigrants from which country settled La Réunion?

| UNIT 1 | UNIT 2 | UNIT 3 |
|---|---|---|
| The Land and Early People of Texas | Newcomers to Early Texas | The Republic of Texas |

UNIT 5

# Texas Grows and Changes

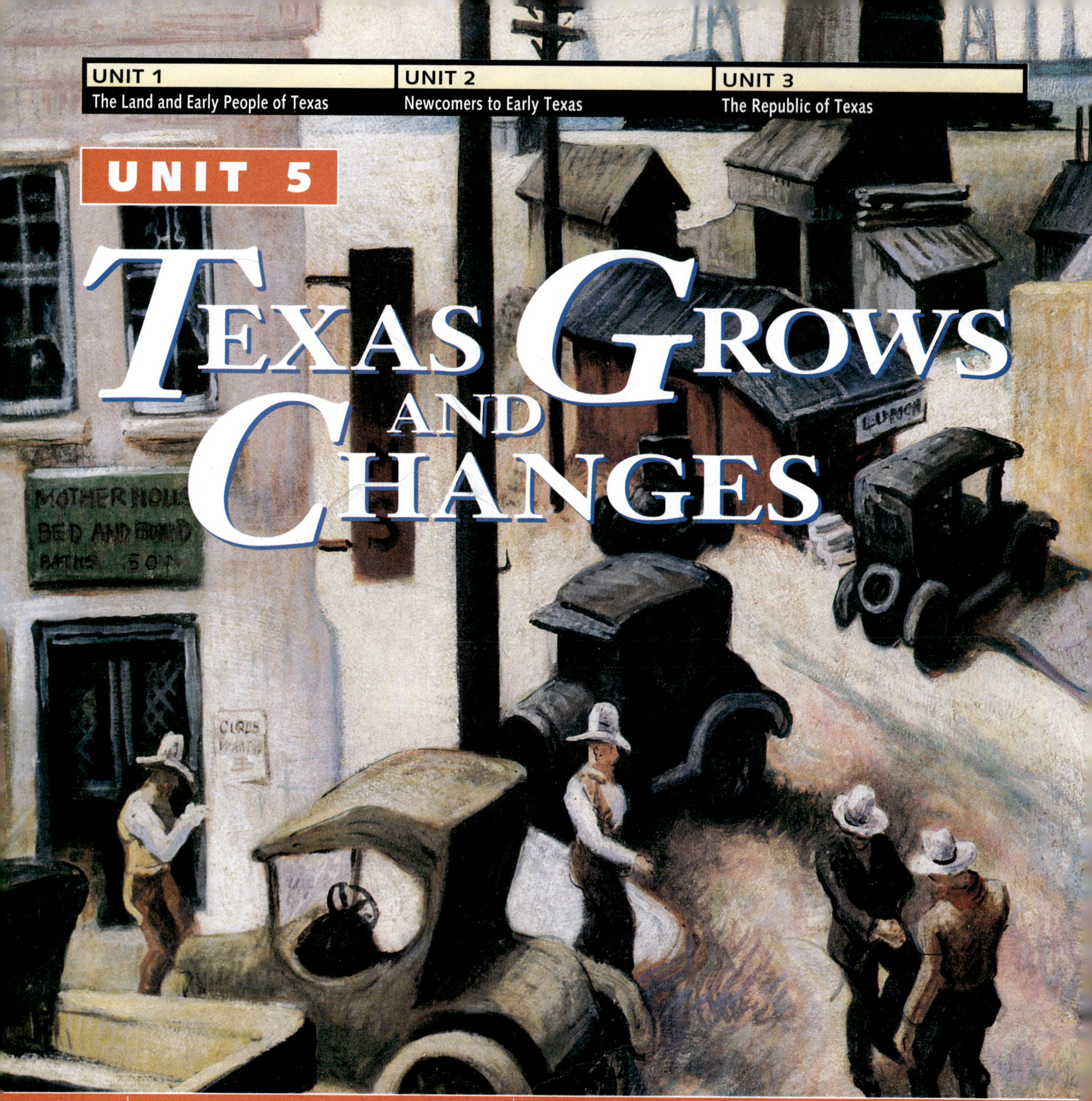


1900

**1901**
Oil is discovered at Spindletop

**1916**
Border conflict begins between Mexico and the United States

**1917**
The United States enters World War I

1920

**1920**
Women in the United States win the right to vote

**1929**
The Great Depression begins

**1930**
East Texas oil field is discovered

1940

**1941**
The United States enters World War II

In the year 1900 four out of five Texans lived on farms or in small towns. Most farmers grew only enough food for their families. Their houses were heated by fireplaces or iron stoves, and their water came from a well. Only the big cities had electricity. Life in Texas in 1900 was hard in some ways, but in other ways it was very peaceful.

In January 1901, however, life in Texas changed suddenly and forever. Oil was discovered near the town of Beaumont on the Gulf Coastal Plain. The quiet farming and ranching state was soon on its way to becoming an industrial state of large cities and modern factories.

**The town in Thomas Hart Benton's painting *Boomtown* was modeled after Borger, Texas. Thousands of people rushed to Borger after oil was discovered there in the late 1920s.**

**1960**

**1961**
The Manned Spacecraft Center is planned in Houston

**1963**
President Kennedy is killed in Dallas

Lyndon B. Johnson becomes President

**1969**
Neil Armstrong walks on the moon

**1980**

**1985**
Texas oil bust causes the price of oil to drop

**1988**
George H. Bush is elected President

**2000**

**1995**
George W. Bush becomes governor of Texas

*SET the SCENE*
*with Literature*

# Spindletop

**by Sibyl Hancock**
**illustrations by Geoffrey P. Smith**

**It was midmorning on January 10, 1901, and workers were drilling for oil on Spindletop hill near Beaumont, Texas. They had been drilling for three months without success. Then suddenly it happened—a gusher! Oil spurted from the ground without being pumped.**

**The following story is about a boy named Jimmy, whose father was one of the workers drilling for oil at Spindletop. Read now what it might have been like to be at Spindletop on that exciting day.**

As the wagon rounded a bend in the road, the top of Spindletop hill came into view. Jimmy could see the tall derrick that stood over the well.

**derrick** a tower built over an oil well to support drilling machines

"I wonder what it's like to strike oil?" Jimmy asked.

"Maybe we'll find out," Papa said.

Papa stopped the wagon at the top of the hill. Jimmy tied [his dog] Susie to one of the big wagon wheels. She had plenty of room to run and play.

"I picked up the new drill bit," Papa called to the men at the derrick.

"Good," Curt called back. "We will really need it."

Jimmy liked Curt. He liked the other men, too, but Curt was special. He wasn't as tall as Papa, but he was very strong. Curt had a wide grin, and he liked to tease Jimmy. Jimmy followed Papa up the steps to the derrick floor.

"Brought your dog today?" Curt asked. He reached over and rumpled Jimmy's hair with his big hand.

"Susie was hiding in the wagon," Jimmy said.

"Smart little dog," Curt said. "But she won't feel very smart if she gets caught in any of this machinery."

Jimmy nodded. "I'll keep her away."

"Let's go to work," Papa said.

Jimmy handed Papa tools. The sharp new drill bit was put onto the end of the pipe that had been drilling far into the ground.

"So far we can't break through that last layer of rock," Curt said.

Jimmy stared at the drill pipe. His heart sank. If they couldn't drill through the rock, then they would never find any oil.

Papa started the machinery, and the clattering, grinding noise began. "The drill is 700 feet down into the ground," Papa said.

Suddenly mud began boiling up past the drill. Then the drill pipe began rising. It went higher and higher and started going through the top of the derrick.

"Run!" Papa yelled. Jimmy scrambled off the derrick floor and ran as hard as he could toward the wagon.

"Look!" Curt shouted. The drill pipe was still coming out of the well. It began to break into pieces and fall to the ground. The last piece of pipe was followed by rocks and a deafening roar of gas.

"Great guns!" Curt exclaimed. "What was that all about?"

"Let's go see," Papa said. "Bring your shovel, Jimmy."

The floor of the derrick was covered with mud. And there was no sign of oil.

"What a mess," Jimmy said.

"Watch out!" Papa shouted. A great chunk of mud flew out of the well with an explosion like a cannon. A cloud of blue gas followed. Jimmy threw down his shovel and ran. The other men were close behind him.

Once again the noise stopped. Slowly the men walked toward the well. Jimmy climbed back onto the derrick floor. He was a little scared, but he wasn't going to let it show.

Papa stood over the well and looked down the hole. They could hear a bubbling sound deep in the earth. Then foamy oil began to pour out of the hole.

"Oil!" Jimmy cried. "It's oil!"

It was as if the well had a heart beating beneath the ground. The oil pushed upward, then settled back. And it kept pushing up a little higher with each great heartbeat.

All at once the oil spurted through the top of the derrick and kept climbing until it reached twice the height of the derrick.

"Ya-hoo!" Curt shouted. Everyone slapped each other on the back. Oil! They had struck oil. Jimmy blinked as the black oil soaked his clothes and sprayed into his face. Never in all his life had he seen anything like this.

CHAPTER 9

# TEXAS IN GOOD TIMES AND BAD

“To a large extent the contempt with which we are viewed . . . comes from the lack of . . . schooling. . . . We can make a vigorous effort . . . to teach our children, and to . . . prevent this harm in the future.”

Jovita Idár, journalist and teacher

Idár started a free kindergarten in San Antonio in 1917. Throughout the early 1900s she was active in causes important to women and Mexican Americans.

LESSON 1

# Oil Changes Texas

## Link to Our World

**How does oil affect your life today?**

***Focus on the Main Idea***
**Read to learn how the discovery of oil affected the lives of Texans in the early 1900s.**

***Preview Vocabulary***

| | |
|---|---|
| **refinery** | **service** |
| **boom** | **free enterprise** |
| **petroleum** | **entrepreneur** |
| **industry** | **wildcatter** |
| **good** | **interdependent** |

The 1900s began with one of the worst natural disasters in United States history. On the morning of September 8, 1900, a hurricane destroyed the city of Galveston. More than 6,000 people died. Texans were in need of some good news. A few months later, that news came from Spindletop—oil had been found in Texas!

The hurricane that struck Galveston on the morning of September 8, 1900, was one of the worst natural disasters in American history. How can people protect themselves from hurricane damage?

## Early Oil Discoveries in Texas

Before the discovery of oil at Spindletop, most people thought that only the eastern United States was rich in oil. Edwin Drake drilled the country's first oil wells in 1859 in Pennsylvania. When oil was first discovered at Spindletop, people learned that it could be found in huge amounts—very deep in the Earth—in other parts of the country, too.

The workers at Spindletop were not the first to find oil in what is now Texas. Indians of the Gulf Coastal Plain had gathered small amounts of oil that seeped out of the ground. They used it for fuel and medicine. The early Spanish settlers had used a solid form of oil called pitch to waterproof their boats.

In 1866 Texans in Nacogdoches County, in East Texas, found traces of oil in a spring. To reach the oil below ground, Lyne Barret used a steam-powered drill. His was the first known oil well in Texas.

At that time, people used oil to make grease for machines and kerosene (KAHR•uh•seen) to burn in lamps. People also used kerosene on roads to hold down the dust.

As more people used oil, the need for oil became greater. New oil fields were discovered in Texas in the 1870s and 1880s. In 1894 oil was discovered in Corsicana while workers were drilling a water well. The first big oil refinery in Texas was built at Corsicana. A **refinery** is a factory where oil is made into products such as grease and kerosene.

By 1900 hundreds of oil wells had been drilled in Texas. But the real **boom**, or fast growth, in oil production was yet to come.

**Where was the first known oil well in Texas?**

## Spindletop

In October 1900 Captain Anthony F. Lucas set up a wooden derrick on a hill 3 miles (5 km) south of Beaumont. Local people had called the hill Round Mound until Lucas set up his drilling rig. After that they laughingly called it Spindletop.

Lucas was a mining engineer born in Europe. He believed that there were pools of oil under the earth in the Gulf Coastal Plain. To reach the oil, Lucas sank pipe hundreds of feet into the ground. On January 10, 1901, his workers drilled into a 40-acre pool of oil under Spindletop.

For nine days the well at Spindletop gushed out of control. The thick, black liquid spouted high in the air, covering everything around it. Word of the oil strike spread quickly. Thousands of people went to see "a gusher gushing in Beaumont." Railroads had to run extra trains to carry all the visitors.

Before workers could control the gusher and store the oil in barrels, it spilled a lake of oil over the countryside. The Lucas well at Spindletop produced more than 75,000 barrels of oil a day. A barrel of oil contains about 42 gallons (159 L). By 1902 Spindletop was producing one-fourth of all the oil sold in the United States!

**When was oil discovered at Spindletop?**

In 1901 Anthony F. Lucas drilled the first well in what became the Spindletop oil field. During the next four years, 12,000 oil wells were drilled there. Spindletop is still a working oil field with about 50 wells.

Lucas's well at Spindletop gushed for nine days and produced 800,000 barrels of oil before workers put a cap on it.

## The First Texas Oil Boom

Soon there was more oil in the United States than people needed. Oil companies had to sell it for very little to get people to buy from them. The price of oil dropped to just three cents a barrel. When new kinds of **petroleum**, or oil, products were invented, the price soon went up again.

Railroads were the first to invent new uses for oil. They used the resource as a fuel for their locomotives. Oil was cheaper than coal and easier to get. Factories also began using oil instead of coal to run machines.

Automobiles were first sold in the early 1900s. Automobiles used gasoline, a fuel made from oil. As more people began driving automobiles, the need for gasoline and other petroleum products grew. This marked the beginning of the first Texas oil boom.

Before long, new oil-drilling companies were started, and the oil **industry**, or business, began to grow. All the new oil derricks, someone said, made Spindletop look like "a big thick forest of drilling rigs." New refineries were built nearby, too. Several large oil companies were started at this time. Texaco and Gulf both grew from the oil discovery at Spindletop.

The oil industry also helped other businesses grow. The oil companies bought lumber from East Texas to build derricks, and they bought pipe to carry the oil. Large ships, called tankers, and railroad tank cars had to be built, too. New factories were built to make all these products.

Thousands of workers in the oil fields and in the new factories needed goods and services. A **good** is a product people buy and sell, such as food or clothing. A **service** is an activity that people do for others, such as cutting hair or repairing shoes. Businesses providing goods and services grew quickly in towns near oil fields and factories.

**How did the oil boom help new businesses in Texas?**

The Spindletop oil field (above) produced 17,420,949 barrels of oil in 1902, one-fourth of the nation's total. In the United States there was little need for oil until the automobile became common (below).

## Free Enterprise and the Oil Industry

The growth of businesses in Texas as a result of the oil boom is an example of how free enterprise works. **Free enterprise** means that people are free to start and run their own businesses.

New businesses are started by entrepreneurs (ahn•truh•pruh•NERZ). **Entrepreneurs** are people who organize and run businesses. To do this, they must have three kinds of resources. They must have natural resources, such as land, water, or fuel. They must have human resources, or workers. They must also have capital resources, or the money, buildings, machines, and tools needed to run a business.

If the business does well, the entrepreneur makes a profit. If people do not want the goods or services the business sells, the business fails. Some entrepreneurs in Texas became rich during the oil boom, while others lost all their money.

During the oil boom, some entrepreneurs made money by renting or selling their land. A few months after the oil strike at Spindletop, the price of land in Beaumont went up. Some land sold for more than $1 million an acre!

**How did entrepreneurs make a profit during the Texas oil boom?**

## Oil and Interdependence

After the discovery at Spindletop, people looked all across Texas for new oil fields. Soon oil was found at Sour Lake and at

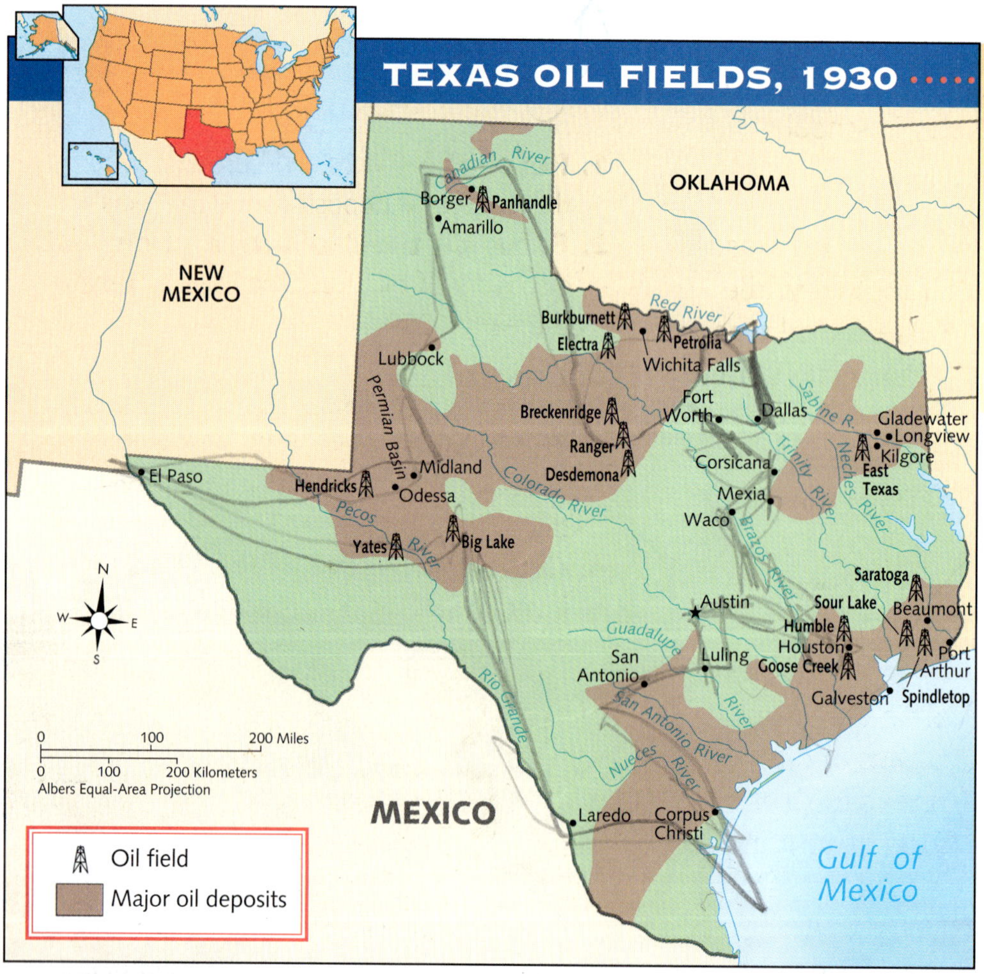


**Map Skill** **REGIONS** The discovery of oil in many areas of Texas led to the building of new towns.

- In what regions of Texas were most oil deposits discovered?

## Who?

### Howard Robard Hughes, Sr. 1869–1924

With the discovery of oil at Spindletop in 1901, Howard Robard Hughes, Sr., saw an opportunity for a new business. He then moved from Missouri to Beaumont, Texas, to set up a drilling business. He quickly learned, however, that much Texas oil lay beneath rock too hard for the tools then in use. In 1908 Hughes invented a new drill bit, or point, that could drill through the hard rock. His invention made him richer than perhaps an oil discovery would have. Howard Robard Hughes used much of his money to help good students stay in school.

Humble, near Houston. In North Texas, W. T. Waggoner found oil in 1904 while drilling for water. In West Texas, oil was found in the 1920s in the Permian Basin of the High Plains near Midland and Odessa. Between 1901 and 1930, oil was discovered in more than 200 of the 254 counties in Texas.

The biggest oil discovery in Texas history was made near Kilgore, in East Texas, by Columbus Marvin "Dad" Joiner. Dad Joiner was a **wildcatter**, a person who searches for new sources of oil. On September 8, 1930, Joiner sank a well into a 200-square-mile (518-sq-km) underground lake of oil. It was the greatest deposit of oil in the world up to that time. The East Texas oil field produced more than 100 million barrels of oil in its first year.

People in other parts of the United States began to depend on Texas for oil. With money from the sale of petroleum products, Texans bought machines, lumber, and other products from other regions in Texas as well as from other states and countries. This trade of oil for other goods made the regions of Texas interdependent. It also made the United States and other countries around the world interdependent. **Interdependent** places, regions, states, or countries depend on one another for goods or services.

**✓ How did the discovery of oil change Texas?**

## LESSON 1 REVIEW

### Check Understanding

1. **Recall the Facts** Where and when was the largest oil deposit found in Texas?
2. **Focus on the Main Idea** How did the discovery of oil affect the lives of Texans in the early 1900s?

### Think Critically

3. **Think More About It** What might Texas be like today if oil had not been discovered in the state?
4. **Cause and Effect** What effect did the invention of the automobile have on the oil industry?

### Show What You Know

**Descriptive-Writing Activity** Imagine that you are a reporter describing what happened on the day of the oil strike at Spindletop. Write an article for your classmates, telling what you saw and heard.

S·K·I·L·L·S

# How To

## Read a Cross-Section Diagram

### Why Is This Skill Important?

Imagine that you make a model of a mountain out of clay. Then you slice through the model by cutting down from the top. What you have is a **cross-section** model. The model shows the inside of the clay mountain. A diagram can also show a cross-section. The diagram on this page is a cross-section of what the Earth under Spindletop might look like. The diagram helps you understand what you cannot see. In this diagram you can see different layers of soil, rock, gas, and oil under the ground.

### Remember What You Have Read

Captain Anthony F. Lucas, the person who discovered oil at Spindletop, believed that there was oil under the ground along the Texas Gulf Coastal Plain. He thought oil might have been trapped in large pools between layers of rock. Often natural gas, another kind of fuel, is trapped along with the oil.

### Understand the Process

A cross-section diagram has parts like those of a map. Knowing what to look for can help you understand what the diagram is showing.

- What do the labels on the diagram tell you?
- How is a cross-section diagram like a map?
- What can a cross-section diagram show that a map cannot show?
- What does the diagram tell you about Lucas's belief that there were pools of oil under the ground?

### Think and Apply

Draw a cross-section diagram of the Earth that is under the ground where you live. There may be water wells, coal mines, caves, or oil wells. You might need to find out more about your region in some reference books. Use your diagram to explain to a classmate what cannot be seen under the ground.

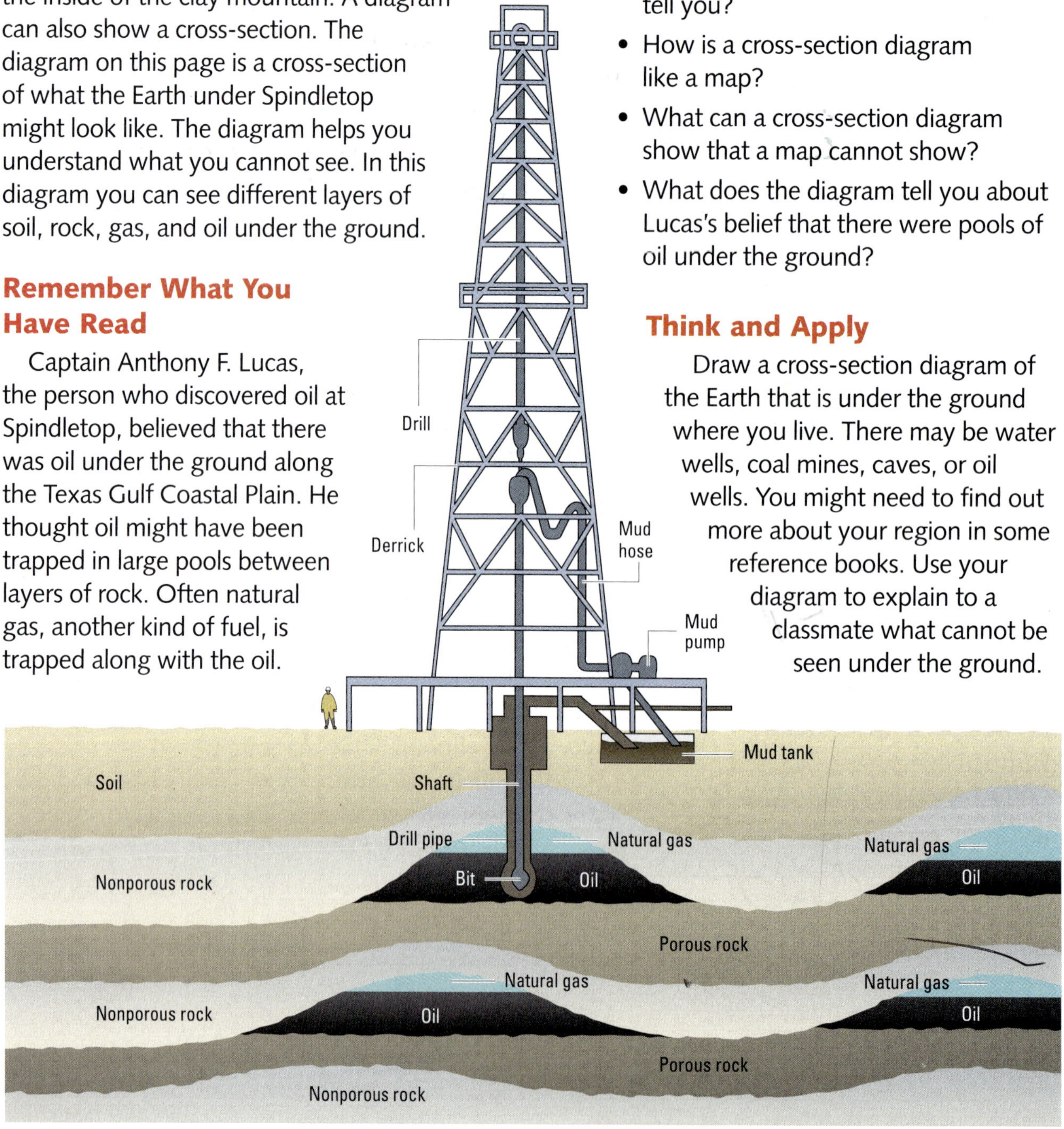

LESSON 2

# Texas in a Changing World

## Link to Our World

**How do events that happen outside the state affect people in Texas today?**

***Focus on the Main Idea***
**Read to find out how events that happened outside Texas affected the lives of many Texans in the early 1900s.**

***Preview Vocabulary***
**civil rights**
**shortage**
**cash crop**
**commercial farm**
**tenant farmer**
**suffrage**
**amendment**

By the early 1900s the United States had become a powerful country. When conflicts with other countries began, Texas became an important part of the events that were happening throughout the world.

## Border Troubles

In 1911 the Mexican president, Porfirio Díaz (pawr•FEER•yoh DEE•ahs), was overthrown in a revolution. Two new leaders fought for control of the government. Both Venustiano Carranza (veh•noos•tee•AH•noh kah•RAN•zah) and Francisco "Pancho" Villa (VEE•yah) wanted to be president. The civil war in Mexico led to trouble in Texas and other states along the border of Mexico.

When the United States recognized Carranza as Mexico's new president, Pancho Villa became angry. He and his soldiers attacked towns in Texas and New Mexico. They killed 66 United States citizens.

In 1916 President Woodrow Wilson sent United States soldiers into northern Mexico to capture Pancho Villa. They did not catch him, but their invasion caused bad feelings between Mexico and the United States for many years. However, the two countries did not get into another war with each other like the one they had fought in 1846.

To many Mexicans, Francisco "Pancho" Villa was a hero of the revolution.

The United States' invasion of Mexico was one more sign of trouble between Anglo Texans, or Anglos, and Mexican Texans, or Tejanos. In South Texas, in the Rio

Grande Valley, some Anglo farmers tried to make Tejano ranchers sell their land. Many Tejano families had been living on the same land in the Valley since before the Texas Revolution.

The Tejanos formed groups to work peacefully for their **civil rights**, the rights of citizens to vote and own property. Some Tejanos, however, wanted to secede from Texas and set up their own republic.

Fighting broke out between the Anglos and the Tejanos and hundreds of people were killed. "The conflict turned the Valley into a virtual war zone," said one historian. In the end, thousands of Tejanos were made to sell their land to Anglos and leave Texas.

Later, in 1929, the League of United Latin American Citizens (LULAC) was formed. Today, this group continues to work for the civil rights of all Mexican American citizens.

**What caused conflict between Tejanos and Anglos?**

This arch was built in San Antonio to welcome the soldiers returning from World War I.

## World War I

The United States' invasion of Mexico in 1916 prepared some American soldiers for more fighting. In 1917 the United States entered a war in Europe. It was later called World War I.

Texas had a very important part in the war. Four training centers—Camp Bowie in Fort Worth, Camp Travis in San Antonio, Camp Logan in Houston, and Camp MacArthur in Waco—were set up to teach soldiers how to work together. Many pilots were trained in San Antonio, where Marjorie and Katherine Stinson and their family ran the Stinson Flying School.

The return home from war was not joyous for some soldiers. This soldier lost his leg in the war.

More than 200,000 Texans from all ethnic groups went to Europe to fight in the war. Those at home helped fight the war in other ways. They raised money for the soldiers. Some women took jobs in factories when men left to fight.

The war caused shortages of food and other goods. A **shortage** of something means that there is not enough of it for everyone. People were asked to use less flour and other foods so there would be enough for the soldiers.

The war ended in 1918. More than 5,000 Texans had died in the fighting. Many soldiers returned home wounded. People thought that the war would bring a lasting peace.

**How did Texans at home help the soldiers in World War I?**

## The Growth of Farms

Ever since the start of the oil industry, farms all over the United States had been changing. Many large farms began using gasoline-powered machines to get more work done by fewer people. New harvesters made gathering crops easier. New kinds of fertilizer were used. Better ways to irrigate made it possible to grow more crops in dry parts of the state.

By the end of World War I, these changes in farming had made cotton and wheat the most important cash crops in Texas. A **cash crop** is one sold to earn money. In the early 1900s farmers began to grow a new cash crop. Seito Saibara (SAY•toh sy•BAH•rah) moved to Texas from Japan to farm rice in Texas. With his family and friends, he grew rice on land near Houston.

Meanwhile, in South Texas, on land where Tejano ranchers once grazed their cattle, Anglo farmers set up commercial farms. A **commercial farm** grows only cash crops. These farmers grew huge amounts of vegetables and citrus fruits. The commercial farmers depended on workers from Mexico to harvest the crops.

Although there were many commercial farms by the 1920s, many of the state's farmers were **tenant farmers**. They farmed on land rented from others. Many tenant farmers did not earn enough money to buy the kinds of machines and fertilizers the large commercial farms used. So they did not prosper.

**What crops did Texas farmers raise?**

## The Growth of Cities

With the new ways of farming came larger farms and more crops. Modern farming methods also led to the growth of cities. Cities in Texas became centers of trade and transportation. Dallas became an important market for lumber from the forests of East Texas and for cotton. The cotton and rice from Southeast Texas contributed to Houston's growth.

> ***"Houston is the only city that dared to dig a ditch to the sea."***
>
> Will Rogers

Something else that helped Houston grow was the construction of a wider, deeper channel along Buffalo Bayou to connect Houston to Galveston Bay. In 1914 the 57-mile (92-km) Houston Ship Channel was opened to ocean ships. Writer Will Rogers said, "Houston is the only city that dared to dig a ditch to the sea." The Houston Ship Channel gave the city a link to the Gulf of

New gasoline-powered equipment helped farmers produce more food with less labor.

## TEXAS CITIES WITH POPULATIONS OF 25,000 OR MORE

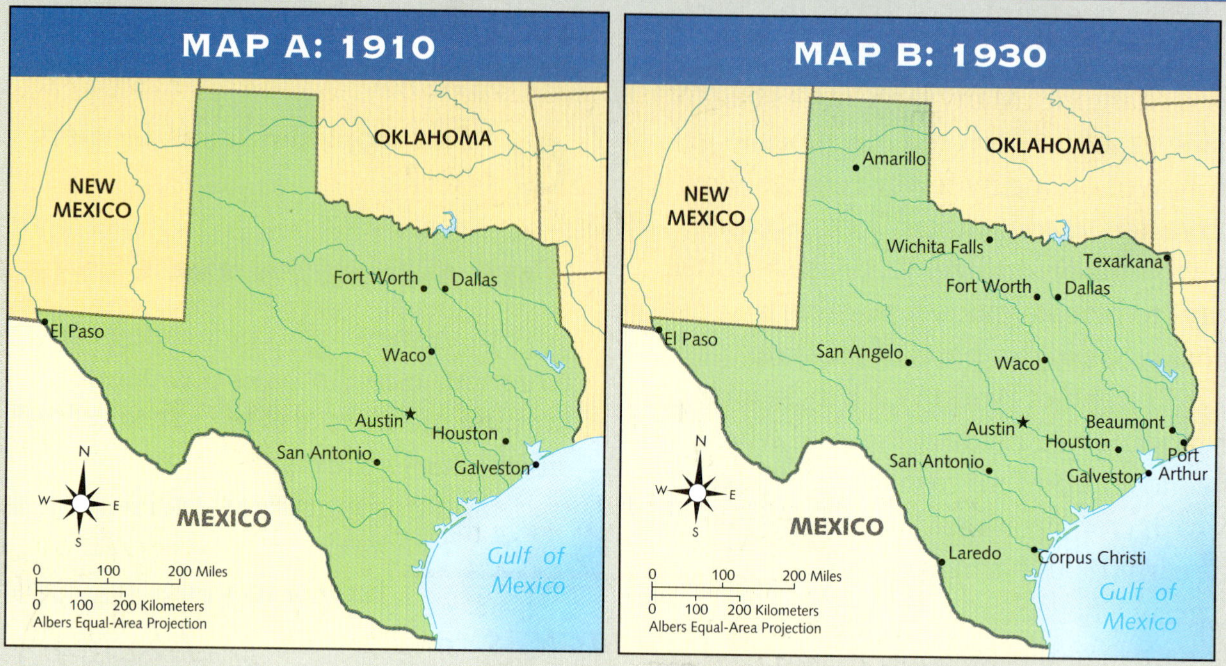


Map Skill

**HUMAN-ENVIRONMENT INTERACTIONS** In 1910 most Texans lived on farms or in small towns. But by 1930 Texas had become a more urban state.

- What might have been some reasons Corpus Christi was a large city by 1930?

Mexico and to markets all over the world. In the United States today only New York City and New Orleans are busier port cities.

Many Texas cities grew because of the oil industry. Between 1900 and 1930, Beaumont, Houston, Port Arthur, Midland, and Odessa grew the fastest. People from other states came to these cities to find work in the oil fields. Among these people were many French-speaking Cajuns from Louisiana. They brought to Texas their food, music, and customs.

San Antonio grew when the United States government set up military training centers there during World War I. These centers remained open after the war, providing jobs and bringing many new people to San Antonio.

**Which cities grew the fastest between 1900 and 1930?**

## Texas Women Get the Right to Vote

Before 1920 women in the United States were not allowed to vote. Women in Texas had begun working for **suffrage** (SUH•frij), or the right to vote, as early as 1893. They set up a group called the Texas Equal Rights Association. Its goal was "to advance education and equal rights for women and to secure suffrage." When the group made women's suffrage its chief goal, it changed its name to the Texas Equal Suffrage Association.

Leaders for women's suffrage, such as Christia Adair, Mary Eleanor Brackenridge, Minnie Fisher Cunningham, and Jovita Idár (oh•VEE•tah ee•DAR), led meetings and wrote for newspapers across the state to let people know it was important for women to have the right to vote. In 1918, Texas lawmakers voted to give women the right to vote in some state elections.

Women all over the United States were working for suffrage during this time too. In 1919 the Texas legislature agreed to the Nineteenth Amendment to the United States Constitution. An **amendment** is a change in the Constitution. When the Nineteenth Amendment was approved in 1920, women across the country at last had the right to vote in all elections.

In 1924 Miriam "Ma" Ferguson was elected governor of Texas. She was the wife of former governor James E. "Pa" Ferguson, who was elected in 1914. Miriam Ferguson was the country's second woman governor. Nellie Tayloe Ross of Wyoming, the country's first woman governor, had been elected two weeks earlier.

**How did women work for the right to vote?**

## Who?

### Christia Adair 1893–1990

Christia Adair played an important role in the struggle to give women the right to vote. The women of the Texas Equal Suffrage Association would not let Adair join their group because she was an African American. Instead, she went on her own from house to house collecting signatures on petitions for women's suffrage. When white Texas women got the right to vote in 1918, Adair and other black women still were not allowed to vote. Adair did not give up. She continued to work so that African American women could enjoy the same rights as all other Texans.

## LESSON 2 REVIEW

### Check Understanding

1. **Recall the Facts** In what ways did Texans support the United States in World War I?
2. **Focus on the Main Idea** How did events that happened outside Texas in the early 1900s affect the lives of Texans?

### Think Critically

3. **Cause and Effect** How did new machines and fertilizers bring about change on Texas farms?
4. **Explore Viewpoints** Imagine that you are a Tejano living in South Texas in the early 1900s. Why might you support setting up a republic for Tejanos?

### Show What You Know

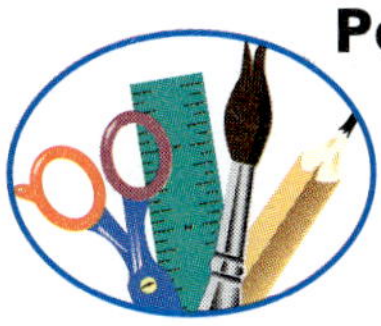

**Poster Activity** Make a poster that asks Texans to support the Nineteenth Amendment. Display your poster in the classroom.

# THE GREAT DEPRESSION AND WORLD WAR II

LESSON 3

## Link to Our World

**How might people today act in hard times?**

***Focus on the Main Idea***

**Read to learn how Texans faced the Great Depression and World War II.**

***Preview Vocabulary***

**depression**
**conserve**
**unemployment**
**reservoir**
**synthetic**

The 1920s was a good time for many Texans. People had extra money to spend. By 1926 there were more than 1 million automobiles in Texas. New oil fields were found, and the oil industry boomed again. In 1929, however, hard times took the place of good times for many people in Texas and the rest of the United States.

### THE GREAT DEPRESSION

Poor business decisions by many people led to problems for the nation in 1929. Banks that had loaned too much money had to close. When the banks failed, many people lost their savings. Because people had little money, they bought few goods and services. More businesses failed. Workers lost their jobs. Many people became homeless.

Mrs. Ollie Prince remembers how her family in Texas lived without much money to buy clothing. They used the cloth sacks that flour, salt, and animal feed came in.

> "We used feed sacks for just about everything we made. This included towels, sheets, pillowcases, cup towels, dishrags, quilt linings, and window curtains. . . . We made shirts for men; baby clothes and diapers; dresses, bonnets, and hats; tablecloths and chair cushions. Feed sacks were put to use for just about everything we needed. We didn't have the money to buy cloth or storemade clothes; we were glad to have those feed sacks."

Soup kitchens, like this one in San Antonio, provided free meals to people left poor by the Great Depression. What other kinds of help would people have needed during the Great Depression?

This period of hard times was called the Great Depression. A **depression** is a time when jobs are scarce and people have little money. The Great Depression lasted for nearly ten years.

**What problems did the Great Depression cause?**

## The Dust Bowl

Many of the farmers in Texas were hit hard by the Great Depression. By the 1930s prices for most crops had dropped. Cotton sold for as low as five cents a pound. Some Texas farming towns held money-raising drives to keep the commercial farms from going out of business.

During the Great Depression, farmers in Texas were also hit with natural disasters. Years of drought ruined many farms in the Texas Panhandle. Strong winds caused huge dust storms that blew away the dry soil. Parts of the Texas Panhandle and nearby Oklahoma, Kansas, Nebraska, Colorado, and New Mexico became known as the Dust Bowl.

One Sunday afternoon in April 1935, a dust storm hit near Perryton, in the Panhandle. Many people were outside when the dust clouds swept in. At that time a young songwriter named Woody Guthrie lived in Pampa, south of Perryton. He later wrote a song about what he saw.

> "A dust storm hit and it hit like
> thunder;
> It dusted us over and covered us
> under;
> Blocked out the traffic and blocked
> out the sun.
> Straight for home all the people did
> run, singing:
> So long, it's been good to know yuh."

Pauline Robertson was 13 years old when the first great dust storm hit Amarillo. She was playing outside.

> "We were running away from it and toward home when the wind hit, pelting our bare legs with gravel. We choked and gasped and ran as the air thickened with brown dust."

In time it began to rain, and people took action to **conserve**, or save, the land. They planted trees to serve as windbreaks. Farmers used better plowing methods to stop soil erosion. By the time the Dust Bowl years ended, many people had left Texas.

**What was the Dust Bowl?**

**Map Skill** **REGIONS** The Dust Bowl covered about 50 million acres of land, mainly in Colorado, Kansas, New Mexico, Oklahoma, and Texas.

- Which state has the most of its total land area in the Dust Bowl region?

## Help for the People

For much of the 1930s, **unemployment**, or the number of people without jobs, was high in Texas. To help people find jobs, Governor James Allred set up a state commission. He also set up a pension, or retirement, plan to help take care of older citizens.

During the Great Depression, Texans also received help from the federal government. Through programs set up by President Franklin D. Roosevelt, Texans received more than $50 million from the federal government. The money was used to help farmers keep their land and for projects that gave people jobs. These workers built hundreds of dams and reservoirs in Texas. A **reservoir** is a lake that stores water held back by a dam. Workers also built many post offices, schools, and other government buildings.

### When?

#### 1936, the Texas Centennial

In the middle of the Great Depression, Texas celebrated its centennial (sen•TEH•nee•uhl), or one-hundredth birthday. The main event celebrating 100 years of Texas independence took place in Dallas, where workers built Fair Park. The Texas State Fair is still held in Fair Park each year in October. In other parts of the state, Texans put up statues and historic markers to observe the Centennial.

The tall tower at the University of Texas at Austin was built with money from the federal government. So were the San Jacinto monument near Houston and the River Walk in San Antonio.

Many well-known Texans served in the United States government at this time. John Nance Garner of Red River County served as Roosevelt's Vice President. Representative Sam Rayburn of Bonham was a leader in Congress, helping to pass new laws. Before he became President, Lyndon B. Johnson headed a work program for young people in Texas.

By 1940 the United States began to come out of the Great Depression. Businesses opened again, and more people were able to find jobs. By this time, however, several countries in Europe were at war again. Soon Americans, including Texans, were fighting in a second world war.

**How did the state and federal governments help people who were unemployed?**

## Texans and World War II

On the morning of December 7, 1941, Japanese planes attacked United States Navy ships in Pearl Harbor, Hawaii. A sailor from Waco, Doris Miller, better known as "Dorie" by his shipmates, was aboard the USS *West Virginia* in Pearl Harbor. As the first bombs were dropped, Miller shot down four of the Japanese planes.

When the attack was over, the Japanese had destroyed most of the ships. The following day, President Franklin D. Roosevelt asked Congress to declare war

From the very first battle, Texans took an important part in World War II. Dorie Miller (right) from Waco was a hero at Pearl Harbor (above).

on Japan. The United States entered World War II, joining the side of the Allies—Britain, France, and the former Soviet Union—against Japan, Germany, and Italy.

As it had in World War I, Texas served as a training center for soldiers and fighter pilots. More than 1 million Americans—one of every ten who fought in World War II—received their training in Texas.

More than 750,000 Texas men and women served in the armed forces during World War II. Many received awards. At 20 years of age, Audie Murphy from Farmersville had won more medals than any other American soldier in the war. In one battle Murphy held off a whole company of more than 80 enemy soldiers by himself.

Some of the war's best-known leaders were Texans. General Dwight D. Eisenhower, who was born in Denison, commanded the combined armies of France, Britain, and the United States in Europe. Admiral Chester W. Nimitz of Fredericksburg was in charge of the United States Navy in the Pacific Ocean. Colonel Oveta Culp Hobby of Houston led the United States Women's Army Corps, or WAC.

By the end of the war in 1945, more than 23,000 Texans had died for their country. Among them was Dorie Miller, the hero at Pearl Harbor. He died late in the war when his ship was sunk in the Pacific.

✓ **In what ways did Texans serve in World War II?**

These women pilots at Waco Air Field were among the 25,000 women who joined the Women's Air Force Service Pilots, or WASPS.

Thousands of Texans at home helped the United States fight the war. In steel mills, aircraft factories, and shipyards, women workers largely replaced the men, who had gone off to war.

## Industry Grows During the War

World War II helped bring Texas out of the Great Depression. Almost everything Texas produced was needed for the war. More than half the oil used during the war for ships, planes, and tanks came from Texas. Texas beef and food crops fed the soldiers and the people at home. Texas cotton was used to make uniforms.

The war also brought new industries to Texas, and new factories were built all over the state. Airplane factories were built at Fort Worth, Garland, and Grand Prairie. In the Gulf Coast cities such as Galveston, Port Arthur, Brownsville, and Rockport, shipyards sent out ships as quickly as they could be built. Steel mills in Houston and Daingerfield provided the steel for the planes and ships. Refineries near the oil fields in Beaumont, Borger, and Houston made **synthetic**, or human-made, rubber from oil. This product was used to make tires and lifeboats.

During World War II the number of people working in Texas factories tripled as more farmers, many of them tenant farmers, left the land to find factory jobs in the cities. By the war's end, for the first time more Texans lived in cities than on farms. This change from a rural, farming state to an urban, industrial state was one of the greatest changes in all of Texas history.

**How did World War II help change Texas from a rural, farming state to an urban, industrial state?**

## Lesson 3 Review

### Check Understanding

1. **Recall the Facts** What caused the United States to enter World War II?
2. **Focus on the Main Idea** How did Texans face the Great Depression and World War II?

### Think Critically

3. **Think More About It** Why was East Texas not a part of the Dust Bowl?
4. **Link to You** The federal government helped people during the Great Depression. How does the government help citizens today in natural disasters and in other hard times?

### Show What You Know

**Simulation Activity** Imagine that you and a partner are tenant farmers in the Texas Panhandle in the Dust Bowl. Role-play a conversation in which you talk about the problems the dust storms have caused and about whether you should leave Texas.

S·K·I·L·L·S

# How To

## Tell Primary from Secondary Sources

### Why Is This Skill Important?

People who study history learn about the past in different ways. The best way to learn about the past is from a primary source. A **primary source** gives the real words and pictures of people who were actually there and saw what happened. Their words may be found in diaries or journals, in interviews, and in many other records. Their photographs may show people or events as they really were.

Sometimes the only way to learn about the past is from a secondary source. A **secondary source** gives information written at a later time by someone who did not see what happened. Your social studies book is one kind of secondary source. Encyclopedias and other reference books are also secondary sources.

### Remember What You Have Read

Primary sources let a reader "hear the voices" of people using their own words to tell about the past. Your social studies book uses many primary sources. In this lesson you "heard" Mrs. Ollie Prince tell how she and her neighbors used feed sacks during the Great Depression. You "heard" Woody Guthrie sing about the Dust Bowl.

You also read much information about World War I and World War II. Most of this information came from secondary sources.

### Understand the Process

The words used in a source can sometimes help you tell if the source is primary or secondary. Words like *I, we, my,* and *our* are often found in primary sources.

Each kind of source is helpful. A primary source can give a reader the feeling of being there. A secondary source may give more facts—names and dates.

Each kind of source also creates problems in learning about the past. Primary sources might give just one person's view. The people writing secondary sources might not understand what had happened, since they were not there.

In this 1936 poster, artist Ben Shahn captured the mood of many Texans during the Great Depression.

### Think and Apply

Write a short journal entry telling what you thought and did during one afternoon. Then trade journal entries with a classmate. Write a paragraph about what your classmate thought and did. Compare the primary sources with the secondary sources.

BUILDING CITIZENSHIP

# CHAPTER 9 REVIEW

## CONNECT MAIN IDEAS

Use this organizer to show that you understand how the chapter's main ideas are connected. First copy the organizer onto a separate sheet of paper. Then complete it by writing a sentence telling how each event affected the lives of Texans in the 1900s.

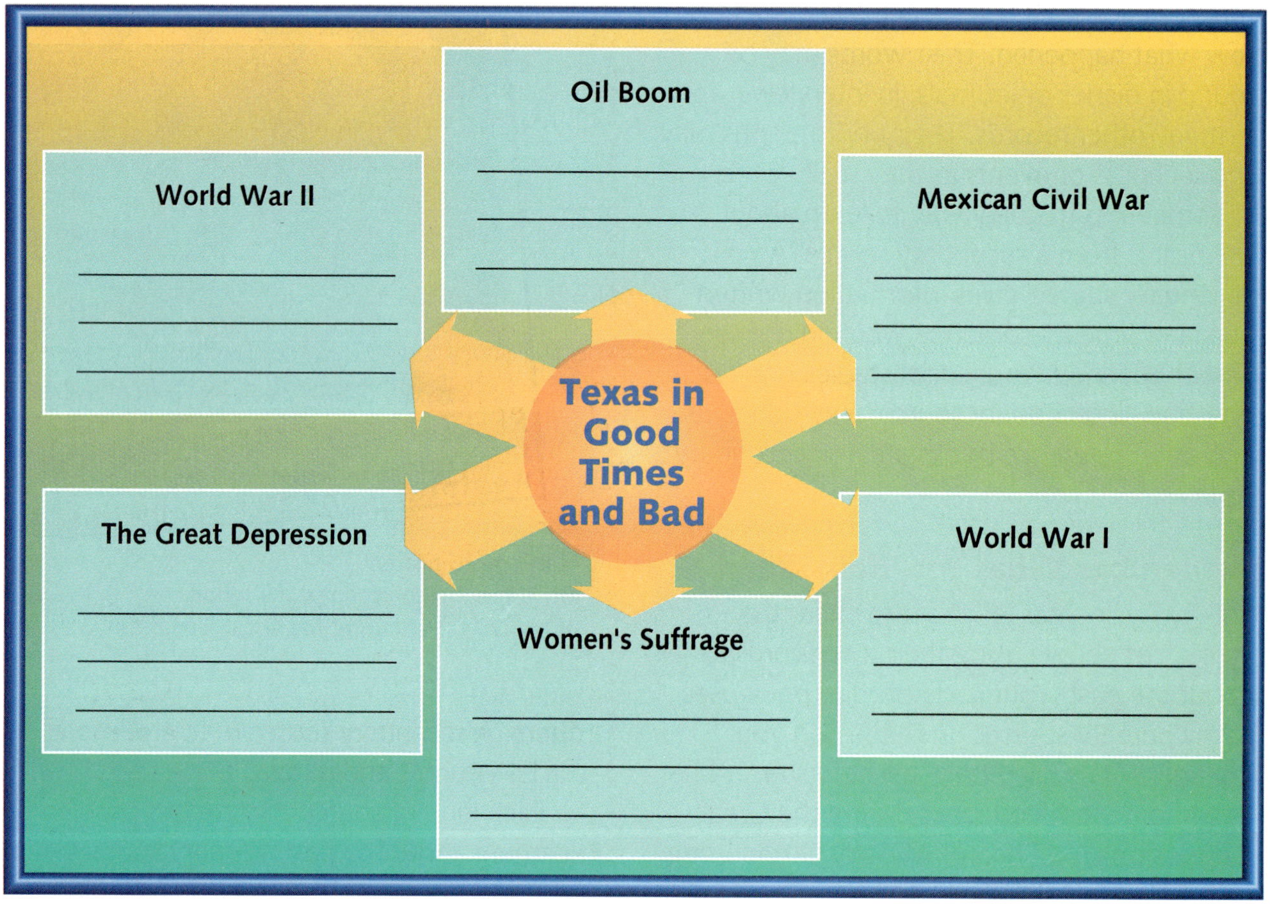


## WRITE MORE ABOUT IT

1. **Write a Letter** Imagine that you live on a farm in Texas. As you are watching your father dig a well for water, he accidentally strikes oil. Write a letter to a friend or relative describing what happened.
2. **Write a Newspaper Headline** Write two newspaper headlines that might have been seen following Pancho Villa's attacks on towns in Texas. The first should be a headline for a newspaper in Texas. The second should be a headline for a newspaper in Mexico.
3. **Write a Poem** Think about Texans who served in the United States armed forces in World War II. Write a poem that describes some of the feelings they may have had.

## USE VOCABULARY

For each group of vocabulary words, write a sentence or two to show how they are related.

1. refinery, petroleum, boom
2. industry, good, service
3. cash crop, commercial farm, tenant farmer
4. suffrage, amendment
5. depression, unemployment

## CHECK UNDERSTANDING

1. When was oil discovered at Spindletop?
2. What events helped start the first oil boom in Texas?
3. What resources do entrepreneurs need to run a business?
4. What businesses helped the oil industry?
5. What is a wildcatter?
6. How did the discovery of oil make Texas interdependent with the rest of the world?
7. Why were there bad feelings between Mexico and the United States in 1916?
8. How did Texans help in World War I?
9. What caused farms in Texas to change in the early 1900s?
10. What major crops did Texas farmers grow in the early 1900s?
11. When were all women first allowed to vote?
12. What caused the Great Depression?
13. How did people try to conserve the land in the Dust Bowl?
14. What new industries started in Texas during World War II?

## THINK CRITICALLY

1. **Think More About It** The automobile industry helped the oil industry boom. Did the oil industry help the automobile industry grow? Explain your answer.
2. **Cause and Effect** How did the new ways of farming lead to the growth of cities in Texas in the early 1900s?
3. **Link to You** In the supermarket you can see potatoes from Idaho, maple syrup from Vermont, bananas from Costa Rica, and ham from Poland. How do these products show interdependence?

## APPLY SKILLS

**How to Read a Cross-Section Diagram** Many petroleum products are transported from the refinery to markets by oil tankers. Research how oil is carried in the tankers. Draw a cross-section diagram to show where the oil would be stored inside a tanker.

**How to Tell Primary from Secondary Sources** Choose a quotation from page 256 or page 257. Write the words that tell you that it is a primary source. How does this source give you the feeling of being there?

## READ MORE ABOUT IT

*Dwight D. Eisenhower: Man of Many Hats* by Kenneth M. Deitch and JoAnne B. Weisman. Discovery Enterprises. This book tells about the events in Eisenhower's life. It is illustrated with many paintings and photographs.

*Exploring Energy: Oil and Natural Gas* by Philip Sauvain. Schoolhouse Press. This book explains how workers find and drill for oil and gas beneath land and water. Photographs illustrate the processes.

CHAPTER 10

# INTO MODERN TIMES

Why has Texas produced so many national leaders?

“There is something about Texans, a strong, independent streak. You really want to be able to do it yourself.”

Barbara Jordan,
a Texas leader, 1990

LESSON 1

# FROM OIL TO ASTRONAUTS

## Link to Our World

**How is Texas changing today?**

***Focus on the Main Idea***
**Read to learn about the changes that took place in Texas after World War II.**

***Preview Vocabulary***
**tideland**
**commute**
**leisure time**
**segregation**
**integrated circuit**
**astronaut**

The population of Texas jumped from about 5.8 million in 1930 to about 7.7 million by the end of the 1940s. Many people came from other states to try to find jobs in Texas industries. For the first time, more Texans lived in cities and towns than on farms. One city that grew fast was Houston. In the years after World War II, Houston became the largest city in the state. Houston grew because of the new industries of the war years and because of the East Texas oil boom.

## THE TIDELANDS DISPUTE

Oil remained the most important industry in Texas after World War II. New oil fields were found on land, but some scientists believed that more oil lay under the Texas tidelands. **Tidelands** are the lands that lie under the water just off a coast. Soon the Texas government let oil companies drill for oil in the tidelands in exchange for money.

The United States government and the Texas government both said they owned the tidelands. The federal government said that Texas had given up this public land when it joined the United States in 1845. But Texans said that the Texas government had been an independent country when it joined the Union and that it had never given up its tidelands. The United States Supreme Court was asked to settle the case. In 1950 the Court agreed with the federal government.

Shallow-water drilling rigs called jack ups were used to drill for oil in the tidelands off the coast of Texas.

After World War II, Texas changed rapidly from a rural state to an urban state. This 1945 photograph shows a cowhand watching cattle in the shadows of Dallas's growing skyline.

The loss of the tidelands hurt the Texas economy. Texans had come to depend on the money they got from oil. This money came from renting public land to oil companies. The state also got money for the oil the companies pumped from that land. They used it to pay for public schools and other government services.

Owning the tidelands was so important to Texans that it affected the way they voted in the 1952 election for President of the United States. In that election more Texans voted than ever before. Many voted for Dwight D. Eisenhower, who was born in Texas. He said the tidelands should be under Texas's control.

Shortly after Eisenhower became President, Congress passed a law returning the tidelands to Texas. Some people in the federal government did not agree with the new law and again asked the Supreme Court to decide the case. This time the Supreme Court decided that Texas owned the tidelands.

**What caused the problem about who owned the tidelands?**

## New Ways of Living

Life was good for many Texans in the years after World War II. New industries provided more jobs that paid higher wages. New ways of living took shape.

Many Texans moved to suburbs, or smaller towns and cities on the edge of large cities. With higher wages people were able to afford automobiles. People in the suburbs **commuted**, or drove to and from work in the cities. The first freeways and shopping malls were built during this time.

In 1945 there were fewer than 10,000 television sets in the United States. Five years later that figure had soared to about 6 million. Today nearly 100 million households in the United States have at least one television set.

## URBAN AND RURAL POPULATIONS IN TEXAS, 1930 AND 1950

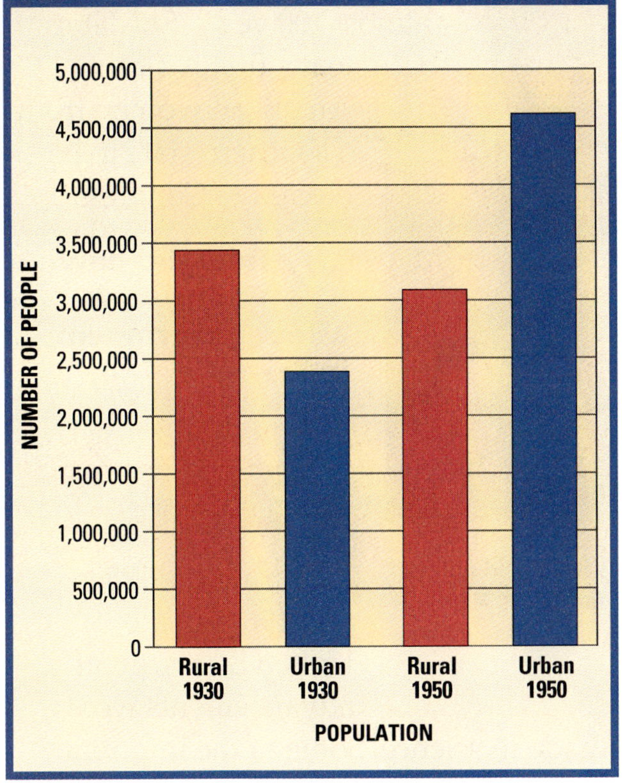


**LEARNING FROM GRAPHS** Between 1930 and 1950 the Texas population shifted from rural to urban.
- By about how much did Texas's urban population grow between 1930 and 1950?

As people made more money, they were able to work fewer hours. This gave them more **leisure time**, or time away from work or school. Many enjoyed watching television and movies. They visited large amusement parks. They played and watched sports.

The first major league sports teams in Texas were formed in the years after World War II. Major league teams are made up of the highest level of professional, or paid, players. In 1952 Dallas had the first major league football team in Texas, but the Dallas Texans lasted only one season. The Dallas Cowboys and Houston Oilers began playing football in 1960. Major league baseball came to Texas in 1962 with the Houston Colt .45s. After the new Astrodome arena was built in 1965, the Colt .45s became known as the Astros. In 1972 the Texas Rangers baseball team came to Arlington, in North Texas. During the 1960s and 1970s, the first major league basketball teams in Texas were formed in Dallas, Houston, and San Antonio.

**What changes in ways of life took place in Texas after World War II?**

## The Fight for Civil Rights

Not everyone shared in the good times that followed World War II. In Texas many of those who were left out were African Americans and Mexican Americans.

Many African Americans and Mexican Americans lived with low wages, poor schools, and segregation. **Segregation** is keeping people apart because of their culture or race. State law also made it hard for African Americans and Mexican Americans to vote. It also kept other civil rights from them.

People in Texas formed groups to work for their civil rights. James Farmer

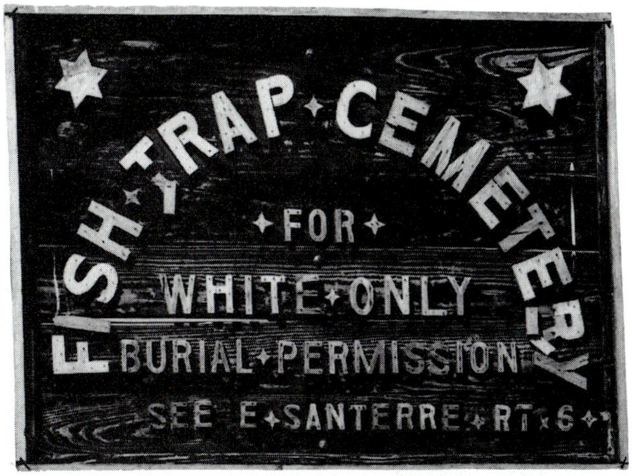


Even cemeteries in Texas were once segregated.

of Marshall helped start the Congress of Racial Equality, or CORE, which worked for the rights of African Americans. Dr. Hector P. García of Corpus Christi started a group that worked for the Spanish-speaking people in the United States.

The fight for civil rights gained attention all over the country through the work of a Georgia minister, Dr. Martin Luther King, Jr. Millions of Americans wanted to help King. With this support, he tried to get the country's leaders to work for change all over the United States.

Thousands of Mexican Americans have held political office in Texas. One of the most famous is Henry B. González of San Antonio.

In the 1950s and 1960s, new federal laws stated that segregation was against the law and made it possible for more people to vote. African Americans and Mexican Americans voted in large numbers, electing their own leaders at the local, state, and national levels of government.

In 1959 Henry B. González (gohn•ZAH•lays) of San Antonio became the first Mexican American elected to the Texas Senate in more than 100 years. In 1961 González was the first Mexican American ever elected to the United States House of Representatives. He was joined in Congress in 1965 by Eligio "Kika" de la Garza of Mercedes.

African American leaders were elected all over the country in the 1960s. One of the best known in Texas was Barbara Jordan of Houston. In 1966 she was the first African American to be elected to the Texas Senate in almost 100 years. She later became the first African American woman from a southern state to be elected to Congress.

**How did new voting laws affect government in Texas?**

## Texas in the Space Age

During the 1950s and 1960s in the United States, great advancements were made in science. Some of the important inventions of this period were made by Texans. In 1959 Jack Kilby, a Dallas engineer for the Texas Instruments Corporation, invented the integrated circuit. An **integrated circuit** is a microchip that can run electronic systems in everything from hand-held calculators to computers. Integrated circuits in computers made it possible to design and fly rockets and other spacecraft.

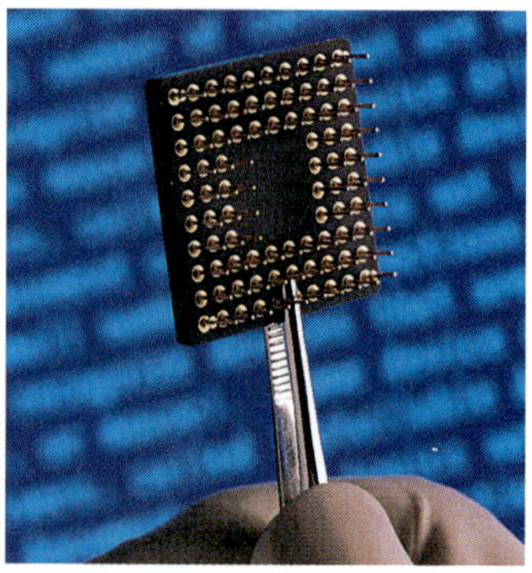

Many computers use a microprocessor that is in the form of a very small chip.

In 1961 the federal government decided to build the Manned Spacecraft Center in Houston. The center would be part of the National

Lesson 2

# Recent Booms and Busts

## Link to Our World

**How do changes in the state or national economy affect you and your family?**

***Focus on the Main Idea***
**Read to learn how changes in the Texas economy affected Texans in the 1970s and 1980s.**

***Preview Vocabulary***
**demand**
**Rust Belt**
**Sun Belt**
**supply**
**diverse**
**service industry**
**high-tech**

The story of Texas in the 1900s includes periods of growth and failure—nicknamed *boom and bust*—in the oil industry. The 1970s and 1980s repeated the ups and downs of good times and bad for many Texans.

### Boom Years in the 1970s

In the 1970s money from oil brought good times to Texas. Greater **demand**, or desire, for oil in the United States and in the rest of the world caused the price of oil to rise to almost $40 a barrel.

As oil prices rose, money from the oil fields made the state's economy boom. Banks loaned money freely to new businesses, and much construction, or building, took place. Many of the shining glass office towers of Dallas and Houston were built during this time. Filling the new office towers were many businesses that moved from the **Rust Belt**, a nickname for the older states of the Northeast and Middle West, where industries used a lot of iron and steel. The businesses that moved to Texas wanted to take part in the economic boom in the **Sun Belt**, a nickname for the states of the South and West.

Many of the towering skyscrapers in Dallas were built during the economic boom in Texas during the 1970s.

As more people came to Texas in the 1970s looking for jobs, the state's population grew. It jumped from about 11 million in 1970 to more than 14 million in

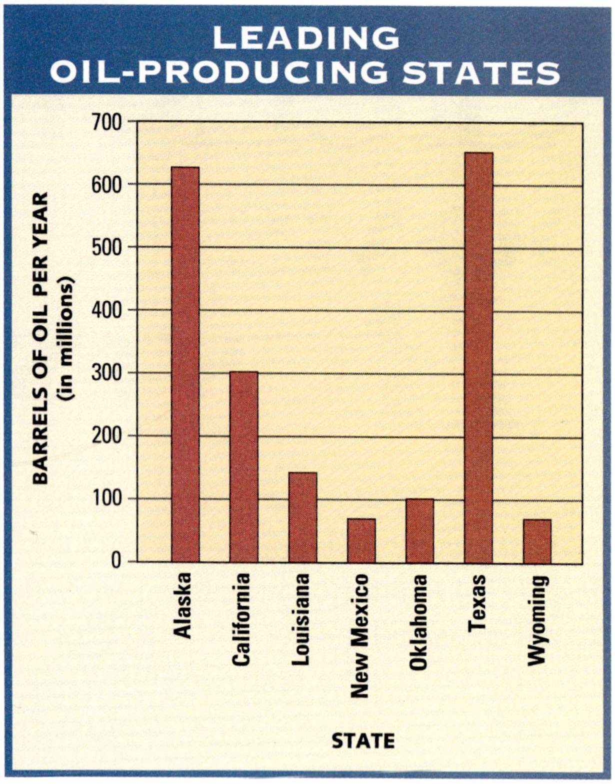


**LEARNING FROM GRAPHS** Texas is still the leading state in the production of oil.

- About how many more barrels of oil a year does Texas produce than California?

1980. A large number of people came from Michigan, in the Rust Belt, where the automobile industry had not been doing well in the 1970s.

During the oil boom Texas made more money by helping other places in the world produce oil. Texas trained oil workers in Alaska, Mexico, Venezuela, Nigeria, Indonesia, Saudi Arabia, Kuwait, and the United Kingdom. Texas also sold oil-drilling tools.

Many people from other parts of the world moved to Texas. People from India, Pakistan, the Philippines, and Korea came to Texas in large numbers during the 1970s to take part in the oil boom. People from Laos, Cambodia, and Vietnam, however, came to escape wars being fought in their countries. Today there are more Texans from Vietnam than from any other country in Asia.

**✓ Name two things that happened in Texas because of the oil boom of the 1970s.**

## A Texas Wheat Boom

The 1970s saw a boom for Texas wheat farmers, too. By the early 1980s the amount of wheat grown on the Texas plains had jumped to five times more than it was in 1971—from about 31 million bushels to about 150 million bushels.

When the price of wheat went up, many farmers stopped growing cotton,

At shipyards in Galveston, wheat for export is loaded onto ships that will sail to faraway countries.

## OIL-PRODUCING REGIONS OF THE WORLD

**REGIONS** Oil deposits are found on every continent.

■ Where are most of the oil-producing regions in South America?

soybeans, and other crops. They began to grow wheat to make more money. Wheat growing spread from the High Plains into the southern and eastern parts of the state.

The price of wheat kept going up as the demand for wheat became greater around the world. Some countries needed Texas wheat because their farmers had poor harvests. The former Soviet Union was one of these countries. The United States government agreed to sell wheat to the Soviet Union. In the 1970s wheat became one of the most important farm products shipped through Texas ports to other countries.

**Why did more Texas farmers start to grow wheat in the 1970s?**

## "Gone Bust" in the 1980s

In the early 1980s the Texas oil industry went from a boom to a bust. This started when other oil-producing countries began selling more of their oil in the United States. The **supply**, or amount of oil for sale, was greater than the demand, or need for it. To get Americans to buy Texas oil, Texas oil companies had to lower their prices. By 1985 the price of oil had dropped from about $30 a barrel to less than $15.

This price drop hurt the Texas economy. With less money from oil, most new construction stopped. Many new office towers stood empty because businesses could not pay the high rents. Banks that had loaned money freely in the 1970s

In the early 1980s oil from countries in Southwest Asia such as Yemen brought down the price of U.S. oil.

found themselves with not enough money in the 1980s. Many businesses closed and unemployment in the state went up. In 1985 Texas had one of the country's highest numbers of unemployed people. By the late 1980s one of every four children in Texas was poor.

The drop in oil prices also affected the state government. Money from oil had paid for government services. To make up for the lost oil money, the Texas legislature in 1987 made taxes higher. Many people did not like this because Texas had always had low taxes.

While Texas was suffering through the oil bust, Mexico, its neighbor to the south, was having its own economic problems. Many Mexicans left their country to try to find jobs in Texas and in other states along the border with the United States. More than one million Mexican citizens came to the United States to find work.

**Name two ways that the oil bust of the 1980s affected Texas.**

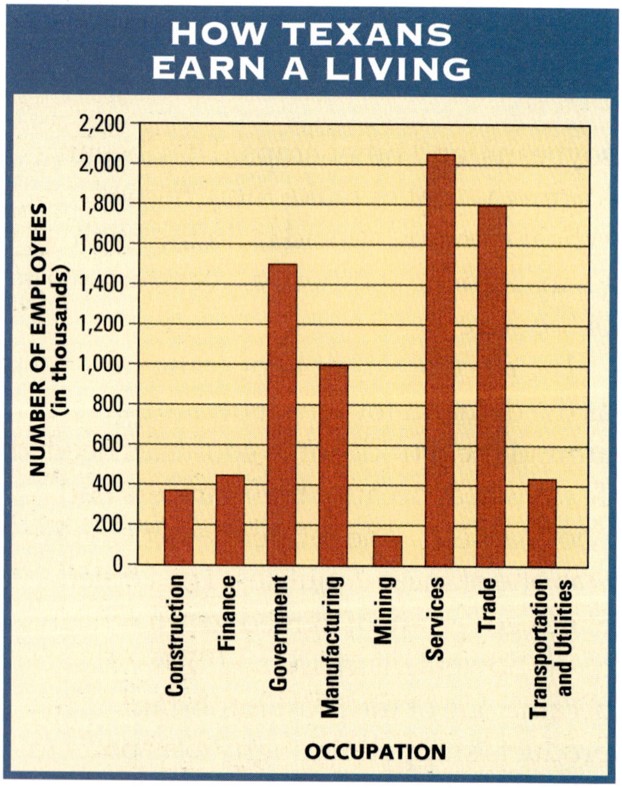


**LEARNING FROM GRAPHS** Today more people in Texas are employed in service industries than in any other kind of industry.

- About how many people in Texas are employed in manufacturing industries?

**Map Skill** **REGIONS** In addition to leading the country in oil production, Texas also leads the country in the production of cattle, sheep and wool. ■ What products are found near Brownsville?

## New Industries for Texas

In the late 1980s the Texas economy began to improve. New businesses opened, and companies moved to Texas from other states, bringing with them many new jobs. In 1988 the J. C. Penney Company moved its offices to North Texas. With the company came almost 4,000 new jobs.

New businesses helped the Texas economy become more **diverse**. That means that the Texas economy was made up of many kinds of industries. It no longer depended mostly on the oil industry.

Some Texas industries make goods such as chemicals, airplanes, paints, clothing, and food products. Others sell goods and provide services. Among these **service industries** are hotels, amusement parks, law offices, and hospitals. More than 50,000 service workers have jobs at the Texas Medical Center in Houston.

High-technology industries make the state's economy even more diverse. So-called **high-tech** businesses are those that invent, build, and use computers and other electronic equipment. At first, computers were used only by scientific centers such as the Johnson Space Center in Houston. Then companies in Texas and other places invented smaller and less-expensive computers. By the late 1980s more people were using computers in their businesses, schools, and homes. The demand for computers went up. To meet the greater demand, the supply of high-tech inventions and services has grown. The city of Austin has become an important center for the computer industry. Several large computer companies are located there.

**How has the Texas economy changed since the late 1980s?**

## What?

### The Texas TENET

The Texas Education Network, called TENET, helps people in Texas get information through a computer network. A computer network links computers so they can share information. The computers can be anywhere in the state, the nation, or the world. The Texas TENET helps Texans get information about schools, government services, and places to visit. People can use the information for anything from finding a job to learning about Texas state parks.

TENET can be a valuable learning tool for students in Texas.

## LESSON 2 REVIEW

### Check Understanding

1. **Recall the Facts** Why was the supply of oil greater than the demand for it in the 1980s?
2. **Focus on the Main Idea** How did changes in the Texas economy affect Texans in the 1970s and 1980s?

### Think Critically

3. **Link to You** What high-tech inventions do you use at home or at school?
4. **Cause and Effect** How have changes in supply and demand of oil affected the price of oil in the United States?
5. **Personally Speaking** If you were a government leader, what would you have done with the extra wheat that Texas grew?

### Show What You Know

**Time Line Activity** Make a time line that lists events in United States space exploration. Begin by using the events and years given in this chapter. Use reference books to find out more about space history to add other events. Include drawings, and display your time line in the classroom.

Lesson 3

# Texans Leading the Nation

## Link to Our World

**What qualities do you think make a good leader?**

***Focus on the Main Idea***

**Read to learn about some leaders from Texas.**

***Preview Vocabulary***

**interstate highway system**
**politics**
**landslide victory**

The 1990s began with a Texan as President of the United States. Since the end of World War II, several Texans have served as Presidents or Vice Presidents. In 1953 Dwight D. Eisenhower took office and became the first Texas-born President. In the 1960s Lyndon B. Johnson served as Vice President and later as President. In 1980 George Bush of Houston became Vice President. He was elected President of the United States in 1988 and served until 1993.

In the 1952 presidential election, more Texans voted than ever before. Dwight D. Eisenhower easily defeated his opponent, Adlai E. Stevenson.

### President Eisenhower

Dwight D. Eisenhower, the thirty-fourth President, was born in Denison, Texas, in 1890. When he was a baby, his parents moved from Texas to Abilene, Kansas. After "Ike," as he was called, finished high school, he went to college at the United States Military Academy in New York. Then, in 1915, the Army sent him to Fort Sam Houston, near San Antonio.

As a young Army officer in 1919, Captain Eisenhower made a long, hard automobile trip across the United States. He said that the trip started him thinking about the importance of good highways. Later, when he was President, Eisenhower helped set up an **interstate highway system** made up of four-lane roads connecting all the states except Alaska and Hawaii. More than 3,000 miles (4,828 km) of highway were built in Texas, giving the state more miles of interstate highway than any other state.

Eisenhower greeted these supporters in Kansas during his campaign for the presidency.

During World War II, General Eisenhower was in charge of armies in Europe. Several years after the war, he was asked to run for President. People elected Eisenhower in 1952 because during the war he had been a leader they could trust. "I like Ike" was his election slogan. Eisenhower was President until 1961, serving two terms. He died in 1969.

**What does the interstate highway system connect?**

## President Johnson

Lyndon Baines Johnson was born in 1908 in the town of Stonewall, near the Pedernales River in Central Texas. LBJ, as he was known, first became interested in **politics**, the running of the government, by helping other people get elected. In 1937 Johnson was elected to the United States Congress. He served first as a representative and then as a senator. People knew him as a man who could get things done.

Johnson was elected Vice President in 1960. On November 22, 1963, Johnson and President John F. Kennedy arrived in Dallas for a visit. While they were driving through the city, President Kennedy was shot and killed. Texas Governor John Connally, who was in the President's car, was badly wounded.

After President Kennedy's death, Lyndon Baines Johnson became the thirty-sixth President. The following year, 1964, was an election year. Johnson ran for President and won a **landslide victory**. That means he was elected by many more votes than his opponent received.

All through his government career, Johnson worked to see that African Americans and Mexican Americans had the same rights as others. As President he helped Congress pass the Civil Rights Act of 1964. This act made all practices of segregation against the law. It also said that people of all races must have the same job opportunities. President Johnson worked to improve schools and to clean up the air and water.

Lyndon B. Johnson was sworn in as President of the United States aboard the President's airplane by U.S. District Judge Sarah T. Hughes. Among the witnesses were Mrs. Johnson and Mrs. John F. Kennedy.

President Johnson supported the work of Martin Luther King, Jr., by signing the Civil Rights Act of 1964.

Texans have honored President Johnson by making his birthday, August 27, a state holiday. There are many Americans, however, who remember him for being President during the Vietnam War, an unpopular war that the United States fought in Asia. Many American soldiers were injured or killed in this war.

The worry of the war made Johnson decide not to run for President again in 1968. He returned to his family ranch on the Pedernales River with Lady Bird, his wife. He died at his ranch in 1973.

**How is Lyndon B. Johnson remembered in Texas and in the rest of the country?**

## President Bush

The latest President of the United States who came from Texas is George Herbert Walker Bush. The forty-first President was born in Massachusetts in 1924, but he later chose to live in Texas.

During World War II, 19-year-old Bush was the youngest fighter pilot in the United States Navy. After the war Bush moved to West Texas to work in the oil industry. In 1953 he started his own oil company and moved the headquarters to Houston in 1959.

In the 1960s Bush became interested in politics. He ran for the United States Senate in 1964 but lost. Two years later he was elected to the House of Representatives, where he served two terms. He ran for the Senate once more in 1970 but lost again.

President Bush and Barbara, his wife, spent Thanksgiving with U.S. troops in Kuwait during the Persian Gulf War.

Because Bush was such a hard worker, Presidents asked him to serve the country in many kinds of jobs. During the 1970s Bush was the United States representative to the United Nations and later to China. He was also director of the Central Intelligence Agency, or CIA. In 1980 Bush was elected Vice President with President Ronald Reagan of California. In 1988, George Bush was elected President.

During his time as President, Bush called on Americans to make "a kinder and gentler nation." At times, however, he had to be firm. In 1991 President Bush sent American soldiers to Southwest Asia to help Kuwait in a war with Iraq. Iraq had attacked Kuwait to take away its oil fields. After losing the 1992 election to Bill Clinton of Arkansas, Bush returned to Houston, where he and Barbara, his wife, now live. In 1995 their son, George W. Bush, became governor of Texas.

Texas businessperson H. Ross Perot caused much excitement during the 1992 presidential election.

**Why did George Bush first come to Texas?**

## Some Other Well-Known Texas Leaders

In recent years many other Texas leaders have become known all over the United States. In 1984 Phil Gramm was elected to the United States Senate. Today, Gramm is one of the most powerful people in the Senate. Business leader H. Ross Perot, who was born in Texarkana, ran for President in 1992. In 1993 Lloyd Bentsen of Mission, Texas, became a member of President Bill Clinton's Cabinet, as secretary of the Department of the Treasury.

Before being elected to the United States Senate, Phil Gramm served for five years in the United States House of Representatives.

Not long after Henry Cisneros of San Antonio finished high school, he set for himself the goal of becoming the mayor of his city. He thought a lot about his goal throughout his college years. Finally, in 1981 he was the first Mexican American elected mayor of San Antonio since Juan Seguín in the 1840s. He was also the first Mexican American mayor of a large United States city. Henry Cisneros also became a member of President Clinton's Cabinet. He became secretary of the Department of Housing and Urban Development.

Many Texas women also became well-known leaders in the 1990s. Ann Richards of Waco became governor of Texas in 1990. Before that, she served as the state treasurer and was the first woman to be elected to state office since Governor Miriam Ferguson in the 1930s. Like Ferguson, Ann Richards was quick to see problems and work to solve them. When she became governor, some people called her Action Annie because she was able to get so much done.

After serving eight years as the mayor of San Antonio, Henry Cisneros joined President Clinton's cabinet as the secretary of the Department of Housing and Urban Development.

Ann Richards was one of many women who took part in Texas politics in the 1990s. In 1993 Kay Bailey Hutchison of Dallas, who had also been a state treasurer, was elected to the United States Senate. Senator Hutchison has a link with Texas history. She is the great-great-great-great-granddaughter of Charles S. Taylor, who signed the Texas Declaration of Independence in 1836.

✓ **Name two Texas leaders of the 1990s.**

Former Texas State Treasurer Kay Bailey Hutchison was elected to the U.S. Senate in 1993.

## LESSON 3 REVIEW

### Check Understanding

1. **Recall the Facts** Which two Presidents were born in Texas?
2. **Focus on the Main Idea** What characteristics made the Texans in this lesson good leaders?

### Think Critically

3. **Personally Speaking** Who are the leaders in your school and community? What do you think makes them good leaders?
4. **Past to Present** Compare and contrast present-day Texas leaders with leaders of the past, such as Stephen F. Austin and Sam Houston.

### Show What You Know

**Writing Activity** Imagine that you are running for governor of Texas. Write a short speech to tell Texas citizens why they should vote for you. Be sure to write about the things you will do to help Texas. Share your speech with your classmates.

S·K·I·L·L·S

# HOW TO

## Use Maps with Different Scales

### Why Is This Skill Important?

A map scale can help you find out how far apart two places are from each other in the real world once you know how far apart they are on the map. A map scale shows you that a certain distance on a map stands for a longer, real distance on Earth. Map scales are different, depending on how big an area the map shows. Knowing about map scales can help you choose a map that will give you the information you need.

### Understand the Process

Look at the map below and at the maps on page 283. Map A shows the United States and part of the interstate highway system. It shows a large area, so it uses a large scale. Map B shows the state of Texas and the interstate highways in the state. This map shows a much smaller area than that shown on Map A. The scale on Map B is smaller than the Map A scale. Map C shows only San Antonio and the surrounding area. Its scale is even smaller. Each map is helpful. Follow the numbered steps to find out how to use the map scale and to determine when each map would be most helpful.

1. Look at Map A. Find the map scale. Use a ruler to measure the exact length of the top line of the map scale, or use a pencil and paper to mark off the length. The top line of the map scale shows the scale for miles. The bottom line shows the scale for kilometers. How long is the line that stands for 500 miles in the real world? It is one inch long.

MAP A: THE UNITED STATES

2. Still using Map A, find El Paso and San Antonio. Use your ruler, or the paper you marked, to measure how far it is on the map between these two cities along Interstate 10. How many times can you fit your 500-mile scale, end to end, between El Paso and San Antonio? Use the map scale to find out how many miles this length stands for in the real world. What is the real distance between El Paso and San Antonio? It is about 500 miles.

3. Look at Map B. Find the map scale. How long is the line that represents 300 miles in the real world? Now measure how far it is on this map between El Paso and San Antonio on Interstate 10. How many times can you fit your 300-mile scale, end to end, between the two cities? How many miles is it between El Paso and San Antonio in the real world?

4. Do both Map A and Map B show the same distance between El Paso and San Antonio? You will see that even when map scales are different, the distances represented on the maps are the same.

5. Study all three maps. Which map would be most helpful in finding out how far it is between San Antonio and cities outside the state of Texas? Which map would be most helpful in finding out how far it is between San Antonio and Corpus Christi? Which map would you use if you wanted to know how far San Antonio International Airport is from New Braunfels?

## Think and Apply

Map Skill

Write a paragraph to explain to a classmate when it would be helpful to use the United States map, the Texas map, and the San Antonio map.

**MAP B: TEXAS**

**MAP C: SAN ANTONIO AREA**

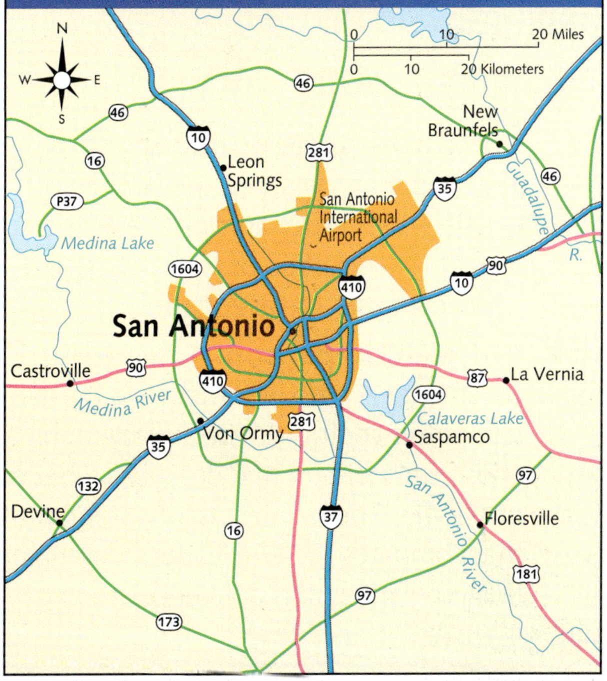

CHAPTER 10

# REVIEW

## CONNECT MAIN IDEAS

Use this organizer to show that you understand how the chapter's main ideas are connected. First copy the organizer onto a separate sheet of paper. Then complete it by listing people or events that were a part of the history of Texas in the 1950s, 1960s, 1970s, 1980s, or 1990s.

### Into Modern Times

**1950s**

**1960s**

**1970s**

**1980s**

**1990s**

## WRITE MORE ABOUT IT

1. **Write a Newspaper Report** Write a newspaper article about the landing of United States astronauts on the moon. Include a description of the landing and interviews with the astronauts.
2. **Write a Comparison** Choose two Texas leaders who were active in the last half of this century. Write a paragraph about each person that describes what he or she did. Then write a third paragraph that compares the two leaders, describing their similarities and differences.

## USE VOCABULARY

Each of the following sentences is false. Replace the underlined word or words to make each sentence true.

1. Both Texas and the federal government claimed to own the Gulf Coastal Plain.
2. Because of leisure time, many African Americans could not live wherever they wanted.
3. By the 1960s the United States had sent several wildcatters into space and to the moon.

4. In the 1970s many Americans moved from the Sun Belt to the Rust Belt to look for jobs.

5. In the 1980s the demand for oil was greater than the supply.

6. Hotels and hospitals are a few examples of politics in Texas today.

7. Eisenhower set up an integrated circuit that connected all the states except Alaska and Hawaii.

## CHECK UNDERSTANDING

1. Who claimed to own the Texas tidelands?
2. Why did the way of life change for many Texans after World War II?
3. How did Texans fight for civil rights?
4. How did people working at the Manned Spacecraft Center in Houston help in the first moon landing?
5. Why did many Texas farmers stop growing cotton and soybeans in the 1970s?
6. Why did unemployment in Texas go up in the early 1980s?
7. What new industries were started in Texas in the late 1980s?
8. What are some of the things that Dwight D. Eisenhower did to help Texas?
9. Name three recent Texas leaders, and tell what they did.

## THINK CRITICALLY

1. **Past to Present** In the 1960s sending a person to the moon was a great scientific achievement. What do you think is a great scientific achievement today?
2. **Explore Viewpoints** Why do you think some people fought to make segregation against the law?
3. **Cause and Effect** What happens to the price of oil if countries produce more oil than people want?
4. **Think More About It** Why is it important to have a good interstate highway system?
5. **Personally Speaking** Which recent Texas leader do you admire the most? Why?

## APPLY SKILLS

**How to Tell Fact from Opinion** Read several paragraphs from an article in the editorial section of a newspaper. Underline all the phrases or sentences that are facts. Circle the opinions. Write a paragraph explaining why you made the choices that you did.

Map Skill

**How to Use Maps with Different Scales** The maps on pages 282 and 283 show different areas and use different scales. Use Map A, Map B, or Map C to answer these questions: How far is it from San Antonio to Houston? From Dallas to Austin? Which map did you use? Why did you choose that map?

## READ MORE ABOUT IT

*The Civil Rights Movement* by Stuart Kallen. Abdo and Daughters. Interesting pictures and text tell the story of the civil rights movement, from its leaders to its important events.

*The Picture Life of George Bush* by R. Schneiderman. Franklin Watts. This book presents a detailed picture of George Bush's life.

MAKING SOCIAL STUDIES RELEVANT

# SPORTS TEAMS IN TEXAS

It started in the 1950s. Major league sports came to Texas and a history of championship sports teams in Texas began. Texans remain great fans of major league sports, especially of football, basketball, and baseball. Many of the sports teams in Texas have names based on things that are special to Texans and to their past.

The Texas Rangers baseball team was named for the legendary Texas Rangers, who have served the state as peace officers since the 1800s. The San Antonio Spurs, Dallas Mavericks, and Dallas Cowboys get their names from the state's cattle-ranching era. The Astros and the Rockets of Houston point to Texas's contributions in space exploration.

Some of these teams have made sports history, and their players and coaches are sometimes honored as Texas heroes. The Dallas Cowboys have been Super Bowl champions, and the Houston Rockets have won national basketball championships.

## Think and Apply

Imagine that a new sports team will be formed in your hometown. With a partner, brainstorm a list of names for the team. The name should reflect something from Texas history from 1900 to the present. Share your list with the class, and explain why you chose each name. Hold a class election to choose the best name.

This cowhand probably never imagined that his line of work would inspire the name of one of the nation's best-known football teams.

UNIT 5

# Story Cloth

Follow the pictures shown in this story cloth to help you review the events in Unit 5.

## Summarize the Main Ideas

1. A new century brought great change to Texas. The discovery of oil at Spindletop in 1901 changed the lives of Texans.
2. In 1911 a civil war in Mexico created trouble between the United States and Mexico. Mexican revolutionary Pancho Villa raided towns in Texas, Arizona, and New Mexico.
3. Women in Texas and across the country worked for suffrage. After World War I, women won the right to vote.
4. Texans were hurt by the Great Depression and the Dust Bowl. Many did not have enough food or even a place to live.
5. Texans at home helped the United States fight World War II. They worked in steel mills, aircraft factories, and shipyards.
6. After World War II, oil remained important in Texas. By the end of the 1940s, more Texans lived in cities than on farms.
7. When astronauts landed on the moon in 1969, they were guided by Mission Control at the Johnson Space Center in Houston. President Lyndon B. Johnson was a strong supporter of the space industry.
8. New technology has brought wealth to Texas, a leader in high-tech industries.

**Choose an Event** From this story cloth choose the event that you think has had the most significant effect on your life today. Write a paragraph to explain your choice.

VOTE
TODAY!
VOTE
BOX

UNIT 5

# REVIEW

## COOPERATIVE LEARNING WORKSHOP

**Remember**

- Share your ideas.
- Cooperate with others to plan your work.
- Take responsibility for your work.
- Show your group's work to the class.
- Discuss what you learned by working together.

**Activity 1**

### Create a Time Line

With a group of classmates, create a time line that tells the story of oil in Texas. Make your time line show important events, from the first use of oil in Texas to the oil bust in the 1980s. Each person in the group can choose one event on the time line. On a separate sheet of paper, write a paragraph about the event you have chosen. Draw a picture to illustrate your event, and place your work on the time line in the proper order. Use the time line to tell the story to the rest of the class.

**Activity 2**

### Put on a Puppet Show

Choose a person who would have lived during the time period of this unit, and make a puppet to represent him or her. With classmates, write a short play in which your characters tell the class about their lives. Afterward, other classmates may wish to ask questions of the puppets.

**Activity 3**

### Conduct an Interview

Work with a group of classmates to find a World War II veteran who you can interview. A local chapter of the Veterans of Foreign Wars or a senior citizens' center may be able to help you. Have each group member write at least two questions for the interview. Assign one or two people to ask all the questions. The rest of the group should take notes during the interview. Afterward, you should write a thank-you note to the person you interviewed. Report the results of the interview to the class. If possible, use a map to show where that person was stationed during the war.

## USE VOCABULARY

Use each vocabulary word in a sentence that helps explain its meaning.

1. boom
2. petroleum
3. free enterprise
4. civil rights
5. commercial farm
6. suffrage
7. unemployment
8. leisure time
9. segregation
10. demand
11. service industry
12. politics

## CHECK UNDERSTANDING

1. What happened at Spindletop?
2. How did the railroad and automobile industries help start the first Texas oil boom?
3. Why did conflict occur between Tejanos and Anglos in South Texas?
4. How did the Houston Ship Channel help businesses in Houston?
5. What law stated that women in the United States had the right to vote?
6. What caused the Dust Bowl?
7. What was under the tidelands that made them valuable?
8. What caused the Texas oil bust of the 1980s?
9. What are Presidents Johnson and Bush remembered for?

## THINK CRITICALLY

1. **Cause and Effect** Before World War II, most people lived close to where they worked. What made it possible for people who worked in the city to live in the suburbs in the years after World War II?
2. **Personally Speaking** Imagine you are a Texas entrepreneur in the early 1900s. Describe the business you plan to set up.
3. **Think More About It** Why did Neil Armstrong say the word *Houston* in his famous quote from the moon?

## APPLY GEOGRAPHY SKILLS

**How to Use Maps with Different Scales** After World War II, people had more leisure time to travel. Use the map below and the maps on pages 282 and 283 to answer the questions that follow.

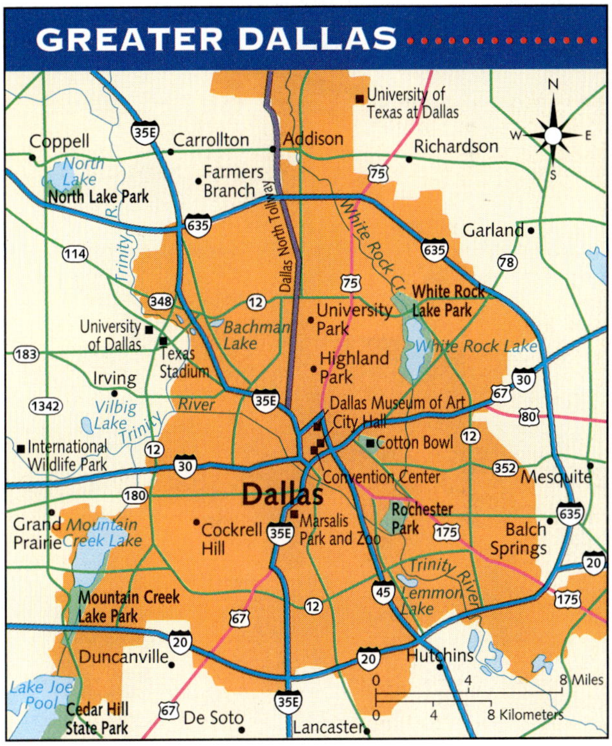


1. How far is it from the Cotton Bowl to the International Wildlife Park?
2. The Tigua Indian Reservation is in El Paso. Which map would best show a route from Texarkana to the reservation?
3. Your family is planning a vacation to visit relatives in three different states. Which map will you use?

# UNIT 6

# TEXAS TODAY

## CHALLENGES

dealing with growth

improving education

protecting the environment

In the 1930s and 1940s, Texas began to change from a farming and ranching state to an industrial and service industry state. This change is still taking place today. As more and more people move to the state, Texas must meet the needs of a fast-growing urban population. The environment must be protected, and there must be education for all. Meeting these needs is the challenge of all Texas citizens and their governments. Texans are ready to address any problems the state's growth may bring—just as they have solved other problems in the past.

◂ Restaurants, shops, and hotels line Paseo del Rio, the River Walk in San Antonio.

## GOVERNMENT

state

local

citizens

# Texas,

**by Gladys Yoakum Wright and William J. Marsh**

**In 1929 a contest to write a state song was held in Texas. The Texas Legislature chose the winner, "Texas, Our Texas." The song shows the pride that Texans feel toward their state and its rich heritage.**

Texas, our Texas! All hail the mighty State!
Texas, our Texas! So wonderful, so great!
Boldest and grandest, Withstanding ev'ry test;
O Empire, wide and glorious,
You stand supremely blest.

God bless you, Texas!
And keep you brave and strong,
That you may grow in pow'r and worth
Thruout the ages long.

# Our Texas

Texas, O Texas! Your freeborn Single Star
Sends out its radiance To nations near and far.
Emblem of Freedom! It sets our hearts aglow
With tho'ts of San Jacinto
And glorious Alamo.

Texas, dear Texas! From tyrant grip now free;
Shines forth in splendor Your Star of Destiny!
Mother of Heroes! We come, your children true,
Proclaiming our allegiance,
Our Faith, our Love for you.

The mockingbird, the bluebonnet, the Lone Star flag, and the San Jacinto Monument are all symbols of the state of Texas.

# The Star-Spangled

## by Francis Scott Key

**The United States Congress agreed in 1931 to accept "The Star-Spangled Banner" as the national anthem. It had been written, however, more than 100 years earlier, during the War of 1812, between Great Britain and the United States. After a British attack on Fort McHenry in Baltimore, Maryland, Francis Scott Key was thrilled to see the American flag still waving. He wrote these words to show pride in his country and in the flag for which the Americans had fought so hard.**

Oh! say, can you see, by the dawn's early light,
What so proudly we hailed at the twilight's last gleaming?
Whose broad stripes and bright stars, thro' the perilous fight,
O'er the ramparts we watched were so gallantly streaming?
And the rockets' red glare, the bombs bursting in air,
Gave proof thro' the night that our flag was still there.
Oh! say, does that star-spangled banner yet wave
O'er the land of the free and the home of the brave?

On the shore, dimly seen thro' the mists of the deep,
Where the foe's haughty host in dread silence reposes,
What is that which the breeze, o'er the towering steep,
As it fitfully blows, half conceals, half discloses?
Now it catches the gleam of the morning's first beam,
In full glory reflected, now shines on the stream.
'Tis the star-spangled banner. Oh! long may it wave
O'er the land of the free and the home of the brave!

# Banner

And where is that band who so vauntingly swore
That the havoc of war and the battle's confusion
A home and a country should leave us no more?
Their blood has washed out their foul footstep's pollution.
No refuge could save the hireling and slave
From the terror of flight or the gloom of the grave,
And the star-spangled banner in triumph doth wave
O'er the land of the free and the home of the brave.

Oh! thus be it ever when freemen shall stand
Between their loved home and the war's desolation,
Blest with vict'ry and peace, may the Heav'n-rescued land
Praise the Pow'r that hath made and preserved us a nation.
Then conquer we must, when our cause it is just,
And this be our motto, "In God is our Trust."
And the star-spangled banner in triumph shall wave
O'er the land of the free and the home of the brave.

**The Liberty Bell, the bald eagle, the United States flag, and the Statue of Liberty are all symbols of the United States of America.**

HAPTER 11

# CHALLENGES FOR TEXAS TODAY

"Life is a challenge. There is no end to learning."

Rose Chin Wong, Austin artist

# THE CHALLENGE OF GROWTH

## Link to Our World

**How is the population of your community changing?**

***Focus on the Main Idea***
**Read to find out how the state's growing population has become a challenge for the citizens of Texas.**

***Preview Vocabulary***
**census**
**multicultural**

Every ten years the United States government takes a **census**, or population count. In 1990 the United States Census counted nearly 17 million people in Texas. Only California and New York had more people. Today the population of Texas is more than 18 million people. Only California now has more people. By the next census, in the year 2000, there may be nearly 20 million people in Texas. Most of the growth is taking place in a triangle-shaped area in the middle of the state. This triangle stretches from the Dallas–Fort Worth area south to Houston and west to San Antonio and Austin.

In completing census forms, families help the government gather information about the population.

### Reasons for Growth

Many of the reasons for population growth in Texas today are the same as those of the past. Not only are more people being born in the state, but more people are moving to Texas from other places.

When Texas was part of New Spain, and later part of Mexico, people came from the south to Texas to build cities and start ranches. Today people from Mexico and South America come to Texas to search for jobs. Many do not have government papers allowing them to live in the United States. They often take the low-paying jobs no one else wants. Because of this, they have become important to the economy in Texas. Many work on the large commercial farms and in the construction and service industries.

Many Vietnamese Americans in Texas make their living by fishing.

When Texas was a Mexican colony, and later a republic, many people moved to Texas from the United States. People still come today. Some businesses have moved their offices to Texas from northern states, bringing workers with them. Older people from other states move to Texas because of its mild climate and its many recreation areas, which are good for their health.

When Texas was a republic and then a new state, many immigrants came from Europe. People from Germany, Poland, and other European countries came to Texas to make a better life for themselves and for their children and grandchildren. Today the largest group of newcomers to Texas from outside the Western Hemisphere is from Asia. People from Vietnam, China, India, the Philippines, Korea, Japan, Laos, Cambodia, and Thailand have settled mainly along the Gulf coast and in the large cities of Texas.

Weak economies and the poor living conditions in other countries have made many people leave their homes and come to the United States. People both in Mexico and in the United States are hoping that the North American Free Trade Agreement, or NAFTA, will make Mexico's economy stronger so that fewer immigrants will come to Texas and other border states.

Mexico, Canada, and the United States, the three largest countries in North America, signed NAFTA in 1994. They agreed to reduce taxes on the goods they import from one another. That way, businesses in the three countries will be able to compete more equally with one another. This is important to all three countries because it means more jobs for their workers.

**What are two reasons for today's growth in the population of Texas?**

## Growth of Cities

With its growing population, Texas has 6 of the 30 largest United States cities. They are Houston, Dallas, San Antonio, El Paso, Austin, and Fort Worth. Few other states have as many cities this large. As Texas cities keep growing, they must be able to provide city services. Among these are water, garbage pickup, and police and fire protection.

Traffic is a problem. Growing numbers of people using their automobiles mean that more roads and highways must be built. Some cities have tried to get people to use public transportation, such as buses.

Crime is another problem. Dropping out of school, not having a job, and using drugs all seem to lead to crime. Texas cities are trying to solve crime problems by looking at the causes.

As Texas cities continue to grow, they will need more police officers to protect the growing populations.

**✓ What problems do Texas cities face as they continue to grow?**

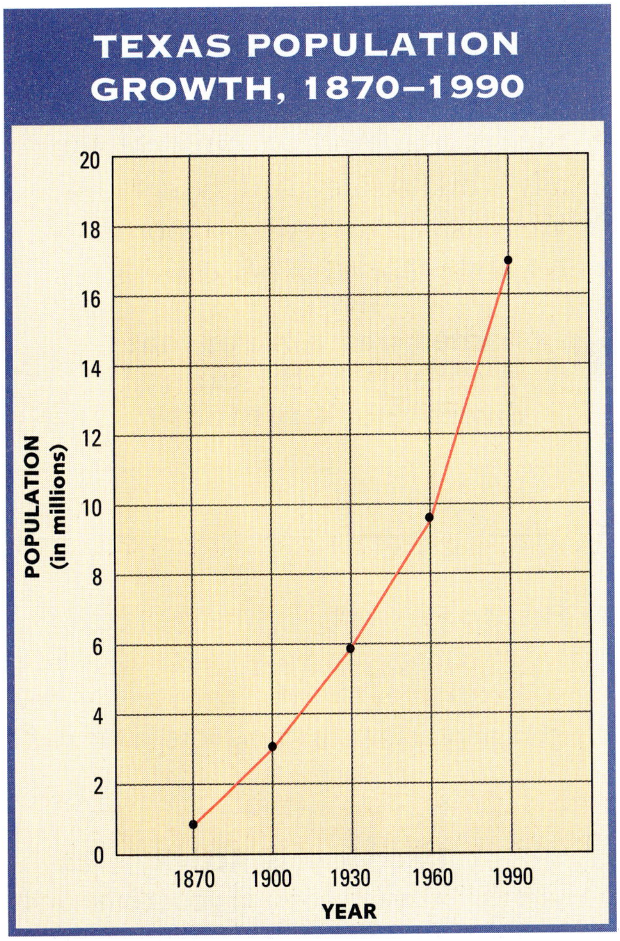


**LEARNING FROM GRAPHS** In 1970 Texas was fourth in population among the states. Today it ranks second.

- Between what years did Texas show the greatest growth in population?

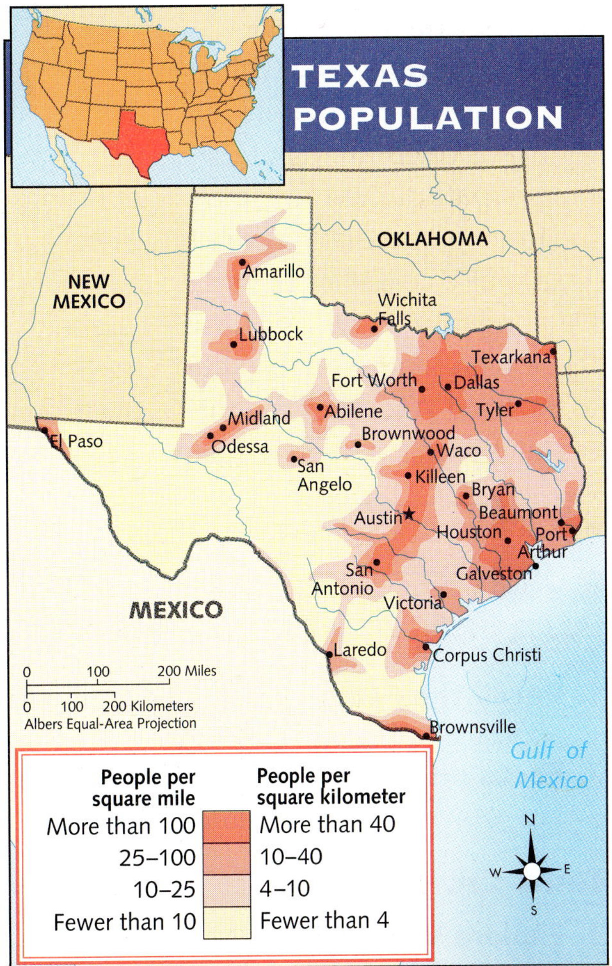


**PLACE** Most of the people in Texas live in urban areas.

- What areas of Texas are the least populated?

Mexican Americans in Texas celebrate *Cinco de Mayo*, which honors the overthrow of French rule in Mexico.

## Cultural Diversity

The many people who have come to live in Texas give the state an interesting blend of diverse, or different, cultures. This blend of cultures has resulted in a mix of customs and traditions. Many Texans eat Mexican foods such as tacos and burritos. Chili is the state dish. Yet German and Chinese foods are also popular in Texas.

Texans celebrate Juneteenth, or Emancipation Day, a holiday celebrating the freeing of enslaved Africans in Texas. Texans also celebrate Confederate Heroes Day on January 19. This day remembers those who fought on the side of the South in the Civil War. They fought for the rights of states to make their own laws.

Former Governor William P. Clements, Jr., once said, "The greatest strength of Texas has long been the vitality and diversity of its people." But having a **multicultural** state, or a state with people of many cultures, can have its problems. Governor Clements also said,

> "We must respect the rights of all Texans. Regardless of their cultural background. And, we must continually work to safeguard those rights. We must see that equal opportunity is a reality for all of our citizens."

**Name three cultures that contribute to the cultural diversity of Texas today.**

## Lesson 1 Review

### Check Understanding

1. **Recall the Facts** What is the estimated population of Texas today?
2. **Focus on the Main Idea** How has the fast-growing population affected the state?

### Think Critically

3. **Explore Viewpoints** What problems do you think people might face when moving to Texas from another country? What problems might Texans have with newcomers whose cultures are not like their own?
4. **Past to Present** In what ways are today's immigrants like immigrants earlier in Texas history? In what ways are the new immigrants different from those in the past?

### Show What You Know

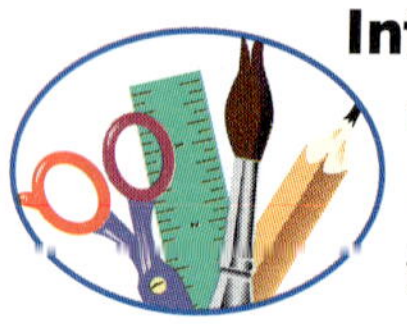

**Interviewing Activity** Talk with people in your community to find out when they or their families came to Texas. With your classmates, prepare a presentation describing the cultures in your community.

S·K·I·L·L·S

# How To

## Use a Pictograph

### Why Is This Skill Important?

Graphs can help you compare amounts. Some graphs use bars or lines. **Pictographs** use symbols to stand for amounts. The graph on this page compares the populations of the largest cities in Texas with those of other cities in the Western Hemisphere. From the pictograph, you can easily see which cities are the largest.

### Understand the Process

The pictograph makes it easy to compare populations, but it does not give exact population numbers. On this pictograph each symbol stands for about 500,000 people. Half of a symbol stands for about 250,000 people. Two symbols are shown for Dallas. To find the population these symbols stand for, you must multiply 500,000 by 2. The answer is 1 million. So the population of Dallas is about 1 million people.

Now use the pictograph to answer these questions.

1. How many symbols are shown for Buenos Aires, Argentina?
2. What is the population of Buenos Aires?
3. How many symbols are shown for El Paso?
4. What is the population of El Paso?
5. Which city, El Paso or Buenos Aires, has more people?
6. Which cities have about the same number of people?

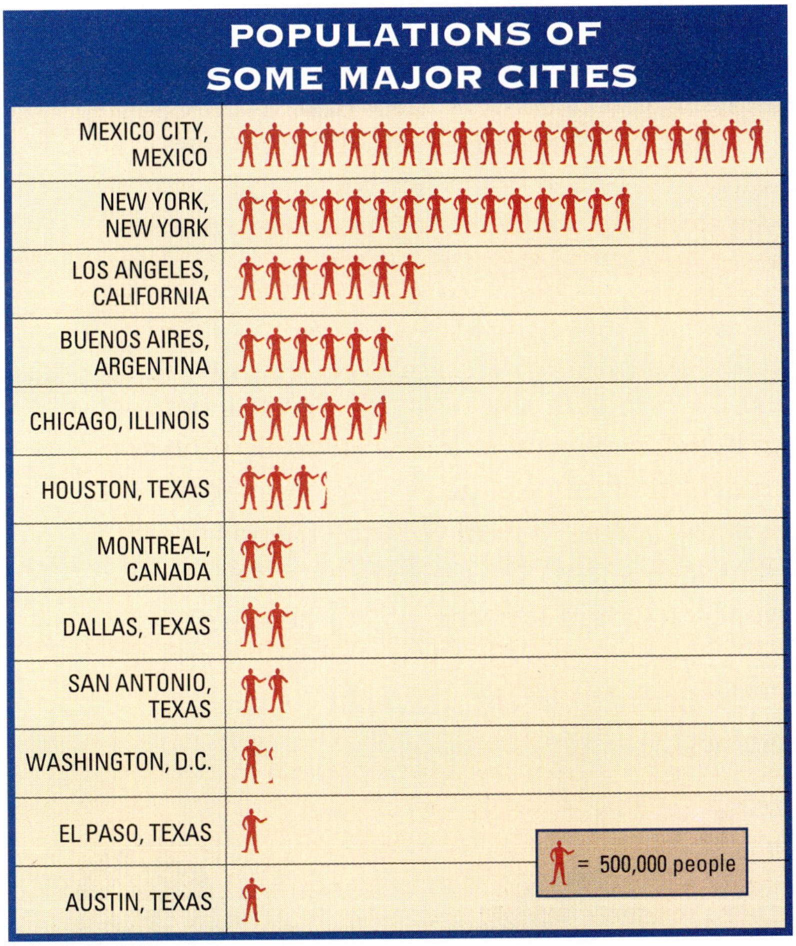


### Think and Apply

Cotton, wheat, and rice are three important cash crops grown in Texas today. Make a pictograph to compare the amounts of money these three crops make for Texas. Draw a different picture symbol to stand for each crop. Let each symbol stand for $100 million.

Use the following information to make your graph:

- cotton — $800 million
- wheat — $400 million
- rice — $150 million

LESSON 2

LEARN with LITERATURE

Focus on Texas as a Multicultural State

# The Courage Seed

by Jean Richardson    illustrations by Pat Finney

**Mary Manygoats has just moved to Houston from a Navajo Indian village in New Mexico. Mary is shy and has a hard time facing school in a new place. In her old school all the students were Navajo. In her new school the students are from places all over the world. On the first day of school, Mary's teacher asks the students to tell the class about themselves. Mary is afraid no one will like her because she is different. The students in the story are based on real people who once went to Townewest Elementary School in Sugar Land, Texas.**

A small girl sitting on the front row nearest the door was the first to speak. Mary couldn't hear a word the girl was saying because her own heart was pounding in her ears. Several students stood up, one at a time, before Mary could quiet her thumping heart enough to hear. How she longed to be back at the Navajo school with the friends she had known all her life. At that school, only the teachers were strangers.

Mary began to wonder what she would say when it was her turn. . . . She didn't have any hobbies, unless herding the Churro sheep could be called a hobby. Perhaps if she listened closely, she could get some ideas from the other students.

A tall boy named Rishi was telling about the home he remembered in India. He described in great detail a beautiful palace he had visited in the city of Agra. As Mary listened, she imagined that she could see the Taj Mahal shimmering above his head.

Next a girl from Colombia told about the home she hadn't seen since she was small. She spoke of the cobblestone streets and the wrought-iron balconies on the buildings. But especially she remembered the wild orchids. Mary could almost smell the sweet fragrance of the blossoms as the girl talked.

When the teacher called "Chris," two boys jumped up. They were both named Chris, and they were both from England. They looked enough alike to be brothers. They had met out on the playground and already were friends.

The two boys took turns telling about their favorite places in London, where they both were born. They talked about Big Ben, the largest bell in the Clock Tower of the Houses of Parliament. They described Trafalgar Square, Charing Cross, the Tower of London, and Piccadilly Circus. When they were finished, everyone wanted to go to London.

April, a small girl with dark brown hair braided in tiny cornrows, was next. She was from the island of Jamaica. She told of the city houses where her aunts and cousins lived, but mostly she remembered life on her grandmother's farm.

She talked about the chickens, goats, and pigs her grandmother raised. She remembered the colorful flowers that grew near their home in the Blue Mountains. In vivid detail she described the tall hibiscus plants with their pink and white blossoms. She missed all those things, but most of all she missed her grandmother.

Philippines

Jason, a boy from the Philippines, came after April. He described his home on stilts, the long front porch, and the swaying palm trees all around his house. He said the family used sleeping mats that were rolled up in a corner.

Jason also explained how the carabao, or water buffalo, did most of the work in the rice fields. And he described the caramata, or two-wheeled cart, which was used to transport almost anything.

"But my caramata now is a bicycle," he said. "I'm going to be a famous bicycle racer when I grow up!"

Netherlands

The next student was a very blonde girl from the Netherlands. "Some people call it Holland," she said, "but the real name, Netherlands, means 'the low countries.' And it *is* a low country. Most of our land was reclaimed from the sea by building dikes to keep the water out. We are most famous for our windmills and tulips. For special occasions we put on our lace caps and wooden shoes. I still have my wooden shoes. Maybe one day I could bring them to school."

**reclaimed** brought into a condition to be used for farming

**dikes** dams

The boy next to her stood up and pointed to his chest when it was his turn. "My name is Syngman, but my sister calls me 'Dragonfish' and my dad calls me 'Young Dragon.' We are Korean, but I do not remember Korea because I was born in America. I have seen pictures of the pagodas and the royal tombs at Kokuryo. Someday I would like to go there to visit."

**pagodas** tower-like temples

Korea

"I have a funny name too," the next boy said. "I live in Pakistan, and my name is Iskander. You can call me 'Ike.' My parents are here on a grant from the university where my father teaches. We live in East Pakistan [present-day Bangladesh], which is flat country covered with bamboo, mango, coconut palm, and date palm trees. Our forests have leopards, bears, and tigers. We don't have to go to a zoo to see those animals."

**grant** gift

The next girl stood up and twirled around in her colorful, full skirt. "My mama let me wear this special dress for the first day of school," she said. "It's a dress I would wear in Mexico for fiesta. My favorite places in Mexico are the churches and the plazas. We visit our relatives often, but America is our home."

**fiesta** festival

Ramzi was the next to speak. "My parents came from Lebanon many years ago. I've never been there, but I've seen pictures of the palaces, with their high arches and the thick stone walls for shade."

The next girl's name was Kimberly. "My grandparents fled Viet Nam in a small sampan after the war. Sometimes they talk about the houses with thatched roofs and the flowers that grew wild. But I don't know of those things. I'm an American."

**sampan** boat

**thatched** made of grass

Tyler said, "I'm an American too. My ancestors came here from Ireland many years ago. I've never been there, but I've heard about the 100-year-old cottages with thatched roofs. Some people call it the 'Emerald Isle' because it's so green."

"My name is John and I'm from Nigeria," said the next boy. "I'm wearing a tie-dyed shirt that my aunt made especially for me. It has a Nigerian design."

"My name is Abi, and I'm from Nigeria too," said the boy across the aisle. "Many people think of Nigeria as a poor country, but we also have modern cities there. We have many of the same things as an American city."

Mary began to look around the room with more interest. These were certainly not the classmates she had expected. She began to wonder: What does a real American look like? Did anyone here really look like the children she had seen on Aunt Betsy's TV set?

The girl sitting next to her on the right was pretty enough to be on television. She had long, blonde hair and beautiful, blue eyes. Her expensive clothes made her look like an advertisement for a department store. Mary thought that if she only looked like that girl, her problems would be over.

The blonde girl's name was Jessica. She told the class about her father, who worked at NASA. She talked about a trip she had made to Florida to watch a shuttle launch.

But Mary wasn't listening. A tiny tear trickled down her face and landed on the desk silently. At that very moment she heard the teacher call her name.

"Mary, you are last. But I'm sure you have some interesting things to tell us."

In the silence that followed, Mary thought of something her grandfather once told her. "You can be brave," he told her when she was very small and had been afraid of the dark. "Look in your mind for the tiny seed of courage."

"Do I have seeds in my mind?" Mary had asked.

"Everyone does," Grandfather replied. "The seeds for love, hope, and courage are all there. But they will never grow big and strong unless you tend them well. Brave deeds help the courage plant grow strong, just as rain helps plants in the desert."

Mary took a deep breath and stood up. "My name is Mary Manygoats," she said. Mary was surprised by the clear, calm sound of her own voice. "I am a Navajo from Shiprock, New Mexico."

Every head in the room turned and looked curiously in her direction. Mary bravely continued. "My grandfather, Night Singer, was a shaman and a great storyteller of the Dineh, our people. My grandmother, Dawn Woman, was famous for the beautiful patterns and brilliant colors in the blankets she wove. My old hobby was herding Churro sheep, but now I have to find a new hobby."

"Thank you, Mary," the teacher said when Mary quit speaking. But Mary did not sit down. Looking all around the room at the expectant faces, she smiled shyly.

"On behalf of my entire tribe," she said in a voice that sounded very much like her grandfather's, "I'd like to welcome all of you to America."

Native American

## Literature Review

1. What were some of the countries the students or their parents came from?
2. In what ways were the students' stories alike? How were the stories different?
3. Make a map with pictures to show the places where the students or their parents were born. In each place, add a symbol that stands for the culture of that country.

S·K·I·L·L·S

# HOW TO

# Use a Map to Show Movement

## Why Is This Skill Important?

People need a way to know which direction to follow on a map, so mapmakers add a drawing called a compass rose. The compass rose on a map helps you identify both the **cardinal directions**, labeled *N, S, E,* and *W,* and the **intermediate directions**, labeled *NE, SE, SW,* and *NW.* The compass rose can help you describe the direction of movement shown on a map.

## Understand the Process

The map on this page shows the countries that the students in Mary's class or their parents came from. First, read the map key to learn that an arrow stands for the movement of people. Trace each arrow from beginning to end with your finger.

1. In which countries do the arrows begin?
2. To which place do the arrows go?

Now trace the arrows again with your finger. Look at the compass rose to see the direction of each arrow from where it starts to where it ends in Texas. In which direction does the arrow go to Texas from each of the countries listed below? Use both cardinal and intermediate directions in your answers.

- Mexico
- Lebanon
- Vietnam
- Nigeria
- England
- Colombia

## Think and Apply

With a partner, draw a map of your community. Show your school in the middle of the map, and show the houses or neighborhoods where some of your classmates live. Be sure to draw a compass rose on your map. Then draw arrows from the houses and neighborhoods to the school. Write a sentence that tells in which direction most of the students travel to get from home to school.

## IMMIGRATION TO TEXAS

# Lesson 3 Education for All

## Link to Our World

**Why is it important to get a good education?**

***Focus on the Main Idea***
**Read to learn how education helps the state of Texas.**

***Preview Vocabulary***
**human resource**
**informed citizen**
**TAAS**

Education has always been important in Texas history. Among the earliest Native Americans who lived in what is now Texas, young people learned from older people the skills of hunting and growing food. In their missions the Spanish taught Native Americans both the Catholic religion and the skills for farming and ranching. During the time when Texas was a republic and in its early days as a state, most Texans went to one-room schools. There they learned the basics of reading, writing, and mathematics. Texas leaders Sam Houston, William B. Travis, Lyndon B. Johnson, and Ann Richards all were once teachers. Today education helps prepare Texans for new ways of life.

Providing a good education for children is one of the most important goals of the Texas state government.

## The Importance of Education for Texans

The Texas economy has become more diverse. In addition to oil, cattle, and farming, the new high-technology industries have also become important in Texas. High-tech businesses use newly discovered knowledge and newly invented tools, such as computers and other electronic equipment.

People who work in these new industries must have a good education. When people get a good education, they are more likely to find good jobs. An educated worker is a valuable **human resource**.

Besides being important to the economy, an educated citizen is important in a democracy. An educated citizen is an informed citizen. An **informed citizen** is one who understands why things happen in the community, the state, the nation, and the world. An informed citizen is more likely to have the skills needed to take part in the community. An informed citizen is also more likely to understand other people's values and opinions.

Reading a newspaper and talking about current events with an adult are good ways to become an informed citizen.

**Why is education important?**

## Improving Education

In 1984 Governor Mark White wanted to know how good the public education was in Texas. He set up a committee to study the needs and the problems of the education system in the state. The committee decided that to be well-educated, Texans had to have the skills and knowledge needed to find good jobs. The committee also found that good schools helped bring new businesses to Texas. People want to live and work in a state where their children can get a good education.

Because of the committee's reports, the state government passed laws to make the public schools stronger. It called for better-trained teachers. In addition, high school students had to learn more to graduate.

You are a citizen of Texas. How is your education preparing you to be a good citizen?

To check whether the schools are improving, the state government requires that all students take tests in the basic skills of reading, writing, and other school subjects. These tests are called the Texas Assessment of Academic Skills, or **TAAS**. The word *assessment* can mean "test."

**Why must Texas students take TAAS tests?**

## Lesson 3 Review

### Check Understanding

1. **Recall the Facts** Why did Governor Mark White set up a committee to study the education system in Texas?
2. **Focus on the Main Idea** How does education help the state of Texas?

### Think Critically

3. **Personally Speaking** Do you think you are learning what you will need to know as an adult in the future? Explain your answer.

### Show What You Know

**Poster Activity** Identify a job or career that you might like to have as an adult. Prepare a poster showing people doing this kind of work. Write a paragraph about the knowledge or skills that are needed to do this job.

# LESSON 4 THE CHALLENGE OF THE ENVIRONMENT

## Link to Our World

**How do people in your community affect their environment?**

***Focus on the Main Idea***
**Read to find out what problems the growing population causes for the environment in Texas.**

***Preview Vocabulary***
**pollute**
**recycle**
**landfill**

When Lyndon and Lady Bird Johnson returned to Texas in 1969 after Johnson had finished his term as President of the United States, they found that much of the land looked different. Lady Bird said she saw at that time that "the meadows and hillsides were all being replaced by highway grids and shopping malls." She worried about seeing litter and too many billboards.

In 1982 Lady Bird Johnson started the National Wildflower Research Center near Austin. One purpose of the center is to find simple ways to conserve and protect the environment. Planting wildflowers is one way to do this. As Lady Bird said, "We in Texas are blessed with what we have. I just want Texas to keep on looking like Texas."

Texans are proud of their state and are serious about keeping it clean and beautiful. "Don't Mess With Texas" has been the slogan of one of the nation's most successful campaigns against littering.

## Conserving Valuable Resources

Texans today depend on the land, the air, and the water as much as Texans of the past did. Today, however, most Texans understand that the state's environment must be conserved. The Dust Bowl of the 1930s showed them what can happen when people do not conserve and protect the state's resources.

Since the Dust Bowl days, Texas, with help from the federal government, has set up soil conservation districts. These districts work with farmers and ranchers to stop

## What?

### National Wildflower Research Center

Texas has more wildflowers than any other state—about 5,000 different kinds have been counted. During spring, colorful wildflowers cover fields all along the highways of Texas. There are so many of these wildflowers partly because of the National Wildflower Research Center. The center, which was founded by Lady Bird Johnson in 1982, is located near Austin. Its researchers study the uses and benefits of wildflowers.

The center, the first of its kind in the country, was founded because preserving wildflowers is a simple and effective way to protect our environment. Wildflowers reduce soil erosion and protect the land against pollution from chemical fertilizers. They help preserve native plant and animal life. Also, it takes little labor to keep wildflowers growing, and they use little water and no fertilizer.

Lady Bird Johnson, who has spent much of her life working to help the environment, summed up her belief on wildflowers. "We cannot manage [public land] in the old way, which meant heavy use of mowing, manpower, fertilizer," she said. "We've got to crank in some use of our native wildflowers, grasses, and shrubs."

soil erosion, save water, and reduce the damage from chemical fertilizers that **pollute**, or spoil, the environment.

Stopping pollution is important in all parts of Texas, not just on farms and ranches. The federal and state governments have passed laws against dumping harmful wastes. People are helping the environment by not littering and by obeying laws passed to cut down on pollution.

**How does a soil conservation district protect the environment?**

## Recycling Is Good Business

Recycling is one way people in Texas cut down on pollution. To **recycle** means to use materials again instead of wasting them. People can take metal cans, glass

Recycling saves both energy and natural resources. Every day, the average person in the United States produces a little more than 4 pounds (2 kg) of garbage. The energy saved by recycling one aluminum can instead of making a new one could run your television for three hours.

bottles and jars, plastic containers, and newspapers to recycling centers. The centers sell these items to companies that use them to make new products.

Most Texas cities and towns now have recycling centers and factories that use recycled materials instead of new ones. One business in Houston even recycles old computers and other electronic equipment. An entrepreneur named Michael Filandro started the company when he realized that some people would pay to have their old or outdated computers taken away.

The disposal of old computers had been causing a problem for the environment. The machines took up landfill space. A **landfill** is a place where garbage and litter from a community are buried. Some parts of the computers were also polluting the water.

So Filandro found ways to recycle the old computers. He sells the plastic coverings, which are melted down and made into other products. He sells the gold and silver used in the computers to jewelers, dental manufacturers, and makers of coins. He even found ways to use the microchips in making new computers and repairing old ones.

"As far as we know, we're the only ones in the United States doing this," says Filandro.

**How does recycling help prevent pollution?**

Leaders in Texas have passed laws to protect the state's water supply. It is hoped that these laws will soon stop the kind of pollution shown here.

## Water: A Most Important Resource

Water is one of the most important natural resources in Texas. People need water to live. Where water is scarce, there are likely to be few cities, farms, ranches, or factories. As more people come to live in Texas, more water is needed. Texans must find a way to provide enough water for all the state's people.

Texans get most of their water from two sources—underground aquifers and reservoirs. Rainfall adds water to the aquifers and reservoirs. If it does not rain, however, water levels drop. When the water from aquifers and reservoirs runs low, state and local governments often ask Texans to conserve water by not watering lawns or washing cars.

Aquifers and reservoirs may even go dry. Some parts of Texas run short of water every time there is a severe drought. Then there is not even enough water for necessary uses, such as irrigating crops or drinking and bathing.

As the Texas population grows, so does the problem of water pollution. Some rivers flow near cities and factories. Sometimes wastes are dumped into rivers. These wastes pollute the water. People can become sick when they drink the water or bathe in it.

Many people are working to clean up Texas rivers and other water sources. State government, businesses, and local communities are working together on large cleanup projects. One of the largest projects is the cleanup of the Rio Grande, which has become very polluted. People on both sides of the river, in Mexico and in the United States, depend on the river. Farmers in South Texas and northern Mexico use the river's water to irrigate crops. Factories in both countries use the water in manufacturing. People living along the Rio Grande use it in their homes.

The Rio Grande project may take many years to complete. However, it shows that Texans can work together and with their neighbors in Mexico to conserve resources and protect the environment. Everybody can help keep Texas a clean, healthful, and beautiful place to live.

**Why is water such an important resource?**

Map Skill **PLACE** Most of the underground water used in Texas comes from nine aquifers.
■ From which aquifer do the people of Lubbock get their water?

## LESSON 4 REVIEW

### Check Understanding

1. **Recall the Facts** How are Texas citizens protecting their environment?
2. **Focus on the Main Idea** What problems does the growing population cause for the environment in Texas?

### Think Critically

3. **Link to You** What can you do to help conserve resources and protect the environment in your community?
4. **Cause and Effect** How could water pollution affect birds and other animals?

### Show What You Know

**Research-and-Report Activity** Use your library to find out more about the pollution of water, land, and air. Present your findings in a report to the class. Include ways in which citizens are working to solve pollution problems.

S·K·I·L·L·S

# How To

# Solve a Problem

## Why Is This Skill Important?

In coming years, you will face problems that are different from those you face today. Learning how to solve difficult problems today will help you solve other problems in the years to come.

## Remember What You Have Read

Think about what you have read about the pollution problem faced by people who live along the Rio Grande. These people depend on the river's water in many ways. Factory owners need it to make goods. Farmers need it to irrigate their crops. Many people need it to drink and use in their homes.

To keep the river clean, all these people need to work together to solve the problem. But solving this problem is difficult because some businesses dump waste into the river. Some farmers still allow chemical fertilizers to run off into the river. Other people continue to dump their garbage along the riverbanks.

## Understand the Process

There are steps you can follow to solve most problems, even those that affect the environment.

1. State the problem. In the case of the Rio Grande, the problem can be stated "The river is polluted."
2. Divide the problem into smaller parts. The Rio Grande problem might be divided into two parts. Why is the river polluted? How can we keep it from getting more polluted?
3. Work to solve the problem one part at a time. One way to keep the Rio Grande from getting more polluted might be for groups of people to pick up the litter along the riverbanks.
4. Check to see if what you are doing is working. People might walk along the river each week to see if less litter is found.
5. Work to solve the other parts of the problem.

## Think and Apply

With a partner, identify an environmental problem in your community. Watch television reports, read the newspapers, or talk with community leaders to see how they are working to solve the problem. Identify the steps they are using. Follow up on their progress periodically. Then discuss with your partner how you would work to solve the problem.

How would you persuade people living along the Rio Grande to stop dumping trash into the river?

COUNTERPOINTS

# WATER

# PUBLIC PROPERTY OR PRIVATE PROPERTY?

The Edwards Aquifer is the main source of water for much of Central Texas. The aquifer provides water for more than 1,500 corn and cotton farms, more than 40,000 businesses, and many towns and cities, among them San Antonio. People who depend on the Edwards Aquifer have different ideas about how the water should be used.

An aquifer that people use is like a glass of water with many straws in it. Each straw comes from a user who competes with others for the water supply. The underground water of aquifers in Texas is **private property**. Individual people own it, and they can use as much water as they want. Surface water in rivers and lakes, however, is **public property**. All the people of the state own it, and the state government controls how people use it. Some people in Texas think underground water should remain private property. Others think laws should make underground water public property. They think the state should control how it is used.

In 1991 Ronnie Pucek, Jr., dug a well into the Edwards Aquifer for water to start a catfish farm near New Braunfels. "Texans eat 40 percent of the catfish consumed nationwide, and we didn't have any growers or processors down here," he said. Pucek drew out more than 43 million gallons a day. This caused the water level in the aquifer and nearby wells to drop.

Now read the following opinions. Decide what each person might think about underground water being public or private property.

**Paul Grohman**
Former City Manager, New Braunfels

"It's a travesty [ridiculous]. That catfish farm will use as much as eight times more water than does this city of more than 30,000 people."

**Ken Kramer**
Director, Lone Star Chapter, Sierra Club

"The aquifer is as important to the economy of the region as it is to the environment of the region. . . . Continued overpumping of water from the Edwards [Aquifer] would be a recipe for disaster."

**Ronnie Pucek, Jr.**
Owner, The Living Waters Artesian Catfish Farm

"At the time this well was dug, there was no regulation of pumping of the Edwards Aquifer. A surface landowner had a right to any and all groundwater his well could produce, so long as he used it legally and for a beneficial purpose."

## COMPARE VIEWPOINTS

1. Which side do you think each person would take in discussing whether underground water should be public property? Give your reasons.
2. Does Ronnie Pucek agree with Paul Grohman? How do you know?
3. How does Ronnie Pucek defend what he is doing?
4. Which side do you take? Give reasons for your answer.

## THINK -AND- APPLY

Think of a way for Texans to have more water without changing the laws. Then explain how your idea would affect people who depend on the Edwards Aquifer. How do you think Paul Grohman, Ken Kramer, and Ronnie Pucek would feel about your idea? Why?

# CHAPTER 11 REVIEW

## CONNECT MAIN IDEAS

Use this organizer to show that you understand how the chapter's main ideas are connected. First copy the organizer onto a separate sheet of paper. Then complete it by writing one or two sentences that describe how Texans are working to meet each challenge.

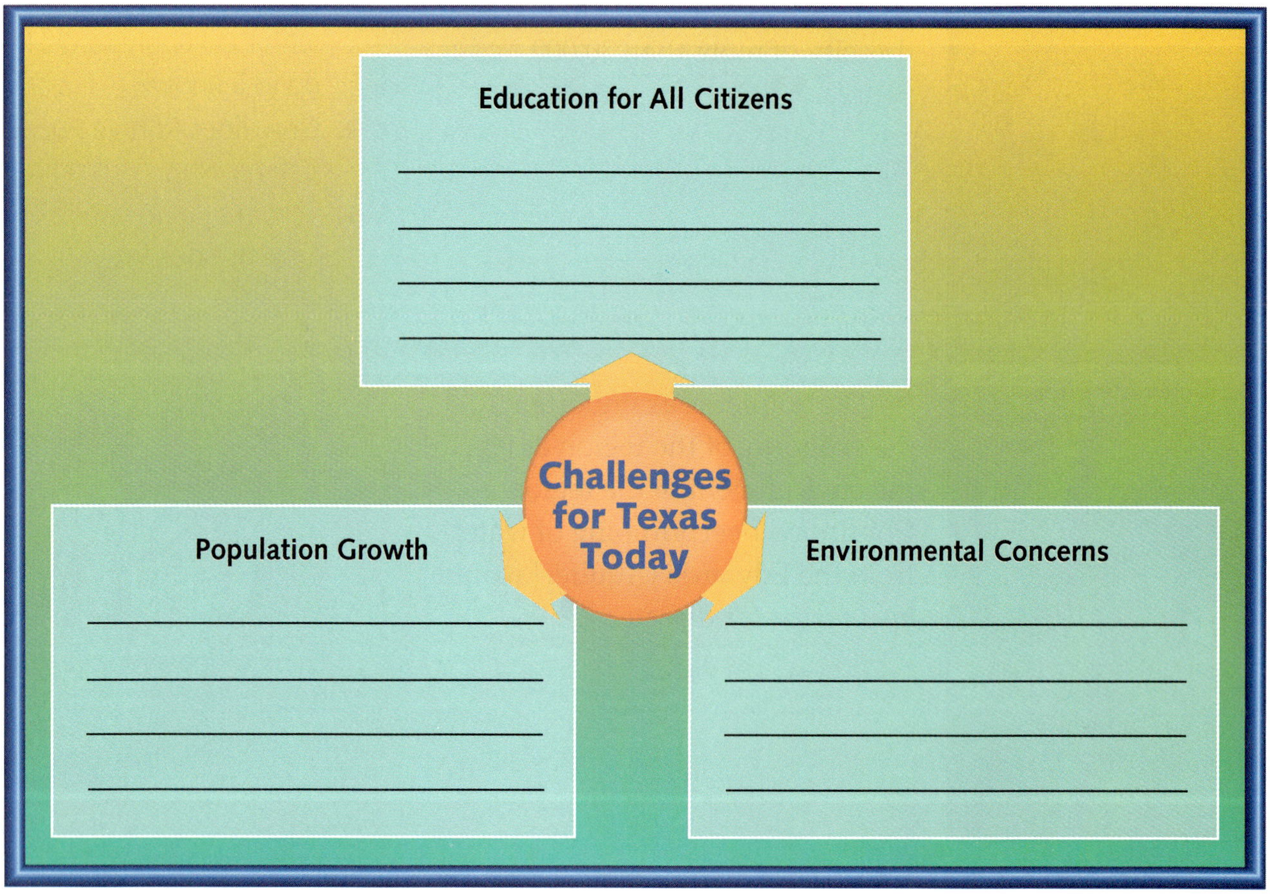


## WRITE MORE ABOUT IT

1. **Write an Advertisement** Imagine that you are starting a recycling center and you want people to bring in their recyclable goods. Write an advertisement that tells about your center and how recycling will help the citizens and the community. Share your advertisement with the class.

2. **Write a Comparison** How do you think living in a large city compares with living in a small town? What are the good points and bad points about each?

3. **Write a Summary** In one paragraph, tell how you think getting a good education will help you face challenges in the future.

## USE VOCABULARY

Use each vocabulary word in a newspaper headline that helps explain the meaning of the word.

1. census
2. multicultural
3. informed citizen
4. TAAS
5. recycle
6. landfill

## CHECK UNDERSTANDING

1. Give two reasons for Texas's population growth in recent years.
2. What are some problems faced by citizens of large Texas cities?
3. What cultures can be seen in Texas today?
4. Why is it important to be an informed citizen?
5. How did Governor White's committee improve the education system in Texas?
6. What does a soil conservation district do?
7. How does recycling help the environment?
8. Name several ways water is used.

## THINK CRITICALLY

1. **Cause and Effect** How has the growth of cities caused problems for Texas?
2. **Think More About It** In what ways is cultural diversity good for Texas?
3. **Explore Viewpoints** Why do you think Governor White wanted to improve the education system in Texas?
4. **Personally Speaking** Do you think you will continue your education after high school? Why or why not?
5. **Link to You** In what ways can you help reduce pollution and conserve water in your community?
6. **Personally Speaking** What do you think is the greatest challenge facing Texas today?

## APPLY SKILLS

**How to Use a Pictograph** Look in old newspapers or magazines for a pictograph. Clip out the graph, and tape it onto a sheet of paper. Below the graph, write a short paragraph describing the information that is shown.

**How to Use a Map to Show Movement** Draw a map that shows your classroom and several other places in your school. Add a compass rose to your map. Then draw arrows from your classroom to the other places shown. Write a sentence that tells in which direction you travel as you walk from one place to another.

**How to Solve a Problem** Reread the literature selection *The Courage Seed*, on pages 304–309. What problem did Mary face in the beginning of the story? What steps did she use to solve her problem? How did her solution work?

## READ MORE ABOUT IT

*From Sea to Shining Sea: Texas* by Dennis Brindell Fradin. Childrens Press. This colorfully illustrated book traces the history of Texas and describes the Texas of today.

*Water: What It Is, What It Does* by Judith S. Seixas. Greenwillow. This book explains what water is, how it is used, and why it is important to conserve it. The easy experiments with water are fun to do.

CHAPTER 12

# TEXAS GOVERNMENT

> "I share the sense of dedication that other . . . Governors must have felt. Like them, I understand that I am responsible to all the people of Texas."
>
> George W. Bush,
> Governor of Texas, 1995

# State Government in Texas

## Link to Our World

**Why is it important for people to share control in government?**

***Focus on the Main Idea***

**Read to find out how the work of the Texas state government is shared.**

***Preview Vocabulary***

**Bill of Rights**
**legislative branch**
**budget**
**executive branch**
**veto power**
**agency**
**judicial branch**
**appeal**
**jury trial**

In 1995 George W. Bush, son of former President George Bush, became governor of Texas. He said, "When I took the oath of office, I pledged to defend two Constitutions, those of the United States and of Texas." The United States Constitution, which became law in 1789, is the law of the nation. The Texas Constitution of 1876 set up the state government that Texans have today. Both constitutions list the rights of citizens and describe how the government should work.

Texans are citizens of both the United States and Texas.

### The Texas Constitution

The Texas Constitution begins with a **Bill of Rights**, or list of freedoms, held by every Texas citizen. It lists many of the freedoms that are found in the United States Bill of Rights—freedom of speech, freedom of the press, freedom of assembly, and freedom of religion.

The Texas Bill of Rights lists the rights of people who are victims of crimes and the rights of those accused of crimes. It also lists the rights of property owners. It states that all these rights can never be taken away.

Like the United States Constitution, the Texas Constitution calls for three branches, or parts, of government. Each branch has its own job. One branch makes the laws. A second branch sees that the laws are obeyed. And a third branch decides if the laws are fair.

✓ **What freedoms does the Texas Bill of Rights protect?**

## THE LEGISLATIVE BRANCH

The Legislature of the State of Texas is the name of the legislative (LEH•juhs•lay•tiv) branch of the state government. The **legislative branch** makes, or passes, the laws.

Two parts, or houses, make up the Texas Legislature—the House of Representatives, sometimes called the House, and the Senate. The Texas House of Representatives has 150 members. The Texas Senate has 31. Voters elect the members of both houses.

The two most important members of the legislature are the lieutenant (loo•TEH•nuhnt) governor and the speaker of the House. The lieutenant governor heads the state Senate. The speaker of the House heads the House of Representatives. The lieutenant governor is elected by the people of Texas. The speaker of the House is elected by the members of the House of Representatives.

Every two years members of the House and the Senate meet at the Texas capitol to pass new laws. The laws they pass help protect the lives, freedoms, and property of Texans.

The members of the Texas House of Representatives meet every two years for no more than 140 days.

The Texas Legislature also makes state tax laws. State taxes pay the costs of running the state government. The legislature must make a plan for spending tax money in the best ways. The plan for spending money is called a **budget**.

State tax money is used to pay for building and repairing state roads and state highways. It is used to keep state parks clean and safe. Almost half of the state tax money is spent on public schools and on state colleges and universities. State taxes pay the teachers and buy the books for Texas schools. The state also uses tax money to help people who cannot earn enough money to pay for their own food, shelter, or health care.

**What are the two parts of the Texas Legislature?**

The Texas state capitol is the largest state capitol building in the country. Its length is equal to about two football fields. Its width and height are each equal to the length of one football field. The building has almost 500 rooms.

## The Executive Branch

The state seal of Texas includes a five-pointed star surrounded by a live oak branch and an olive branch. The live oak branch stands for strength, and the olive branch stands for peace. Why do you think these symbols were chosen for the state seal?

The Texas Constitution gives the **executive branch** of the state government the power to make sure that state laws passed by the legislature are obeyed. The governor of Texas is the head of the state's executive branch.

As head of the executive branch, the governor can suggest new laws to the legislature. The governor shows that he or she agrees with a new law by signing it. The governor also has **veto power**. This means that the governor can refuse to sign a new law. The legislature can still pass a law vetoed by the governor if two-thirds of its members vote to do so, but this does not happen very often.

The governor shares the work of the executive branch with other officers. Like the governor, most are elected by Texas voters every four years. The only executive officer who is appointed is the secretary of state.

Besides the governor, the executive branch has about 200 **agencies**, or groups of state officials who see that laws passed by the legislature are obeyed. More than 190,000 people work for these state agencies in Texas. One of the most important is the Texas Railroad Commission. It was started in the 1890s by Governor James S. Hogg to make rules for all the railroads in the state. Today it also makes rules for the oil industry.

## What?

### The Governor's Mansion

The governor's mansion in Austin has been the home of Texas governors since 1855. Governor Elisha Pease chose the location, less than 300 yards (274 m) from the capitol building. Workers who built the two-story brick house hauled the pine logs that were made into the huge front columns. They painted the walls white and the window shutters green—the same colors they are painted today. The workers also planted the mansion's garden with fig, pecan, and elm trees. Since that time, each governor's family has added to the gardens at the mansion. The mansion is open to the public, and many people visit. Three Texas Rangers guard the grounds at all times.

✓ **Who is the head of the executive branch of the Texas state government?**

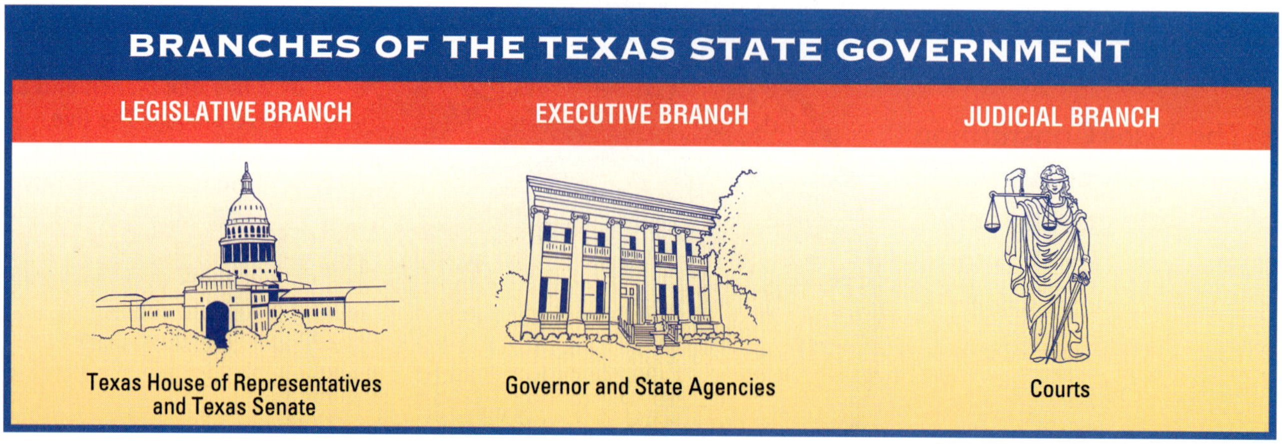


**LEARNING FROM DIAGRAMS** No one branch of the Texas state government is more powerful than another.

- Why do you think the state government is separated into three branches?

## The Judicial Branch

The third branch of the Texas state government is the judicial branch. As in the federal government, the state **judicial branch** is made up of courts and judges who hear and decide law cases. The judges make sure that Texas laws are used fairly.

The two highest courts in Texas are the Texas Supreme Court and the Court of Criminal Appeals. The Texas Supreme Court decides questions about the Texas Constitution and the rights of Texas citizens. The Texas Court of Criminal Appeals is the highest court in Texas to which a person who has been found guilty of a crime can appeal. In law, to **appeal** is to ask for another trial. The Texas Court of Criminal Appeals decides if a lower court was correct in finding a person guilty.

Below the Supreme Court and the Court of Criminal Appeals are the district courts of Texas. Jury trials are often held in district courts. In a **jury trial** a group of citizens decides if a person accused of a crime is guilty or innocent. If a person is found guilty of breaking the law, the jury decides what the punishment will be.

**What are the two highest Texas courts?**

## Lesson 1 Review

### Check Understanding

1. **Recall the Facts** What freedoms are Texans guaranteed by the Texas Bill of Rights?
2. **Focus on the Main Idea** What work does each branch of the Texas state government do?

### Think Critically

3. **Personally Speaking** Describe three ways state tax money is spent in your community.
4. **Think More About It** What might happen if one branch of the state government had more power than the others?

### Show What You Know

**Simulation Activity** With two partners, role-play the governor of Texas, a member of the Texas Legislature, and a judge on the Texas Supreme Court. In front of the class, hold a conversation in which each of you describes your work in the government.

SKILLS HOW TO

# Use a Flow Chart

## Why Is This Skill Important?

Some information is easier to understand when it is explained in a drawing. The drawing on this page is a type of flow chart. A **flow chart** is a drawing that shows the order in which things happen. Arrows on a flow chart show the reader how to follow each step in the correct order. The flow chart on this page can help you understand how the Texas Legislature makes a new law.

## Understand the Process

Start at the top of the chart to see the first step in passing a law. The first step is to make a plan. During this step, leaders in the legislature explain their idea for a new law. A plan for a new law is called a **bill**. Follow the arrow to the next step. The bill is given a number and sent to a special committee. The committee is a small group of members of the legislature who study the bill and tell what they think of it. What is the next step for a bill to become a law?

Read the other steps. What happens after the Senate and the House of Representatives agree to the bill? How can a bill become a law if the governor vetoes it?

## Think and Apply

Work with a partner to list the steps for making something, such as a peanut butter and jelly sandwich. Write each step on a strip of paper. Then put the steps in order. Paste the strips on a sheet of posterboard, and add arrows to make a flow chart. Give your flow chart a title, and display it on a bulletin board in the classroom.

**HOW A BILL BECOMES A LAW**

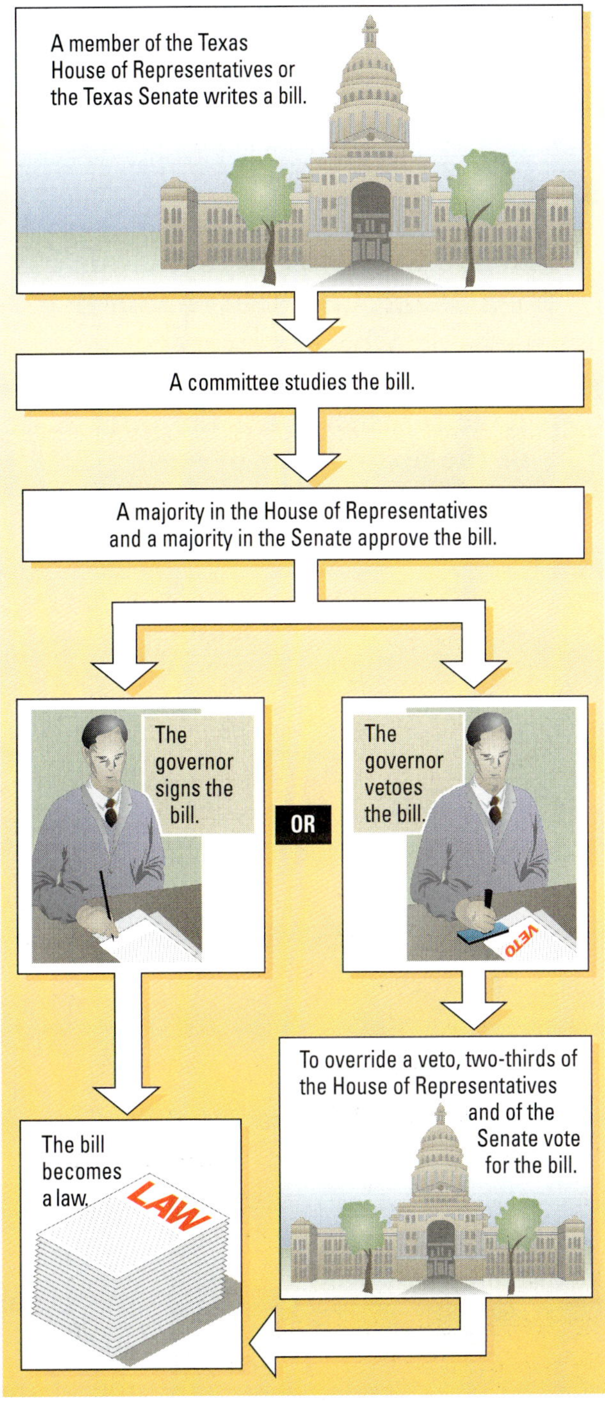

LESSON 2

# Local Governments in Texas

## Link to Our World

**What forms of government make the laws where you live?**

***Focus on the Main Idea***
**Read to learn about the work of the many forms of local government in Texas.**

***Preview Vocabulary***
**special district**
**county seat**
**commissioners court**
**enforce**
**municipal**
**school board**

Texans are ruled by local governments as well as a state government. Local governments make laws, see that laws are obeyed, and decide if laws are fair in cities, towns, and counties. Texas has more than 4,000 local governments. Of that number, 254 are county governments. More than 1,100 are city or town governments. And 2,700 are **special districts**, which each deal with one kind of problem or service. More than 1,000 of these special districts are school districts.

## County Governments

Texas is divided into 254 counties—the largest number of any state. One town in each county is the county seat. A **county seat** is the town or city that is the center of government for that county.

County governments in Texas work differently from the state government. Instead of having separate legislative and executive branches, each county in Texas has a **commissioners court** that does the work of these two branches.

The commissioners court does not act as a regular court, however. It is made up of an elected county judge and four commissioners. Among the many things that this group does is to make sure that elections in the county are run fairly. It sees that the county court and the jail are run properly and that county roads are built and repaired. The commissioners court decides how much county taxes citizens will be required to pay and how the tax money will be spent.

Gonzales County Courthouse

Voters elect a number of county officials. The best-known is the sheriff. The sheriff of each county **enforces** the laws, or sees that they are obeyed. It is the sheriff's job to protect people in the county and keep them safe. The sheriff also runs the county jail. If a county has no tax collector, the sheriff may also collect county taxes. Other elected county officials include the county treasurer, who pays the county's bills, and the county clerk, who keeps county records. Among the county records is information on births, deaths, and marriages.

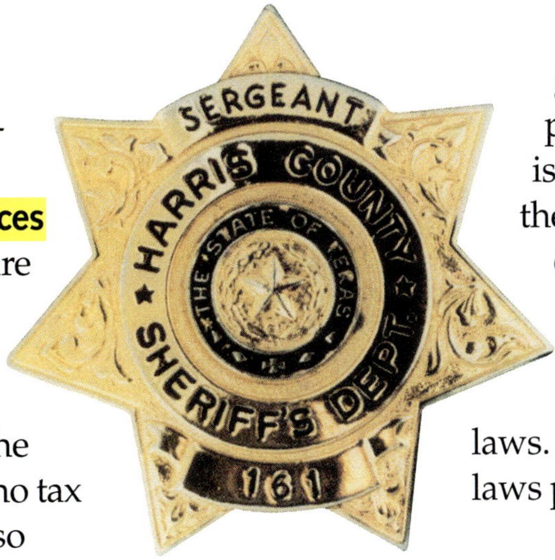

The sheriff in most Texas counties heads a department made up of many law enforcement officers.

Each county also has a judicial branch of government. These county courts are usually run by a justice of the peace. The justice of the peace is a judge who hears and decides only cases for which the fine for breaking the law is $200 or less. A justice of the peace may also perform marriages.

**A commissioners court combines the work of what two branches of government?**

## City Governments

Four out of every five Texans live in cities. Each city has a government that makes laws, enforces laws, and hears and decides some court cases. People living in cities depend on **municipal**, or city, governments for services such as fire and police protection and garbage collection.

Some cities have a mayor-council form of municipal government. The city council is the legislative branch of a municipal government, which passes laws. The mayor is elected by voters or the council to head the executive branch of municipal government. The mayor chooses people to enforce the laws. The mayor can also veto laws passed by the city council.

Most cities have a council-manager form of municipal government. The elected city council members still make the laws. Instead of an elected mayor, however, there is a city manager, who enforces the laws passed by the council. The city council hires the city manager, who runs the city the way the council wants. The head of the city council in a council-manager form of government is often called the mayor. This mayor's main duty is to run the city council meetings.

Other cities have a commission form of municipal government. This kind of city government was formed after the Galveston hurricane of 1900. The people of Galveston thought the city government they had could not handle the problems caused by the hurricane. To rebuild the city, they set up a totally new form of municipal government.

The people of Galveston elected a commission consisting of five members. Each member was in charge of a different department, such as water services or police and fire protection. The Galveston Plan, which combines the legislative and executive branches, was later used by many other cities all over the United States.

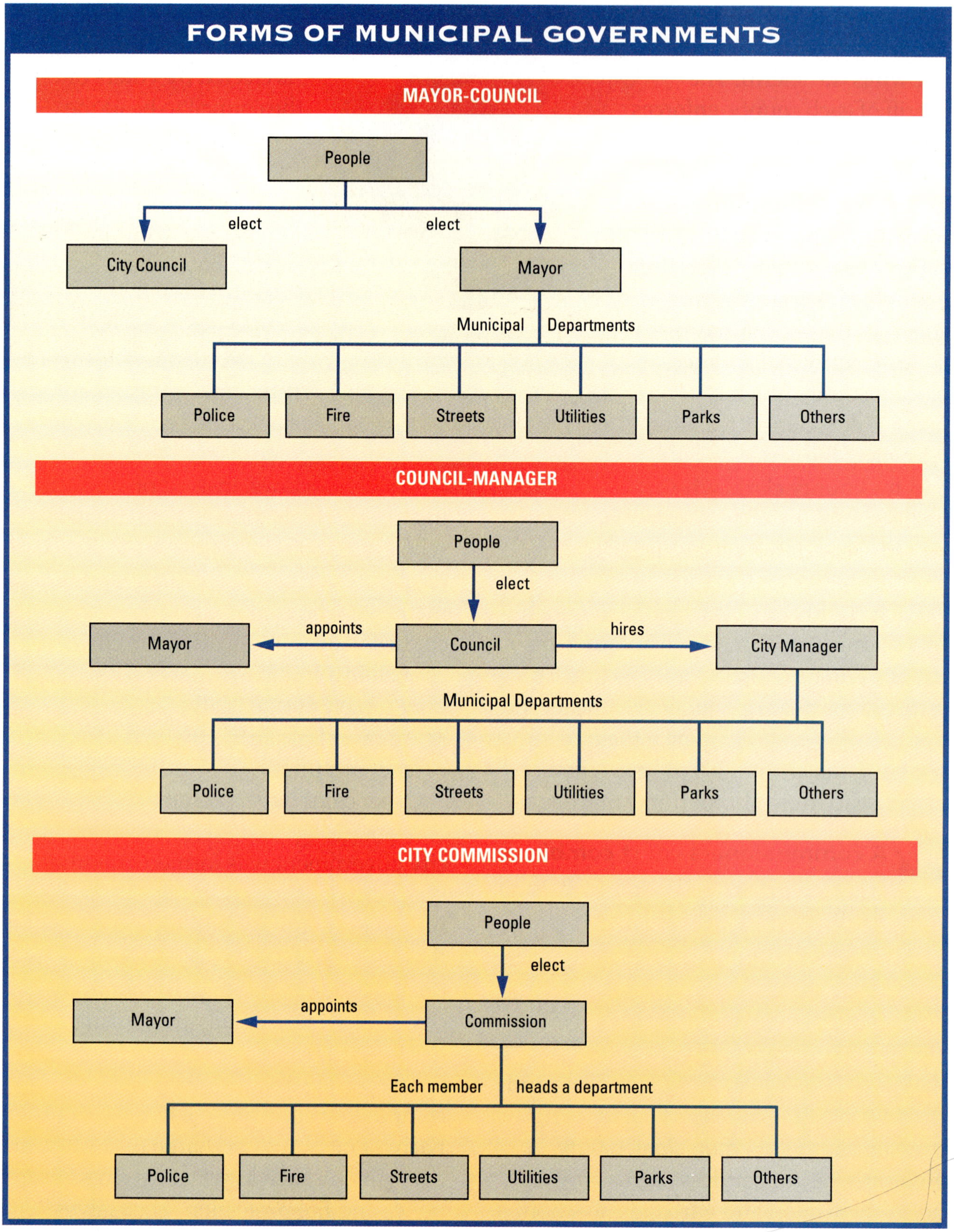


**LEARNING FROM DIAGRAMS** In Texas, towns with populations of more than 5,000 choose their own form of government.

- In which form of municipal government do the people elect both a mayor and a city council?

Cities in Texas have different ways to make and enforce laws, but they all have a similar way of handling people who break city laws. The judicial branch of most city governments is the municipal court. These city courts deal with people who break traffic laws and other city laws. Other kinds of crimes are handled by county or district courts.

These workers for the Lower Colorado River Authority water district are testing Lake Buchanan for water pollution.

**Name three forms of municipal government in Texas cities.**

## Special Districts and School Districts

Of all the types of local governments in Texas, special districts are the greatest in number. Special districts each take care of one particular problem or service. A special district may be smaller than a county, or it may be made up of many counties.

One kind of special district in Texas deals with water problems. Often there is not enough water in the state. Water districts make sure that people use water carefully and do not waste it. Water districts also look for new sources of water, and they work to solve water-pollution problems.

Another kind of special district is the school district. There are 1,045 school districts in Texas. A **school board**, whose members are elected by voters in each school district, makes decisions about running the schools. The Texas Education Agency, a part of the state government, sets many of the rules that the school districts must follow.

**What is the purpose of a special district?**

## Lesson 2 Review

### Check Understanding

1. **Recall the Facts** Name three forms of local government.
2. **Focus on the Main Idea** What do the different forms of local government do?

### Think Critically

3. **Think More About It** How is the county commissioners court different from the branches of state government?
4. **Cause and Effect** When can a justice of the peace deal with a person accused of a crime?

### Show What You Know

**Chart-Making Activity** Look at the chart on page 330. Work with a partner to make a similar chart, using the names of people in your local government. If there is not a city government where you live, make a chart showing the people in your county government. Share your chart with your classmates.

S·K·I·L·L·S

# How To

# Make Economic Choices

## Why Is This Skill Important?

When you buy something at a store or decide what to order at a restaurant, you are making an economic choice. Some economic choices are difficult to make. To buy one thing, you may have to give up buying something else. This is called a **trade-off**. What you give up is the **opportunity cost** of what you get. Knowing about trade-offs and opportunity costs can help you make thoughtful economic decisions.

## Remember What You Have Read

Like people, governments have to make many economic choices. They, too, face trade-offs and opportunity costs.

You have read that municipal governments must provide certain services, such as police and fire protection, road repair, and public libraries. It costs money to provide these services. A city government pays for these services by taxing the city's residents. Often, governments do not have enough money to pay for everything that needs to be done.

## Understand the Process

Imagine you are the mayor of a rapidly growing town in Texas. You have to make a choice. Should you pay to have Main Street widened to help reduce the growing traffic problems? Or should you buy more garbage trucks and hire more sanitation workers to help keep your growing town clean?

1. **Think about the trade-off.** To do this, you must figure out the advantages and disadvantages of each choice. Traffic jams happen every day on Main Street. Widening the street would allow more traffic to drive down the street more safely. The trade-off is that it would cost a lot of money. Buying more garbage trucks and hiring more workers would keep the town clean and would cost less money than widening the street. The trade-off for that choice is that the town would still have traffic problems.
2. **Think about the opportunity costs.** You do not have enough money to pay for both projects, so you have to give up one. If you choose to widen the street, the opportunity costs are the garbage trucks and the extra money that would have been left over. If you choose to buy the garbage trucks, the opportunity costs are the road-widening project and the risk of having more traffic accidents. What choice should you make?

Because you usually cannot have everything you want, you will often face opportunity costs as you trade off one product for another. This does not mean that the product you give up has no value. It means that at the time, another product or another action has more value to you.

## Think and Apply

Imagine that you have $10 to spend. You want to buy some comic books. But you also want to see a movie. You do not have enough money to pay for both. Explain to a partner the trade-offs and opportunity costs of your choices.

LESSON 3

# TEXAS CITIZENSHIP

## Link to Our World

**What does it mean to be a citizen?**

***Focus on the Main Idea***
**Read to learn about the rights and responsibilities of citizens of the United States and of Texas.**

***Preview Vocabulary***
**responsibility**
**naturalized citizen**
**register**

Since Texas became a state in 1845, Texans have been citizens of the United States and of the state of Texas. The word *citizen* means "member." As members of a country and a state, citizens have rights that noncitizens do not. At the same time, citizens also have responsibilities. A **responsibility** is a duty people are required to do.

### BECOMING A CITIZEN

The United States Constitution says,

"All persons born or naturalized in the United States . . . are citizens of the United States and of the State wherein they reside."

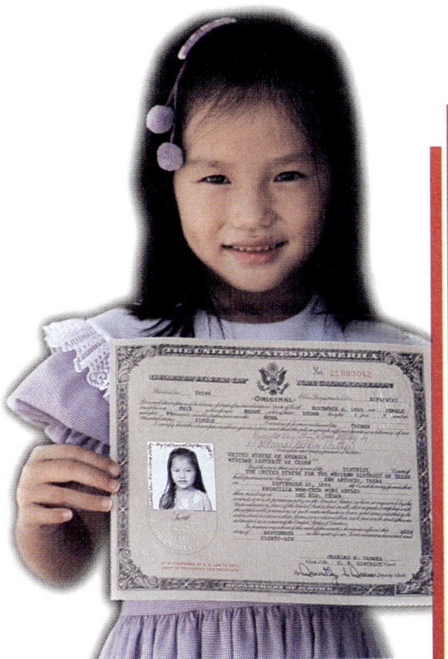

Children under 18 years old automatically become citizens when their parents do.

A **naturalized citizen** is an immigrant who becomes a citizen by taking steps described in the law. When adults become United States citizens, their children under 18 years of age become citizens as well.

Becoming a naturalized citizen is a three-step process. First, a person who has lived in the United States for at least five years must ask a judge in writing to become a citizen. Second, the person must meet the requirements of education. The person must pass a test about United States history and how the United States government works. The final step is a ceremony in which the person promises to be a loyal citizen. Many ceremonies take place on September 17, Citizenship Day.

**✓ How can immigrants become citizens of the United States?**

## The Rights of Citizens

Citizens of Texas have the freedoms and rights granted in both the United States and Texas constitutions. These include freedom of speech, freedom of the press, freedom of religion, and freedom to gather in groups. Citizens have the rights to vote and to hold public office. They have the right to travel through the state and all over the United States. Laws passed by Congress and the Texas Legislature can give citizens other rights.

A citizen's rights cannot be taken away, but governments can place certain limits on citizens. A citizen must be at least 18 years old to vote. States can limit a citizen's right to vote by requiring people to **register**, or sign up, to vote.

Noncitizens have many of the same rights as citizens. However, noncitizens cannot vote, hold public office or certain jobs, or be a member of a trial jury.

**What documents give Texas citizens their rights?**

## The Responsibilities of Citizens

Responsibilities come with having rights. The responsibility to vote comes with the right to vote. The responsibility to be an informed citizen and learn about public problems comes with freedom of speech and freedom of the press.

Some responsibilities are stated in laws. United States and Texas laws state that it is a citizen's responsibility to pay taxes, obey laws, and be loyal. One way that citizens of the United States show their allegiance, or loyalty, to their country is with a pledge, or promise. The Pledge of Allegiance says that people of the United States promise loyalty to their flag, to their country, and to the ideas of freedom and fairness.

> "I pledge allegiance to the Flag of the United States of America, and to the Republic for which it stands, one Nation under God, indivisible, with liberty and justice for all."

Many students begin each school day by reciting the Pledge of Allegiance. Think about the words to the Pledge of Allegiance. What do they mean to you?

Texans have a long history of volunteerism. In 1917 these American Junior Red Cross volunteers (left) helped people in Weatherford. These young people assisting an elderly woman (below) are carrying on Texas's long tradition of volunteerism.

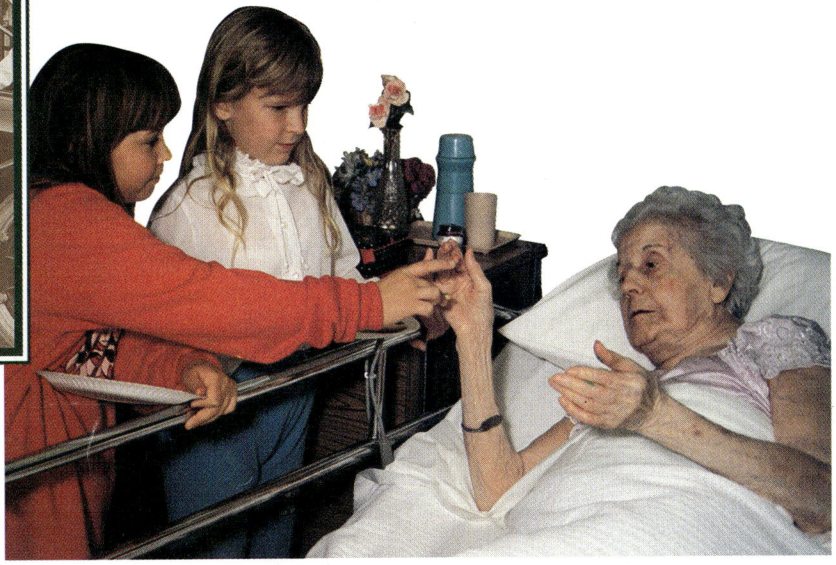

Texans also promise to respect their flag and to be loyal to the state.

> "Honor the Texas Flag;
> I pledge allegiance to thee,
> Texas, one and indivisible."

Some people take on responsibilities that help make communities better places to live. Volunteers, or helpers, work without pay in places like schools and hospitals. Some volunteers take part in community cleanup projects. Helping an older neighbor with yard work is one way to volunteer and to show responsibility as a citizen.

When he became governor of Texas in 1995, George W. Bush called on all Texans to be responsible citizens. He said, "I will call upon the best within every Texan as we confront our challenges." In the long history of Texas, Texans have always shown pride in their state and in their abilities. Texans will need to continue to do this as Texas meets the challenges of the future.

**✓ Why do citizens have responsibilities?**

## LESSON 3 REVIEW

### Check Understanding

1. **Recall the Facts** At what age can citizens first vote?
2. **Focus on the Main Idea** What are some rights and responsibilities of citizens of the United States and of Texas?

### Think Critically

3. **Think More About It** Why do people need to be loyal to be responsible citizens?
4. **Cause and Effect** How does being a responsible citizen affect the country and the state?

### Show What You Know

**Poster Activity** Make a poster of ways you can be a responsible citizen. You can include newspaper pictures of other people being responsible citizens. Display your poster in the classroom.

CHAPTER 12

# REVIEW

## CONNECT MAIN IDEAS

Use this organizer to show that you understand how the chapter's main ideas are connected. First copy the organizer onto a separate sheet of paper. Then complete it by listing the duties and structure of each part of the Texas government.

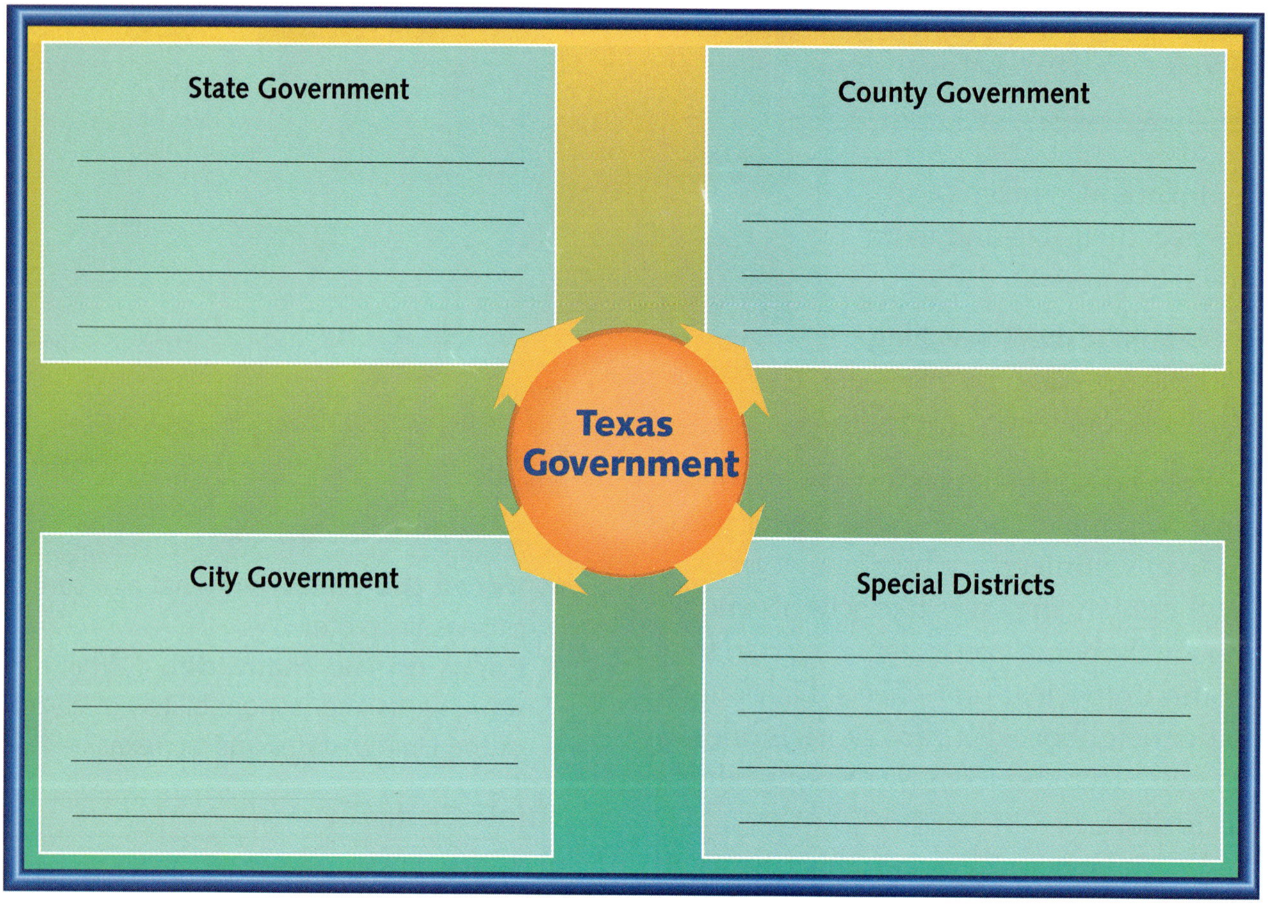


## WRITE MORE ABOUT IT

1. **Write a Journal Entry** Imagine that you are an immigrant to Texas and have just become a naturalized citizen of the United States. Write a journal entry that describes the steps you went through and how you feel about being a citizen. Share your entry with a classmate.

2. **Write a Want Advertisement** Imagine that your county needs a new sheriff. As a member of the commissioners court it is your job to hire this person. Write a classified advertisement for the job. Be sure to describe the work of a county sheriff.

## USE VOCABULARY

On a separate sheet of paper, write the word or phrase that completes each of the sentences that follow.

**Bill of Rights**
**executive branch**
**judicial branch**
**legislative branch**
**naturalized citizen**
**special district**

1. The list of freedoms in the Texas Constitution is called the ________.
2. The ________ of the Texas state government makes laws.
3. The governor is head of the ________ of the Texas state government.
4. Courts and judges who hear and decide law cases make up the ________ of the Texas state government.
5. A ________ takes care of one kind of problem or service.
6. An immigrant who becomes a United States citizen is a ________.

## CHECK UNDERSTANDING

1. Name some of the rights of citizens listed in the Texas Bill of Rights.
2. What are the main duties of the Texas Legislature?
3. What are some duties of the governor?
4. Name the two highest courts in Texas.
5. Name the three forms of municipal government in Texas cities.
6. Give an example of a special district in Texas.
7. What are some of the responsibilities of citizens?

## THINK CRITICALLY

1. **Think More About It** Why do you think the Texas Constitution is similar to the United States Constitution?
2. **Explore Viewpoints** Why do some immigrants want to become citizens of the United States?
3. **Think More About It** Why do you think it is important for citizens to have both rights and responsibilities?
4. **Personally Speaking** Do you think you will vote regularly once you are old enough to do so? Explain your answer.

## APPLY SKILLS

**How to Use a Flow Chart** Think about something you do often, such as getting ready for school or playing a game. List the steps you follow when performing this task. Then make a flow chart of the task, placing each step in order. Add arrows and a title to your flow chart.

**How to Make Economic Choices** Imagine that you need to choose between buying a video game or getting a new pair of soccer shoes. How would you go about making this economic choice? Identify the trade-offs and the opportunity costs.

## READ MORE ABOUT IT

*Getting Elected: How Politics Works* by Philip Seib. Hendrick-Long. This book tells about elections and election day.

*Our Constitution* by Linda Carlson Johnson. Millbrook. The Texas Constitution takes many ideas from the United States Constitution. This book tells about the United States Constitution and the ideas in it.

## Making Social Studies Relevant

# C.O.P.S. in San Antonio

More than 20 years ago the people of the south and west sides of San Antonio decided that something had to be done about the problems that faced their neighborhoods. Houses and schools were run down, streets became flooded when it rained, and the roads needed repairing. The city government was doing very little to take care of these problems. Residents of the neighborhood, organized by Ernesto Cortés, Jr., came to realize that taking action to solve these problems was not only the responsibility of the government, but the responsibility of the citizens. So Cortés and his neighbors organized COPS, or Communities Organized for Public Service.

COPS has helped many San Antonio neighborhoods with flood control. It has also helped neighborhoods get new sewers, streets, sidewalks, parks, libraries, and medical clinics. The group has helped families build or repair more than 1,000 houses and apartments, making San Antonio a better place to live.

How has COPS done all this? The members have taken an active role in city government. They have attended meetings and informed city leaders about problems. They have studied the city budget and made suggestions for change. By taking responsibility for their communities, these citizens have shown that they have the power to achieve their goals.

Ernesto Cortés summed up the organization's accomplishments. "COPS has won its victories not by speaking for ordinary people but by teaching them how to speak, to act, and to engage in politics for themselves."

## Think and Apply

Think about how the members of COPS have been active citizens. Identify some citizens in your own community who have worked in similar ways to solve problems. Learn more about their work by asking them to speak to your class. Before their visit, prepare a list of questions.

COPS get things done by encouraging people to vote and to voice their opinions at city government meetings

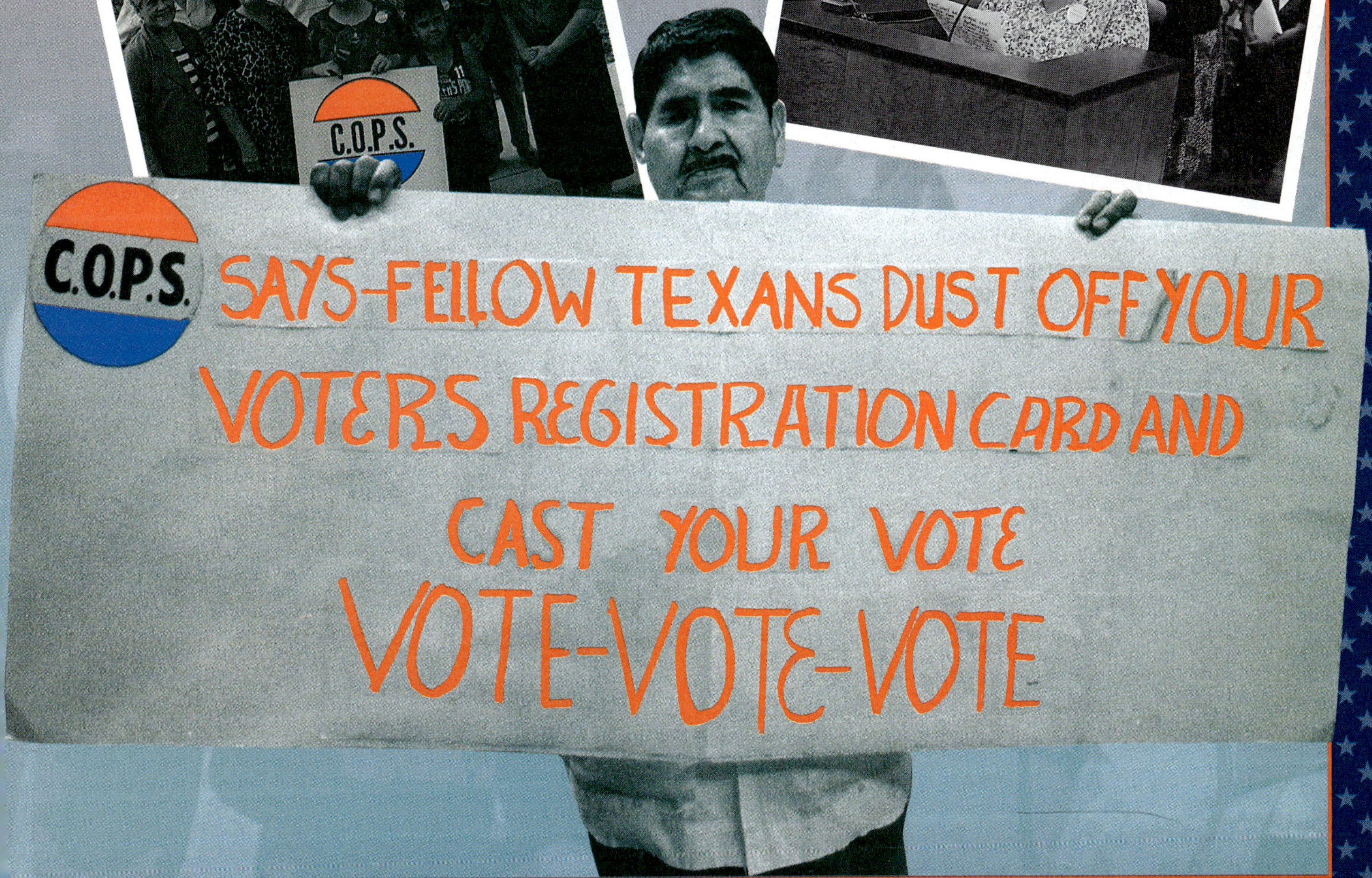

## UNIT 6

# STORY CLOTH

Follow the pictures shown in this story cloth to help you review Unit 6.

## Summarize the Main Ideas

1. Texas is working to meet the needs of its growing population. This growth is happening because more people are being born in Texas and more are moving to Texas from other places.
2. The Texas state government has passed laws to make public schools stronger. Educated citizens are important in a democracy. They help build the economy of Texas.
3. Texans are working to improve the environment and use its resources wisely—through both conservation and recycling.
4. The state government of Texas has three branches—the executive, the legislative, and the judicial.
5. A city council or a commission is the legislative branch of a municipal government. City governments provide services for the citizens of Texas.
6. Citizens of Texas have the rights given in the Texas Constitution. They also have responsibilities, such as voting and helping make their communities better places to live.

**Create a Mural** Celebrate the different cultures of Texas by creating a class mural. Cover a bulletin board with paper. Then use art materials to show things from each culture, such as food, clothing, musical instruments, and language. Invite other classes to see the mural.

THE STATE OF TEXAS

# UNIT 6 REVIEW

## COOPERATIVE LEARNING WORKSHOP

**Remember**

- Share your ideas.
- Cooperate with others to plan your work.
- Take responsibility for your work.
- Show your group's work to the class.
- Discuss what you learned by working together.

Activity 1

### Make a Poster

Work with several classmates to make a poster that shows how recycling can help the environment. You can draw or cut out pictures of recyclable materials to put on the poster. Add a title or slogan that will help people remember the importance of recycling.

Activity 2

### Design a Brochure

As a class, create a brochure that explains how to become a United States citizen. Include a list of things an immigrant must do to become a citizen, and tell about the rights and responsibilities of United States citizens. Draw or find pictures to illustrate the brochure.

Activity 3

### Perform a Simulation

Work with several other classmates to prepare a skit in which the main characters are members of the branches of Texas state government. There should be at least one character from each branch, such as a state senator, the governor, and a Texas Court of Criminal Appeals judge. Write a scene in which the characters talk about their jobs in state government. Make name tags that list the branch and job title for each character.

Activity 4

### Plan a Multicultural Presentation

Work with several classmates to research a cultural group that is part of the diverse population of Texas. Find out about the country they came from, their native dress, special foods they eat, what they do for work and fun, their holidays and celebrations, and other special facts. Make posters, drawings, or models to show what you have learned. Share your presentation with the rest of the class.

## USE VOCABULARY

For each pair of terms, write a sentence that explains how they are related.

1. responsibility, naturalized citizen
2. informed citizen, human resource
3. pollute, recycle
4. legislative branch, budget
5. executive branch, veto power

## CHECK UNDERSTANDING

1. Why has the population of Texas grown in recent years?
2. Why is education good for the economy and the community?
3. What is the purpose of the Texas Assessment of Academic Skills (TAAS)?
4. Why is recycling important?
5. Describe three ways to conserve water.
6. What are some freedoms listed in the Texas Bill of Rights?
7. List the three branches of state government.
8. What are some responsibilities of a commissioners court?
9. What three things do immigrants have to do to become United States citizens?
10. What are some responsibilities of United States citizens?

## THINK CRITICALLY

1. **Link to You** Think of four things you can do every day to help the environment.
2. **Explore Viewpoints** Why do you think some people and businesses choose to pollute and not recycle?
3. **Personally Speaking** What job in the Texas state government do you think you would like to have? Why?

## APPLY GEOGRAPHY SKILLS

Map Skill

**How to Use a Map to Show Movement** In the late 1800s, Dallas began holding an annual fair. Now known as the Texas State Fair, it is one of the attractions at Fair Park. People come from near and far each year to visit the fair and the park's other attractions.

**MOVEMENT OF PEOPLE TO DALLAS**

In which directions do the arrows go to Fair Park from each of the following cities?

1. Amarillo
2. Austin
3. El Paso
4. Little Rock, Arkansas
5. Oklahoma City, Oklahoma
6. Shreveport, Louisiana

*Defenders of the Alamo*

# FOR YOUR REFERENCE

Stephen F. Austin

Texas state capitol dome

## CONTENTS

# How to Gather and Report Information

To write a report, make a poster, or do many other projects in your social studies class, you may need information that is not in your textbook. You can gather this information from reference books, electronic references, or community resources. The following guide can help you gather information from many sources and report what you find.

## How to Use Reference Tools

Reference works are collections of facts. They include books and electronic resources, such as almanacs, atlases, dictionaries, and encyclopedias. Books in libraries are organized through a system of numbers. Every book in a library has its own number, called a call number. The call number on the book tells the librarian where in the library the book can be found. In a library a reference book has an *R* or *REF* for *reference* on its spine along with the call number. Most reference books are for use only in the library. Many libraries also have electronic references on CD-ROM and the Internet.

## When to Use an Encyclopedia

An encyclopedia is a good place to begin to look for information. An encyclopedia has articles on nearly every subject. The articles are arranged in alphabetical order by subject. Each article gives basic facts about people, places, and events. Some electronic encyclopedias allow you to hear music and speeches and to see short movies related to the subject.

## When to Use a Dictionary

A dictionary gives information about words. Dictionaries explain the meanings of words and show how the words are pronounced. A dictionary is a good place to check the spelling of a word. Some dictionaries also include the origins of words and lists of foreign words, abbreviations, well-known people, and place names.

## When to Use an Atlas

You can find information about places in an atlas. An atlas is a book of maps. Some atlases have road maps. Others have maps of countries around the world. There are atlases with maps that show where certain crops are grown and where certain products are produced. Some atlas maps show the population of different places. Ask a librarian to help you find the kind of atlas you need.

## When to Use an Almanac

An almanac is a book or electronic resource of facts and figures. It shows information in tables and charts. The population of a city or the largest industries of a country are the kinds of facts contained in an almanac. However, the subjects in an almanac are not listed in alphabetical order. You would need to use the almanac's index, which lists the subjects in alphabetical order. Most almanacs are brought up-to-date every year. So an almanac can give you the latest information on a subject.

## How to Find Nonfiction Books

Nonfiction books give facts about real people and things. Fiction books tell stories that are made up. In a library, all nonfiction books are placed in order on the shelves according to their call numbers. You can find a book's call number by using a card file or a computer catalog. To find this number, you need to know the book's subject, author, or title. Here are some sample cards for a book on Texas civilizations.

**Subject Card**

**TEXAS--CIVILIZATION.**

JUV
976.4
STAN

Stanush, Barbara Evans.
Texans : a story of Texan cultures for young people / Barbara Evans Stanush. -- 1st ed. -- [San Antonio] : University of Texas Institute of Texan Cultures at San Antonio, 1988.

122 p. : ill. (some col.) ; 27 cm. -- (The Texians and the Texans) -- (Stories for young readers)

**Author Card**

JUV
976.4
STAN

Stanush, Barbara Evans.
Texans : a story of Texan cultures for young people / Barbara Evans Stanush. -- 1st ed. -- [San Antonio] : University of Texas Institute of Texan Cultures at San Antonio, 1988.

122 p. : ill. (some col.) ; 27 cm. -- (The Texians and the Texans) -- (Stories for young readers)

Includes bibliographical references.

JUV
976.4
STAN

Stanush, Barbara Evans.
Texans : a story of Texan cultures for young people
(Card 2)

**Title Card**

**Texans : a story of Texan cultures for young people**

JUV
976.4
STAN

Stanush, Barbara Evans.
Texans : a story of Texan cultures for young people / Barbara Evans Stanush. -- 1st ed. -- [San Antonio] : University of Texas Institute of Texan Cultures at San Antonio, 1988.

122 p. : ill. (some col.) ; 27 cm. -- (The Texians and the Texans) -- (Stories for young readers)

ISBN 0-86701-040-1

F395.A1S73 1988

JUV 976.4
88-50983/AC

On the following page are sample computer catalog screens for a book on Texas civilizations.

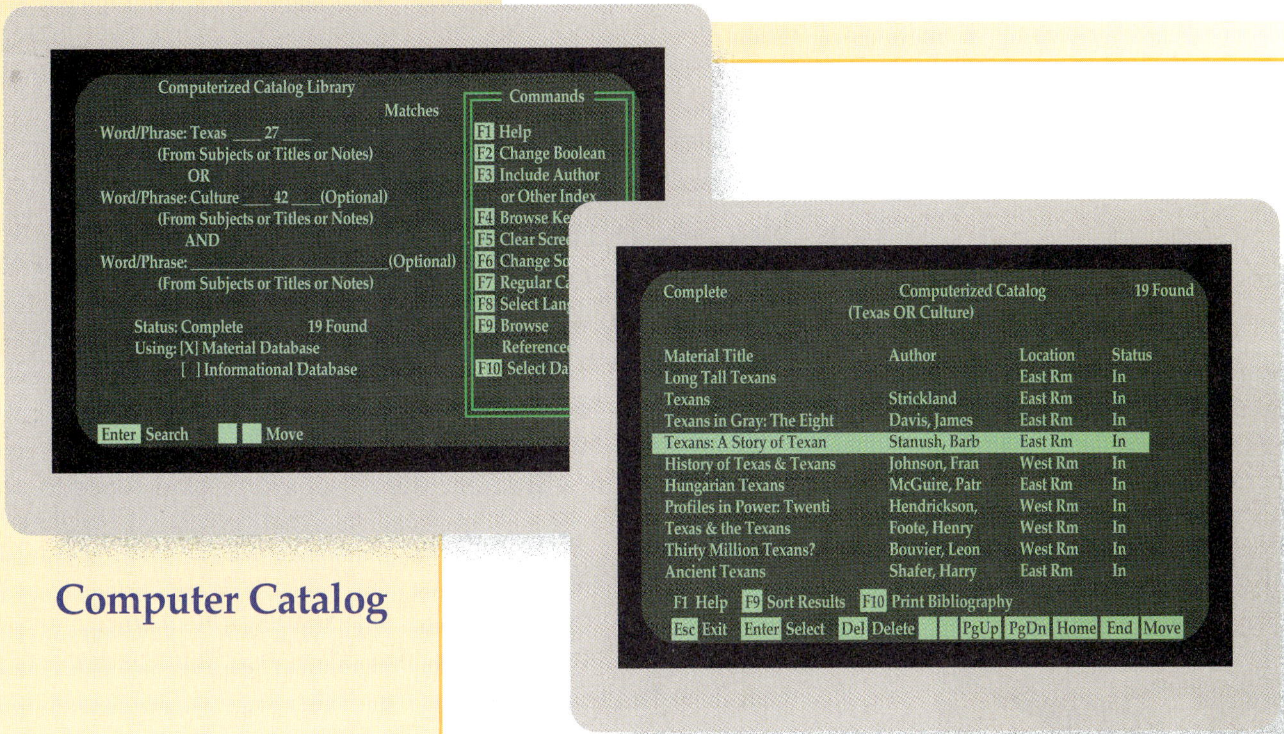


## Computer Catalog

## How to Find Periodicals

Libraries have special sections for periodicals — newspapers and magazines. A periodical, which is published every day, week, or month, is a good source for the most up-to-date information. You might find topics in periodicals that may not be found in books. The latest editions of periodicals are usually displayed on a rack. Older issues are stored away, sometimes on film. Most libraries have an index that lists magazine articles by subject. The most widely used indexes are the *Children's Magazine Guide* and the *Readers' Guide to Periodical Literature.* A librarian can help you use an index to find magazine articles.

The entries in these guides are listed in alphabetical order by subject and author, and sometimes by title. Abbreviations are used for many parts of an entry, such as the name of the magazine and the date of the issue. Here is a sample entry for an article on Native Americans in Texas.

**NATIVE AMERICANS IN TEXAS**
Urban Indians: Trails of Hope, *Texas Highways* 10 95: pp 32-41

**Heading:** The topic you are researching

**Title:** The title of the article

**Name:** The name of the periodical

**Date:** The date of the periodical in which the article appears

**Page Number(s):** The page(s) on which the article appears

## How to Conduct an Interview

Conducting interviews, or talking with people, is a good way to get facts and points of view on a topic.

### Planning an Interview

1. Make a list of people to interview. Think about who the experts are on the subject you are researching.
2. Call or write to each person to request an interview. When you contact the person, identify yourself, and let the person know what you want to talk about.
3. Ask the person you will interview to set a time and place to meet.

### Before the Interview

1. Read more about your topic and, if possible, about the person you are interviewing. That way you will be better able to talk with the person.
2. Make a list of questions to ask.

### During the Interview

1. Listen carefully. Do not interrupt or argue with the person.
2. Take notes during the interview, and write down the person's exact words.
3. If you want to use a tape recorder, first ask the person if you may do so.

### After the Interview

1. Before you leave, thank the person you interviewed.
2. Follow up by writing a thank-you note.

## How to Conduct a Survey

A good way to get information about the views people in your community have is to conduct a survey.

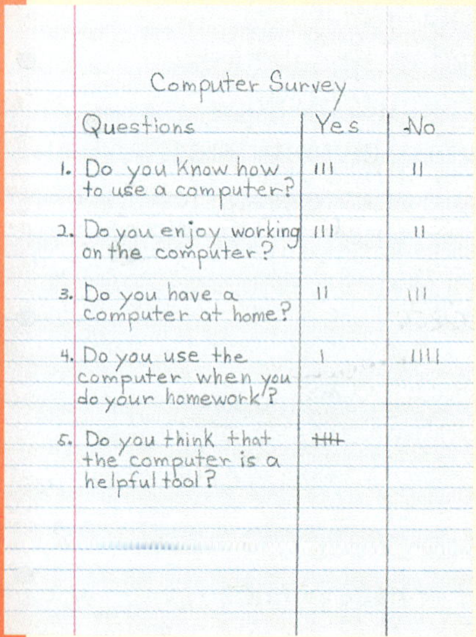

Computer Survey

| Questions | Yes | No |
|---|---|---|
| 1. Do you know how to use a computer? | III | II |
| 2. Do you enjoy working on the computer? | III | II |
| 3. Do you have a computer at home? | II | III |
| 4. Do you use the computer when you do your homework? | I | IIII |
| 5. Do you think that the computer is a helpful tool? | ++++ | |

1. Identify your topic, and make a list of questions. Write the questions so that they can be answered with "yes" or "no" or with "for" or "against." You may also want to give a "no opinion" or "not sure" choice.
2. Make a tally sheet on which to record your responses.
3. Decide how many people you will ask and where you will conduct your survey.
4. During the survey, record your responses on the tally sheet carefully.
5. When you have finished your survey, count the responses, and write a summary statement or conclusion that your survey supports.

## How to Write for Information

You can write a letter to ask for information. When you write, be sure to do these things:

- Write neatly or use a word processor.
- Say who you are and why you are writing.
- Make your request specific and reasonable.
- Provide a self-addressed, stamped envelope for the answer.

You may or may not get a reply, but if you do, you may find that it was worth your time to write.

## How to Write a Report

You may be asked to write a report on the information you have gathered. Knowing how to write a report will help you make good use of the information you have collected. There are a number of steps that should be taken when writing a report.

### Gather and Organize Your Information

- Gather information about your topic from reference books, electronic references, or community resources.
- Take notes that you need for your report.
- Review your notes to make sure that you have all the information you want to include.
- Outline your information.
- Make sure the information is in the correct order.

### Draft Your Report

- Review your information. Decide if you need more.
- Remember that the purpose is to share information.
- Write a draft of your report. Put all your ideas on paper. Present your ideas in a clear and interesting way.

### Revise

- Check that you have followed the order of your outline. Move sentences that seem out of place.
- Add any information that seems needed.
- Add quotations that show people's exact words.
- Reword sentences if too many follow the same pattern.

### Proofread and Publish

- Check for errors.
- Make sure nothing has been left out.
- Make a clean copy of your report .

# ALMANAC

## FACTS ABOUT TEXAS

## Did You Know?

Texas is one of four states in the region called the Southwest. The other southwestern states are Arizona, New Mexico, and Oklahoma.

# TEXAS

### LAND

**Highest Point:**
Guadalupe Peak in West Texas 8,749 feet (2,667 m)

**Lowest Point:**
Texas Gulf Coast sea level

### SIZE

**Area:**
266,807 square miles (690,977 sq km)

**Distance North/South:**
737 miles (1,186 km)

**Distance East/West:**
774 miles (1,246 km)

### CLIMATE

**Highest Recorded Temperature:**
120° F (49°C) at Seymour on August 12, 1936

**Lowest Recorded Temperature:**
-23°F (-31°C) at Tulia on February 12, 1899, then again at Seminole on February 8, 1933

**Average Temperature:**
83°F (28°C) in July, 46°F (8°C) in January

**Average Yearly Rainfall:**
27 inches (69 cm)

Climate varies widely.

### POPULATION*

18,496,000*

*the most recent figure available

### LEADING PRODUCTS AND RESOURCES

**Crops:**
cotton, watermelons, rice, peanuts, pecans, hay, grapefruit, cucumbers, oranges, sugar beets, tomatoes, lettuce

**Fishing:**
shrimp, crabs, oysters, red snapper, trout, drum, flounder

**Livestock:**
beef cattle, horses, sheep, hogs, goats, turkeys, chicken

**Manufacturing:**
chemicals, processed food, electronic equipment, petroleum products, machines, ships and boats

**Mining:**
oil, natural gas

Houston is the largest city in the state of Texas. It was founded in 1836 by brothers Augustus C. and John K. Allen and served as the capital of the Republic of Texas from 1837 to 1839.

# THE UNITED STATES

At 313 feet (95 m) tall, the Texas State Capitol stands 6 feet (2 m) higher than the United States Capitol.

Texas has more than 4,000 elementary schools.

# Almanac

## Facts About Texas Counties

| County | Population* | County Seat |
|---|---|---|
| Anderson | 49,050 | Palestine |
| Andrews | 14,452 | Andrews |
| Angelina | 73,925 | Lufkin |
| Aransas | 20,785 | Rockport |
| Archer | 7,941 | Archer City |
| Armstrong | 2,076 | Claude |
| Atascosa | 32,875 | Jourdanton |
| Austin | 21,780 | Bellville |
| Bailey | 6,746 | Muleshoe |
| Bandera | 12,523 | Bandera |
| Bastrop | 42,587 | Bastrop |
| Baylor | 4,262 | Seymour |
| Bee | 23,845 | Beeville |
| Bell | 215,480 | Belton |
| Bexar | 1,280,062 | San Antonio |
| Blanco | 7,062 | Johnson City |
| Borden | 767 | Gail |
| Bosque | 16,166 | Meridian |
| Bowie | 83,579 | Boston |
| Brazoria | 211,524 | Angleton |
| Brazos | 130,387 | Bryan |
| Brewster | 8,761 | Alpine |
| Briscoe | 1,809 | Silverton |
| Brooks | 8,266 | Falfurrias |
| Brown | 35,271 | Brownwood |
| Burleson | 14,678 | Caldwell |
| Burnet | 25,375 | Burnet |
| Caldwell | 28,062 | Lockhart |
| Calhoun | 20,403 | Port Lavaca |
| Callahan | 12,278 | Baird |
| Cameron | 299,584 | Brownsville |
| Camp | 10,458 | Pittsburg |
| Carson | 6,570 | Panhandle |
| Cass | 30,393 | Linden |
| Castro | 8,594 | Dimmitt |
| Chambers | 21,324 | Anahuac |
| Cherokee | 40,812 | Rusk |
| Childress | 6,375 | Childress |
| Clay | 9,976 | Henrietta |
| Cochran | 4,180 | Morton |
| Coke | 3,497 | Robert Lee |
| Coleman | 9,662 | Coleman |
| Collin | 326,153 | McKinney |
| Collingsworth | 3,397 | Wellington |
| Colorado | 18,591 | Columbus |
| Comal | 60,829 | New Braunfels |
| Comanche | 13,449 | Comanche |
| Concho | 3,056 | Paint Rock |

| County | Population* | County Seat |
|---|---|---|
| Cooke | 31,269 | Gainesville |
| Coryell | 71,687 | Gatesville |
| Cottle | 2,065 | Paducah |
| Crane | 4,621 | Crane |
| Crockett | 4,228 | Crockett |
| Crosby | 7,277 | Crosbyton |
| Culberson | 3,261 | Van Horn |
| Dallam | 5,944 | Dalhart |
| Dallas | 1,942,303 | Dallas |
| Dawson | 14,142 | Lamesa |
| Deaf Smith | 19,250 | Hereford |
| Delta | 4,808 | Cooper |
| Denton | 320,123 | Denton |
| DeWitt | 18,438 | Cuero |
| Dickens | 2,437 | Dickens |
| Dimmit | 10,706 | Carrizo Springs |
| Donley | 3,703 | Clarendon |
| Duval | 12,827 | San Diego |
| Eastland | 17,866 | Eastland |
| Ector | 123,128 | Odessa |
| Edwards | 2,934 | Rocksprings |
| Ellis | 91,850 | Waxahachie |
| El Paso | 664,800 | El Paso |
| Erath | 29,575 | Stephenville |
| Falls | 17,850 | Marlin |
| Fannin | 25,083 | Bonham |
| Fayette | 20,888 | La Grange |
| Fisher | 4,442 | Roby |
| Floyd | 8,224 | Floydada |
| Foard | 1,637 | Crowell |
| Fort Bend | 280,026 | Richmond |
| Franklin | 8,654 | Mount Vernon |
| Freestone | 15,762 | Fairfield |
| Frio | 15,357 | Pearsall |
| Gaines | 14,471 | Seminole |
| Galveston | 234,690 | Galveston |
| Garza | 4,810 | Post |
| Gillespie | 18,832 | Fredericksburg |
| Glasscock | 1,442 | Garden City |
| Goliad | 6,080 | Goliad |
| Gonzales | 17,334 | Gonzales |
| Gray | 23,419 | Pampa |
| Grayson | 97,267 | Sherman |
| Gregg | 109,785 | Longview |
| Grimes | 20,634 | Anderson |
| Guadalupe | 70,584 | Seguin |
| Hale | 35,676 | Plainview |
| Hall | 3,750 | Memphis |

*The population figures give the most recent estimates.*

| County | Population* | County Seat |
|---|---|---|
| Hamilton | 7,588 | Hamilton |
| Hansford | 5,403 | Spearman |
| Hardeman | 14,909 | Quanah |
| Hardin | 45,628 | Kountze |
| Harris | 3,045,212 | Houston |
| Harrison | 58,077 | Marshall |
| Hartley | 3,738 | Channing |
| Haskell | 6,530 | Haskell |
| Hays | 74,221 | San Marcos |
| Hemphill | 3,541 | Canadian |
| Henderson | 62,121 | Athens |
| Hidalgo | 461,015 | Edinburg |
| Hill | 28,150 | Hillsboro |
| Hockley | 24,468 | Levelland |
| Hood | 31,537 | Granbury |
| Hopkins | 29,368 | Sulphur Springs |
| Houston | 21,670 | Crockett |
| Howard | 32,125 | Big Spring |
| Hudspeth | 2,911 | Sierra Blanca |
| Hunt | 65,950 | Greenville |
| Hutchinson | 24,867 | Stinnett |
| Irion | 1,671 | Mertzon |
| Jack | 6,888 | Jacksboro |
| Jackson | 13,579 | Edna |
| Jasper | 32,321 | Jasper |
| Jeff Davis | 2,115 | Fort Davis |
| Jefferson | 242,861 | Beaumont |
| Jim Hogg | 5,097 | Hebbronville |
| Jim Wells | 39,390 | Alice |
| Johnson | 104,278 | Cleburne |
| Jones | 16,010 | Anson |
| Karnes | 12,363 | Karnes City |
| Kaufman | 58,271 | Kaufman |
| Kendall | 18,485 | Boerne |
| Kenedy | 427 | Sarita |
| Kent | 959 | Jayton |
| Kerr | 39,553 | Kerrville |
| Kimble | 4,137 | Junction |
| King | 345 | Guthrie |
| Kinney | 3,242 | Brackettville |
| Kleberg | 30,801 | Kingsville |
| Knox | 4,630 | Benjamin |
| Lamar | 44,954 | Paris |
| Lamb | 14,817 | Littlefield |
| Lampasas | 15,268 | Lampasas |
| La Salle | 5,380 | Cotulla |
| Lavaca | 18,594 | Hallettsville |
| Lee | 13,553 | Giddings |
| Leon | 13,570 | Centerville |
| Liberty | 58,033 | Liberty |
| Limestone | 20,913 | Groesbeck |
| Lipscomb | 2,951 | Lipscomb |
| Live Oak | 10,172 | George West |
| Llano | 12,495 | Llano |
| Loving | 137 | Mentone |
| Lubbock | 230,525 | Lubbock |
| Lynn | 6,625 | Tahoka |
| Madison | 11,352 | Madisonville |
| Marion | 10,069 | Jefferson |
| Martin | 14,937 | Stanton |
| Mason | 3,504 | Mason |
| Matagorda | 38,710 | Bay City |
| Maverick | 44,227 | Eagle Pass |
| McCulloch | 8,481 | Brady |
| McLennan | 197,173 | Waco |
| McMullen | 806 | Tilden |
| Medina | 30,446 | Hondo |
| Menard | 2,333 | Menard |
| Midland | 114,165 | Midland |
| Milam | 23,473 | Cameron |
| Mills | 4,686 | Goldthwaite |
| Mitchell | 7,729 | Colorado City |
| Montague | 17,743 | Montague |
| Montgomery | 222,157 | Conroe |
| Moore | 18,890 | Dumas |
| Morris | 13,216 | Daingerfield |
| Motley | 1,378 | Matador |
| Nacogdoches | 56,185 | Nacogdoches |
| Navarro | 140,315 | Corsicana |
| Newton | 13,894 | Newton |
| Nolan | 16,439 | Sweetwater |
| Nueces | 310,881 | Corpus Christi |
| Ochiltree | 8,690 | Perryton |
| Oldham | 2,233 | Vega |
| Orange | 84,253 | Orange |
| Palo Pinto | 25,098 | Palo Pinto |
| Panola | 22,551 | Carthage |
| Parker | 71,303 | Weatherford |
| Parmer | 10,245 | Farwell |
| Pecos | 14,432 | Fort Stockton |
| Polk | 37,280 | Livingston |
| Potter | 102,928 | Amarillo |
| Presidio | 7,425 | Marfa |
| Rains | 7,389 | Emory |
| Randall | 94,107 | Canyon |
| Reagan | 14,523 | Big Lake |
| Real | 2,442 | Leakey |
| Red River | 13,969 | Clarksville |
| Reeves | 15,395 | Pecos |
| Refugio | 7,814 | Refugio |
| Roberts | 996 | Miami |
| Robertson | 15,432 | Franklin |
| Rockwall | 31,398 | Rockwall |
| Runnels | 11,157 | Ballinger |
| Rusk | 44,229 | Henderson |
| Sabine | 10,131 | Hemphill |

*The population figures give the most recent estimates.*

| County | Population* | County Seat |
|---|---|---|
| San Augustine | 7,885 | San Augustine |
| San Jacinto | 18,639 | Coldspring |
| San Patricio | 64,798 | Sinton |
| San Saba | 5,842 | San Saba |
| Schleicher | 2,983 | Eldorado |
| Scurry | 18,202 | Snyder |
| Shackelford | 3,325 | Albany |
| Shelby | 22,322 | Center |
| Sherman | 2,868 | Stratford |
| Smith | 159,000 | Tyler |
| Somervell | 5,712 | Glen Rose |
| Starr | 49,531 | Rio Grande City |
| Stephens | 8,895 | Breckenridge |
| Sterling | 1,536 | Sterling City |
| Stonewall | 1,960 | Aspermont |
| Sutton | 4,299 | Sonora |
| Swisher | 8,293 | Tulia |
| Tarrant | 1,257,189 | Fort Worth |
| Taylor | 121,902 | Abilene |
| Terrell | 1,309 | Sanderson |
| Terry | 12,869 | Brownfield |
| Throckmorton | 1,815 | Throckmorton |
| Titus | 24,469 | Mount Pleasant |
| Tom Green | 101,243 | San Angelo |
| Travis | 646,437 | Austin |
| Trinity | 12,236 | Groveton |
| Tyler | 18,336 | Woodville |
| Upshur | 33,478 | Gilmer |
| Upton | 4,112 | Rankin |
| Uvalde | 24,964 | Uvalde |
| Val Verde | 42,736 | Del Rio |
| Van Zandt | 40,660 | Canton |
| Victoria | 79,437 | Victoria |
| Walker | 53,492 | Huntsville |
| Waller | 25,823 | Hempstead |
| Ward | 12,257 | Monahans |
| Washington | 27,575 | Brenham |
| Webb | 163,062 | Laredo |
| Wharton | 39,964 | Wharton |
| Wheeler | 5,451 | Wheeler |
| Wichita | 124,053 | Wichita Falls |
| Wilbarger | 14,557 | Vernon |
| Willacy | 19,034 | Raymondville |
| Williamson | 172,666 | Georgetown |
| Wilson | 25,811 | Floresville |
| Winkler | 8,094 | Kermit |
| Wise | 37,321 | Decatur |
| Wood | 31,895 | Quitman |
| Yoakum | 8,471 | Plains |
| Young | 17,642 | Graham |
| Zapata | 10,740 | Zapata |
| Zavala | 12,331 | Crystal City |

*The population figures give the most recent estimates.*

## Facts About Texas Governors Since Annexation

| Governor | Term |
|---|---|
| J. Pinckney Henderson | 1846-1847 |
| George T. Wood | 1847-1849 |
| P. Hansborough Bell | 1849-1853 |
| Elisha M. Pease | 1853-1857 |
| Hardin R. Runnels | 1857-1859 |
| Sam Houston | 1859-1861 |
| Francis R. Lubbock | 1861-1863 |
| Pendleton Murrah | 1863-1865 |
| Andrew J. Hamilton | 1865-1866 |
| James W. Throckmorton | 1866-1867 |
| Elisha M. Pease | 1867-1869 |
| Edmund J. Davis | 1869-1874 |
| Richard Coke | 1874-1876 |
| Richard B. Hubbard | 1876-1879 |
| Oran M. Roberts | 1879-1883 |
| John Ireland | 1883-1887 |
| Lawrence S. Ross | 1887-1891 |
| James S. Hogg | 1891-1895 |
| Charles A. Culberson | 1895-1899 |
| Joseph D. Sayers | 1899-1903 |
| S. W. T. Lanham | 1903-1907 |
| Thomas M. Campbell | 1907-1911 |
| Oscar B. Colquitt | 1911-1915 |
| James E. Ferguson | 1915-1917 |
| William P. Hobby | 1917-1921 |
| Pat M. Neff | 1921-1925 |
| Miriam A. Ferguson | 1925-1927 |
| Dan Moody | 1927-1931 |
| Ross Sterling | 1931-1933 |
| Miriam A. Ferguson | 1933-1935 |
| James V. Allred | 1935-1939 |
| W. Lee O'Daniel | 1939-1941 |
| Coke R. Stevenson | 1941-1947 |
| Beauford H. Jester | 1947-1949 |
| Allan Shivers | 1949-1957 |
| Price Daniel | 1957-1963 |
| John B. Connally | 1963-1969 |
| Preston Smith | 1969-1973 |
| Dolph Briscoe | 1973-1979 |
| William P. Clements,Jr. | 1979-1983 |
| Mark White,Jr. | 1983-1987 |
| William P. Clements,Jr. | 1987-1991 |
| Ann Richards | 1991-1994 |
| George W. Bush | 1994- |

# Biographical Dictionary

*The Biographical Dictionary lists many of the important people introduced in this book. The page number tells where the main discussion of each person starts. See the Index for other page references.*



## A

**Adair, Christia** *1893–1990* Worker for women's suffrage in Texas. p. 255

**Adair, John** *?–1885* Co-owner of the JA Ranch in the Texas Panhandle. p. 223

**Aldrin, Edwin E., Jr.** *1930–* United States astronaut who became one of the first humans to set foot on the moon, on July 20, 1969. p. 269

**Allred, James** *1899–1959* Governor of Texas from 1935 to 1939. He set up a commission to help people find jobs and a pension plan for senior citizens. p. 258

**Alvarez, Francisca** Mexican nurse who became known as the Angel of Goliad after she protected some Texas soldiers from the massacre at Goliad. p. 155

**Armstrong, Neil** *1930–* United States astronaut who became one of the first humans to set foot on the moon, on July 20, 1969. p. 269

**Ashworth, Aaron** Early African American rancher who owned a large ranch in Jefferson County in Southeast Texas. p. 221

**Austin, Moses** *1761–1821* Missouri business person who received a grant from the Spanish government to bring settlers into Texas. p. 107

**Austin, Stephen F.** *1793–1836* Known as the "Father of Texas," he brought the first 300 families of settlers into Texas. He fought for Texas independence. The city of Austin is named for him. pp. 106, 122, 162

## B

**Barret, Lyne** *1832–1913* Drilled the first known oil well in Texas, in 1866. p. 245

**Bentsen, Lloyd** *1921–* Secretary of the treasury in President Clinton's Cabinet; former United States senator from Texas. p. 280

**Bonavide, Florencia** One of the first women in Texas to be a cattle rancher. p. 224

**Bonham, John** *1807–1836* Volunteer who fought for Texas independence. p. 144

**Borland, Margaret Heferman** One of the first women in Texas to be a cattle rancher. She went on the long cattle drives to Kansas. p. 224

**Bowie, James** *1796–1836* Volunteer who fought for Texas independence. p. 144

**Brackenridge, Mary Eleanor** *1837–1924* Worker for women's suffrage in Texas. p. 255

**Burnet, David** *1788–1870* Chosen as the first president of the Republic of Texas. pp. 150, 161

**Bush, George Herbert Walker** *1924–* 41st President of the United States of America; President during the Persian Gulf War. p. 279

**Bush, George W.** *1946–* Became governor of Texas in 1994. He is the son of George Herbert Walker Bush. pp. 322, 335

## C

**Cabeza de Vaca, Álvar Núñez** *1490–1557* Spanish explorer who traveled across present-day Texas, New Mexico, and Mexico. p. 90

**Carranza, Venustiano** (kah•RAN•zah, veh•noos•tee•AH•noh) *1859–1920* Gained control of the Mexican government in 1911. p. 251

**Carson, Samuel** *1798–1838* A signer of the Texas Declaration of Independence. p. 149

**Childress, George** *1804–1841* Headed the group that wrote the Texas Declaration of Independence. pp. 147, 149

**Chisholm, Jesse** (CHIH•zuhm) *?–1868* Rancher for whom the Chisholm Trail is named. p. 223

**Chisum, John** *1824–1884* Set up one of the first ranches in North Texas. p. 222

**Cisneros, Henry** *1947–* Secretary of the Department of Housing and Urban Development in Clinton's Cabinet. p. 280

**Clements, William P., Jr.** *1917–* Governor of Texas from 1979 to 1983; 1987 to 1991. p. 302

**Clinton, Bill** *1946–* 42nd President of the United States of America. p. 280

**Collins, Albert** African American blues musician from Texas. p. 233

**Connally, John B.** *1917–* Governor of Texas from 1963 to 1969. p. 278

**Coronado, Francisco** (kawr•oh•NAH•doh) *1510?–1554* Spanish explorer who led an expedition in 1540 in search of Cíbola. p. 94

**Cortés, Ernesto, Jr.** Mexican American activist who helped organize C.O.P.S. (Communities Organized for Public Service). p. 338

**Cortés, Hernando** *1485–1547* Spanish conquistador who conquered what is now central and southern Mexico. p. 92

**Cós, Martín Perfecto de** (KOHS, mar•TEEN pair•FEK•toh day) Mexican general who sent soldiers to Goliad and San Antonio during the Texas Revolution. p. 143

**Crockett, Davy** *1786–1836* Pioneer who fought for Texas independence. p. 144

**Cunningham, Minnie Fisher** *1882–1964* Worker for women's suffrage in Texas. p. 255

# D

**de León, Martín** (day lay•OHN, mar•TEEN) *1765–1833* Tejano who started a colony in Texas with 200 Mexican families. p. 112

**DeWitt, Green** *1787–1835* Empresario who started a settlement in Texas with 100 families from Missouri. p. 111

**De Zavala, Lorenzo** *1788–1836* Mexican who supported the Texas struggle for independence. He was later elected vice president of the Republic of Texas. pp. 124, 142, 147, 150

**Díaz, Porfirio** (DEE•ahs, pawr•FEER•yoh) *1830–1915* Mexican president who was overthrown in a revolution in 1911. p. 251

**Dickenson, Susanna** *?–1883* A survivor of the Battle of the Alamo. She was sent by Mexican general Santa Anna to tell Texas leaders about the fall of the Alamo. pp. 138, 146

**Dodson, Sarah** *1812–1848* Early settler in Texas who designed a flag on which the Texas state flag is based. p. 165

**Drake, Edwin** *1819–1880* Drilled the country's first oil well in 1859 in Pennsylvania. p. 245

# E

**Eberly, Angelina** *early 1800s–1860* Austin business person who led the citizens of Austin in the brief Archives War of 1842. p. 164

**Edwards, Benjamin** *?–1837* American who was given a land grant to start a settlement near Nacogdoches. He led the Fredonia Rebellion in 1825. p. 121

**Edwards, Haden** *1771–1849* American who was given a land grant to start a settlement near Nacogdoches. p. 121

**Eisenhower, Dwight D.** *1890–1969* 34th President of the United States of America and, earlier, commander of all Allied armies in Europe during World War II. pp. 259, 266, 277

**Ellis, Richard** *1781–?* A signer of the Texas Declaration of Independence. p. 149

**Esparza, Gregorio** *1803–1836* A Tejano defender of the Alamo. p. 138

**Estéban** (ehs•TAY•bahn) African who explored Texas and the Southwest United States. Also known as Estevanico. p. 91

# F

**Fannin, James** *1804–1836* A Texas leader during the Texas Revolution. He and 300 of his soldiers were killed by Mexican soldiers at Goliad on March 27, 1836. p. 154

**Farmer, James** *1920–* Helped start the Congress of Racial Equality, or CORE. p. 267

**Ferguson, James E. ("Pa")** *1871–1944* Governor of Texas from 1915 to 1917. p. 254

**Ferguson, Miriam ("Ma")** *1875–1961* Governor of Texas from 1925 to 1927 and from 1933 to 1935. p. 255

**Forbes, John** *1797–1880* A Texas leader during the Texas Revolution. p. 160

# G

**García, Hector P.** Started a group after World War II that worked for the rights of Spanish-speaking people in the United States. p. 268

**Garner, John Nance** *1868–1967* Vice President of the United States from 1933 to 1941 under President Franklin D. Roosevelt. p. 258

**Garza, Eligio ("Kika") de la** *1927–* Mexican American from Mercedes who was elected into Congress in 1965. p. 268

**Glenn, John** *1921–* First American to circle the Earth in space. p. 269

**Glidden, Joseph** *1813–1906* Began the widespread use of barbed-wire fences. p. 225

**González, Henry B.** (gohn•ZAH•lays) *1916–* The first Mexican American ever elected to the United States House of Representatives. p. 268

**Goodnight, Charles** *1836–1929* Co-owner of the JA Ranch in the Texas Panhandle. p. 223

**Goyens, William** *1794–1856* Free African business person from Nacogdoches who helped work out a peace treaty with the Cherokees during the Texas Revolution. p. 170

**Gramm, Phil** *1942–* United States senator, elected in 1984, from College Station. p. 280

**Granger, Gordon** *1822–1876* United States Army general who proclaimed all slaves in Texas free on June 19, 1865. p. 205

**Guthrie, Woody** *1912–1967* Folksinger and composer from Pampa. p. 257

## H

**Harris, Dilue Rose** *1825–1914* Texas settler whose family was a part of the Runaway Scrape during the Texas Revolution. p. 154

**Hidalgo, Miguel** (ee•DAHL•goh) *1753–1811* Mexican priest who led the first Mexican rebellion against Spain in 1810. p. 108

**Hobby, Oveta Culp** *1905–1996* First director of the Women's Army Corps (WACs), and the first woman to hold the rank of colonel in the United States armed forces. p. 259

**Hogg, James S.** *1851–1906* Governor of Texas from 1891 to 1895. He established the Texas Railroad Commission. p. 228

**Houston, Sam** (HYOO•stuhn) *1793–1863* Commander of the Texas forces at San Jacinto; the first president of the Republic of Texas; one of the first United States senators from Texas; elected governor of Texas in 1859. pp. 149, 160, 178, 204

**Hughes, Howard Robard, Sr.** *1869–1924* American who became a millionaire after inventing, in 1908, a new drill bit for oil drilling. p. 249

**Hutchison, Kay Bailey** *1943–* United States senator from Dallas and great-great-great-great-granddaughter of Charles S. Taylor, a signer of the Texas Declaration of Independence. p. 281

## I

**Idár, Jovita** (ee•DAR, oh•VEE•tah) *1885–1946* Activist for causes important to women and Mexican Americans. pp. 244, 254

## J

**Johnson, Claudia Alta ("Lady Bird")** *1912–* Wife of Lyndon Baines Johnson, the 36th President of the United States of America. She founded the National Wildflower Research Center near Austin. pp. 38, 313

**Johnson, Lyndon Baines** *1908–1973* 36th President of the United States of America. He expanded the Vietnam War. pp. 269, 277

**Joiner, Columbus Marvin ("Dad")** *1860–1947* Made one of the biggest oil discoveries in Texas history, in 1930. p. 249

**Jones, Anson** *1798–1858* Last president of the Republic of Texas. p. 174

**Jordan, Barbara** *1936–1996* First African American woman to represent a southern state in the United States Congress. pp. 264, 268

## K

**Kennedy, John F.** *1917–1963* 35th President of the United States of America. pp. 269, 278

**Kian** (KEE•uhn) Enslaved African who settled in Texas with Jane Long, one of the Old Three Hundred. Also known as Kiamatia. p. 111

**Kilby, Jack** *1923–* Inventor of the integrated circuit. p. 268

**King, Henrietta** *1832–1925* Wife of Richard King. After her husband died, she managed and expanded the King Ranch. p. 221

**King, Martin Luther, Jr.** *1929–1968* African American minister who was the main leader of the civil rights movement in the United States during the 1950s and 1960s. pp. 268, 279

**King, Richard** *1825–1885* Started one of the largest and best-known ranches in Texas. p. 221

## L

**La Salle, Sieur de** (luh•SAL) *1643–1687* French explorer, also known as René-Robert Cavelier, who set up the Fort St. Louis colony. p. 98

**Lamar, Mirabeau** (luh•MAR, MIR•uh•boh) *1798–1859* The first elected vice president of the Republic of Texas. Later, in 1838, he was elected president of Texas. pp. 161, 169, 178

**Lee, Robert E.** *1807–1870* Confederate army commander during the Civil War. p. 204

**Lincoln, Abraham** *1809–1865* 16th President of the United States of America and signer of the Emancipation Proclamation. p. 203

**Lone Wolf** Kiowa leader. p. 214

**Long, Jane** *1798–1880* One of the Old Three Hundred and wife of James Long. She first settled on Point Bolivar and later joined the Austin colony. p. 110

**Love, Nat** *1854–1921* African American cowhand who worked on the great cattle drives from Texas until 1889. p. 224

**Lucas, Anthony F.** *1855–1921* Engineer who in 1901 drilled the first well in the Spindletop oil field. p. 246

## M

**Mackenzie, Ranald S.** *1840–1889* Officer who led the surprise attack on the Indians at Palo Duro Canyon on September 28, 1874. p. 214

**Martínez, Antonio** *?–1823* Spanish governor of Texas who in 1820 granted Moses Austin the land to set up the territory's first colony. p. 107

**McCulloch, Samuel** *1810–1893* Free African who was the only Texas soldier wounded at the Battle of Goliad. p. 144

**McGloin, James** *1801–1856* Empresario who set up an Irish colony in Texas in 1828. p. 111

**McMullen, John** *1785–1853* Empresario who set up an Irish colony in Texas in 1828. p. 111

**Meusebach, John** (MOY•zuh•bahk) *1812–1897* German immigrant who led the Society for the Protection of German Immigrants. p. 171

**Miller, Dorie** *1919–1943* Sailor from Waco who shot down four Japanese planes during the attack on Pearl Harbor. p. 258

**Moczygemba, Leopold** (moh•sheh•GEM•bah) *1825–1891* Priest who encouraged Polish people to immigrate to Texas and helped set up the village of Panna Maria. p. 199

**Murphy, Audie** *1924–1971* Soldier from Farmersville who won more medals in World War II than any other American soldier. p. 259

**Músquiz, Manuel** Started one of the first large ranches in West Texas. p. 222

## N

**Narváez, Pánfilo de** *1478–1528* Spanish explorer who traveled through Florida in 1528. p. 90

**Navarro, José Antonio** (nah•VAR•roh, hoh•SAY ahn•TOH•nee•oh) *1795–1871* A signer of the Texas Declaration of Independence. p. 147

**Nimitz, Chester W.** *1885–1966* Commander of the United States Pacific fleet from 1941 to 1945, during World War II. p. 259

**Nocona, Peta** *?–1860* Comanche chief and father of Quanah Parker. p. 217

## O

**Oñate, Juan de** (ohn•YAH•tay) *1549–1628* Spanish conquistador who claimed the land north of the Rio Grande. He started settlements along the Chama River. p. 96

## P

**Parker, Cynthia Ann** *1827–1864* Mother of Quanah Parker. After being taken from her home by the Comanches in 1838, she married Peta Nocona. p. 217

**Parker, Quanah** *1845–1911* Chief of the Quohada Comanche tribe. He worked for peace between the whites and the Indians. p. 214

**Parmer, Martin** *1778–1850* A signer of the Texas Declaration of Independence. p. 149

**Pease, Elisha** *1812–1883* Governor of Texas from 1853 to 1857; 1867 to 1869. p. 325

**Perot, H. Ross** *1930–* Texas business leader who ran for President in 1992. p. 280

**Peterson, Pat Lester** *1948–* Choctaw Indian who lives in Dallas. p. 82

**Pike, Zebulon** *1779–1813* Explorer of the western frontier of the United States in 1806. p. 135

**Piñeda, Alonzo Alvarez de** (pin•YAY•dah) Spanish explorer who in 1519 might have been the first European to land on Texas soil. p. 90

**Potter, Robert** *1799–1842* A signer of the Texas Declaration of Independence. p. 149

**Pryor, Harriet** One of the Old Three Hundred. She and her family left Alabama in 1821 to settle in the Austin colony. p. 115

## R

**Rayburn, Samuel T.** *1882–1961* Politician who was elected to the Texas legislature in 1906 and then to the United States Congress in 1912. p. 258

**Reagan, Ronald** *1911–* 40th President of the United States of America. p. 280

**Richards, Ann** *1933–* Governor of Texas from 1991 to 1994. She was the first woman to be elected to state office since Miriam Ferguson in the 1930s. p. 281

**Rodriguez, Paula** One of the first women in Texas to be a cattle rancher. p. 224

**Roosevelt, Franklin D.** *1882–1945* 32nd President of the United States of America. He formed work programs that helped the nation out of the Great Depression. p. 258

**Ross, Nellie Tayloe** *1876–1977* First woman to be a governor in the United States. p. 254

**Ruiz, José Francisco** (roo•EES, hoh•SAY frahn•SEES•koh) *1783–1840* A signer of the Texas Declaration of Independence. p. 147

## S

**Saibara, Seito** (sy•BAH•rah, SAY•toh) Japanese farmer who owned large rice farms near Houston in the early 1900s. p. 253

**Santa Anna, Antonio López de** *1794–1876* General in the Mexican army who took over as dictator of the Mexican government in 1835. pp. 122, 138, 155, 161

**Satanta** *1807?–1878* Kiowa chief also known as White Bear. p. 210

**Scott, Winfield** *1786–1866* United States Army general who captured Mexico City, ending the Mexican-American War. p. 176

**Seguín, Erasmo** (say•GEEN, ay•RAHS•moh) *1782–1857* Tejano rancher who befriended colonists in the Austin colony. p. 112

**Seguín, Juan** *1806–1889* Tejano who joined the Texans in their fight for independence. He was a son of Erasmo Seguín. pp. 112, 144

**Selena** *1971–1995* Grammy-winning Mexican American pop singer; known as the Queen of Tejano. p. 232

**Smith, Erastus** *1787–1837* Scout in General Houston's army during the Texas Revolution. He was also known as "Deaf Smith." p. 152

**Smithwick, Noah** *1808–1899* Early settler of Texas who opposed annexation of Texas by the United States. pp. 108, 179

**Stevenson, Adlai E.** *1900–1965* Politician who ran against Dwight D. Eisenhower in the 1952 and 1956 Presidential elections. p. 277

**Stinson, Katherine** *1891–1977* Aviator who trained pilots during World War I. p. 252

**Stinson, Marjorie** *1895?–1975* Aviator who trained pilots during World War I. p. 252

## T

**Taylor, Charles S.** *1808–1865* A signer of the Texas Declaration of Independence. p. 281

**Ten Bears** Comanche chief. p. 212

**Travis, William B.** *1809–1836* Commander of the Texas forces at the Alamo. pp. 127, 144

## U

**Urrea, José** (oor•RAY•ah, hoh•SAY) Mexican general who ordered the massacre of 300 Texas soldiers at Goliad. p. 154

## V

**Vaughan, Stevie Ray** *1954–1990* Grammy-winning blues guitarist from Dallas. p. 233

**Villa, Francisco ("Pancho")** (VEE•yah) *1877–1923* Mexican leader and bandit who raided towns in Texas and New Mexico after he failed to gain control of the Mexican government in 1911. p. 251

**Villareal, Margarita** One of the first women in Texas to be a cattle rancher. p. 224

## W

**Waerenskjold, Elise** *1815–1895* Norwegian immigrant to Texas. p. 194

**Waggoner, W. T.** *1852–1934* Found oil in Texas in 1904 while drilling for water. p. 249

**Wallace, Daniel Webster** *1860–1939* African American cattle rancher in Texas. p. 223

**White, Edward** *1930–1967* The first astronaut to "walk" in space, in 1965. p. 269

**White, James Taylor** Cattle rancher in Texas during the 1840s. p. 172

**White, Mark, Jr.** *1940–* Governor of Texas from 1983 to 1987. p. 312

**Williams, Lizzie Johnson** One of the first women in Texas to be a cattle rancher. She went on the long cattle drives to Kansas. p. 224

**Williamson, Robert M.** *1804–1859* Editor of *The Texas Gazette,* the first newspaper published in the Austin colony. p. 111

**Wilson, Woodrow** *1856–1924* 28th President of the United States of America. p. 251

# GAZETTEER

*The Gazetteer is a geographical dictionary that will help you locate places discussed in this book. The page number tells where each place appears on a map.*



## A

**Abilene** A city in Central Texas. (32°N, 100°W) p. 29

**Adobe Walls** The site of a battle in the War on the Plains. p. 213

**Agua Dulce** (AHG•wah DOOL•see) The site of a battle in the Texas Revolution. p. 153

**Amarillo** The commercial and industrial center of the Texas Panhandle. (35°N, 102°W) p. 29

**Arlington** A city in northern Texas. (33°N, 97°W) p. 29

**Austin** The capital of Texas; named after Stephen F. Austin. (30°N, 98°W) p. 29

## B

**Balcones Escarpment** (bal•KOH•nays) A long wall of steep cliffs in Texas that separates the High Plains from the Gulf Coastal Plain. p. 42

**Bandera** A city in southwestern Texas; located on the Medina River. (30°N, 99°W) p. 222

**Bangladesh** (bang•gluh•DESH) A nation in southern Asia; located on the Bay of Bengal. p. 310

**Bastrop** A city in South-Central Texas; one of the oldest settlements in Texas. (30°N, 97°W) p. 123

**Beaumont** (BOH•mahnt) A city in southeastern Texas; located on the Neches River. (30°N, 94°W) p. 29

**Borger** (BAWR•ger) A city in the Panhandle of Texas. (36°N, 101°W) p. 248

**Brazoria** (brah•ZOHR•ee•ah) A settlement established in 1828 in southeastern Texas. (29°N, 96°W) p. 123

**Brazos River** (BRAH•zohs) A river in Central Texas; flows southeast into the Gulf of Mexico. p. 47

**Brownsville** A city in southern Texas; located on the Rio Grande. (26°N, 97°W) p. 29

**Brownwood** An industrial city in Central Texas. (32°N, 99°W) p. 29

**Bryan** A city in East-Central Texas. (31°N, 96°W) p. 29

**Buffalo Bayou** A stream that flows through Houston and into San Jacinto Bay. p. 156

**Burnet** A city in Central Texas. (31°N, 98°W) p. 29

## C

**Canadian River** A river that flows through the Panhandle of Texas and into the Arkansas River. p. 47

**Cap Rock Escarpment** A long wall of steep cliffs in Texas that separates the Central Plains from the High Plains. p. 42

**Castroville** A town in southern Texas settled by French immigrants. (29°N, 99°W) p. 237

**Central Plains** One of the natural regions of Texas; part of the Interior Plains of the United States. p. 40

**Chisos Mountains** (CHEE•sohs) A mountain chain located in the southern part of the Mountains and Basins region of Texas. p. 42

**Cíbola** (SEE•boh•lah) A region in what is now New Mexico; included the "Seven Cities of Cíbola" which Spanish explorers believed held many treasures. p. 99

**Colombia** A nation in northwestern South America. p. 310

**Colorado River** A river in Texas that flows southeast into the Gulf of Mexico. p. 47

**Columbia** A town in eastern Texas; the first capital of the Republic of Texas. (30°N, 96°W) p. 123

**Columbus** A town in Texas settled in 1823 by members of Stephen F. Austin's colony. (30°N, 97°W) p. 123

**Comfort** A town in Central Texas settled by German immigrants. (30°N, 99°W) p. 237

**Corpus Christi** A city in southeastern Texas; located on Corpus Christi Bay, at the mouth of the Nueces River. (28°N, 97°W) p. 29

**Corsicana** A city in northeastern Texas. (32°N, 96°W) p. 248

## D

**Dallas** A city in northeastern Texas; located on the Trinity River. (38°N, 97°W) p. 291

**Davis Mountains** A mountain chain located in the center of the Mountains and Basins region of Texas. p. 42

## E

**Edwards Plateau** (pla•TOH) A major plateau located in the southern part of the High Plains region of Texas. p. 42

**El Paso** A city at the western tip of Texas; located on the Rio Grande. (32°N, 106°W) p. 29

**El Paso del Norte** Original name of El Paso. p. 123

**England** A nation in Europe; located in the southern part of the island of Great Britain. p. 310

# F

**Fayetteville** A town in southeastern Texas settled by German immigrants. (30°N, 97°W) p. 237

**Fort Belknap** A United States military post in northern Texas, built to protect the frontier during the War on the Plains. p. 213

**Fort Bend** A fort in southeastern Texas used during the Texas Revolution. p. 153

**Fort Bliss** A United States military post near El Paso, built to protect the frontier during the War on the Plains. p. 213

**Fort Concho** A United States military post in Central Texas, built to protect the frontier during the War on the Plains. p. 213

**Fort Davis** A United States military post in western Texas, built to protect the frontier during the War on the Plains. p. 213

**Fort Duncan** A United States military post in southern Texas, built to protect the frontier during the War on the Plains. p. 213

**Fort Elliot** A United States military post in northern Texas, built to protect the frontier during the War on the Plains. p. 213

**Fort Griffin** A United States military post in Central Texas, built to protect the frontier during the War on the Plains. p. 213

**Fort Richardson** A United States military post in northern Texas, built to protect the frontier during the War on the Plains. p. 213

**Fort St. Louis** A French colony in Texas founded by the explorer Sieur de La Salle. p. 99

**Fort Stockton** A city in western Texas. (31°N, 103°W) p. 29

**Fort Worth** A city in northern Texas; located on the Trinity River. (33°N, 97°W) p. 29

**Fredericksburg** A town in Central Texas settled by German immigrants. (30°N, 99°W) p. 237

# G

**Galveston** A city located on Galveston Island in Galveston Bay. (29°N, 95°W) p. 29

**Galveston Bay** An inlet of the Gulf of Mexico on the southeastern coast of Texas. p. 150

**Garland** A city in northeastern Texas; located near Dallas. (33°N, 97°W) p. 29

**Gladewater** A city in northeastern Texas. (33°N, 95°W) p. 248

**Goliad** (GOH•lee•ad) A city in southeastern Texas; the site of a battle in the Texas Revolution. (29°N, 98°W) p. 123

**Gonzales** (gohn•ZAH•lays) A city in South Texas; the site of the first battle of the Texas Revolution. (29°N, 98°W) p. 123

**Groce's Plantation** A plantation in southeastern Texas that served as a campsite for the Texas army during the Texas Revolution. p. 153

**Guadalupe Mountains** (gwah•dah•LOO•pay) A mountain chain located in the northern part of the Mountains and Basins region of Texas. p. 42

**Guadalupe Peak** The highest point in Texas; part of the Guadalupe Mountains. p. 42

**Guadalupe River** A river that flows through southeastern Texas into the San Antonio River. p. 47

**Gulf Coastal Plain** One of the natural regions of Texas; covers almost one-third of the state. p. 40

**Gulf of Mexico** A body of water off the southwestern coast of North America; opens onto the Atlantic Ocean; surrounded by the United States, Cuba, and Mexico. p. 273

# H

**Harrisburg** One of the first settlements built in Texas. (31°N, 94°W) p. 123

**High Plains** One of the natural regions of Texas; stretches from Central Texas to Canada. p. 40

**Houston** The largest city in Texas; third-largest port in the United States; capital of Texas from 1836 to 1839. (30°N, 95°W) p. 29

**Hutto** A town in eastern Texas settled by German immigrants. (31°N, 98°W) p. 237

# I

**India** A nation located in southern Asia. p. 310

**Indianola** One of the earliest settlements in Texas. p. 199

**Industry** A town in eastern Texas settled by German immigrants. (30°N, 96°W) p. 237

**Ireland** A nation located to the west of Great Britain. p. 310

**Irving** A city in northeastern Texas; located near Dallas. (33°N, 97°W) p. 29

# J

**Jamaica** An island nation in the West Indies. p. 310

**Jonesborough** One of the first Anglo-American settlements in Texas. p. 123

# K

**Karnack** A city in northeastern Texas; located near the Louisiana-Texas border. (33°N, 94°W) p. 40

**Kilgore** A city in northeastern Texas; known as the "Oil City of the World." (32°N, 95°W) p. 248

**Killeen** A city in Central Texas, north of Austin. (31°N, 95°W) p. 29

# L

**La Bahia** A settlement near Matagorda Bay established by the Spanish in 1722. (30°N, 97°W) p. 102

**La Grange** (luh GRAYNJ) A city in southwestern Texas; located on the Colorado River. (30°N, 97°W) p. 123

**La Réunion** A town in northeastern Texas settled by French immigrants. p. 237

**Laredo** (luh•RAY•doh) A city in southern Texas; located on the Rio Grande. (27°N, 99°W) p. 29

**Lebanon** (LEB•uh•nuhn) A nation in the Middle East; located on the Mediterranean Sea. p. 310

**Liberty** A city in eastern Texas; one of the first settlements in the state. (30°N, 95°W) p. 123

**Llano Estacado** (YAH•noh es•tah•KAH•doh) A major plateau in the southwestern United States; part of the High Plains in Texas. p. 96

**Longview** A city in northeastern Texas. (32°N, 95°W) p. 29

**Lubbock** A city in northwestern Texas. (34°N, 102°W) p. 29

**Luling** A city in South-Central Texas. (30°N, 98°W) p. 248

**Lynchburg** A town in southeastern Texas; located on the San Jacinto River. (30°N, 95°W) p. 156

# M

**Matagorda** (mat•uh•GAWR•duh) A town on the Gulf Coast of Texas; settled in the early 1800s. (29°N, 96°W) p. 123

**McAllen** A city in southern Texas. (26°N, 98°W) p. 29

**McClellan Creek** The site of a raid during the War on the Plains. p. 213

**Mexia** (muh•HAY•uh) A city in East-Central Texas. (32°N, 96°W) p. 248

**Mexico** A Spanish-speaking nation in North America, south of the United States. p. 28

**Mexico City** The capital of Mexico. (19°N, 99°W) p. 99

**Midland** A city in western Texas; a major oil-producing and cattle-ranching area. (32°N, 102°W) p. 29

**Mississippi River** The largest river in the United States; it flows from Lake Itasca, Minnesota, into the Gulf of Mexico. p. 28

**Mountains and Basins** One of the natural regions in Texas; the highest and driest part of the state. p. 40

# N

**Nacogdoches** (nah•koh•DOH•ches) A city in eastern Texas; began as a Spanish mission in 1716. (32°N, 95°W) p. 102

**Neches River** (NAY•chehs) A river that flows through eastern Texas and into Sabine Lake. p. 47

**Netherlands** A nation in northwestern Europe; borders the North Sea, Germany, and Belgium. p. 310

**New Braunfels** (BRAWN•fuhlz) A city in South-Central Texas settled by German immigrants. (30°N, 99°W) p. 199

**New Sweden** A town in Central Texas settled by Swedish immigrants in the mid-1800s. (30°N, 97°W) p. 199

**Nigeria** (ny•JIR•ee•uh) A nation in western Africa on the Gulf of Guinea. p. 310

**North America** One of the seven continents; contains Canada, the United States, and Mexico. p. 237

**Nueces River** (noo•AY•says) A river that flows through southern Texas and into Nueces Bay. p. 47

# O

**Odessa** A city in western Texas. (32°N, 102°W) p. 29

# P

**Palmito Ranch** The site of a battle in the Civil War; located near Brownsville. p. 207

**Palo Duro Canyon** A large canyon located on the Red River in northwestern Texas. p. 99

**Panna Maria** A town in southern Texas settled by Polish immigrants in 1854. (29°N, 98°W) p. 199

**Pecos** A city in western Texas; located near the Pecos River. (31°N, 103°W) p. 222

**Pecos River** A river that flows through eastern New Mexico and western Texas and into the Rio Grande. p. 47

**Philippines** A nation made of more than 7,000 islands in southeastern Asia. p. 310

**Pikes Peak** A peak in the Rocky Mountains; named for Zebulon Pike. (39°N, 105°W) p. 135

**Point Bolivar** The southern tip of the Bolivar Peninsula on the Texas coast. p. 123

**Port Arthur** A city in southeastern Texas; located on Sabine Lake. (30°N, 94°W) p. 29

**Praha** A town in southern Texas settled by Czech immigrants. (30°N, 97°W) p. 199

**Presidio** (pray•SEE•dee•oh) One of the earliest settlements in southwestern Texas. (30°N, 104°W) p. 123

# R

**Red River** A tributary of the Mississippi River; begins in eastern New Mexico and flows into the Mississippi River; forms the Texas-Oklahoma border. p. 47

**Refugio** A town in southern Texas; one of the earliest settlements in the state. (28°N, 97°W) p. 123

**Rio Grande** A river that flows through the southwestern United States; begins in the Rocky Mountains in Colorado and flows into the Gulf of Mexico; forms the Texas-Mexico border. p. 47

**Rockport** A city in southern Texas; located near Aransas Bay. (28°N, 97°W) p. 29

# S

**Sabine Pass** An outlet for the Sabine River; extends from Sabine Lake to the Gulf of Mexico; site of a Civil War battle. p. 207

**Sabine River** The river that forms part of the Texas-Louisiana border; empties into the Gulf of Mexico. p. 47

**San Angelo** A city in West-Central Texas. (31°N, 100°W) p. 29

**San Antonio** A city in Central Texas; located on the San Antonio River; started as the Spanish settlement San Antonio de Bexar in 1718. (29°N, 99°W) p. 283

**San Antonio de Bexar** A Spanish settlement in Texas founded in 1718 as a mission and presidio; later became known as San Antonio. p. 102

**San Antonio de Valero** A Spanish mission in Texas, built in 1718. p. 102

**San Antonio River** A river that flows through southern Texas and into the San Antonio Bay. p. 47

**San Augustine** One of the earliest settlements in eastern Texas. (32°N, 94°W) p. 123

**San Felipe** A settlement in southeastern Texas. (30°N, 96°W) p. 199

**San Felipe de Austin** (SAN fay•LEEP•ay day AWS•tuhn) A town set up by Stephen F. Austin in 1823 as the capital of an American colony in Spanish Texas. p. 123

**San Francisco de los Tejas** A Spanish mission in eastern Texas; active during the 1600s and 1700s. p. 102

**San Jacinto** (SAN jah•SIN•toh) The site of the last battle of the Texas Revolution; located near the point where the San Jacinto River meets Galveston Bay. p. 156

**San Jacinto Bay** A bay at the mouth of the San Jacinto River; connects the river with Galveston Bay. p. 156

**San Jacinto River** A river that flows through southeastern Texas; flows into the Galveston Bay. p. 150

**San Juan Bautista** A Spanish settlement in southern Texas; active in the 1600s and 1700s. p. 102

**San Patricio** A settlement in southern Texas; active in the early 1800s. p. 123

**San Saba** A town in Central Texas; located on the San Saba River. p. 102

**San Xavier** A Spanish mission in eastern Texas; active in the 1600s and 1700s. p. 102

**Santa Fe** The capital of New Mexico. (36°N, 106°W) p. 97

**Serbin** A town in Texas settled by Wend immigrants in 1854. (30°N, 97°W) p. 237

**South America** The fourth-largest continent on Earth. p. 273

**South Korea** A nation in eastern Asia. p. 310

**Spindletop Field** The first major oil field discovered in Texas; located near the city of Beaumont. p. 248

# T

**Texarkana** A city on the Texas-Arkansas border. (33°N, 94°W) p. 29

**Texas** A state in the southwestern United States; the second-largest state in the country. p. 29

**Trinity River** A river that flows through eastern Texas; formed where the West Fork and Elm Fork rivers meet. p. 47

**Tule Canyon** The site of a battle in the War on the Plains. p. 213

**Tyler** A city in northeastern Texas. (32°N, 95°W) p. 29

# U

**United States** A nation in North America. p. 28

# V

**Velasco** (vay•LAS•koh) The site of the signing of the Treaty of Velasco, which ended the Texas Revolution. p. 123

**Victoria** A city in southern Texas; located near Matagorda Bay. (29°N, 97°W) p. 29

**Vietnam** (vee•et•NAHM) A nation in southeastern Asia. p. 310

# W

**Waco** A city in Central Texas; located on the Brazos River. (32°N, 97°W) p. 29

**Washington, D.C.** The capital of the United States; located on the Potomac River in a special district that is not part of any state. (39°N, 77°W) p. 282

**Washington-on-the-Brazos** A city in eastern Texas; site of the signing of the Texas Declaration of Independence. p. 150

**Waterloo** A settlement in Texas located on the Colorado River; chosen as the capital of Texas in 1839 and renamed Austin. (30°N, 98°W) p. 123

**Wichita Falls** A city in northern Texas. (34°N, 98°W) p. 29

# Y

**Ysleta** (ees•LAY•tah) The first Spanish mission in Texas; located in West Texas. p. 102

# Glossary

*The Glossary contains important social studies words and their definitions. Each word is respelled as it would be in a dictionary. When you see this mark ´ after a syllable, pronounce that syllable with more force than the other syllables. The page number at the end of the definition tells where to find the word in your book.*

add, āce, câre, pälm; end, ēqual; it, īce; odd, ōpen, ôrder; tŏŏk, pōōl; up, bûrn; yōō as *u* in *fuse*; **oi**l; p**ou**t; ə as *a* in *above*, *e* in *sicken*, *i* in *possible*, *o* in *melon*, *u* in *circus*; **ch**eck; ri**ng**; **th**in; **th**is; **zh** as in *vision*



## A

**abolish** (ə•bol´ish) To put an end to. p. 149

**adapt** (ə•dapt´) To fit ways of living to the land and its resources. p. 77

**adobe** (ä•dō´bā) Clay brick. p. 77

**agency** (ā´jən•sē) A group of state officials. p. 325

**ally** (al´ī) A partner or helper. p. 78

**amendment** (ə•mend´mənt) A change in the Constitution. p. 255

**analyze** (an´ə•līz) To break something down into its parts and look closely at how those parts are connected. p. 25

**ancestor** (an´ses•tər) A family member from long ago. p. 79

**Anglo** (ang´glō) A person whose ancestors came from Britain. p. 110

**annex** (ə•neks´) To add on. p. 174

**appeal** (ə•pēl´) To ask for another trial. p. 326

**aquifer** (ak´wə•fər) Underground pool of water between layers of rock and sand. p. 46

**archives** (är´kīvz) Government records. p. 164

**astronaut** (as´trə•nôt) A space explorer. p. 269

**auction** (ôk´shən) A public sale. p. 196

## B

**band** (band) A small group of families that live and work together. p. 63

**barbed wire** (bärbd wīr) A twisted wire with sharp points. p. 225

**basin** (bā´sən) Low, bowl-shaped land with higher ground all around it. p. 43

**bill** (bil) A plan for a new law. p. 327

**Bill of Rights** (bil uv rīts) A list of freedoms in the Constitution. p. 323

**blockade** (blo•kād´) To close off a place, so nothing can get through. p. 204

**boom** (bōōm) A fast growth. p. 246

**boundary** (boun´drē) The border or edge around a place. p. 175

**brand** (brand) A symbol marked on cattle that shows ownership. p. 224

**breed** (brēd) A kind of a particular animal. p. 223

**budget** (buj´it) A plan for spending money. p. 324

## C

**cabinet** (kab´ə•nit) A group of people that help the head of state. p. 161

**canyon** (kan´yən) A narrow valley with steep sides. p. 48

**capital** (kap´ə•təl) The center of government. p. 108

**cardinal directions** (kär´də•nəl di•rek´shənz) The four main directions: north, south, east, and west. p. 310

**cash crop** (kash krop) A crop sold to make a profit. p. 253

**cattle drive** (kat´(ə)l drīv) The way cowhands drove, or moved, cattle to market. p. 222

**cause** (kôz) Something that makes something else happen. p. 125

**census** (sen´səs) A population count. p. 299

**century** (sen´chə•rē) A unit of time that is 100 years. p. 76

**channel** (chan´əl) The path of a river through the land. p. 46

**citizen** (sit´ə•zən) A member of a town, state, or country. p. 19

**civics** (siv´iks) The study of citizenship and the ways in which citizens govern themselves. p. 30

**civil rights** (siv´əl rīts) The rights of all citizens to be treated equally. p. 252

**civil war** (siv´əl wôr) A fight between groups of citizens in the same country. p. 202

**civilization** (siv•ə•lə•zā´shən) A culture that has large cities and highly developed arts and sciences. p. 66

**climate** (klī´mit) The kind of weather a place has most often, year after year. p. 50

**coastal plain** (kōs´təl plān) Low, mostly flat land that lies alongside an ocean. p. 39

**colony** (kol´ə•nē) A settlement ruled by a faraway country. p. 97

**commercial farm** (kə•mûr´shəl färm) A farm that grows only cash crops. p. 253
**commission** (kə•mish´ən) A special committee. p. 228
**commissioners court** (kə•mish´ən•ərz kôrt) A group that acts as the legislative and executive branch in each Texas county. p. 328
**commute** (kə•myo͞ot´) To drive to and from work. p. 266
**Confederacy** (kən•fed´ər•ə•sē) The group of southern states that made up the Confederate States of America. p. 203
**confederation** (kən•fed•ə•rā´shən) A group made up of different, smaller groups who join to help one another. p. 69
**conflict** (kon´flikt) A disagreement. p. 121
**congress** (kong´gris) A law-making branch of government. p. 147
**conquistador** (kon•kēs´tə•dôr) A Spanish conqueror. p. 93
**conserve** (kən•sûrv´) To save. p. 257
**constitution** (kon•stə•t(y)o͞o´shən) A written plan of government. p. 150
**cotton gin** (kot´(ə)n jin) A machine that separates seeds from cotton fibers. p. 196
**council** (koun´səl) A group of leaders. p. 75
**county seat** (koun´tē sēt) The town or city that is the center of government for a county. p. 328
**crop** (krop) Plants grown for food. p. 73
**cross-section** (krôs•sek´shən) A slice or piece of something that shows its insides. p. 250
**culture** (kul´chər) A group's way of dressing, speaking, behaving, and believing. p. 66

## D

**dam** (dam) A wall built across a river or stream to help control flooding. p. 49
**declaration** (dek•lə•rā´shən) An announcement of a fact. p. 147
**demand** (di•mand´) A desire or need. p. 271
**democracy** (di•mok´rə•sē) A government in which the people make decisions or elect leaders to make decisions. p. 123
**depression** (di•presh´ən) A time when jobs are scarce and people have very little money. p. 257
**desert** (dez´ərt) A dry area with few plants. p. 57
**dictator** (dik´tā•tər) A government leader who makes all the decisions for an entire country. p. 123
**diverse** (di•vûrs´) Made up of many different kinds. p. 275
**drought** (drout) A long period of very little or no rain. p. 52

## E

**economy** (i•kon´ə•mē) The way people use their resources to meet their needs. p. 30
**effect** (i•fekt´) What results from a cause. p. 125
**election** (i•lek´shən) When citizens make choices about their government by voting. p. 161
**elevation** (el•ə•vā´shən) The height of the land above sea level. p. 40
**empire** (em´pīr) A country that has other lands under its rule. p. 179
**empresario** (em•prā•sä´rē•ō) A person with a land grant from the Mexican government and the right to sell the land at low cost. p. 111
**enforce** (in•fôrs´) To see that laws are obeyed. p. 329
**entrepreneur** (än•trə•prə•nûr´) A person who organizes and runs a business. p. 248
**environment** (in•vī´rən•mənt) The surrounding land and climate. p. 64
**equator** (i•kwā´tər) An imaginary line that runs east and west around the middle of the Earth. p. 44
**erosion** (i•rō´zhən) The wearing away of the land's surface. p. 48
**escarpment** (es•kärp´mənt) A long wall of steep cliffs where the elevation of the land changes. p. 41
**exchange** (iks•chānj´) To trade. p. 69
**executive branch** (ig•zek´yə•tiv branch) The branch of government with the power to make sure that laws passed by the legislature are obeyed. p. 325
**expedition** (ek•spə•dish´ən) A journey into an area to learn more about it. p. 94

## F

**fact** (fakt) A statement that is supposed to be true and can be checked. p. 270
**federal** (fed´ər•əl) Having to do with the national government. p. 202
**fertile** (fûr´təl) Rich soil. p. 65
**filibuster** (fil´ə•bus•tər) A soldier in a private army. p. 111
**floodplain** (flud´plān) Low, flat land along a river. p. 49
**flow chart** (flō chärt) A drawing that shows the order in which things happen. p. 327
**free enterprise** (frē en´tər•prīz) When people are free to start and run their own businesses. p. 248
**free state** (frē stāt) A state in which there were no slaves. p. 173

**frontier** (frun•tir´) The place where settled land ended and wilderness began. p. 107

# G

**geography** (jē•og´rə•fē) The study of many different settings around the world. p. 26

**good** (gŏŏd) A product people buy and sell. p. 247

**government** (guv´ər(n)•mənt) A group of people who lead a village, city, state, or country. p. 79

**grant** (grant) A gift of land. p. 107

# H

**heritage** (her´ə•tij) The culture people today have gained from people in the past. p. 103

**high-tech** (hī•tek´) Technology having to do with computers and electronics. p. 275

**history** (his´tə•rē) What happened last month and last year as well as in the long-ago past. p. 23

**horizontally** (hôr•ə•zon´təl•lē) From left to right. p. 157

**human resource** (hyōō´mən rē´sôrs) An educated worker. p. 311

**humid** (hyōō´mid) Air that has a lot of moisture, or water, in it. p. 51

**hurricane** (hûr´ə•kān) A very strong storm with high winds and heavy rains. p. 53

# I

**immigrant** (im´ə•grənt) A person who moves into a country from another country. p. 171

**independence** (in•di•pen´dəns) Freedom from someone else's control or from some other country's control. p. 147

**industry** (in´dəs•trē) A group of companies that make up one type of business. p. 247

**informed citizen** (in•fôrmd´ sit´ə•zən) A citizen who understands why things happen in the community, the state, and the world. p. 312

**inland** (in´lənd) Away from the coast. p. 39

**inset map** (in´set map) A small map within a larger map. p. 29

**integrated circuit** (in´tə•grāt•əd sûr´kit) A microchip that can run electronic systems. p. 268

**interdependent** (in•tər•di•pen´dənt) Depending on each other for goods and services. p. 249

**intermediate directions** (in•tər•mē´dē•it di•rek´shənz) Directions between the cardinal directions: northeast, northwest, southeast, and southwest. p. 310

**interstate highway system** (in´tər•stāt hī´wā sis´təm) Four-lane roads connecting all the states except Alaska and Hawaii. p. 277

**irrigate** (ir´ə•gāt) To move water from nearby rivers and streams to the crops. p. 77

# J

**judicial branch** (jōō•dish´əl branch) The branch of government made up of courts and judges who hear and decide cases. p. 326

**Juneteenth** (jōōn•tēnth´) June 19, the day slaves were freed in Texas. p. 205

**jury trial** (jŏŏr´ē trī´əl) A trial in which a group of citizens decides if a person accused of a crime is guilty or innocent. p. 326

# L

**landfill** (land´fil) A place where garbage and litter from a community are buried. p. 315

**landslide victory** (land´slīd vik´tər•ē) An election in which a candidate receives many more votes than the opponent. p. 278

**latitude** (lat´ə•t(y)ōōd) An imaginary line that runs east and west around the Earth. p. 44

**legislative branch** (lej´is•lā•tiv branch) The branch of government that makes, or passes, laws. p. 324

**leisure time** (lē´zhər tīm) Time away from work or school. p. 267

**location** (lō•kā´shən) Where a place is. p. 45

**long drive** (lông drīv) A trip when cattle were driven on long trails to market. p. 223

**longhorn** (lông´hôrn) A breed of Texas cattle that has large horns. p. 220

**longitude** (lon´jə•t(y)ōōd) An imaginary line that runs north and south around the Earth between the North Pole and the South Pole. p. 44

# M

**majority** (mə•jôr´ə•tē) The greater part. p. 173

**marsh** (märsh) An area of flat land often covered with water because the land is low. p. 58

**massacre** (mas´ə•kər) The killing of people who have no chance to fight back. p. 155

**mesquite** (me•skēt´) A treelike bush with long roots that search for water. p. 57

**mestizo** (mes•tē´zō) A person whose ancestors were Spanish and Indian. p. 102

**militia** (mə•lish´ə) A group of unpaid citizens that acts as an army. p. 108

**mission** (mish´ən) A religious settlement. p. 100

**missionary** (mish´ən•er•ē) A religious worker. p. 94
**multicultural** (mul•ti•kul´chər•əl) Including many different cultures. p. 302
**municipal** (myōō•nis´ə•pəl) Having to do with city government. p. 329

# N

**natural region** (nach´ər•əl rē´jən) A part of the Earth that has one major kind of natural feature. p. 39
**naturalized citizen** (nach´ər•əl•īzd sit´ə•zən) An immigrant who becomes a citizen by taking steps described in the law. p. 333
**nomad** (nō´mad) A person who moves from place to place. p. 70
**northers** (nôr´thərz) Blasts of cold wind blowing from the north. p. 51

# O

**opinion** (ə•pin´yən) Something a person believes or thinks to be true. p. 270
**opportunity cost** (op•ər•t(y)ōō´nə•tē kôst) The cost of giving up one thing to get another. p. 332

# P

**panhandle** (pan´han•dəl) A narrow strip of land that is joined to a bigger piece of land. p. 41
**petroleum** (pə•trō´lē•əm) Oil. p. 247
**pictograph** (pik´tə•graf) A graph that uses symbols to stand for numbers. p. 303
**plantation** (plan•tā´shən) A very large farm with a crop tended by laborers who live there. p. 172
**plateau** (pla•tō´) Land that is high and flat like a table. p. 41
**plaza** (plaz´ə) Town square. p. 101
**point of view** (point uv vyōō) A person's set of beliefs shaped by certain factors. p. 25
**policy** (pol´ə•sē) A plan or way of action. p. 169
**political region** (pə•lit´i•kəl rē´jən) The area occupied by a city, state, or nation. p. 177
**politics** (pol´ə•tiks) The running of the government. p. 278
**pollute** (pə•lōōt´) To spoil the environment or make it dirty. p. 314
**population** (pop•yə•lā´shən) The number of people who live in a place. p. 114
**prairie** (prâr´ē) Flat grasslands. p. 56
**precipitation** (pri•sip´ə•tā•shən) Rain, sleet, hail, or snow. p. 51
**presidio** (prā•sē´dē•ō) A fort. p. 101
**primary source** (prī´mer•ē sôrs) A source that gives the real words of people who actually saw what happened. p. 261
**prime meridian** (prīm mə•rid´ē•ən) An imaginary line that runs north and south around the Earth. It is the starting point for measuring lines of longitude. p. 44
**private property** (prī´vit prop´ər•tē) Property that individual people own. p. 318
**prosperity** (pros•per´ə•tē) Material wealth and success. p. 199
**public property** (pub´lik prop´ər•tē) Property that all people of a state or country own. p. 318

# R

**recognize** (rek´əg•nīz) To accept as true. p. 162
**Reconstruction** (rē•kən•struk´shən) The period after the Civil War when people had to reconstruct, or rebuild, the way they lived. p. 205
**recycle** (rē•sī´kəl) To use materials again instead of wasting them. p. 314
**redback** (red´bak) A Republic of Texas dollar bill that was red. p. 171
**refinery** (ri•fī´nər•ē) A factory where oil is made into products such as grease and kerosene. p. 246
**region** (rē´jən) An area on the Earth whose features make it different from other areas. p. 27
**register** (rej´is•tər) To sign up, or enter one's name, to vote. p. 334
**republic** (ri•pub´lik) A government in which the people are free to choose their leaders. p. 150
**reservation** (rez•ər•vā´shən) Land set aside only for American Indians. p. 211
**reservoir** (rez´ər•vwär) A lake that stores water held back by a dam. p. 258
**responsibility** (ri•spon•sə•bil´ə•tē) A duty people are required to do. p. 333
**retreat** (ri•trēt´) To pull back or withdraw. p. 154
**revolution** (rev•ə•lōō´shən) A change of government made by force, usually a war. p. 143
**rights** (rīts) Freedoms. p. 120
**river system** (riv´ər sis´təm) A river and all its tributaries. p. 48
**route** (rōōt) A path. p. 99
**Rust Belt** (rust belt) A nickname for the states of the Northeast and Middle West, where industries use a lot of iron and steel. p. 271

# S

**scarce** (skârs) Hard to find or get. p. 64
**school board** (sko͞ol bôrd) A group elected by voters in each school district to make decisions about running the schools. p. 331
**scout** (skout) A person who is sent ahead to explore areas and gather information about the land and the enemy. p. 152
**sea level** (sē lev´əl) Land the same height as the surface of an ocean. p. 40
**secede** (si•sēd´) To leave or withdraw from a union. p. 203
**secondary source** (sek´ən•der•ē sôrs) A source written at a later time that gives information by someone who did not see what happened. p. 261
**segregation** (seg•rə•gā´shən) Keeping people apart from others because of their culture or race. p. 267
**service** (sûr´vis) An activity that people do for others. p. 247
**service industry** (sûr´vis in´dəs•trē) An industry that provides services. p. 275
**shaman** (shä´mən) A religious leader who takes care of the sick and keeps a group's traditions alive. p. 71
**sharecropper** (shâr´krop•ər) A person who rents farmland and pays the rent with a share of the crops. p. 205
**shortage** (shôr´tij) When there is not enough for everyone. p. 252
**slave** (slāv) A person who is owned by another person and made to work. p. 110
**slave state** (slāv stāt) A state in which people could own slaves. p. 173
**special district** (spesh´əl dis´trikt) A district that deals with one problem or service. p. 328
**specialize** (spesh´əl•īz) To work on one job. p. 66
**stampede** (stam•pēd´) To run away wildly. p. 224
**suffrage** (suf´rij) The right to vote. p. 255
**Sun Belt** (sun belt) A nickname for states with sunny climates. p. 271
**supply** (sə•plī´) The amount available for use. p. 273
**surrender** (sə•ren´dər) To give up. p. 145
**symbol** (sim´bəl) A sign that stands for something else. p. 168
**synthetic** (sin•thet´ik) Produced artificially rather than occurring naturally. p. 260

# T

**TAAS** (täs) Texas Assessment of Academic Skills—tests Texas students take so the state can see if schools are improving. p. 312
**Tejano** (tā•hä´nō) A Mexican settler who moves to Texas. p. 112
**temperature** (tem´prə•chər) The measure of how warm or cold a place is. p. 50
**temple** (tem´pəl) A building in which people worship or pray. p. 69
**tenant farmer** (ten´ənt fär´mər) A farmer who rents land from someone else. p. 253
**tepee** (tē´pē) A cone-shaped shelter made of animal hides. p. 74
**term** (tûrm) Period of time. p. 169
**textile mill** (teks´tīl mil) A factory where cloth is made. p. 196
**tidelands** (tīd´landz) The lands that lie under the water just off a coast. p. 265
**time line** (tīm līn) A graph that shows units of time. p. 76
**time zone** (tīm zōn) A region where all the people use the same time. p. 229
**title** (tīt´(ə)l) Ownership of land or property. p. 169
**tornado** (tôr•nā´dō) A funnel-shaped storm with swirling winds. p. 53
**trade-off** (trād´ôf) What one gives up to buy something else. p. 332
**treason** (trē´zən) Working against one's country. p. 123
**treaty** (trē´tē) A written agreement between two or more groups. p. 161
**tribe** (trīb) A group of many bands who share land and a way of life. p. 66
**tributary** (trib´yə•ter•ē) A river or stream that flows into a larger river or stream. p. 48

# U

**unemployment** (un•im•ploi´mənt) The condition of being without a job. p. 258
**Union** (yo͞on´yən) The United States of America. p. 203

# V

**vaquero** (bä•kā´rō) Spanish or Indian cowhand. p. 100
**vegetation** (vej•ə•tā´shən) Plant life. p. 55
**vertically** (vûr´ti•kəl•lē) From top to bottom. p. 157
**veto power** (vē´tō pou´ər) The power to refuse to sign a new law. p. 325
**volunteer** (vol•ən•tir´) A person who offers help, usually without pay. p. 144

# W

**wildcatter** (wīld´kat•ər) A person who searches for new sources of oil. p. 249

# INDEX

*Page references for illustrations are set in italic type. An italic m indicates a map. Page references set in boldface type indicate the pages on which vocabulary terms are defined.*



# A



# B



# C

# H



# I



# J



# K

## O



## P



## Q



## R



## S

For permission to reprint copyrighted material, grateful acknowledgment is made to the following sources:

*Eakin Press, an imprint of Sunbelt Media, Inc.*: From *Spindletop* by Sibyl Hancock. Text copyright © 1980, 1984 by Sibyl Hancock and Patty L. Rucker. From *Texas Footprints* by Rita Kerr. Text copyright © 1988 by Rita Kerr. From *Sarah's Flag for Texas* by Jane Alexander Knapik. Text copyright © 1993 by Jane Alexander Knapik. From *The Courage Seed* by Jean Richardson, illustrated by Pat Finney. Copyright © 1993 by Jean Richardson.

*Folkways Music Publishers, Inc., New York*: From "SO LONG It's Been Good To Know Yuh" ("Dusty Old Dust") by Woody Guthrie. TRO—lyrics © copyright 1940 (Renewed) 1950 (Renewed) 1963 (Renewed).

*Gertrude Lerner Kerman Furman*: From *Cabeza de Vaca: Defender of the Indians* by Gertrude Kerman. Text copyright © 1974 by Gertrude Lerner Kerman.

*Harcourt Brace & Company*: From *The Armadillo from Amarillo* by Lynne Cherry. Copyright © 1994 by Lynne Cherry. From *Quanah Parker* by Len Hilts. Text copyright © 1987 by Len Hilts. From *Susanna of the Alamo: A True Story* by John Jakes, illustrated by Paul Bacon. Text copyright © 1986 by John Jakes; illustrations copyright © 1986 by Paul Bacon.

*Mary C. Hearne and Owen Edward Thomas*: Texas State Song, "Texas, Our Texas," by William J. Marsh. Lyrics copyright © 1925 by W. J. Marsh; lyrics copyright renewed 1953 by William J. Marsh. Published by Southern Music Company.

*Hendrick-Long Publishing Co., Dallas, TX*: From *Johnny Texas* by Carol Hoff.

## ILLUSTRATION CREDITS:

Page 76 Steve Gardner, Hankins & Tegenborg Ltd.; 84-85 David Henderson, Mendola Ltd.; 132-133 Steve Gardner, Hankins & Tegenborg Ltd.; 145 Tom Powers, The Ivy League of Artists; 165 The Mazer Corporation; 184-185 Dan Andreason, Publishers' Graphics Inc.; 190-193 Fred Willingham, PCI ARTsource; 234-235 David Henderson, Mendola Ltd.; 240-243 Geoffrey P. Smith; 250 The Mazer Corporation; 288-289 Steve Gardner, Hankins & Tegenborg Ltd.; 318 The Mazer Corporation; 327 The Mazer Corporation; 340-341 Bill Maughan, Mendola Ltd.; all charts, graphs, diagrams, tables, and time lines, The Mazer Corporation.

## COVER CREDIT:

Keith Gold & Associates

**All maps by GeoSystems**

## PHOTO CREDITS:

**Page Placement Key:** (t)-top (c)-center (b)-bottom (l)-left (r)-right

**Table of Contents**

Page iii Zigy Kaluzny/Gamma Liaison; iv (t) Lawrence Migdale; iv (b) The Granger Collection, New York; v (t) Archives Division, Texas State Library; v (b) Archives Division, Texas State Library; Photographed by Eric Beggs; vi (t) Archives Division, Texas State Library; vi (b) The Norwegian Historical Association; vii (t) Smithsonian Institution; vii (b) The Institute of Texan Cultures, San Antonio, Texas; viii (t) Bob Daemmrich Photography; viii (b) Patrick Wong; ix Bob Daemmrich/Sygma.

**Introduction**

Page 20 Star of the Republic Museum, Washington, Texas; 23 (t) Bettmann; 24 (t) The Institute of Texan Cultures, San Antonio, Texas; 24 (b) Bob Daemmrich Photography; 25 Texas State Library, Archives Division; 30 (t) Bob Daemmrich Photography; 30 (c) Bruce Byers/FPG International; 30 (b) Lee Snider Photo Images; A1 David Wagner/Phototake.

**Harcourt Brace & Company Photos**

18 Victoria Bowen; 19; 21 Victoria Bowen; 22 Victoria Bowen; 23 (b) Eric Camden; 31 Victoria Bowen; 73 (inset) Black Star/Lisa Rudy/Courtesy Tonkawa Tribal Museum; 86 Eric Camden; 134 Eric Camden; 186 Eric Camden; 189 (bl) Don Couch Photography/Courtesy of the Railroad Pioneer Museum; 224 (c) Victoria Bowen; 224 (b) Victoria Bowen; 236 Eric Camden; 270 (r) Reprint courtesy of the Fort Worth Star-Telegram/Eric Camden; 290 Terry D. Sinclair; 292 (bcb); 292 (bcr); 292 (bcb) Rich Franco; 311 (b); 311 (b); 312 (t) Terry D. Sinclair; 319 (c) Kevin Vandivier/Black Star; 319 (b) Michael Klein/Black Star; 342 Victoria Bowen; R2 Eric Camden; R3 Eric Camden; R6 Terry D. Sinclair; R7 Terry D. Sinclair.

**Unit 1**

Page 32 (b) Lee Boltin; 32-33 David Muench; 33 (bl) Mark Gulezian/QuickSilver Photography; 33 (br) Mickey Gibson/Animals Animals; 38 Zigy Kaluzny/Gamma Liaison; 39 Dan Richards/Stock Options; 41 Laurence Parent; 42 David Muench; 46 Willard Clay/Dembinsky Photo Associates; 47 David Muench; 48 Carol Barrington/TexStock Photo; 49 (t) Murray Getz/The Stockhouse; 49 (inset) Bob Daemmrich Photography; 50 Karen Dickey/Texas Dept. of Agriculture; 51 William A. Logan/The Image Bank; 52 Kim Todd/The Stockhouse; 53 Wichita Falls Times Record News; 54 NOAA/Photo Researchers; 55 National Wildflower Research Center; 56 (t) Joe McDonald/Animals Animals; 56 (b) James A. Ellenburg/The Stockhouse; 57 (t) David Northcott/Superstock; 57 (b) Doug Sokell/Tom Stack & Associates; 57 (inset) Karl H. Switak/Photo Researchers; 58 David Muench; 59 (l) Jack Hollingsworth/Stock Options; 59 (r) James A. Ellenburg/The Stockhouse; 62 Lawrence Migdale; 63 Lee Boltin; 64 From THE INDIANS OF TEXAS: FROM PREHISTORIC TO MODERN TIMES by William W. Newcomb, Jr., © 1961, renewed 1989. By permission of the University of Texas Press.; 65 (r) Mark Gulezian/QuickSilver Photography; 65 (l) Detail from "The Huaxtec Civilization, And The Cultivation Of The Corn,"mural by Diego Rivera/Ulrike Welsch/Photo Researchers; 66 Will & Deni McIntyre/Photo Researchers; 67 Kjell B. Sandved/Smithsonian Institution, Washington D.C./Photo Researchers; 68 Randall S Mallory; 69 Institute of Texan Culture San Antonio; 71 From THE INDIANS TEXAS: FROM PREHISTORIC TO MO ERN TIMES by William W. Newcomb, Jr., (C) 1961, renewed 1989. Permission of the University of Texas Press.; 72 Breck P. Kent/Animals Animals; 73 Courtesy of The Witte Museum, San Antonio, Texas; 74 From THE WORLD BOOK ENCYCLOPEDIA., 1995 World Book, Inc., By permission of the publisher.; 75 Royal Ontario Museum; 77 Salinas Pueblo Missions/United States Department of the Interior; 78 (t) Bob Daemmrich Photography; 78 (b) Farrell Grehan/FPG International; 79 Stephen Trimble; 82 (inset) Texas Department of Transportation, Travel and Information Div., Audiovisual Branch; 82-83 Scott Berner/The Stockhouse; 83 (inset) Texas Depart-ment of Transportation, Travel and Information; 83 Texas Department of Transportation.

**Unit 2**

Page 88 (l) Stock Montage; 88 (r) (C) 1986 The Mel Fisher Heritage Museum Society, Key West, FL. Photo by S. Nierling; 88-89 Daughters of the Republic of Texas Library, Gift of the Yanaguana Society; 89 (l) Texas Department of Transportation; 89 (r) David R. Frazier Photolibrary; 90 Painting by Louis S. Glanzman/National Park Service; 92 The Granger Collection, New York; 93 Boltin Picture Library; 94 The British Library; 95 The Granger Collection, New York; 96 Bob Waterman/West Light; 98 The Granger Collection, New York; 100 Superstock; 101 Art by Richard Williams/National Park Service; 102 (inset) The Granger Collection, New York; 102 Detail from Fandango, painting by Theodore Gentilz, Yanaguana Society gift, The Daughters of the Republic of Texas Library; 103 Alan Smith/Tony Stone Images; 106 Archives Division, Texas State Library; 107 Archives Division, Texas State Library; 108 Mural by Diego Rivera/Carl Frank/Photo Researchers; 109 (t) Library of Congress; 109 (b) David R. Frazier Photolibrary; 110 (inset) Prints and Photographs Collection, Jane Long File, The Center for American History, The University of Texas at Austin, #CN07361; 110 Courtesy of the Rosenberg Library, Galveston, TX; 111 (inset) Texas Newspaper Collection Nacogdoches, Texas, The Center for American History, The University of Texas at Austin, #CN 02349; 111 Archives Division, Texas State Library, Austin; 112 Institute of Texan Cultures, San Antonio, Texas; 113 Star of the Republic Museum; 115-119 (border) Courtesy of The Witte Museum, San Antonio, Texas; 116-117 The Granger Collection, New York; 118-119 Texas Highway Department; 118 (b) The Granger Collection, New York; 120 San Jacinto Museum of History, Houston, Texas; 121 Prints & Photographs Collection, The Center for American History, University of Texas at Austin; 122 Amon Carter Museum, Fort Worth, Texas; 124 Archive Photos; 126 Texas Department of Transportation; 127 (t) Archives Division, Texas State Library; 127 (b) Archives Division, Texas State Library; 130-131 Superstock; 130 Louis H. Jawitz/Image Bank; 131 (t) John Warden/Tony Stone Image; 131 (cl) Scott Berner/The

Stockhouse; 131 (cr) Bob Abraham/ The Stock Market; 131 (b) Nicole Galeazzi/Omni-Photo.

**Unit 3**

Page 136 (l) Texas Department of Transportation; 136 (r) Star of the Republic Museum; 136-137 Friends of the Governor's Mansion, Austin; 137 (l) Archives Division, Texas State Library; 137 (r) The Granger Collection, New York; 142 Archives Division, Texas State Library; Photographed by Eric Beggs; 143 Texas Department of Transportation; 144 Archives Division, Texas State Library, Austin; 146 (t) The Granger Collection, New York; 146 (b) Superstock; 147 Prints & Photographs Collection/The Center for American History/The University of Texas at Austin/CN01094; 148 Courtesy, Special Collections Division, The University of Texas Arlington Libraries, Arlington, Texas; 149 (inset) The Daughters of the Republic of Texas Library at the Alamo, San Antonio, Texas; 149 Star of the Republic Museum, Washington, Texas; 151 (l) Bettmann; 151 (c) The Granger Collection, New York; 151 (r) Archives Division, Texas State Library; 152 Bettmann; 154 (t) San Jacinto Museum of History; 154 (b) From The Collections of the Dallas Historical Society, photo by Stock Yard; 155 (t) Archives Division, Texas State Library. Photo by Eric Beggs; 155 (b) From the collections of the Dallas Historical Society; 161 (l) Archives Division, Texas State Library; 161 (r) Texas Rangers file/The Center for American History, The University of Texas at Austin, CN #01069; 161 Archives Division, Texas State Library; 162 Archives Division, Texas State Library; 163 The Granger Collection, New York; 164 Archives Division, Texas State Library; 166-167 Star of the Republic Museum; 167 Capitols File, The Center for American History, The University of Texas at Austin; 168 (all) Texas Department of Transportation; 169 San Jacinto Museum of History, Texas; 170 Texas Southern University, Art Department; 171 Archives Division, Texas State Library; 172 The Daughters of the Republic of Texas Library; 173 Bettmann; 174 (inset) Archives Division, Texas State Library; 174 Prints & Photographs Collection, Annexation File, The Center for American History, The University of Texas at Austin, CN03085; 176 The Granger Collection, New York; 178 (l) Archives Division, Texas State Library; 178 (r) Texas State Archives Prints & Photographs Collections; 179 Archives Division, Texas State Library; 182 (inset) Marty Snortum; 182-183 Bob Daemmrich Photography; 182-183 (r) inset The Stockhouse, Inc.; 182-183 (c) inset Dick Loman/Unicorn Stock Photos; 183 (inset) Robert E. Daemmrich/Tony Stone Images.

**Unit 4**

Pages 188, 189 (t) Thomas Gilcrease Institute of American History and Art, Tulsa, Oklahoma; 188 (bl) Bob Daemmrich Photography; 188 (bc) The Museum of the Confederacy, Richmond, Virginia, Photography by Katherine Wetzel; 188 (br) Nawrocki Stock Photo; 189 (br) Railroad and Pioneer Museum; 194 Norwegian-American Historical Association; 195 Smithsonian Institution; 196 The Carnegie Museum of Art, Pittsburgh; Gift of Mrs. [illegible]tch Ingersoll, 58.4; 197 North Wind Pictures; 198 Courtesy of Sophienburg Museum & Archives, New Braunfels, Texas; 199 (t) Archives & Manuscripts Division of the Oklahoma Historical Society, #8527; 200 The Institute of Texan Cultures, San Antonio, Texas. Courtesy: Carl T. Widen; 202 (all) The Museum of the Confederacy, Richmond, Virginia, Photography by Katherine Wetzel; 203 (t) Nawrocki Stock Photo; 203 (c) Library of Congress; 203 (b) Culver Pictures; 204 Archives Division, Texas State Library; 205 Courtesy Houston Metropolitan Research Center, Houston Public Library; 206 The Granger Collection, New York; 210 Smithsonian Institution; 211 National Museum of the American Indian/Smithsonian Institution #s2698; 212 (t) National Museum of American Art/ Art Resource, NY; 212 (inset) National Archives; 213 (t) National Museum of the American Indian/Smithsonian Institution #s3476; 213 (b) Archives Division, Texas State Library, Austin; 214 (t) Richard Stockton/The Stockhouse; 214 (b) Western History Collections, University of Oklahoma Library; 214 (inset) National Archives; 215 The Granger Collection, New York; 216 National Cowboy Hall of Fame/Tom McHugh/PhotoResearchers; 217 The Granger Collection, New York; 218 Bettmann; 218-219 (Background) Smithsonian Institution, Photo No. 1778A; 219 (t) Archives & Manuscripts Division of the Oklahoma Historical Society, #8527; 219 (b) Smithsonian Institution, Photo No. 50322; 220 Bob Daemmrich Photography; 221 California Historical Society; 222 (t) Courtesy of Panhandle-Plains Historical Society, Canyon, Texas; 223 (t) Courtesy of Panhandle-Plains Historical Society, Canyon, Texas; 223 (b) T. Algire/H. Armstrong Roberts; 224 (t) The Bettmann Archive; 225 The Granger Collection, New York; 226 The Granger Collection, New York; 227 (t) Archives Division, Texas State Library; 227 (b) Charles B. Turrill Collection, The Center for American History, The University of Texas at Austin; 228 Archives Division, Texas State Library; 232 Robert E. Daemmrich/Tony Stone Images; 233 (tl) Pam Francis/Gamma Liaison; 233 (tr) Michael Grecco/Sygma; 233 (c) Lee Snider Photo Images; 233 (bl) Pat Harbran/Outline Press Syndicate; 233 (br) Bob Daemmrich Photography.

**Unit 5**

Pages 238-239 (t) Memorial Art Gallery of the University of Rochester; Marion Stratton Gould Fund, 51.1; 238 (bl) Culver Pictures; 238 (br) Sophia Smith Collection, Smith College; 239 (bl) NASA; 239 (br) NASA; 244 The Institute of Texan Cultures, San Antonio, Texas; 245 Courtesy of Rosenberg Library, Galveston, Texas; 246 (b) Brown Brothers; 247 (t) Brown Brothers; 247 (b) Wide World Photos; 249 The Howard Hughes Corporation; 251 Brown Brothers; 252 (t) Schuchard, Pioneer Flour Mills album, p. 59, DRT Library at the Alamo; 252 (b) UPI/Bettmann Newsphotos; 253 Brown Brothers; 255 (t) Sophia Smith Collection, Smith College; 255 (b) Texas Women's University; 256 The San Antonio Light Collection. The Institute of Texan Cultures; 257 Culver Pictures; 258 From the Collections of The Dallas Historical Society; 259 (t) Culver Pictures; 259 (b) Department of the Air Force; 259 (inset) The Granger Collection, New York; 260 (t) AP/Wide World; 260 (inset) AP/Wide World Photos; 261 The Granger Collection, New York; 264 Bob Daemmrich Photography; 265 The Stockhouse; 266 (t) Collections of the Library of Congress; 266 (b) Culver Pictures; 267 From the Collection of the Texas/Dallas History and Archives Division, Dallas Public Library; 268 (t) Wide World Photos; 268 (b) Reg Watson/Tony Stone Images; 269 (t) NASA; 269 (b) NASA; 270 (l) The Dallas Morning News; 271 Bob Daemmrich Photography; 272 (t) David R. Frazier Photolibrary; 274 Tony Stone Images; 276 David Young-Wolff/PhotoEdit; 277 Culver Pictures; 278 (t) AP/Wide World Photos; 278 (b) Archive Photos; 279 (t) UPI/Bettmann; 279 (b) Diana Walker/ Gamma Liaison; 280 (t) Donna West/Stock Options; 280 (b) Brooks Kraft/Sygma; 281 (t) Robert E. Daemmrich/Tony Stone Images; 281 (b) Wide World Photos; 286 (inset) Miller/Focus on Sports; 286-287 (border) Cowgirl Stock Photography; 286-287 Bettmann; 287 (b) (inset) Chuck Solomon/Focus on Sports; 287 (t) (inset) Bettmann.

**Unit 6**

Pages 292-293 (t) John M. Roberts/The Stock Market; 292 (bl) McNee/The Stockhouse; 292 (bct) Dennis O'Clair/Tony Stone Images; 292 (bcl) Micheal Simpson/FPG International; 292 (br) Barbara Filet/Tony Stone Images; 293 (bl) Texas Highway Dept.; 293 (bc) Bob Daemmrich Photos; 293 (br) Dallas Morning News/Rick Moon; 294 (b) Willard Clay/FPG International; 294 (tl) Brian Kenney/Natural Selection; 294-295 Bruce Senior/The Stockhouse; 295 (r) Ray Soto/TexStock Photo; 296 (l) Reza Estakhrian/Tony Stone Images; 296-297 (b) Ken Biggs/Tony Stone Images; 296 (tr) Daniel J. Cox/Natural Selection; 297 (r) Richard Laird/FPG International; 298 Patrick Wong; 299 Bob Daemmrich Photography; 300 H. Kokojan/Black Star; 301 Bob Daemmrich Photography; 302 (t) & (inset) Bob Daemmrich Photography; 311 (t) Dennis O'Clair/Tony Stone Images; 311 (l) Micheal Simpson/FPG International; 312 (b) Frank Siteman/ Light Sources; 313 Stock Yard; 314 (l) Mark Lewis/Tony Stone Images; 314 (r) Bob Daemmrich Photography; 315 Chris Holmes/Masterfile; 317 Jim Richardson; 319 (t) City of Pearland, Texas; 322 Bob Daemmrich/Sygma; 323 Bob Daemmrich Photography; 324 (t) Robert E. Daemmrich/ Tony Stone Images; 324 (b) Scott Berner/ The Stockhouse; 325 (t) Texas Highway Dept.; 325 (b) Andre Jenny/The Stockhouse; 328 Bob Daemmrich Photos; 329 Harris County Sheriff's Department; 331 Bob Daemmrich Photography; 332 Bruce Byers/ FPG International; 333 Robert E. Daemmrich/Tony Stone Images; 334 Jeffry W. Myers/FPG International; 335 (l) Myrleen Ferguson/PhotoEdit; 335 (r) American Red Cross; 338-339 (all) Alan Pogue; 344 Bob Daemmrich Photography.

**Reference**

Page R1 (t) Bob Daemmrich Photography; R1 (b) The Stockhouse; R8 R. Reagan Atkinson/The Stockhouse; R9 (l) Tom Overton/The Stockhouse; R9 (r) Richard Hutchings/Photo Researchers.